SCIENCE AND NATURE

Science and Nature: Past, Present, and Future brings together the work and insights of historian Carolyn Merchant on the history of science, environmental history, and ethics. The book explores her ideas about the interconnections among science, women, nature, and history as they have emerged over her academic lifetime. Focusing on topics such as "The Death of Nature," the Scientific Revolution, women in the history of science and environment, and partnership ethics, it synthesizes her writings and sets out a vision for the twenty-first century. Anyone interested in the interactions between science and nature in the past, present, and future will want to read this book. It is an ideal text for courses on the environment, environmental history, history of science, and the philosophy of science.

Carolyn Merchant is Professor of Environmental History, Philosophy, and Ethics at the University of California, Berkeley. She is the author of *The Death of Nature*, *Ecological Revolutions*, *Reinventing Eden*, and *Autonomous Nature*, among other books. She is a past president of the American Society for Environmental History; a recipient of the Society's Distinguished Scholar Award and its Distinguished Service Award; a former Guggenheim fellow; and a fellow of the American Association for the Advancement of Science.

RELATED TITLES FROM ROUTLEDGE

SCIENCE AND NATURE

Past, Present, and Future

Carolyn Merchant

Routledge
Taylor & Francis Group

NEW YORK AND LONDON

First published 2018
by Routledge
711 Third Avenue, New York, NY 10017

and by Routledge
2 Park Square, Milton Park, Abingdon, Oxon, OX14 4RN

Routledge is an imprint of the Taylor & Francis Group, an informa business

© 2018 Taylor & Francis

Library of Congress Cataloging-in-Publication Data
Names: Merchant, Carolyn, author.
Title: Science and nature : past, present, and future / by Carolyn Merchant.
Description: New York, NY : Routledge, 2017. | Includes bibliographical references and index.
Identifiers: LCCN 2017026337 | ISBN 9781138084049 (hardcover : alk. paper) | ISBN 9781138084056 (pbk. : alk. paper) | ISBN 9781315111988 (ebook)
Subjects: LCSH: Science, Renaissance. | Force and energy. | Women in science. | Ecology. | Environmental protection.
Classification: LCC Q125.2 .M47 2017 | DDC 509.2/24—dc23
LC record available at https://lccn.loc.gov/2017026337

ISBN: 978-1-138-08404-9 (hbk)
ISBN: 978-1-138-08405-6 (pbk)
ISBN: 978-1-315-11198-8 (ebk)

Typeset in Times New Roman
by Apex CoVantage, LLC

Printed and bound by CPI Group (UK) Ltd, Croydon, CR0 4YY

For David and John

"The product of a rich life of intellect and activism, this book is a must read for anyone concerned with nature, gender, and the future of life on our planet."

Londa Schiebinger, author of *The Mind Has No Sex?*,
Nature's Body, and *Has Feminism Changed Science?*

"Carolyn Merchant has been one of the true pioneers of environmental history, making important contributions for more than four decades. This collection will enable readers to sample and savor the wide-ranging nature of her work over the full sweep of her career."

William Cronon, author of *Changes in the Land* and *Nature's Metropolis*

"*Science and Nature* is a wide-ranging feast of scholarship from early modern mechanics, natural philosophy, and sociology of knowledge to eco-feminism and environmental history. The broad topical scope is marked by a strong and masterfully argued thematic coherence. Carolyn Merchant's trenchant critique of the grand narrative of the Scientific Revolution is prerequisite to her critical analysis of contemporary environmental justice and her offering of a new and visionary ethic of partnership with Nature."

Francesca Rochberg, author of *Before Nature* and *The Heavenly Writing*

"Dating from the early seventies to the present, this collection of lively essays, artfully revised to create a coherent whole, demonstrates Carolyn Merchant's lucid mastery and synthesis of the full spectrum of the environmental humanities. Centrally, they trace the history of the revolution in Western natural philosophy (aka the "Scientific Revolution") to what is in effect a second such revolution epitomized by ecology, relativity/quantum physics, and chaos/complexity mathematics. This dramatic engagement of often hubristic Science with obdurate Nature is critically examined through the moral lens of feminism and environmental ethics."

J. Baird Callicott, author of *In Defense of the Land Ethic* and *Thinking Like a Planet*

CONTENTS

FIGURES

DIAGRAMS AND TABLE

SOURCES

5. Newton

Carolyn [Merchant] Iltis. "The Leibnizian-Newtonian Debates: Natural Philosophy and Social Psychology." *British Journal for the History of Science* 6, no. 4 (December 1973): 343–377.

6. D'Alembert

Carolyn [Merchant] Iltis. "D'Alembert and the *Vis Viva* Controversy." *History and Philosophy of Science* 1, no. 2 (1970): 135–144.

III. WOMEN AND THE SCIENTIFIC REVOLUTION

7. Margaret Cavendish

Carolyn Merchant. *The Death of Nature: Women, Ecology, and the Scientific Revolution* (San Francisco: HarperCollins, 1980), pp. 268–274 and Keynote Address to Margaret Cavendish Society, June 2017.

8. Anne Conway

Carolyn Merchant. "Anne Conway, Quaker and Philosopher," in *Perspectives on the Seventeenth Century World of Viscountess Anne Conway, Guilford Review* 23, no. 1 (Spring 1986): 2–13; Merchant, "The Vitalism of Anne Conway: Its Impact on Leibniz's Concept of the Monad." *Journal of the History of Philosophy* 17, no. 3 (July 1979): 255–69; Merchant, "The Vitalism of Francis Mercury van Helmont: Its Influence on Leibniz." *Ambix* 26, no. 3 (November 1979): 170–182.

9. Emilie du Châtelet

Carolyn [Merchant] Iltis. "Madame du Châtelet's Metaphysics and Mechanics." *Studies in History and Philosophy of Science* 8, no. 1 (May 1977): 29–48.

IV. ECOLOGY AND CONSERVATION

10. Ecological Revolutions

Carolyn Merchant. "The Theoretical Structure of Ecological Revolutions." *Environmental Review* 11, no. 4 (Winter 1987): 265–74.

11. Shades of Darkness: Race and Environmental History

Carolyn Merchant. "Shades of Darkness: Race and Environmental History." *Environmental History* 8, no. 3 (July 2003): 380–94.

12. Restoring Nature

Carolyn Merchant. "Perspective: Restoration and Reunion with Nature." *Restoration and Management Notes* 4 (Winter 1986): 68–70.

V. ENVIRONMENTAL ETHICS

13. Is It Time for an Earth Ethic?

Carolyn Merchant. "Is it Time for an Earth Ethic?" *Vassar Quarterly* 86, no. 2 (Spring 1990): 10–14. Also "Fish First!: The Changing Ethics of Ecosystem Management." *Human Ecology Review*, special issue on "Emerging Ecological Policy: Winners and Losers" 4, no. 1 (Spring/Summer 1990): 25–30.

14. Ecofeminism and Feminist Theory

Carolyn Merchant. "Ecofeminism and Feminist Theory," in Irene Diamond and Gloria Ornstein, eds., *Reweaving the World: The Emergence of Ecofeminism* (San Francisco: Sierra Club Books, 1990), 100–105.

15. Partnership Ethics

Carolyn Merchant. "Partnership Ethics: Business and the Environment," in Patricia Werhane, ed. *Environmental Challenges to Business*, 1997 Ruffin Lectures, University of Virginia Darden School of Business (Bowling Green, OH: Society for Business Ethics, 2000), pp. 7–18.

VI. CONCLUSION

16. Conclusion: Science for the Twenty-First Century

Carolyn Merchant. *Reinventing Eden*, "Order out of Chaos," (New York: Routledge, 2004), Ch. 10 revised.

PREFACE

In 1979, I began a fabulous new position as Professor of Environmental History, Philosophy, and Ethics at the University of California, Berkeley. I was one of three women hired to teach in the new Department of Conservation and Resource Studies (CRS)—an innovative program designed for undergraduates who wished to create their own majors. The students could invent a title for their major and take eight upper-level courses from any department on the campus—as long as they fit into an environmental theme. The popular major had attracted around 400 students and the men who had started it were successful in getting approval for the three positions. All went to women. Prophetically, they were the last recruitments ever approved for the major. Soon, it was under review and threatened with extinction. But another woman—Cal's first woman provost—stepped in and saved the major. She cut it down to 120 students and tightened the requirements. A decade later, its faculty and students were merged into a larger department dedicated to the theme of Environmental Science, Policy, and Management (ESPM). But the CRS major was allowed to continue and to this day, it still takes on the task of saving the world.

My new position allowed me to meld my background and passion for the history of science, in which I had obtained my doctorate from the University of Wisconsin, Madison, and my position at the University of San Francisco teaching physics for non-science students and history of science with my new job at UC Berkeley. This book, *Science and Nature: Past, Present, and Future*, reflects that synthesis. My overall goal is to explore the interconnections among topics in science, women, nature, and history in Europe and the United States as they have emerged over my academic lifetime.

The book consists of five parts, each three chapters long, with an Introduction, Conclusion, and Epilogue. They have been selected from peer-reviewed articles, updated, and organized to bring together my ideas and interests. The Introduction elaborates on my own intellectual history and how I came to write *The Death of Nature* (1980) and other works. The Conclusion and Epilogue present my vision for the future of science and nature.

Part I on "The Scientific Revolution" focuses on "The Death of Nature" and "Francis Bacon" from a 2005 twenty-fifth anniversary celebration of the book's 1980 publication. The chapter "Isis Consciousness Raised" (Egyptian patroness of the History of Science Society and its journal *Isis*) sets out my lifelong concern with the role of women in science and nature (that ultimately led to the concept of ecofeminism discussed in Part V). In these chapters, I accept the idea that a major transformation known as the "Scientific Revolution" occurred during the sixteenth and seventeenth centuries in the ways that science and nature were understood.

Part II, "On Energy and Momentum," focuses on the remarkable, often bitter controversy that raged for several decades among Descartes, Leibniz, Newton, and their followers over whether what is now known as kinetic energy and momentum were both conserved. But the larger argument entailed the role of God in the universe. Did God show his power and care by intervening to set the planets back in their orbits when perturbed by a passing comet (Newton) or did He create such a perfect cosmos that everything unfolded forever in a pre-established harmony (Leibniz)? These chapters show that larger metaphysical beliefs influenced the ways in which scientists accepted or rejected supposedly "objective" scientific laws and concepts.

Part III is devoted to three pioneering women who explored the foundations of science during the Scientific Revolution—Margaret Cavendish, Anne Conway, and Emilie du Châtelet. Each of these upper-class women was highly educated and ahead of her time in studying and engaging with the issues in science and nature that were gripping learned society at the turn of the seventeenth century. Margaret Cavendish wrote a book about and was enamored by the new "experimental philosophy" and insisted on visiting and observing the experiments created by the all-male Royal Society of London that had been established in 1660. Anne Conway, despite debilitating headaches that devastated her life, studied the origins of philosophy and hypothesized a vitalistic cosmos that was a major influence on Leibniz. Gabrielle Emilie du Châtelet was the brilliant follower of Leibniz and lively mistress of Voltaire, competing with him by secretly entering scientific contests sponsored by the French Academy of Sciences, and translator of Newton's *Principia Mathematica* into French (still the standard translation). Together, these studies show that women engaged in and contributed to the Scientific Revolution in ways that pioneered subsequent investigations by women historians of science.

In Part IV, I bring my concept of the European "Scientific Revolution" to bear on the American environment. I investigate the ways in which the organic view of nature and society in Renaissance Europe influenced European communities in the New World and how those views were then transformed by the Industrial Revolution. In "Shades of Darkness," I analyze how racial ideas helped to form the views of conservationists such as Henry David Thoreau, John Muir, and Mary Austin. I also look at the idea of "restoring nature" (as it existed in the past) through science and ecology.

In Part V on "Environmental Ethics," I ask "Is it Time for an Earth Ethic?" Here I open up connections between people and the land and how we can treat nature with care and respect. I examine linkages between feminism and ecology as they have merged into what is now known as ecofeminism. Finally, I argue that we need a new ethic that I call "Partnership Ethics" and set out what it would look like and why it is needed. In the Conclusion, I explore a new vision for the twenty-first century based on the new sciences of chaos and complexity. As a whole, the book presents my synthesis of themes ranging from the "death of nature" in the Scientific Revolution to new theories of "science and nature" for the future of humanity.

The book's cover image comes from a large poster that hung on the walls of my office for many years. It symbolizes my interests in both the history of science and environmental history. A man peers out from the edge of the earth's atmosphere and the sphere of the moon into the spheres of the planets, the ether, and the heavens beyond. The water and earth at his feet contain plants, trees, fields, and houses. The poster depicts humanity's curiosity, vision, and quest for knowledge. The origins of the image, however, have been debated. It was originally published as a black and white engraving by Camille Flammarion in his 1888 book *The Atmosphere: Popular Meteorology* (*L'atmosphère: météorologie populaire*, Paris: Librairie Hachette, 1888, p. 163). But whether he himself created it from a description, from a group of images, from a similar Renaissance image, or whether he commissioned the painting is not known. The image was rendered in color by UC Berkeley's Roberta Weir in 1970 (see https://en.wikipedia.org/wiki/Flammarion_engraving).

In producing this book, I am grateful to Berkeley colleague Laura Nader and my intellectual companion from college days, Judith Oppenheimer Loth, both of whom suggested that I bring my ideas and writings together in a single volume. I am indebted to my husband, Charles Sellers, whose depth of knowledge about American history, interest in the environment, and fascination with bird life has provided a multitude of ideas and approaches without which I would not have produced the books and articles that have defined my career. My sons David Iltis and John Iltis have engaged me in intense, stimulating discussions over many years as my thoughts have developed and matured. My sister Ann Merchant Boesgaard, an astronomer at the University of Hawaii, has been a role model who shares my interests in the history of astronomy and science. I especially thank my friends, students, and colleagues in my department, on campus, and around the world from whom I have gained numerous insights and had enlightening conversations over the past several decades.

Carolyn Merchant
Berkeley, California

FIGURE 0.1 The Hoodoos in Bryce Canyon

INTRODUCTION

A Look Back*

The shadows lengthened on the red, yellow, and brown pillars of the canyon walls. A panoply of moving colors bathed hundreds of eroded limestone spires as the sun sank over the sculpted peaks. In front of me, my two young sons, 11 and 13 years old, picked their way along a narrow trail across a maze of rock outcrops that dropped precipitously to the river below. We watched as a red-tailed hawk ascended the updrafts to an aerie on the high peaks. The view was breathtaking, the colors magnificent, the rocks vibrant and alive.

It was the summer of 1975; the place was Bryce Canyon, Utah, and the three of us were exploring the canyonlands of the American west. After our evening meal in the park campground, the boys fell into an exhausted slumber. I lay awake pondering the irony of the living rocks. Science viewed them as dead and inert, yet for much of human history those very rocks had been alive—growing and reproducing like plants and animals. It was then that the title of a book I had been sculpting for several years emerged into clear relief. *The Death of Nature* was christened.[1]

Thinking back on that summer of magic, I am awed by the concatenation of personal, intellectual, and social events that led to the formation of the book's thesis. The influences on my life and their intersections with history seem an odd coupling of chance occurrences, mundane events, and strange flashes of understanding. During the 1960s and 1970s, the women's movement sparked by Betty Friedan's *Feminine Mystique* (1963), the environmental movement propelled by Rachel Carson's *Silent Spring* (1962), and the social upheavals of the civil rights and anti-war movements formed my nascent social consciousness.[2]

I entered the environmental movement in the fall of 1959 in a baptism by fire. On my first date with my ex-husband, we went out and burned a Wisconsin prairie. The following spring, a multicolored carpet of exquisite native wildflowers adorned a hillside that had been nearly obliterated by encroaching aspens. Working together to save native prairies for the Nature Conservancy, debating the consequences of Rachel Carson's exposé of pesticides, and pondering the impact of the world population on food supplies, I absorbed an environmental ethic early on in the emerging ecological movement.

I spent most of the 1960s as a graduate student in the University of Wisconsin's provocative program in the History of Science studying the origins of the modern Scientific Revolution and drafting a dissertation on Gottfried Wilhelm Leibniz's concept of living force.[3] I had always been in love with science, especially physics, and was awed by the beauty of its mathematical derivations, simplicity of explanation, and clarity of worldly description. My childhood and high school joy over biology turned to a fascination with chemistry in college, ultimately leading me to the pursuit of physics and then history of science in graduate school. Raising two sons sensitized me to the problems of housewife and career and I devoured Friedan's *Feminine Mystique* when it appeared. I applied for and received one of the nation's first fellowships designed to support women with children who were attempting to finish graduate school, at which task I ultimately succeeded.

By the late 1960s, the stage was set for the three themes that that would subsequently comprise the subtitle of *The Death of Nature*—women, ecology, and the Scientific Revolution. Lacking, however, was the conceptual glue that would soon knit them together. The events of the 1970s in my new home in Berkeley, California, would provide that sinew. I began teaching physical science at the University of San Francisco (USF) amid the social turmoil over the bombing of Cambodia, the emergence of Earth Day 1970, and the questioning of the role played by science in the new electronic battlefield directed at North Vietnam. With our Chinese-American neighbors, my sons and I joined in San Francisco peace marches and worked to integrate the Berkeley schools.

As a young woman on fire with the conventional beauty of science, I was poised at a unique moment in which my personal experiences came into juxtaposition with the social implications of the scientific domination of nature. I began investigating the character of science in terms of its implications for women and nature.

Inspired by the widespread questioning of 1950s' assumptions about science, society, and mainstream values, I started re-evaluating the meaning of my earlier work in the history of science. The history of mechanics as a system of matter in motion on which I had done my graduate work took on new implications when set against a Renaissance cosmology of animate spirits and ensouled beings in which everything was alive. What role did the history of the Scientific Revolution play in the way we in the late twentieth century world were conducting our lives? What historical alternatives, both real and utopian, had challenged some of the excesses of mainstream society? Such questions stimulated my work as a teacher and I turned to students, colleagues, and friends in seeking answers.

At USF, I introduced a new course on science and society and began teaching the social context of the rise of modern science in my history of science courses. Then in the summer of 1972, I traveled to Italy to participate in the Enrico Fermi Institute's course on the "History of Twentieth Century Physics" in which issues of the social responsibility of science took center stage. From Marxist philosopher of physics Robert Cohen, I learned that the Scientific Revolution had been explained by historian Boris Hessen (1931) and sociologist Edgar Zilsel (1953) as phenomena arising out of early capitalist development and emerging middle-class crafts and trades. Cohen also introduced me to William Leiss's new book, *The Domination of Nature*, which appeared in the fall of 1972. I began to understand some of the specific ways in which economic and social changes could influence the choices and underlying assumptions available to scientists as they pursued their theoretical work.[4]

That fall, two additional events conspired to change my outlook and launch the writing of the book. While teaching my new science and society course, I heard high praise from science writer Daniel Greenberg for Theodore Roszak's *Where the Wasteland Ends*.[5] Not only was Roszak's book a startling critique of mechanistic science and an exploration of alternative timetold approaches such as the Gnostic tradition and William Blake's art and poetry, but it heralded a new holistic ecological worldview. It was through Ted Roszak's subsequent kindness that the manuscript of *The Death of Nature* made its way to the desk of my editor, John Shopp of Harper, San Francisco.

On the very same day that I learned of Roszak's remarkable book, I also met fellow historian of science David Kubrin. David, who had done a graduate dissertation on Isaac Newton and published a highly regarded article on "Newton and the Cyclical Cosmos" (1967),[6] attended a lecture given by our British colleague, Peter Harman. Peter noticed a guy in the audience sewing patches on his clothing and from the nature of his post-lecture question deduced that this must indeed be the well-known Kubrin. Early the next year, I began attending a small class on the rise of modern science given by Kubrin at an alternative school in San Francisco. David introduced me and others to the pamphlet *Witches, Midwives, and Nurses* by Barbara Ehrenreich and Deirdre English as well as ideas that took seriously the work of the alternative magical tradition in science history.[7] It was David's idea that the key concept of early modern science was that matter was dead. In a 1972 article entitled "How Sir Isaac Newton Helped Restore Law 'n' Order to the West" and a later article called "Newton's Inside Out" (1981), Kubrin explored the role that Newton played in suppressing magical and alchemical ideas in society and in his own mind and promoting the mechanical view of nature.[8] My work on Leibniz and David's work on Newton provided grist for an emerging analysis of the rise of modern science in which a world of living, vital forces gave way to a dead mechanical system that supported the new capitalist tendencies of early modern society.

What ultimately emerged as *The Death of Nature* began as a series of three essays I started writing in the summer of 1973. The first was on women and witches in the sixteenth and seventeenth centuries, the second interpreted the change from magic to mechanism, and the third rethought the meaning of science and utopias from Campanella and Andrae to Francis Bacon. I began giving papers on "women and nature" and on "natural philosophy and the environmental crisis" to local, national, and international meetings of the History of Science Society and the American Historical Association.

Under the threat of recessionary layoffs at USF in 1976, I applied for and received four fellowships and grants that enabled me to rework and expand the initial essays into a book-length manuscript that covered the period of the entire Scientific Revolution. Despite the economic hardships of the layoffs and part-time employment, the times were intellectually heady. With great excitement, I read and absorbed hundreds of articles and books on the period. Everything seemed to fit together and to make sense of a period I had begun to know intimately and love deeply. As the book neared completion, I accepted employment at the University of California, Berkeley, in an environmental studies program in the College of Natural Resources. After revisions and final editing, *The Death of Nature* was launched in June 1980.

The book's debut was surprising. A friend invited me to take a tour of Berkeley's Telegraph Avenue where it was displayed in several bookstore windows. Another friend who gave me a book party reported the incredulity of a local bakery: "You want 'death' on a cake?" I gave talks that week on the UC campus to the Women's Studies program and at Cody's bookstore to large numbers of people. The *California Monthly* featured an early review. I was soon asked to give an endowed lecture at Harvey Mudd College, the first of many such invitations over the years. For an academic book, which my editor said was ahead of its time, this response was gratifying. There were three obvious audiences for its themes: feminists, environmentalists, and historians of science and technology. Yet the book also garnered interest from political scientists, sociologists, philosophers, geographers, English teachers, and scientists. Over one hundred reviews of the book have appeared during its lifetime. Among those who appraised, reviewed, or discussed the book were: Christopher Hill, Everett Mendelsohn, Houston Baker, Jr., Fritjof Capra,

Walter Pagel, Evelyn Fox Keller, Donna Haraway, Helen Longino, Susan Griffin, Stephen Brush, Joan Rothschild, Margaret Jacob, Bruno Latour, Nina Gelbart, Tore Frängsmyr, Ronnie Ambjörnsson, Shigeru Nakayama, John Perkins, Audrey Davis, Margaret Osler, Rita Arditti, Joseph Meeker, Harold Gilliam, Murray Bookchin, Jim Swan, Kirkpatrick Sale, David Ray Griffin, and Jerry Mander.[9]

The early reviews focused on the connections between science and the domination of nature and on the relationships between women and nature. Reviewers emphasized the argument that the mechanistic worldview laid open a new and brutal exploitation of the environment, animals, and a living, vital nature. The shift was part of a rejection of the feminine as a constitutive part of reality and a concomitant oppression of women. The machine metaphor redefined reality as controlling heretofore unruly events. There was praise for the integration of topics as diverse as ecology, natural magic, utopias, witch trials, midwives, women scientists, and for the recasting of the work of such founders of modern science as Francis Bacon, René Descartes, William Harvey, Thomas Hobbes, Isaac Newton, and Gottfried Wilhelm Leibniz. Some commentators admired its lively style and correlated illustrations, while others found it dry and academic in tone.

More controversial was the issue of how historical events were related to each other and especially to ideas. One reviewer noted that the ideas explored in the book sometimes reflected social values and sometimes seemed to trigger changes. Yet this was a proverbial problem for historians, she stated, and the strength of the argument was that it avoided simple causations and hasty conclusions. Plausibility, associated values, compatibility, and the simultaneity of events made for a rich and complex argument. Others agreed that this approach resisted an easy determinism in favor of subtlety. Still others were concerned that the book's crusading tone and feminist orientation might create opposition. Yet another objection lay in the problem of the precise relationship between female metaphors that described nature and the social subjection of women.

The book soon found an audience beyond academia. It made its way into congressional circles at a House of Representatives hearing on energy research and production in 1980; was addressed by Ronald Reagan's science advisor, George A. Keyworth II, in 1982; and was picked up by *Newsweek* in a 1983 discussion of the mainstreaming of feminist scholarship. The book made its television debut in the British production of *Crucible: A History of Nature* by Central Television in January 1983, the first third of which was based on *The Death of Nature*.[10]

Soon foreign journals and newspapers began to take notice of the book and its thesis. Early in 1981, Tore Frängsmyr introduced the topic to the Swedish audience and the publicity he gave it was followed by reviews in the *Gothenburg Post* and Stockholm's *Dagens Nyheter* later that year. The book was reviewed in France in 1981, Japan in 1982, Poland in 1983, and in Denmark, France, and Germany in 1984. India gave it a central place in its 1984–85 report on *The State of India's Environment*, and in 1986, it received attention in Australia. With its translation into Japanese (1985), German (1987, with a mass market edition in 1994), Italian (1988), Swedish (1994), and Chinese (Green Classics Library, 1999), additional foreign language reviews followed. In 1990, a tenth-anniversary second edition appeared in English.[11]

In assessing the impact of the book's lifespan, three contributions seem to stand out. The book was an early critique of the problems of modernism and especially mechanistic science and its associated worldview that lent grist to the postmodern deconstruction of Enlightenment optimism and progress. Second, as ecofeminism gained attention in the 1980s and 1990s, the book came to be viewed as an early classic statement of the women-nature relationship. Third, the book pointed the way toward a reassessment of the human ethical relationship to nature by moving away from ideas of domination and toward a new dynamic partnership between people and their environment. Over the years, at numerous gatherings and lectures on several continents, people have told me that *The Death of Nature* has affected their lives, even changed their whole way of thinking. For this I am very grateful.

Since 1980, my own work has moved beyond *The Death of Nature's* assessment of the Scientific Revolution and toward a reassessment of the book's implications for American history, the current environmental movement, and a new environmental ethic. In *Ecological Revolutions: Nature, Gender, and Science in New England* (1989), I asked how the issues discussed in seventeenth-century Europe were played out in America.[12] I attempted to develop a more precise approach to the interactions between ideas, the material world, and social and economic change by articulating a model of revolutionary transformations based on ecology, production, reproduction, and consciousness. These American "ecological revolutions" bore similarities to the change from an organic to a mechanical worldview brought about by early capitalist development discussed in *The Death of Nature*. In *Radical Ecology* (1992), I expanded the idea of ecological revolutions to an analysis of the environmental movement of the past thirty years and in *Earthcare: Women and the Environment* (1996), I attempted to develop more precise relationships between women's involvement in environmental movements and symbols of nature as female.[13] In *Reinventing Eden: The Fate of Nature in Western Culture*, I worked out the details of a partnership ethic between people and the non-human environment that removes some of the stigmas associated historically with nature as female and men as agents of domination and draws on some of the newer developments in the sciences such as chaos and complexity theory.[14] And with my most recent book, *Autonomous Nature: Problems of Prediction and Control from Ancient Times to the Scientific Revolution*, I have come full circle back to the issues of the European transformation. Here I emphasize the aspect of nature that is unruly, unlawful, rambunctious, and recalcitrant as manifested in the unpredictability of volcanoes, earthquakes, tsunamis, and plagues.[15]

In thinking back to the poignancy of that summer of 1975 in Bryce Canyon and to my many subsequent encounters with the birds and mountains of the world, accompanied by loved family members and friends, I am brought increasingly to appreciate the power of life on the planet and the need for an ethic of earthcare. If *The Death of Nature* contributes even in some small way to a new environmental consciousness, its legacy will live on.

NOTES

* From Carolyn Merchant, "The Death of Nature: A Retrospective," Organization and Environment 11, no. 2 (June 1998): 198–206. Reprinted by permission of Sage Publications, Inc.
1. Carolyn Merchant, *The Death of Nature: Women, Ecology, and the Scientific Revolution* (San Francisco, CA: HarperCollins, 1980; 2nd ed. 1990).
2. Betty Friedan, *The Feminine Mystique* (New York: Dell, 1963); Rachel Carson, *Silent Spring* (Boston: Houghton Mifflin, 1962).
3. Carolyn [Merchant] Iltis, "The Controversy Over Living Force: Leibniz to D'Alembert," Doctoral Dissertation, University of Wisconsin, Madison, 1967.
4. Boris Hessen, *The Social and Economic Roots of Newton's 'Principia'*, with a new introduction by Robert S. Cohen (New York: Howard Fertig, 1971 [1931]); Edgar Zilsel, "The Genesis of the Concept of Scientific Progress," in Philip P. Wiener and Aaron Noland, eds., *The Roots of Scientific Thought* (New York: Basic Books, 1957): 251–75; William Leiss, *The Domination of Nature* (New York: George Braziller, 1972).
5. Theodore Roszak, *Where the Wasteland Ends: Politics and Transcendence in Post-Industrial Society* (Garden City, NY: Doubleday, 1972).
6. David Kubrin, "Newton and the Cyclical Cosmos: Providence and the Mechanical Philosophy," *Journal of the History of Ideas* 28 (July–September 1967): 325–46.
7. Barbara Ehrenreich and Deirdre English, *Witches, Midwives, and Nurses* (Old Westbury, NY: Feminist Press, 1973).
8. David Kubrin, "How Sir Isaac Newton Helped Restore Law 'n' Order to the West," *Liberation* 16, no. 10 (March 1972): 32–41; David Kubrin, "Newton's Inside Out! Magic, Class Struggle, and the Rise of Mechanisms in the West," in Harry Woolf, ed., *The Analytic Spirit: Essays on the History of Science in Honor of Henry Guerlac* (Ithaca, NY: Cornell University Press, 1981), pp. 96-121.
9. See Carolyn Merchant's website, "Reviews of Her Books," https://ourenvironment.berkeley.edu/people/carolyn-merchant; for the reviews, see https://nature.berkeley.edu/departments/espm/env-hist/reviews.html.
10. Mick Gold (producer), *Crucible: A History of Nature*, TV series episode (January 16, 1983; England: Central Television), Television.
11. See Carolyn Merchant's website, "Reviews of Her Books"; "The Second Citizen's Report," in Anil Agarwal, ed., *The State of India's Environment, 1984–85* (New Delhi: Centre for Science and Environment, 1985), p. 370; Carolyn Merchant, *The Death of Nature: Women, Ecology, and the Scientific Revolution* (London: Wildwood House, 1983); Carolyn Merchant, *The Death of Nature: Women, Ecology, and the Scientific Revolution*, Japanese

translation (Tokyo: Kousakusha, 1985); Carolyn Merchant, *Der Tod der Natur: Ökologie, Frauen und neuzeitliche Naturwissenschaft* (Munich: C. H. Beck, 1987); Carolyn Merchant, *La Morte Della Natura: Donne, ecologia e Rivoluzione scientifica* (Milan: Garzanti Editorial, 1988); Carolyn Merchant, *Der Tod Der Natur* (Munich: C.H. Beck, mass market paperback, 1994); Carolyn Merchant, *Naturens Död: Kvinnan, Ekologin och den Vetenskapliga Revolutionen* (Stockholm, Stegag: Symposion, 1994); Carolyn Merchant, *The Death of Nature: Women, Ecology, and the Scientific Revolution*, Chinese translation (Beijing: Jilin Peoples' Publishing House, 1999).

12. Carolyn Merchant, *Ecological Revolutions: Nature, Gender, and Science in New England* (Chapel Hill, NC: University of North Carolina Press, 1989).

13. Carolyn Merchant, *Radical Ecology: The Search for a Livable World* (New York: Routledge, 1992); Carolyn Merchant, *Earthcare: Women and the Environment* (New York: Routledge, 1996).

14. Carolyn Merchant, *Reinventing Eden: The Fate of Nature in Western Culture* (New York: Routledge, 2003; 2nd ed. 2013). Text added to original article.

15. Carolyn Merchant, *Autonomous Nature: Problems of Prediction and Control from Ancient Times to the Scientific Revolution* (New York: Routledge, 2016). Text added to original article.

Part I

THE SCIENTIFIC REVOLUTION

"The world we have lost was organic." So begins my book *The Death of Nature: Women, Ecology, and the Scientific Revolution*, which first appeared in 1980. In it I argue that roughly between the time of Nicolaus Copernicus's *On the Revolutions of the Heavenly Spheres* in 1543 and Isaac Newton's *Principles of Mathematical Philosophy* in 1687, a fundamental transformation took place. A world that was structured by close-knit, organic communities, an earth that was alive and filled with living things (including minerals and metals) that grew in "her" womb, and an earth-centered cosmos comprising a body, soul, and spirit became a machine. By the late seventeenth century, matter was made up of "dead" inert corpuscles (or atoms), God was a clockmaker, an engineer, and a mathematician, and the human body was like a machine or as Thomas Hobbes's put it, "What is the heart, but a spring; the nerves, but so many strings; and the joints but so many wheels?"[1] Under pre-industrial capitalism, a new world was explored and exploited, machines extracted metals from the earth, and nation states were based on competitive self interest in which one mixed one's labor with the soil and gained title to the land.

In Chapter 1 of this section, I offer a twenty-five year retrospective (from 2005) on the contributions that *The Death of Nature* made to ecofeminism, environmental history, and reassessments of the Scientific Revolution. I also respond to challenges to my argument that Francis Bacon's rhetoric legitimated the control of nature. Although Bacon did not use terms such as the torture of nature, his followers, with some justification, interpreted his rhetoric in that light.

In Chapter 2, originally published in 2008, I continue to engage with the work of Francis Bacon on the domination of nature. Bacon's use of metaphors to characterize his nascent concept of experimentation must be interpreted within attempts to "penetrate" the "secrets of nature" prevalent during his time. His language should be placed in the context of settings such as the courtroom, the anatomy theater, and the laboratory. Here I look specifically at the history of the anatomy theater as an arena for dissecting the human body and by extension the body of nature.

In Chapter 3, "Isis Consciousness Raised," published in 1982, soon after *The Death of Nature* appeared, I focus on how a feminist perspective on the history of science can impact the field. I examine three aspects of the connections between women and science. First, how can a feminist perspective help to analyze the Western scientific worldview and its historical origins? Second, what is the role of image, language, and metaphor in writing the history of science? Third, how were the roles of women and women scientists portrayed by historians of science before widespread consciousness about the role of women in science began to emerge in the 1980s and beyond by women historians of science?

Together, the chapters in Part I, "The Scientific Revolution," bring together thoughts and ideas that emerged in my scholarly work after the publication of *The Death of Nature* and reflect on research and reactions to the book.

NOTE

1. Thomas Hobbes, *Leviathan or the Matter, Forme, and Commonwealth Ecclesiasticall, and Civil* (New York: Dutton, 1950), "The Introduction," p. 3.

FIGURE 1.1 The Earth-Centered Cosmos

Source: Robert Fludd, *Utriusque Cosmi Maioris Scilicet et Minoris Metaphysica* (Oppenheim, Germany, 1617–1621), vol. 1, p. 3, engraved by Johann Theodore de Bry. Public domain.

1

THE DEATH OF NATURE*

In 1980, the year *The Death of Nature* appeared, Congress passed the Super-fund Act, ecofeminists held their first nationwide conference, and environmentalists celebrated the tenth anniversary of Earth Day. *The Death of Nature*, subtitled "Women, Ecology, and the Scientific Revolution," spoke to all three events. The chemicals that polluted the soil and water symbolized nature's death from the very success of mechanistic science. The 1980 "Women and Life on Earth: Ecofeminism in the '80s" conference heralded women's efforts to reverse that death. Earth Day celebrated a decade of recognition that humans and ecology were deeply intertwined. The papers in this chapter reflect the themes of the book's subtitle, and I shall comment on each of them in that order. I shall also elaborate on my analysis of Francis Bacon's rhetoric on the domination and control of nature.[1]

When *The Death of Nature* appeared in 1980, the concept of ecofeminism was just emerging (see Chapter 14 in this volume). The 1980 conference organized by Ynestra King and others seemed to me to offer an antidote to the death of nature and the basis for an activist movement to undo the problems that the Scientific Revolution had raised for contemporary culture in the form of the environmental crisis. Moreover, it connected the effects of nuclear fall-out and chemical pollutants on women's (and men's) reproductive systems to the relations between production and reproduction I had discussed in *The Death of Nature*.[2]

Ecofeminism linked the domination of women with the domination of nature and recognized the values and activities associated with women, including childbearing and nurturing. Ecofeminism, however, faced a critique by academic women during the 1980s and 1990s that it was essentialist in its conflation of women with nature, implying not only that women's nature is to nurture, but also that women's role is to clean up the environmental mess made by men. Critics pointed out that women who came to the defense of nature were actually cementing their own oppression in the very hierarchies that (as anthropologist Sherry Ortner had argued) identified men with culture and women with nature.[3]

My own efforts to deal with the problems of essentialism and nature/culture dualism led me to develop a form of ecofeminism rooted not in dualism but in the dialectics of production and reproduction that I had articulated in *The Death of Nature*. There I argued that nature cast in the female gender when stripped of activity and rendered passive could be dominated by science, technology, and capitalist production. During the transition to early modern capitalism, women lost ground in the sphere of production (through curtailment of their roles in the trades), while in the sphere of reproduction, William Harvey and other male physicians were instrumental in undermining women's traditional roles in midwifery and hence women's control over their own bodies.[4] During the same period, Francis Bacon advocated extracting nature's secrets from "her" bosom through science and technology. The subjugation of nature as female, I argued, was thus integral to the scientific method as power over nature: "As woman's womb had symbolically yielded to the forceps, so nature's womb harbored secrets that through technology could be wrested from her grasp for use in the improvement of the human condition."[5]

The dialectical relationships between production and reproduction became for me the basis for a form of socialist ecofeminism grounded in material change. I also addressed the related problem of nature depicted as female, and its conflation with women, by advocating the removal of gendered terminology from the description of nature and the substitution of the gender-neutral term "partner." This led me to articulate an ethic of partnership with nature in which nature was no longer symbolized as mother, virgin, or witch, but as an active partner with humanity.[6]

The role of ecology in the Scientific Revolution was the second of the three themes in *The Death of Nature*'s subtitle "Women, Ecology, and the Scientific Revolution." In *The Death of Nature*, a bridge between the history of science and environmental history was developed most explicitly in Chapter 2, "Farm, Fen, and Forest," on the ecological and economic changes taking place in Western Europe during the period of the rise of mercantile capitalism and the nation state.[7] That chapter argues that ecological and technological changes in the late sixteenth and early seventeenth centuries helped to create material conditions that made new ideas plausible. I did not argue that material or ecological changes *cause* or *determine* ideological changes. Rather they make some ideas prevalent at the time seem more plausible than others. Some ideas die out or become less compelling (in this case, those associated with natural magic and the organic worldview), while others are developed and accepted, in particular those that led to mechanical explanations for phenomena and the mechanistic worldview. *The Death of Nature* moved back and forth between material and social conditions and ideas about nature and science. Thus ecological and material changes can both be seen as fundamental to understanding the rise of mechanism and to the argument for the links between environmental history and the history of science.[8]

In *The Death of Nature*, I focused on nature symbolized as female, but I did not believe that nature itself was a universal force. Rather nature is characterized by ecological laws and processes described by the laws of thermodynamics and by energy exchanges among biotic and abiotic components of an ecosystem. Any of these components can become an actor or actors in an environmental history of a particular place. In my 1989 book *Ecological Revolutions*, I developed a theory of ecology, production, reproduction, and consciousness in which "material, cultural, and social relations" are all interacting parts of ecological history. While I would still argue that the drivers of change are material (bacteria, insects, plants, and animals—including humans) and economic (explorations, colonization, markets, and capital), new ideas can support and legitimate new directions and actions taken by groups of people, societies, and nations.[9]

The Scientific Revolution is the third theme in the book's subtitle. While *The Death of Nature* in general had an arresting impact in many fields and was used widely in courses, the book also had a substantial audience among historians of science.[10] Although awarded accolades by the field's heavyweights such as Everett Mendelsohn, Walter Pagel, and Frances Yates, the book challenged the pedestal on which historians had tended to place the Scientific Revolution. It questioned the grand narrative of the Scientific Revolution as progress and undermined the valorization of the most revered fathers of modern science—such as Harvey, Bacon, Descartes, and Newton. It argued that seventeenth-century mechanistic science itself contributed to the most pressing ecological and social problems of today and dared to suggest that women were as much the victims as the beneficiaries of the progress of science. The book contributed to a growing body of scholarship that led to the interest of historians of science in the social construction of nature, the importance of the role of women in science, and to the questioning of grand narratives and the ways that science was implicated in ideologies of progress.

In *The Death of Nature*, I focused on the major transformations in science and society that occurred during the sixteenth and seventeenth centuries (1500–1700) from Copernicus to Newton, from Renaissance natural magic to the mechanical worldview, and from the breakup of feudalism to the rise of mercantile capitalism and the nation state. I could also have emphasized the explorations of the New World (depicted as female) as a source of natural resources for the emerging European economies, connections I later developed in *Ecological Revolutions* (1989) and *Reinventing Eden* (2003). An understanding of the ways in which "early modern science" engaged with the everyday world has been enriched by metaphors and emblems of female nature and the female body, as well as by studies of scientific patronage and the witnessing of experiments.[11]

The notion of a "Scientific Revolution" in the sixteenth and seventeenth centuries is part of a larger narrative of Western culture that has propelled science, technology, and capitalism's efforts to "master" nature—a narrative into which most Westerners have unconsciously been socialized and within which we ourselves become actors in a storyline of upward progress. Demoting the "Scientific Revolution" to the mere nomer of "early modern science" obscures the power of dominant narratives, such as colonialism and imperialism, which have helped to shape Western culture since the seventeenth century at the expense of nature, women, minorities, and indigenous peoples. This move hides the political power played by scientific narratives in remaking the earth and its natural resources as objects for human use.[12]

II

Francis Bacon's influence and reputation as a founder of modern science has been the subject of debate in recent years.[13] In *The Death of Nature*, I argued that Bacon's goal was to use constraint and force to extract truths from nature. His choice of words was part of a larger project to create a new method that would allow humanity to control and dominate the natural world.[14]

I stated that "much of the imagery [Bacon] used in delineating his new scientific objectives and methods derives from the courtroom, and, because it treats nature as a female to be tortured through mechanical inventions, strongly suggests the interrogations of the witch trials and the mechanical devices used to torture witches" and quoted a passage from Bacon's *Advancement of Learning*. I also suggested that "the strong sexual implications of the last sentence can be interpreted in the light of the investigation of the supposed sexual crimes and practices of witches."[15]

I did not claim, however, that Bacon himself used the phrases "torture nature" or "putting nature on the rack." He believed that everything in nature should be studied, including those valid things that witches might indeed know about nature. But nature was nevertheless to be studied through interrogation. The goal, as Peter Pesic argued, was to extract the truth.[16] While some scholars read Bacon's passages and methods of interrogation as a benign means of obtaining knowledge, I read them as legitimation for the domination of nature.

******

What were Bacon's views about the torture of nature and witches? It would be naïve to believe that Bacon was ignorant of knowledge of the most severe means of torture or of the methods of examining women's bodies for evidence of consorting with the devil or of James I's early obsession and involvement with these methods. The European Inquisition, torture practices, and death were part of the context of his life and world and were known by that widely read and influential man. In addition to the rack, the instruments of torture included the breast strip, breast press, witches chair, ducking stool, Judas cradle, expanding vaginal pears, the wheel, the ladder, the strangle, the hanging strap, and the funnel and water torture.[17]

Bacon did not advocate the practice of torture or use of the rack on human beings. He nevertheless used imagery drawn from torture in his writings and believed that witchcraft and sorcery could reveal useful information. The method of confining, controlling, and interrogating the human being becomes the method of the confined, controlled experiment used to interrogate nature. The experimental method is superior to that developed by magicians to control nature. A question must be asked and an experiment designed to answer it. For the experimental method to succeed, the experiment must be a closed, isolated system in which variables are controlled and extraneous influences excluded. Witnessing is critical to the process. The trial, i.e., the experiment, must be witnessed by others. Indeed it was one of

FIGURE 1.2 The Rack

Source: Replica of the rack, http://geocities.com/christprise/. Public domain.

Bacon's singular contributions to realize that to understand nature, it must be studied under constrained conditions that can be both witnessed and verified by others. Bacon used metaphor, rhetoric, and myth to develop his new method of interrogating nature. As Peter Pesic notes, "Since he was describing something not yet formed, he used a rich variety of rhetorical figures to express his vision."[18]

Bacon promoted the study and interrogation of sorcerers and practitioners of the occult arts for clues as to how nature worked and how the devil worked through nature. In endeavoring to gain power over nature, he drew heavily on the alchemical and magical traditions for clues that would lead to the human control of nature. He accepted the goal and idea of control, but sought new methods of extracting knowledge. What was true should be sorted out from that which was erroneous. The problem with magic was that it was rooted in individual knowledge and judgment, rather than being subjected to a set of universal rules and agreements. As Paolo Rossi put it, "According to Bacon, magic endeavours to dominate and to improve nature; and for this it should be imitated. Where it needs revising is in its claim to use one man's inspiration instead of the organised efforts of the human race, and to make science serve individual ends rather than mankind."[19]

Even though Bacon opposed the practice of torture, his rhetoric and metaphors for the interrogation of nature under constraint come from the devices of torture in his cultural milieu, the rack being one such device. According to Leonard A. Parry, "Not only was the fabric of a case often built up on the allegations of the hired creatures of the Government, but the existence of the rack gave a preposterous twist to the words of every witness." The rack, he states, was the most frequent method of torture used in England. Introduced during the reign of Henry VI, it consisted of an oak frame three feet above the ground, on or under which the prisoner with hands and feet bound to rollers and levers on each end was placed on his back. The levers were then moved to exert force on the joints and sockets until the prisoner responded to the interrogation.[20]

****

If Bacon did not explicitly state that nature should be put on the rack, however, where did that phrase come from? The rack and its association with Bacon and the torture of nature seem to have been present in cultural exchanges at least by the late seventeenth century. Peter Pesic details the history of the association of Bacon's ideas with the torture of nature and of putting nature on the rack.[21] He points out that its connection to Bacon may first have been put in writing by Gottfried Wilhelm Leibniz. In 1696, Leibniz wrote about "the art of inquiry into nature itself and of putting it on the rack—the art of experiment which Lord Bacon began so ably."[22] Four years later, Jean Baptiste du Hamel, secretary of the Paris Academy of Sciences, wrote, "we discover the mysteries of nature much more easily when she is tortured [torqueatur] by fire or some other aids of art than when she proceeds along her own road."[23] The Latin verb "torqueo" means "to turn, twist, wind, or wrench" and "of torturing on the rack, etc: to rack, wrench," as well as "to rack, torture, torment." Under the word "rack," the *Oxford English Dictionary* includes: "racken 'torquere, tendere, tormentis, experime.' See also . . . racken, to vex, torture (Grimm)." There are thus clear associations between the word torture and the rack.[24] In contrast to Leibniz and Hamel, Wolfgang von Goethe complained that under scientific investigation, "nature falls silent on the rack," and urged that "phenomena must once and for all be removed from their gloomy empirical-mechanical-dogmatic torture chamber."[25]

Later philosophers also associated the torture of nature with Francis Bacon. In 1878, Thomas Fowler wrote that Bacon "insisted, both by example and precept, on the importance of experiment as well as observation. Nature like a witness, when put to the torture, would reveal her secrets."[26] In 1953, Ernst Cassirer noted that Bacon's approach to science was to treat nature as if it were a witness on the rack. Cassirer wrote:

> The very style of Bacon's writing evinces everywhere this spirit. Bacon sits as a judge over reality, questioning it as one examines the accused. Not infrequently he says that one must resort to force to obtain the answer desired, that nature must be 'put to the rack'. His procedure is not simply observational but strictly inquisitorial. The witnesses are heard and brought face to face; the negative instances confront the affirmative ones, just as the witnesses for the defence confront those for the prosecution. After all the available bits of evidence have been gathered together and evaluated, then it is a matter of obtaining the confession which finally decides the issue. But such a confession is not obtainable without resorting to coercive measures. [As Bacon states,] 'For like as a man's disposition is never well known or proved till he be crossed . . . so nature exhibits herself more clearly under the trials and vexations of art than when left to herself.'[27]

And in 1975, historian Charles Webster in *The Great Instauration: Science, Medicine, and Reform, 1626–1660* concurred: "By 'interrogation' applied with extreme determination and cunning, nature would be 'tortured' into revealing her secrets; she would then submit to voluntary 'subjugation.'"[28]

Was Bacon's method of interrogating nature to put it on the rack? These philosophers certainly interpreted him that way. To them, the rack exemplified the constraint of nature in a closed, controlled system responding to questions posed by an inquisitor before witnesses, the very core of experimentation itself. Through metaphor and imagery, Bacon struggled to define experimentation as a new way of learning nature's truths.

A related controversy arises over Bacon's use of the terms "hound," "vex," and the "vexation" of nature. "Even though Bacon's use of vex is occasionally strong," Alan Soble writes, "'vex' does not always or usually carry a pernicious connotation but is meant, innocuously along the lines of his hound and my pester." In a passage from *De Dignitate*, Bacon writes: "For you have but to follow and as it were hound nature in her wanderings, and you will be able when you like to lead and drive her afterward to the same place again." The *Oxford English Dictionary* gives the following definition of the word "hound": "to pursue, chase, or track like a hound, or, as if with hound; esp. to pursue harassingly, to drive as in the chase" and quotes the previous phrase from Bacon's the 1605 *Advancement of Learning* as the first example. Other definitions of hound are equally violent: "to set (a hound, etc.) at a quarry; to incite or urge on to attack or chase anything" and "to incite or set (a person) at or on another; to incite or urge on." Such meanings are reminiscent of the English fox hunt (outlawed by the British Parliament in 2005) for its excessive cruelty to the hounded and tortured foxes. Nature for Bacon, as Soble himself puts it, must be "out-foxed." But, contrary to Soble's desire to read Bacon's rhetoric innocuously, merely "pestering" nature would not produce the results Bacon desired for his new method, i.e., extracting the secrets of nature.[29]

Bacon also used the term "vex" to refer to the interrogation of nature under constraint: "The vexations of art are certainly as the bonds and handcuffs of Proteus, which betray the ultimate struggles and efforts of matter." Art in this context meant *techne* or the technologies used to "vex" nature. The term "vex," meaning "to shake, agitate, disturb," likewise carried connotations of violence, including to aggressively harass, physically distress, to twist, press, and strain, and to subject to violence.[30] All these meanings convey force in ways that range from irritation to inflicting physical pain through intentional violence. All precisely describe much of the early experimentation done on animals and human beings as discussed later.

Vex and torture were closely associated in Bacon's cultural milieu. The French historian Pierre Hadot, in *Le Voile D'Isis: Essai sur l'histoire de l'idée de Nature*, quotes a recent French translation of the *Novum Organum* that renders the English phrase "the vexations of art" in French as "la torture des arts [mécaniques]," i.e., "the torture of the [mechanical] arts." A possible French translation of the English word "vex" is in fact "tormenter."[31]

Soble suggests that Bacon's association of the vexations of art with Proteus does not pertain to nature as female because Proteus was a "guy." Yet Bacon himself compares Proteus to nature in the female gender as was common in the period (translations not withstanding): "For like as a man's disposition is never well known or proved till he be crossed, nor Proteus ever changed shapes till he was straitened and held fast, so nature exhibits herself more clearly under the trials and vexations of art than when left to herself." The verb "straiten" in the seventeenth century meant "to tighten a knot, cord, or bonds—an act that would hold a body fast as on the rollers and levers of the rack." As John C. Briggs, in his discussion of Bacon's use of the Proteus myth, states: "Still the lesson that Bacon draws from the myth turns upon the wise man's power to chain Proteus to the rack so as to force matter 'to extremities, as if with the purpose of reducing it to nothing.'"[32]

For Bacon, the myth of Proteus was a stand-in for the interrogation of nature under constraint. Proteus was a Greek sea god (the prophetic "old man of the sea"), the son of Neptune and herder of Poseidon's seals. He had the gift both of prophecy and of changing his shape at will. He would not share his knowledge of the future and changed his shape to avoid doing so unless held fast. He would reveal the future only to someone who could capture and constrain him. Capturing and constraining was the very method used to extract confessions and secrets from witches. Bacon's use of the terms straiten, held fast, and vexed all indicate violence toward nature and, I would still argue, casting nature in the female gender (both then and now) legitimates the treatment of nature in ethically questionable ways (Proteus being a "guy" notwithstanding).[33]

III

Bacon's words and work influenced the growth of scientific societies and experimentation in the early modern period (even if he himself did not anticipate their development). Although condemned by individuals such as John Locke, John Wesley, Joseph Butler, and Gottfried Wilhelm Leibniz, experiments done on animals during the seventeenth and eighteenth centuries and continuing even to the present could be described as torture. Such experimentation was legitimated by the mechanical philosophy of nature that viewed animals as automata. Both René Descartes and Thomas Hobbes conceptualized the bodies of humans and other animals as machines. Descartes denied thought to animals although he admitted life and sensation. In his *Meditations on the First Philosophy* (1641), he wrote, "if the body of man be considered as a kind of machine, so made up and composed of bones, nerves, muscles, veins, blood, and skin, that although there were in it no mind, it would still exhibit the same motions which it at present manifests involuntarily." In his introduction to *Leviathan* ten years later (1651), Hobbes stated, "For what is the heart, but a spring; and the nerves, but so many strings; and the joints, but so many wheels, giving motion to the whole body, such as was intended by the artificer." If animals or even human bodies were thought of as machines, experimentation could be done with impunity.[34]

In England, the Cambridge Platonist Thomas More objected to Descartes' idea of animal automata, writing in 1648: "I recognize in you not only subtle keenness, but also, as it were, the sharp and cruel blade which in one blow, so to speak, dared to despoil of life and sense practically the whole race of animals, metamorphosing them into marble statues and machines." In his response, Descartes continued to deny a soul to animals, writing, "I speak of cogitation, not of life or sense; for to no animal do I deny life, inasmuch as that I attribute solely to the heat of the heart; nor do I deny sense in so far as it depends upon the bodily organism. And thus my opinion is not so much cruel to wild beasts as favourable to men, whom it absolves . . . of any suspicion of crime, however often they may eat or kill animals." Although objections to the concept of the "beast-machine" were voiced in England, the idea nevertheless lent credence to the notion of animal experimentation.[35]

In his *History of the Royal Society* (1667), Thomas Sprat reported on experiments done on animals under constraint, experiments that could be considered torture: "Experiments of keeping creatures many hours alive, by blowing into the lungs with bellows, after that all the thorax, and abdomen were open'ed and cut away, and all the Intrials save heart, and lungs remov'd: of reviving chickens, after they have been strangled, by blowing into their lungs: to try how long a man can live, by expiring, and inspiring again the same air." Sprat describes the fatal effects on animals of keeping them in rarified air and of investigations into the amount of air necessary for a breathing animal to survive. Experiments were made on living animals kept in a bell jar with candles to see which would expire first and of men living in a leaden bell under water. Vipers, frogs, fish, and insects were subjected both to the removal of air and to increased air pressure.[36]

Experimentation moved from animals to humans. In 1656, Christopher Wren injected a dog's veins with a liquid infusion, witnessed by other members of the Royal Society, including Robert Boyle and John Wilkins. Animals were "purg'd, vomited, intoxicated, kill'd, or reviv'd, according to the quality of the liquor injected." A dog was injected with opium after which it was whipped and beaten to keep it alive. Other dogs and drugs were tested. The experiments soon led to blood transfusions, first on animals and then on humans. Wren used a quill to inject the blood of one animal into another, and Richard Lower described his animal to animal transfusions in 1665 and 1666. In 1667, the blood of a sheep was injected into the veins of a spaniel. In France, Jean Baptiste Denis transferred blood between two dogs, and experimented with introducing calves' blood into dogs. He then injected a lamb's blood into a young woman, and later blood from a sheep's artery into a human "lunatic," who at first improved, but died following a subsequent transfusion.

After charges of poisoning were brought by the man's wife, human transfusions were prohibited.[37]

Historian of science Thomas Kuhn noted that Bacon's method of interrogating nature through constraint influenced seventeenth-century experimenters:

> The attitude towards the role and status of experiment is only the first of the novelties which distinguish the new experimental movement from the old. A second is the major emphasis given to experiments which Bacon himself described as 'twisting the lion's tail.' These were the experiments which constrained nature, exhibiting it under conditions which it could never have attained without the forceful intervention of man. The men who placed grain, fish, mice, and various chemicals *seriatim* in the artificial vacuum of a barometer or an air pump exhibit just this aspect of the new tradition.[38]

Objections to animal torture appeared during the Enlightenment. William Hogarth painted the "Four Stages of Cruelty" in 1751. The series depicted the life and death of criminal Tom Nero in London. The first stage, the St. Giles Charity Schoolyard, shows acts of cruelty against animals. Boys are constraining, binding, cutting, goring, hanging, and shooting dogs, cats, and chickens. In the second stage, animal cruelty spreads to the streets and the larger city of London. Sheep, horses, donkeys, cattle, and humans are tied, beaten, rolled over, and gored. Finally, Nero himself is publicly dissected in a surgeon's hall. The series was meant to raise consciousness against inhumane methods of torture, and it ultimately led to the outlawing of vivisection and the formation of the Society Against Cruelty to Animals.[39]

Objections to experiments on animals in the bell jar were also mounted. Beginning in 1748, James Ferguson constructed scientific instruments and demonstrated them in lectures around England, writing them up in his 1771 *Lectures on Select Subjects*. Although his lectures included "Experiments with the Air Pump," he warned that, "If a fowl, a cat, rat, mouse or bird be put under the receiver, and the air be exhausted, the animal is at first oppressed as with a great weight, then grows convulsed, and at last expires in all the agonies of the most bitter and cruel death. But as this experiment is too shocking to every spectator who has the least degree of humanity, we substitute a machine called the 'lung-glass' in place [of] the animal; which by a bladder within it, shows how the lungs of animals are contracted into a small compass when the air is taken out of them."[40]

Perhaps inspired by Ferguson's lectures, but not heeding his admonitions, Joseph Wright of Derby painted "Experiment on a Bird in the Air Pump" in 1768.[41] In Wright's painting, a pet cockatoo is removed from a cage (shown in the upper right corner), placed in a bell jar, and the air evacuated. The experimenter's hand is placed near the stop cock and he holds the power to halt the evacuation and return air to the jar to revive the bird. An old man stares at a human skull contemplating death. A young girl covers her eyes to avoid viewing the impending horror, while a second girl stares anxiously upwards, and a woman, unable to watch, gazes at the face of another man who views the experiment directly. As Yaakov Garb has pointed out, the men and women have different responses. The women are stereotypically emotional, look-ing in horror at the bell jar, hiding their eyes, or looking at the men, thereby experiencing the results vicariously. The men, on the other hand, control the outcome via the stopcock, stare directly at the experiment with open curios-ity, or contemplate the larger philosophical meaning of death. The men "wit-ness" a scientific truth, the women "experience" a dying bird. The painter has forced social norms about male and female scientific responses to nature onto the audience. The experiment reflects the goals of Francis Bacon's method. A question is asked of nature, a controlled experiment is devised, and the results are witnessed and evaluated for their truth content. Whether a particular experiment reflects the torture or the mere vexation of nature must be left to the individual viewer. (See also Ch. 3 of this book, pp. 51–52.)[42]

Through his use of metaphor, rhetoric, and myth, Francis Bacon developed the idea of the constrained, controlled experiment. Obviously, Bacon cannot be held individually responsible for the positive or negative implications or applications of his ideas. Bacon drew on tendencies existing in his culture and his ideas were augmented by those who followed his direction. Had Bacon lived today, he might or might not have supported genetic engineering, fac-tory farming, and biotechnology as methods of interrogating nature instead of stuffing a chicken with snow to see if putrefaction could be halted. The devel-opment of the scientific method itself was nevertheless strongly influenced by Bacon's rhetoric and his vision of the interrogation of nature.

NOTES

* From Carolyn Merchant, "The Scientific Revolution and the Death of Nature," special Focus section on Carolyn Merchant's *The Death of Nature, Isis* 97, no. 3 (September 2006): 513–33. Copyright 2006 by the History of Science Society, University of Chicago Press. All rights reserved. I have shortened the original article for the purposes of this volume. Those who wish more detail concerning my arguments on Francis Bacon should consult the original article in *Isis*.

1. Carolyn Merchant, *The Death of Nature: Women, Ecology, and the Scientific Revolution* (San Francisco: HarperCollins, 1980; 2nd ed. 1990). For a list of previous reviews and commentaries on the book from 1980 to 1998, see Carolyn Merchant, "The Death of Nature: A Retrospective," in "Symposium on Carolyn Merchant's *The Death of Nature*, Citation Classics and Foundational Works," *Organization and Environment* 11, no. 2 (June 1998): 180–206, with commentary by Linda C. Forbes, John M. Jermier, Robyn Eckers-ley, Karen J. Warren, Max Oelschlaeger, and Sverker Sörlin. See also Kevin C. Armitage, "A Dialectic of Domination: Carolyn Merchant's *The Death of Nature: Women, Ecology,*

and the Scientific Revolution," 2000, online, reviewed for H-Ideas' Retrospective Reviews of "books published during the twentieth century which have been deemed to be among the most important contributions to the field of intellectual history." Also Nöel Sturgeon, Donald Worster, and Vera Norwood, "Retrospective Reviews on the 25th Anniversary of *The Death of Nature*," *Environmental History* 10, no. 4 (October 2005): 805–15.

2. Sherry Ortner's foundational article "Is Female to Male as Nature Is to Culture?," in Michelle Rosaldo and Louise Lamphere, eds., *Woman, Culture, and Society* (Stanford, CA: Stanford University Press, 1974), pp. 67–87, influenced my thinking about women's relationships to nature and culture. I was also influenced by Rosemary Radford Reuther's "Women's Liberation, Ecology & Social Revolution," *WIN* 9 (October 4, 1973): 4–7, and Rosemary Radford Reuther, *New Woman/New Earth: Sexist Ideologies and Human Liberation* (New York: Seabury Press, 1975). Susan Griffin, while writing *Woman and Nature: The Roaring Inside Her* (New York: Harper Collins, 1978), consulted me on some of her ideas. Although Françoise d'Eaubonne had used the term in 1974 in "The Time for Eco-feminism" in her book *Feminism or Death* (*Le Féminisme ou la Mort*), few scholars in the U.S. had heard the word at that time (Paris: Pierre Horay, 1974), pp. 215–52. Ynestra King taught a course on "Ecofeminism" at the Institute for Social Ecology, Plainfield, Vermont, about 1976.

3. Ortner, "Is Female to Male as Nature Is to Culture?" 2. For a history of theories associated with ecofeminism, see Carolyn Merchant, *Radical Ecology: The Search for a Livable World* (New York: Routledge, 1992; 2nd ed. 2005), chap. 8.

4. Harvey argued that the semen of the male as the most perfect animal was the efficient cause, while the egg was mere matter. In fact, the male semen was so powerful that impregnation of the egg could occur without contact with the sperm. "How," he wrote, "should such a fluid [the female's] get the better of another concocted under the influence of a heat so fostering, of vessels so elaborate, and endowed with such vital energy?—how should such a fluid as the male semen be made to play the part of mere matter?" William Harvey, *Works* (London: Sydenham Society, 1847), pp. 298, 299, quoted in Merchant, *Death of Nature*, p. 159. For a recent assessment of scholarship on midwifery, see Monica H. Green, "Bodies, Gender, Health, Disease: Recent Work on Medieval Women's Medicine," *Studies in Medieval and Renaissance History* 3rd ser., 2 (2005): 1–46. (I thank Katharine Park for this reference.)

5. Merchant, *Death of Nature*, p. 169. See also: "For Bacon as for Harvey, sexual politics helped to structure the nature of the empirical method" as power over nature (p. 172).

6. On socialist feminism, see Merchant, *Radical Ecology*, chap 8. On partnership with nature, see Carolyn Merchant, *Reinventing Eden: The Fate of Nature in Western Culture* (New York: Routledge, 2003), chap. 11.

7. I elaborated on these connections at the History of Technology meeting (a 4S meeting) in Toronto in 1980 and in the 1982 article "Hydraulic Technologies and the Agricultural Transformation of the English Fens," *Environmental Review* 7, no. 2 (Summer): 165–77.

8. Merchant, *Death of Nature*, p. 68: "As European cities grew and forested areas became more remote, as fens were drained and geometric patterns of channels imposed on the landscape, as large powerful waterwheels, furnaces, forges, cranes, and treadmills began increasingly to dominate the work environment, more and more people began to experience nature as altered and manipulated by machine technology. A slow but unidirectional alienation from the immediate daily organic relationship that had formed the basis of human experience from earliest times was occurring. Accompanying these changes were alterations in both the theories and experiential bases of social organization which had formed an integral part of the organic cosmos."

9. Carolyn Merchant, *Ecological Revolutions: Nature, Gender, and Science in New England* (Chapel Hill: University of North Carolina Press, 1989).

10. Merchant, "The Death of Nature: A Retrospective," pp. 198–206.

11. Merchant, *Death of Nature*, pp. 131–2, 288; Merchant, *Ecological Revolutions*, pp. 55–6; Merchant, *Reinventing Eden*, pp. 117–23; Katharine Park, "Nature in Person: Medieval

and Renaissance Allegories and Emblems," in Lorraine Daston and Fernando Vidal, eds., *The Moral Authority of Nature* (Chicago: University of Chicago Press, 1994), pp. 50–73; Lorraine Daston and Katharine Park, *Wonders and the Order of Nature, 1150–1750* (Cambridge, MA: MIT Press, 1998); Mario Biagioli, *Galileo, Courtier: The Practice of Science in the Culture of Absolutism* (Chicago: University of Chicago Press, 1993); Steven Shapin and Simon Schaffer, *Leviathan and the Air-Pump: Hobbes, Boyle, and the Experimental Life* (Princeton, NJ: Princeton University Press, 1985).

12. Merchant, *Reinventing Eden*, pp. 1–8.

13. Alan Soble, "In Defense of Bacon," *Philosophy of the Social Sciences* 25 (1995): 192–215, reprinted with additions and corrections in Noretta Koertge, ed., *A House Built on Sand: Exposing Postmodernist Myths about Science* (New York: Oxford University Press, 1998), pp. 195–215, see esp. 203–6; William R. Newman, "Alchemy, Domination, and Gender," ibid., pp. 216–239; Nieves H. De Madariaga Mathews, *Francis Bacon: The History of a Character Assassination* (New Haven: Yale University Press, 1996), chaps. 24, 33; Mathews, "Francis Bacon, Slave-Driver or Servant of Nature? Is Bacon to Blame for the Evils of Our Polluted Age?" http://itis.volta.alessandria.it/episteme/madar1.html; Peter Pesic, "Nature on the Rack, Leibniz's Attitude towards Judicial Torture and the 'Torture' of Nature," *Studia Leibnitiana* 39, no. 2 (1997): 189–97; Peter Pesic, "Wrestling with Proteus: Francis Bacon and the 'Torture' of Nature," *Isis* 90 (1999): 81–94; Iddo Landau, "Feminist Criticisms of Metaphors in Bacon's Philosophy of Science," *Philosophy* 73 (1998): 47–61; Perez Zagorin, *Francis Bacon* (Princeton, NJ: Princeton University Press, 1998), 121–2.

14. Merchant, *Death of Nature*, p. 168: "These social events influenced Bacon's philosophy and literary style. Much of the imagery he used in delineating his new scientific objectives and methods derives from the courtroom, and, because it treats nature as a female to be tortured through mechanical inventions, strongly suggests the interrogations of the witch trials and the mechanical devices used to torture witches." See also p. 172: "The interrogation of witches as symbol for the interrogation of nature, the courtroom as model for its inquisition, and torture through mechanical devices as a tool for the subjugation of disorder were fundamental to the scientific method as power."

15. Merchant, *The Death of Nature*, pp. 168–9.

16. Pesic, see note 13. I have drawn on and respect Pesic's research, although I disagree with his interpretations.

17. Leonard A. Parry, *The History of Torture in England* (Montclair, NJ: Patterson Smith, 1975; originally published, 1934), pp. 76–87, 162–77, 182; George Ryley Scott, *The History of Torture Throughout the Ages*, 2nd ed. (London: Kegan Paul, 2003), pp. 168–255; Merchant, *Death of Nature*, pp. 168–72.

18. Pesic, "Wrestling with Proteus," [13], quotation on p. 81. Pesic's goal in this article, however, is to argue against Bacon's advocacy of torture and against torture as a model for the experimental method.

19. Paolo Rossi, *Francis Bacon: From Magic to Science* (Chicago: University of Chicago Press, 1968), pp. 32–3, quotation on p. 32.

20. Parry, *History of Torture* [17], pp. 180–1, quotation on p. 41, on the use of the rack, see p. 76; Scott, *The History of Torture Throughout the Ages*, pp. 168–80; Francis Bacon, "De Dignitate et Augmentis Scientiarum" ("Of the Dignity and Advancement of Learning," written 1623), in *Works*, vol. 4, quotation on p. 298.

21. Quotations and citations have been compiled by Peter Pesic in "Wrestling with Proteus," [13], p. 82, and "Nature on the Rack," p. 195, n. 29; p. 197, n. 34, 35. I have added to and elaborated on them in what follows.

22. Gottfried Wilhelm Leibniz, *Philosophical Papers and Letters*, ed. Leroy E. Loemker (Chicago: University of Chicago Press, 1956), vol. 2, p. 758.

23. Jean Baptiste du Hamel, *Regiae Scientiarum Academiae Historia*, 2nd ed. (Paris: J. B. Delespine, 1701), p. 16, "sic natura arcana longe facilius deprehendimus, cum per ignem aut alia artis adminicula varie torquetur, quam ubi itinere quodam suo progreditur." Cited

and translated by Stephen Beasley Linnard Penrose, Jr., "The Reputation and Influence of Francis Bacon," Doctoral Dissertation, Columbia University, New York, 1934, pp. 97–8. Interestingly, Penrose [incorrectly] adds, but gives no citation: "Bacon said that nature must be tortured upon the rack to make her give up her secrets. The similarity of expression is striking."

24. For the Latin "*torquere*," see Sir William Smith, *A Smaller Latin-English Dictionary*, rev. ed. John F. Lockwood (New York: Barnes & Noble, 1960), p. 759; for "*torqueo*," see *Cassell's New Latin Dictionary*, rev. ed. D. P. Simpson (New York: Funk & Wagnalls, 1959), pp. 607–8. For the definition of rack, see *Oxford English Dictionary*, compact ed., 2 vols. (Oxford, England: Oxford, 1971), vol. 2, p. 2401.

25. Johann Wolfgang von Goethe, *Maximen und Reflexionen. Nach den Handschriften des Goethe-und Schiller-Archivs herausgegeben von Max Hecker* (Weimar: Goethe-Gesellschaft, 1907), Maxim 115, p. 21: "Die Natur verstummt auf der Folter; ihre treue Antwort auf redliche Frage ist: Ja! ja! Nein! nein! Alles Übrige ist vom Übel." Johann Wolfgang von Goethe, *Sämtliche Werke, Jubiläums-Ausgabe*, ed. Eduard von der Hellen, 40 vols. (Stuttgart and Berlin: J. G. Cotta, 1902–1912), vol. 39, Maxim 430, p. 64: "Die Phänomene müssen ein für allemal aus der düstern empirisch-mechanisch-dogmatischen Marterkammer vor die Jurn des gemeinen Menschen-verstandes gebracht werden." For the English, see Johann Wolfgang von Goethe, *Maxims and Reflections*, trans. Elisabeth Stopp, ed. Peter Hutchinson (London: Penguin, 1998), Maxim 115, p. 14: "Nature grows dumb when subjected to torture; the true answer to honest questioning is yes! yes! no! no! All else is idle and basically evil," and Maxim 430, p. 55: "Phenomena must once and for all be removed from their gloomy empirical-mechanical-dogmatic torture chamber and submitted to the jury of plain common sense." See also Erich Heller, *The Disinherited Mind: Essays in Modern German Literature and Thought* (Cambridge: Bowes & Bowes, 1952), p. 18: "Goethe regards it as his own scientific mission to 'liberate the phenomena once and for all from the gloom of the empirico-mechanico-dogmatic torture chamber,'" as taken from Johann Wolfgang von Goethe, *Jubliäums-Ausgabe* (Stuttgart and Berlin: J. G. Cotta, 1902–1912), vol. 34, p. 64.

26. Thomas Fowler, *Bacon's Novum Organum*, with introduction, notes, etc. (Oxford: Clarendon Press, 1878), p. 124; in the second edition of 1889, see p. 127, as noted in Martha [Ornstein] Bronfenbrenner, *The Role of Scientific Societies in the Seventeenth Century* (New York: Arno Press, 1975), p. 40. In his 1990 film *Mindwalk*, Fritjof Capra used the torture chamber to illustrate the torture of nature under mechanistic science.

27. Ernst Cassirer, *The Platonic Renaissance in England*, trans. James P. Pettegrove (Austin: University of Texas Press, 1953), pp. 47–8; Cassirer cites Bacon, *Works*, vol. 2, chap. ii, *De Augmentis*. For Cassirer's use of the phrase "nature must be put to the rack," see also Pesic, "Wrestling with Nature" [13], p. 82, n. 4.

28. Charles Webster, *The Great Instauration: Science, Medicine, and Reform, 1626–1660* (London: Duckworth, 1975), p. 338. See Pesic, "Wrestling with Proteus" [13], p. 82, n. 4.

29. Soble, "In Defense of Bacon" [13], p. 205; Bacon, *De Augmentis*, *Works*, vol. 4, p. 296; *Oxford English Dictionary*, compact ed., vol. 1, p. 1338.

30. The meanings of "vex" included: a. "to trouble, affect, or harass (a person, etc.) by aggression, encroachment, or other interference with peace and quiet"; "of diseases, etc.: to afflict or distress physically, to afflict with pain or suffering"; and "to disturb by causing physical movement, commotion, or alteration; to agitate, toss about, work, belabour, or tear up; b. to disturb by handling; to twist; c. to press, strain, or urge." Similarly, "vexation" was: "the act of troubling or harassing by agitation or interference"; "the action of troubling, disturbing, or irritating by physical means"; and "the action of subjecting to violence or force." *Oxford English Dictionary*, compact ed., vol. 2, p. 3621.

31. Bacon, "Paraseve," *Works*, vol. 4, p. 257; Pierre Hadot, *Le Voile D'Isis: Essai sur l'histoire de l'idée de Nature* (Paris: Éditions Gallimard, 2004): "De même, en effet, que, dans la vie publique, le naturel d'un individu et la disposition cachée de son esprit et de ses passions se découvrent, lorsqu'il est plongé dans le trouble, mieux qu'à un autre moment, de même les

secrets (*occulta*) de la nature se découvrent mieux sous la torture des arts [mécaniques] que dans son cours naturel" (p. 133) from Francis Bacon, *Novum Organum*, I, sec. 109, p. 165, Malherbe et Pousseur (trad. légèrement modifiée). For the French translation of vex, see E. Clifton and J. McLaughlin, *A New Dictionary of the French and English Languages*, new rev. ed. (New York: David McKay, 1904), p. 630.

32. Soble, "In Defense of Bacon" [13], p. 205; Bacon, *De Dignitate, Works*, vol. 4, p. 298. In the 1605 English edition of *The Advancement of Learning, Works*, vol. 3 (1876), the passage reads: "For like as a man's disposition is never well known till he be crossed, nor Proteus ever changed shapes till he was straitened and held fast; so the passages and variations of nature cannot appear so fully in the liberty of nature, as in the trials and vexations of art" (p. 333). The 1623 Latin edition, *De Augmentis Scientiarum, Works*, vol. 1 (1858), reads: "Quemadmodum enim ingenium alicujus haud bene noris aut probaris, nisi eum irritaveris; neque Proteus se in varias rerum facies vertere solitus est, nisi manicis arcte comprehensus; similiter etiam natura arte irritata et vexata se clarius prodit, quam cum sibi libera permittitur" (p. 500). *Oxford English Dictionary*, compact ed., vol. 2, p. 3080; John C. Briggs, *Francis Bacon and the Rhetoric of Nature* (Cambridge, MA: Harvard University Press, 1989), p. 35.

33. Briggs, *Francis Bacon and the Rhetoric of Nature* [32], pp. 32–8. Such descriptions are particularly relevant to biotechnology today. The name Proteus comes from the Greek word *protos* (also the root of protein) meaning mutable, changeable, versatile, and capable of assuming many forms. The biotechnology company Proteus describes itself as a modern day Proteus: "Proteus discovers and develops biomolecules of primary importance and turns them to any form that meets the needs of the near future. It is the leading provider of wireless applications and carrier connectivity. . . . Some of the popular programming brands that have been extended to a mobile audience through Proteus' services include: HBO's *The Sopranos* and *Sex and the City* and ABC's *The View: His & Her Body Test*." "Proteus," http://proteus.com/home.jsp.

34. Scott, *History of Torture* [17], 138; René Descartes, "Animals Are Machines," in Susan J. Armstrong and Richard G. Botzler, eds., *Environmental Ethics: Divergence and Convergence* (New York: McGraw-Hill, 1993), pp. 281–5, see p. 285; René Descartes, *Meditations and Selections from the Principles of Philosophy* (La Salle, IL: Open Court, 1952), pp. 1–106, quotation on p. 98; Thomas Hobbes, "Leviathan," in William Molesworth, ed., *English Works*, 11 vols., reprint ed. (Aalen, Germany: Scientia, 1966), vol. 3, quotation on p. ix.

35. Leonora D. Cohen, "Descartes and Henry More on the Beast-Machine: A Translation of Their Correspondence Pertaining to Animal Automatism," *Annals of Science* 1 (1936): 48–61, quotations on pp. 50 and 53. Objections to the concept of animals as machines were voiced by Thomas Willis, John Locke, John Keill, John Ray, David Hartley, and David Hume. See also Albert G. A. Balz, "Cartesian Doctrine and the Animal Soul: An Incident in the Formation of the Modern Philosophical Tradition," Columbia Department of Philosophy, ed., *Studies in the History of Ideas* (New York: Columbia University Press, 1935), vol. 3, pp. 117–180.

36. Thomas Sprat, *History of the Royal Society* [1667], eds. Jackson I. Cope and Harold Whitmore Jones (St. Louis: Washington University Press, 1958), pp. 218–19, quotation on p. 218.

37. Dorothy Stimson, *Scientists and Amateurs: A History of the Royal Society* (New York: Greenwood Press, 1968), pp. 84–6; Sprat, *History of the Royal Society*, p. 317; Richard Lower, *Tractatus de corde* (1665); see also Richard Lower (attributed), "The Method Observed in Transfusing the Blood Out of One Animal into Another," *Philosophical Transactions of the Royal Society of London* 1, (December 1666): 353–8; Richard Lower, "Extrait du Journal d'Angleterre, contenant la manière de faire passer le sang d'un animal dans un autre," *Journal des sçavans* (January 31, 1667), as cited and discussed in Harcourt Brown, *Science and the Human Comedy: Natural Philosophy in French Literature from Rabelais to Maupertuis* (Toronto: University of Toronto Press, 1979), pp. 107–25.

38. Thomas S. Kuhn, "Mathematical vs. Experimental Traditions in the Development of Physical Science," *Journal of Interdisciplinary History* 7 no. 1 (Summer 1976): 1–31, quotation on p. 12. Note: Bacon did not use the term "twisting the lion's tail."

39. William Hogarth, "Four Stages of Cruelty," 1751, www.haleysteele.com/hogarth/plates/four_stages.html.

40. James Ferguson, *Lectures on Select Subjects* [1761], as cited in www.mezzo-mondo.com/arts/mm/wright/wright.html.

41. Joseph Wright of Derby, "An Experiment on a Bird in the Airpump," 1768, www.nationalgallery.org.uk/cgi-bin/WebObjects.dll/CollectionPublisher.woa/wa/largeImage?workNumber=NG725.

42. Stephen Daniels, *Joseph Wright* (Princeton, NJ: Princeton University Press, 1999), p. 40; Yaakov Garb, personal communication.

FIGURE 2.1 Francis Bacon (1561–1626)

Source: *Old England's Worthies*, London, 1847, p. 97. Courtesy Getty Images, Hulton Archive 463984775.

2

FRANCIS BACON*

To some scholars, Francis Bacon's writings have represented progress for humanity through science and technology. To others, his rhetoric has been problematical from the perspectives of women and the environment. The rise of modern science in the seventeenth century depended on a transition from occult to public knowledge of nature's secrets, from constraints against the penetration of nature's inner recesses to the assumption that nature herself was willing to reveal her own secrets. That Nature gendered as female held secrets that could be extracted from her womb through "art and the hand of man" and that women held secrets that could be extracted through dissection of her womb and bosom were part of an emerging scientific method—the method of the constrained, controlled experiment that Bacon's rhetoric inspired and that has endured through his legacy.

Francis Bacon rose to power during a period of social and intellectual upheaval. The colonization of the Americas, the rise of mercantile capitalism, the wars of religion, the revival of ancient learning, and skepticism over medieval philosophy made the early seventeenth century particularly transformative. . . .[1]

A deep divide exists between Bacon's supporters and detractors. The deeper roots of this divide lie in perceptions of the Scientific Revolution as a grand narrative of progress and hope versus one of decline and despair. How one views the Scientific Revolution itself is a marker of how one might assess the import of Bacon's contributions. As Eduard J. Dijksterhuis characterized it in the mid-twentieth century:

> That the adoption of the mechanistic view has had profound and far reaching consequences for the whole of society is an historical fact which gives rise to the most divergent opinions. Some commend it as a symptom of the gradual clarification of human thought, of the growing application of the only method that is capable of producing reliable results in every sphere of knowledge. . . . Others, though recognizing the outstanding importance it has had for the progress of our theoretical understanding and our practical control of nature, regard it as nothing short of disastrous in its general influence on philosophical and scientific thought as well as on society.[2]

Views of Francis Bacon as a pivotal figure in the emergence of modern science catalyze these oppositions. The internalist-externalist debates of the 1960s, the social constructivist-realist debates of the 1980s, and the "science wars" of the 1990s reflect the polarizing positions taken by scholars of the Scientific Revolution. Some scholars read Bacon's rhetoric and associated meanings harshly, while others interpret the same phrases and meanings benignly. Perhaps most scholars will find themselves somewhere along a continuum between extremes.

Whether the control of nature leads to human wealth and well-being for the few or to social and ecological decline for the many is an underlying assumption of the narratives told by various scholars. Likewise, the actors in the narratives vary according to the assumed plot: great men as scientists and philosophers building on the knowledge of their predecessors versus historical contextualization by race, gender, and class. Despite three decades of efforts to inject issues raised by feminist scholars into texts and courses, most still focus largely on the great men of the revolutionary era between Copernicus and Newton.[3] Despite two decades of advancement of the field of environmental history, most scholarship and courses on the Scientific Revolution ignore the environment as a major actor.[4]

Bacon's life and work spanned the period in which science (natural philosophy), technology (the mechanical arts), and mercantile capitalism conjoined with religion to make possible a new form of knowledge (an "advancement of learning") in the service of humankind ("the relief of man's estate"). A narrative of progress emerges in which humanity is able to recover that which was lost in the Fall from Eden, giving hope for the betterment of humanity through the control of nature. "Man by the Fall, fell at the same time from his state of innocency and from his dominion over creation. Both of these losses, however, can even in this life be in some part repaired, the former by religion and faith, the latter by arts and sciences," Bacon pronounced.[5] It was through a new knowledge to be gained from science and technology that the lost dominion could be reclaimed: "Let the human race *recover* that right over nature which belongs to it by divine bequest," he asserted.[6]

The new narrative reversed the tragedy of the Fall to a comedy of recovery. The plot of the recovery narrative was an upward or progressive trajectory ending in a new happiness on earth, rather than in the pain of a lost Edenic happiness. The road to recovery lay in the interrogation and cross-examination of nature. "I mean (according to the practice in civil causes) in this great plea or suit granted by the divine favor and providence (whereby the human race seeks to *recover* its right over nature) to examine nature herself and the arts upon interrogatories."[7] The new narrative was made possible by the discoveries of the Americas, the new mechanical devices of early capitalist society, and most importantly for Bacon a new experimental method based on the "disclosing of the secrets of nature."[8]

It was Bacon's singular achievement to demonstrate through rhetoric, metaphor, and vivid example how the "secrets of nature" could be extracted and put into use in the service of humankind.[9] Bacon's thought evolved during a period in which natural magic emerged as a new practical technique for understanding the workings of the natural world through the manipulation of matter. The writings of Della Porta, Agrippa, Ficino, Pico della Mirandola, Paracelsus, Bruno, and John Dee constituted the "scientific" antecedents on which Bacon built his new philosophy. John Drury, Samuel Hartlib, Joseph Glanvill, Thomas More, and Robert Boyle comprized the scientific successors who built on Bacon's inspiration and who along with Bacon transformed the natural magic tradition into a new science based on the experimental method.

The confined, controlled experiment that could be witnessed, replicated, and validated by a multitude of observers replaced the individualistic, arcane secrets known only to the *magus*, the astrologer, and the witch. That new method, I argue in what follows, was rooted, at least in part, in gendered interconnections between the secrets of nature and the secrets of women and in new forms of knowledge extracted from female nature and the female body. By reforming the secrets tradition, the private secrets held by both nature and women could be revealed. The anatomy of nature and the anatomy of the body could be exposed for the benefit of humankind.[10]

It is out of the genre of the "secrets of nature" that Bacon formulated significant aspects of his experimental philosophy. Della Porta's *Natural Magic, or the Secrets and Miracles of Nature* provided numerous examples of "transformations" for the "scientists" of Bacon's "New Atlantis" that would inspire his followers. Bacon drew on the "secrets tradition" when he wrote: "There is much ground for hoping that there are still laid up in the womb of nature many secrets of excellent use having no affinity or parallelism with anything that is now known ... only by the method of which we are now treating they can be speedily and suddenly and simultaneously presented and anticipated."[11]

FIGURE 2.2 "Nature Unveiling Herself to Science" ("La Nature se dévoilant devant la Science"). Francis Bacon and others believed that nature held secrets that could be revealed through scientific examination.

Source: Sculpture by Louis-Ernest Barrias (French, 1841–1905). Ecole de Médecine, Paris. Photograph by Carolyn Merchant.

The secrets tradition for Bacon included "narratives of sorceries, witch-crafts, charms, dreams, divinations, and the like." Out of "speculation" about these, he wrote, "a useful light may be gained, not only for a true judgment of the offences of persons charged with such practices, but likewise for the further disclosing of the secrets of nature."[12] What was useful in the occult sciences should be ferreted out and applied to the benefit of humanity.

William Eamon has analyzed the tradition of natural magic in *Secrets of Nature: Books of Secrets in Medieval and Early Modern Culture.*[13] He argues that "the 'new science' of the seventeenth century has its roots, in part, in the practical activities of artisans, alchemists, and common healers. . . . By publishing the 'secrets' of craftsmen and experimenters, early modern printers created a body of empirical knowledge that became the basis for the 'Baconian sciences' of the seventeenth century."[14] Natural magic was closely bound to the demonic magic banned by the Catholic Church. Eamon points out that "the church condemned all magical activity as heretical. Natural magic was caught up along with popular superstitions, witchcraft, and consort with demons."[15]

The secrets tradition was a "research program" that offered a window into nature and the search for nature's secrets—a tradition that would lead from the natural magic of the sixteenth century, through Bacon's "New Atlantis," which appeared in eight editions between 1626 and 1658, to experimentation on "the hidden causes of things" in the second half of the seventeenth century.[16] Giovan Abioso da Bagnola, a sixteenth-century tutor of Giambattista Della Porta, sought to establish a restoration of human dominion over the natural world—goals echoed by Bacon in the phrases quoted previously. Bagnola's *instauratio magna* (anticipating Bacon's own title) stated that one must turn away from the ancients and "hunt for the new secrets of nature" (*venari nova naturae secreta*).[17] Eamon writes:

According to the epistemology of the hunt, since nature's secrets were hidden beyond the reach of ordinary sense perception, they had to be sought out by extraordinary means. Instruments had to be made, for example, which would enable researchers to 'look out at and look into' (*auspicit et inspicit*) nature, as the motto of the Lincean Academy expressed it. Experiments had to be devised that would enable researchers to penetrate nature's interior, 'Twisting the lion's tail' to make her cry out her secrets. As Bacon expressed it, nature, like Proteus, had to be constrained by experiments that forced it out of its natural condition, for 'the secrets of nature reveal them selves more readily under the vexations of art than when they go their own way.' Finally, new methods of reasoning had to be found to take the place of scholastic logic, which according to the early moderns was incapable of reaching the inner recesses of nature and laying bare its secrets.[18]

That the secrets tradition directly influenced Bacon is clear not only from his references to disclosing the secrets of nature, but to the influence of Agrippa and Della Porta on the transformations of nature depicted in the "New Atlantis." Here "scientists" perfected existing organisms (such as serpents, worms, flies, and fishes), produced entirely new species by "making one plant or tree turn into another," experimented to see what "new dissection and trials" could be "wrought on the body of man," and developed methods to control the weather. Bacon refuted the constraints against such manipulations that had hampered the natural magicians owing to threats by the Inquisition.[19] His objective was to recover "man's right over nature" lost in the Fall. As Bacon put it, "The end of our foundation is the knowledge of causes and secret motions of things and the enlarging of the bounds of human empire, to the effecting of all things possible."[20]

The rise of modern science in the seventeenth century depended on a transition from occult to public knowledge of nature's secrets, from constraints against the penetration of nature's inner recesses to the assumption that nature herself was willing to reveal her own secrets. In 1160, Alain of Lille, of the School of Chartres, recounted an allegory in which *Natura*, God's humble servant, weeps over human failure to obey her laws. As humans aggressively penetrate the secrets of the heavens, they tear her garments of modesty and expose her to the public. Similarly, in 1490–95, an old hermit of Lichtenstat tells a story in which Mother Earth in a tattered green gown is defended against a miner accused of matricide. The miner pleads his case by arguing that Earth is not a real mother, but a wicked stepmother who conceals her bounty in her inner recesses. By contrast, in the nineteenth century, Nature is depicted in sculptures by Louis-Ernest Barrias as removing her own veil and willingly revealing herself to science. Francis Bacon's *Instauratio Magna* lies at the center of this transition from private secrets to public knowledge. The transition itself, however, cannot be understood apart from its context of gendered rhetoric, ways of seeing, and representations of woman and nature.[21]

What was the nature of the "nature" that harbored those secrets? Abundant evidence exists that most thinkers of the Renaissance and Scientific Revolution cast nature in the female gender. This was true, not only because nature was gendered as female in the Romance languages deriving from the Latin *Natura*, but more broadly because of a pervasive worldview, held at all levels of society, that symbolized, allegorized, and characterized Nature as female, virgin, mother, and witch. The earth too was female, having deep recesses, cavities, and wombs in which grew the seeds of living things, including stones and metals.[22] Likewise, abundant evidence exists that, despite courtly traditions, females were held in lower esteem than the men of their class and that, as feminist scholarship has shown, women experienced neither a

Renaissance nor a Scientific Revolution until the emergence—at the upper levels of society—of the learned ladies of the Enlightenment.

Perhaps nowhere is the dichotomy between men's minds and women's bodies so blatant as in depictions of the "anatomy theaters" of early modern Europe that provided the context for Francis Bacon's efforts to create an anatomy of the world that would reveal the secrets of nature. Bacon's (and James I's) physician was William Harvey, who had studied at Padua, and the anatomy theaters of Italy and Leiden were known in English culture. The anatomy theater, the witnessing of the anatomy lesson, and the dissection of nature and the body by hand and mind epitomize the controlled, constrained experimental method toward which Bacon was groping. Knowing Nature's anatomy could lead to the recovery of the knowledge lost in the Fall from Eden. While Bacon does not describe dissections of the female body, he draws on anatomy and dissection in his rhetoric about extracting the secrets of nature.

That women's bodies concealed secrets to be extracted in the service of humanity has been artfully argued by Katharine Park in *Secrets of Women: Gender, Generation, and the Origins of Human Dissection* (2006). In the tradition of the history of "secrets," women both harbored and knew the secrets of nature. As maidens, mothers, midwives, and witches, women knew women's bodies and the herbs and medicines that could be used for all aspects of women's reproduction—from menstruation to fertility, pregnancy, childbirth, and abortion. In the changing history of human dissection from the Middle Ages to the Renaissance, the secrets of women evolved from secrets known only to and by women to the secrets that women's bodies could reveal though the scientific study of female anatomy. While women accumulated a vast reservoir of knowledge that was passed down among neighbors and kin, no formal means of accumulating and recording that knowledge existed until science collected, collated, and publicized the data.[23]

Elaborating on Jonathan Sawday's analysis of the gendered "art of seeing," in Vesalius's *De humani corporis fabrica* (1543, 2nd ed. 1555), Park reveals the hidden meanings in Vesalius's title page that depicted the dissection of a female body and the counterpoint meanings in the accompanying portrait of Vesalius himself. The title page shows the public dissection, in the center of a rotunda, of the body of a female criminal who has been hanged. Her naked, prone body with genitals exposed and reproductive organs dissected lies at the center of a large crowd of male observers with Vesalius himself standing over her and pointing to the secrets of her womb. The active mastery of the standing, gesticulating male voyeurs contrasts with the passivity of the supine female object at center stage. Park observes: "The corpse is displayed in a way calculated to call maximum attention to her genitals, in the style of contemporary erotic prints," such as that of Jacopo Caraglio in *Mercury and Aglaurus*, a graphic of the late 1520s that displayed the female genitals through the open legs of the reclining lover.[24]

The only other clearly identifiable woman in Vesalius's title page stands between two pillars in the background peering from beneath a veil. She may be the midwife who would have examined the condemned woman for evidence of pregnancy before her execution. She exemplifies women's knowledge of women's secrets now exposed to the vulgarity of the raucous crowd.[25]

The iconography of Vesalius's female-centered title page contrasts with the male-dominated iconography of the portrait of Vesalius himself. Vesalius as authorial symbol is shown standing, fully clothed, and in an enclosed, private rather than public space. He gazes with penetrating eyes at the viewer, while grasping the bulging muscles of a standing male corpse, holding the tendons of the corpse's hand in his own, emphasizing his own identity with the male subject, rather than his distance from the female object of the title page. His scalpel and manuscript lie in easy reach on the table before him, ready to record for public consumption the new knowledge of human anatomy. Science, *scientia*, as knowledge of nature available to the many, supplants the secret knowledge of the arcana accessible only to the few. The secrets harbored by women and nature become the revealed secrets of public knowledge.[26]

In the *Fabrica*, Vesalius portrays his anatomical corpses against landscapes that serve as theaters of display. The figures dominate the surroundings—sparse vegetation and distant villages—mastering them by virtue of size and the physicality of musculature. The surroundings mask the violence of the act of dissection and the consenting violent act of the observer. As Devon Hodges puts it, "The anatomist cuts, dissects, flays, tears, and rips the body apart in order to know it."[27] By participating in the seeing, the observer joins in the dissecting. The controlled setting separates the body's parts; the landscaped theater removes the observing subject from the mastered object. In Foucault's terms, to know a dissected body is to "dominate, conquer, master, discipline, and punish it."[28]

Jonathan Sawday analyzes the "culture of dissection" in *The Body Emblazoned: Dissection and the Human Body in Renaissance Culture*, associating it with violence and having a dark side: "[A] dissection might denote not the delicate separation of constituent structures, but a more violent 'reduction' into parts: a brutal dismemberment of people, things, or ideas. . . . Anatomy, too, is an act of partition or reduction and, like dissection, anatomy is associated primarily with medicine. But, just as in the case of dissection, there lurks in the word a constant potential for violence."[29]

Francis Bacon associated dissection with an inquiry into nature's secrets, writing in *The Advancement of Learning*, "In the inquiry which is made by Anatomy, I find much deficience: for they inquire of the *parts*, and their *substances, figures, and collocations*; but they inquire not of the *diversities of the parts*, the *secrecies of the passages*, and the *seats or nestlings of the humours*."[30] The body was made up of a series of cavities that contained secrets to be uncovered through scientific inquiry. As Sawday explains it, "Bacon's demand for anatomies which delved into the secret cavities and receptacles of the body-space was met, in a religious context, by the true anatomist who was a dissecting and punishing God. Divine or sacred anatomy thus entered the body cavity and uncovered the inward configuration of fallen humanity."[31] Just as the anatomy of the New World could be explored on a macrocosmic scale though the voyages of discovery, so the body could be explored on a microscopic scale through the anatomy lesson. The microcosm-macrocosm theory that provided an organizing framework for Renaissance culture took on new meanings as an anatomy of the world.

Bacon drew on metaphors of dissection and anatomy when, in the *Novum Organum*, he announced his intent to create an "anatomy of the world": "For I am building in the human understanding a true model of the world, such as it is in fact, not such as man's own reason would have it to be; a thing which cannot be done without a very diligent dissection and anatomy of the world."[32] Hodges characterizes Bacon's mission as follows:

> Bacon's description of his project is couched in a rhetoric of imperialism. . . . As explorers and colonizers anatomize the world, laying it open to master it, so Bacon will lay open the intellectual world. Such projects, as Timothy Reiss has pointed out, are often imaged as acts of sexual violence; the new scientist 'is conqueror enforcing his will, a man ravishing a woman.'. . . Certainly, the act of vision described as an anatomizing process, to lay a body 'widely open' suggests the violence and disruption involved in such acts of discovery. The conquering power of the eye cruelly violates the integrity of a body.[33]

Renaissance anatomists displayed human bodies as living beings standing in natural or artificial settings and in which portions of the body were laid open with skin peeled back to reveal the interior organs. Female figures in which the observer could see directly into the dissected womb included images from Charles Estienne, "De dissectione" (1545), Berengarius, "Isagoge Breves" (1522), and Spigelius, "De formato foeto" (1627). In 1618, Pietro Berrettini drew a naked maiden holding open the dissected skin of her own stomach and womb in an act of revealing her own interior. Gaetano Petrioli engraved and published Berrettini's figure in 1741 and showed an accompanying inset of a womb containing a fetus. These images were part of a transition in which the arcane and mysterious secrets of the female body became public knowledge revealed through science. Woman's womb, which had defined woman herself as a mysterious and uncontrollable uterine force, now became part of a scientific anatomy lesson that sought to master the body through intellect and art. As Sawday puts it: "Once the uterus was seen, however, it had to be mastered in a complex process of representation. . . . Berrettini's figure peels back the surface tissue of her body . . . as though her body is no more than a vehicle for a vagina. . . . If she is casually made to open herself to the gaze of science, then science could not resist moralizing her body even as it stared into her."[34]

The anatomical theater reflected the microcosm-macrocosm framework of the Renaissance—the anatomy of the world. Moving upward and outward from the female earth at the center of the macrocosm in increasing concentric circles were the four elements—earth, water, air, and fire—followed by orbits of the moon and seven known planets, the *primum mobile*, and the empyrean heaven of God.[35] Moving upward and outward from the supine corpse flayed open on the dissecting table of the Leiden anatomy theater (ca. 1609) were cascading rings of benches occupied by hierarchies of professors, students, and public witnesses of the anatomy lesson, as well as human and animal skeletons. The learned professor stands at center stage just above the body, right hand gesticulating toward an open book of knowledge, while an assistant points to the parts of the body. Above the professor's head, a pair of open compasses (within the instrument cabinet) symbolize the geometrical proportions of body, the theater, and the globe itself and point to skeletons of Adam and Eve (holding spade and apple respectively) flanking the corpse. Adam and Eve as fallen humans who have lost eternal life now contribute to a recovery of knowledge through the dissection of the body.[36]

The anatomy theater as site for dissection and setting for the public gaze was a prototype for an emerging experimental science that could be repeated, verified, and exposed to public scrutiny. Francis Bacon's rhetoric about the constraint of nature sets up the ideal of a new experimental science in controlled conditions that can be witnessed, replicated, and verified by any observer. The anatomy amphitheater is an enclosed, circular, public space where attention can be focused on the experiment being conducted at the center of the theater. The experimenter, scalpel in hand, who stands over the table on which lies the corpse or animal to be dissected, is isolated from the natural environment and constrained by the very bounds of the artificial space. The experimental method that Bacon's work inspired depends on a set of isolated, constrained operations in confined, controlled spaces that can be witnessed, recreated, and repeated at any subsequent time and place.

The modern scientific laboratory, funded by public money and open to the scrutiny of the scientific community and the discerning public, is an offspring of the anatomy theater of the Renaissance. The experiments of the researchers in Bacon's *New Atlantis*, the "searchers and spies of nature" who "hound[ed] nature in her wanderings," and the struggles of Proteus to escape his bonds all formed part of an emerging Baconian experimental method that would be brought to fruition by the scientific societies of the seventeenth century.[37] Observations of the natural world could be assembled, organized, and compared in a central location—a laboratory or research center modeled after Salomon's House in the *New Atlantis*. Zoos and botanical gardens, as central spaces, reassembled and displayed under controlled conditions the species of animals and plants brought by explorers from around the globe. The secrets of the heavens could be observed through telescopes and the secrets of the soil and water through microscopes. The data were meaningless, however, without centralization, comparison, analysis, and publication.[38]

Francis Bacon's achievement was to draw together and ferret out the disparate strands of the occult sciences that delved into the "secrets of nature," transforming them into a new program of experimentation on nature. Magic, superstition, witchcraft, divination, and sorcery were all sources for determining what was useful. Nature under the constraints of art (technology) would reveal possibilities yet to be imagined. That Nature gendered as female held secrets that could be extracted from her womb or bosom through art and observation and that women held secrets that could be extracted through dissection of her womb or bosom were part and parcel of the same tradition and transformation. That those methods of constraint and extraction could be seen as violent were equally a part of the transformation of natural philosophy and the emergence of the experimental method.[39]

Rhetorical meanings and the practical arts melded together across a spectrum of possibilities; the hand (technology) and the eye (observation) functioned together to craft a new empirical methodology. The material and the visual combined to produce power over nature. "By art and the hand of man," Bacon stated, nature can be "forced out of her natural state and squeezed and molded" into revealing her hidden secrets.[40] Under the mechanical arts, he wrote, "nature betrays her secrets more fully . . . than when in enjoyment of her natural liberty." Technological discoveries "help us to think about the secrets still locked in nature's bosom." "They do not, like the old, merely exert a gentle guidance over nature's course; they have the power to conquer and subdue her, to shake her to her foundations."[41] Bacon's new method was part of an emerging framework of science, technology, capitalist development, and Christian religion that provided hope for the recovery of humanity's dominion over nature lost in the Fall from Eden.

Were the results of the new experimental method useful? Did they improve the state of humanity? Unquestionably, the answer is yes. Were there costs for peoples throughout the world, for the environment, and for the laboring classes? That answer, too, must be yes. Francis Bacon alone cannot be held responsible for those outcomes. Yet Bacon was a pivotal figure in a larger movement. He lived during a period of enormous expansion of knowledge, of social and intellectual upheaval, and of the widening and consolidation of political power. That he grasped and reflected those trends eloquently in his writings is to the benefit or, as some might suggest, the detriment of humankind. In either case, however, Bacon stood for the revealing of the "secrets of nature" for all to contemplate, admire, denounce, share, and put to use.

NOTES

* From Carolyn Merchant, "Secrets of Nature: The Bacon Debates Revisited," copyright by the *Journal of the History of Ideas* 69, no. 1 (January 2008): 147–62, used by permission.

1. Brian Vickers, "Francis Bacon, Feminist Historiography, and the Dominion of Nature," *Journal of the History of Ideas* 69, no. 1 (January 2008): 117–41. Vickers' article is, in part, a critique of Carolyn Merchant, "The Scientific Revolution and the Death of Nature," special Focus section on Carolyn Merchant's *The Death of Nature, Isis* 97 (September 2006): 513–33. This article is both a response to Vickers and an exploration of the connections between women and nature as viewed through the "secrets of nature" tradition and the anatomy theater as exemplars of the confined, controlled experimental method developed by Francis Bacon and his followers. I have omitted 2 para. about Vickers from pp. 147–148.

2. Eduard J. Dijksterhuis, *The Mechanization of the World Picture*, trans. C. Dikshoorn (Oxford: Clarendon Press, 1964 [originally published, 1950]), pp. 3–4. Critics of Bacon include: Max Horkheimer and Theodor Adorno, *Dialectic of Enlightenment*, trans. John Cumming (New York: Herder & Herder, 1972); and William Leiss, *The Domination of Nature* (New York: George Braziller, 1972). See also Nieves Matthews, "Francis Bacon: Slave-Driver or Servant of Nature," www.sirbacon.org/mathewsessay.htm: "In 1942 Herbert Marcuse, the patron saint of a generation of leftist extremists, described Bacon as the 'evil animus' of modern science, while Martin Heidegger, who was still celebrating in 1953 what he called 'the inner truth and greatness of Nazism', denounced in Bacon the symbol of a nefarious identification of science with technology. During those same decades Bacon's reputation as a scientist was also at its lowest ebb."

3. For example, see Wilbur Applebaum, *The Scientific Revolution and the Foundations of Modern Science* (Westport, CT: Greenwood Press, 2005). Robert Hatch's website, "The Scientific Revolution," contains a brief biographical list on "women of learning," www.clas.ufl.edu/users/rhatch/pages/03-Sci-Rev/SCI-REV-Home/. Lisa Sarasohn's *The Scientific Revolution* (Boston: Houghton Mifflin, 2006) includes the section "Did Women Have a Scientific Revolution?"

4. Exceptions are Max Oelschlager, *The Idea of Wilderness: From Prehistory to the Age of Ecology* (New Haven: Yale University Press, 1991); and Albert Borgmann, *Crossing the Postmodern Divide* (Chicago: University of Chicago Press, 1992).

5. Francis Bacon, "Novum Organum," in James Spedding, Robert Leslie Ellis, and Douglas Devon Heath, eds., *Works*, 14 vols. (London: Longmans Green, 1875), vol. 4, Bk II, Aphorism 52, pp. 247–8.

6. Ibid., vol. 4, Bk. I, Aphorism 129, p. 115, emphasis added.

7. Bacon, "Preparative Towards a Natural and Experimental History (*Parasceve*)" (1620), in *Works*, vol. 4, p. 263, emphasis added.

8. Carolyn Merchant, *Reinventing Eden: The Fate of Nature in Western Culture* (New York: Routledge, 2003), Ch. 1, 4, and pp. 74–5.

9. Lorraine Daston and Katharine Park write: "Bacon sometimes referred to natural history as a 'warehouse,' one that must be constantly replenished and drawn upon if natural philosophy were ever to fathom the secrets of nature." See Lorraine Daston and Katharine Park, *Wonders and the Order of Nature, 1150–1750* (New York: Zone Books, 1998), p. 224; see

Bacon, "Novum Organum," in *Works*, vol. 4, Bk. 1, Aphorism 18, p. 50. "This is why Bacon contended that 'from the wonders of nature is the nearest intelligence and passage towards the wonders of art: for it is no more by following and as it were hounding Nature in her wanderings, to be able to lead her afterwards to the same place again.'" Daston and Park, *Wonders*, p. 223. See Bacon, *Advancement of Learning* (1605), in *Works*, vol. 3, p. 331; "De Agumentis" (1623), in *Works*, vol. 4, p. 296.

10. In Merchant, "The Scientific Revolution and the Death of Nature," I used the example of the witch and the rack to discuss the emergence of the controlled experiment. Here I provide another context for the controlled, constrained experimental method based on anatomy and dissection.

11. Francis Bacon, "Novum Organum," in *Works*, vol. 4, Aphorism 109, p. 100. For the Latin, see Bacon, "Novum Organum," *Works*, vol. 1, p. 208: "Itaque sperandum omnino est, adhuc esse in naturae sinu multa excellentis usus recondita, quae nullam cum jam inventis cognationem habent aut parallelismum, sed omnino sita sunt extra vias phantasiae." Although Spedding, et al., translate *naturae sinu* as the womb of nature, others translate it as the bosom of nature. One possible, although uncommon, meaning of bosom in the early modern period was uterus; other meanings included a curved recess, cavity, or hollow interior (*Oxford English Dictionary*, compact ed., vol. 1, p. 252). Also, while Spedding, et al., employ the term secrets, other translations use things, matters, or treasures. Secret not only meant hidden from view, but also referred to the sex organs (*OED*, compact ed., vol. 2, p. 2702). Fulton Anderson uses the Spedding translation in Francis Bacon, *The New Organon and Related Writings*, ed. Fulton Anderson (New York: Liberal Arts Press, 1960), Bk. I, Aphorism, 109, p. 102. Basil Montague translates the passage as: "We may, therefore, well hope that many excellent and useful matters are yet treasured up in the bosom of nature, bearing no relation or analogy to our actual discoveries, but out of the common track of our imagination, and still undiscovered." See Francis Bacon, *Novum Organum (1620)*, in Basil Montague, ed. and trans., *The Works*, 3 vols. (Philadelphia: Parry & MacMillan, 1854), vol. 3, Bk. I, Aphorism 109, p. 365. Lisa Jardine and Michael Silverthorne translate the passage as: "Therefore it is very much to be expected that many exceedingly useful things are still hidden in the bosom of nature." See Francis Bacon, *The New Organon*, eds., Lisa Jardine and Michael Silverthorne (Cambridge, England: Cambridge University Press, 2000), Bk. I, Aphorism 109, p. 86.

12. Bacon, *De Dignitate et Augmentis Scientiarum* ("Of the Dignity and Advancement of Learning," written 1623), in *Works*, vol. 4, Bk. II, p. 296. The first edition of the *Advancement of Learning*, written in English in 1605, states: "Yet from the speculation and consideration of them light may be taken, not only for the discerning of the offences, but for the further disclosing of nature." Bacon, *Advancement*, in *Works*, vol. 3, 330–1. The 1623 Latin edition states: "Ideoque licet hujusmodi artium usum et praxim merito damnandum censeamus, tamen a speculatione et consideratione ipsarum (si strenue excutiantur) notitiam haud inutilem consequemur, non solum ad delicta in hoc genere reorum rite dijudicanda, sed etiam ad naturae secreta ulterius rimanda." Bacon, *De Dignitate et Augmentis Scientiarum*, in *Works*, vol. 1, pp. 496, 498. The 1624 French translation states: "Et partant encore que la pratique de telles choses soit à condamner, toutefois de la spéculation & considération d'icelles, l'on peut prendre de la offences, mais pour d'avantage de secourir la nature." Francis Bacon, *Le Progrez et avancement aux sciences diuines & humaines* (Paris: Pierre Billaine, 1624), Bk. 2, Ch. 2, pp. 197, 199–201 (French modernized).

13. William Eamon, *Science and the Secrets of Nature: Books of Secrets in Medieval and Early Modern Culture* (Princeton: Princeton University Press, 1994).

14. Eamon, http://honors.nmsu.edu/weamon/sci_secrets.html.

15. Eamon, *Science and the Secrets of Nature*, p. 195.

16. Ibid., pp. 195, 291. On the complex and differing roles of the occult sciences in the Renaissance and their relationship to early modern science, see William R. Newman and Anthony Grafton, eds., *Secrets of Nature: Astrology and Alchemy in Early Modern Europe* (Cambridge, MA: MIT Press, 2006).

17. Eamon, *Science and the Secrets of Nature*, pp. 197–8.
18. Ibid., p. 285; Bacon, *Novum Organum*, in *Works*, vol. 4, Bk. I, Aphorism 98, p. 95. Lisa Jardine and Michael Silverthorne, eds., *New Organon* (Cambridge, MA: Cambridge University Press, 2000), Bk. 1, p. 81 translate the passage as: "the secrets of nature reveal themselves better through harassments applied by the arts than when they go on in their own way." Fowler's Latin edition, *Novum Organum*, Bk. I, p. 304 states: "Occulta naturae magis se produnt per vexationes artium, quam cum cursu suo meant" and he adds the following footnote (p. 304, note 82): "Nature best discovers her secrets, when tortured by Art. This is an excellent illustration of the advantage which Experiment, at least in many cases, possesses over Observation." Thomas Fowler, ed., *Bacon's Novum Organum*, with introduction and notes, 2nd ed. (Oxford: Clarendon Press, 1889).
19. Merchant, *Death of Nature*, pp. 180–6. Bacon, "New Atlantis," *Works*, vol. 3, 157–9; Giambattista Della Porta, *Natural Magic*, ed. Derek J. Price (facsimile of 1658 edition, New York: Basic Books, 1957; first published 1558), pp. 27, 29, 31–40, 61–2, 73, 74–5, 81, 95–9; Henry Cornelius Agrippa, *The Vanity of Arts and Sciences* (London: R. Everingham, 1694; first published 1530), pp. 252–3.
20. Bacon, "New Atlantis," in *Works*, vol. 3, p. 156. In the *Novum Organum*, he stated it as follows: "But if a man endeavour to establish and extend the power and dominion of the human race itself over the universe, his ambition (if ambition it can be called) is without doubt both a more wholesome thing and a more noble than the other two. Now the empire of man over things depends wholly on the arts and sciences. For we cannot command nature except by obeying her." Bacon, *Novum Organum*, in *Works*, vol. 4, Bk. I, Aphorism 129, p. 114. This last phrase is often used to exonerate Bacon from the charge that his goal was the domination and control of nature by pointing out that, for Bacon, nature must be obeyed. But the experimental method that leads to the control of nature is in no way inconsistent with obeying nature's laws. Indeed science cannot work outside of the laws of nature. It can, however, use those laws to manipulate and control the natural world for human benefit (examples include hydropower, nuclear power, genetic engineering, stem cell research, nanotechnology, and so on).
21. Merchant, *Death of Nature*, pp. 10, 32–3, 190; Carolyn Merchant, *Earthcare: Women and the Environment* (New York: Routledge, 1996), p. 65. See also Ch. 3, this volume, pp. 53–54.
22. Merchant, *Death of Nature*, Ch. 1.
23. Katharine Park, *Secrets of Women: Gender, Generation, and the Origins of Human Dissection* (New York: Zone Books, 2006), p. 256. Park's analysis does not include witches.
24. Park, *Secrets of Women*, pp. 249–59; Jonathan Sawday, *The Body Emblazoned: Dissection and the Human Body in Renaissance Culture* (London: Routledge, 1995); Jonathan Sawday, "The Fate of Marsyas: Dissecting the Renaissance Body," in Lucy Grant and Nigel Llewellyn, eds., *Renaissance Bodies: The Human Figure in English Culture, c. 1540–1660* (London: Reaktion, 1990), pp. 112–35. For the analysis of Vesalius's title page, see also Hillary Nunn, *Staging Anatomies: Dissection and Spectacle in Early Stuart Tragedy* (Burlington, VT: Ashgate, 2005), pp. 12–16. For the image of Mercury and Aglaurus by Jacobo Caraglio after Perino del Vaga, see Park, Figure 5.21, p. 254. Also Bette Talvacchia, *Taking Positions: On the Erotic in Renaissance Culture* (Princeton: Princeton University Press, 1999), Figure 55, p. 157. Caraglio produced a series of images of gods and goddesses *in flagrante delecto*. See Talvacchia, *Taking Positions*, Figs. 35–56, pp. 140–60.
25. Park, *Secrets of Women*, pp. 256–9.
26. Ibid., p. 250.
27. Devon L. Hodges, *Renaissance Fictions of Anatomy* (Amherst: The University of Massachusetts Press, 1985), p. 5.
28. Quoting Hodges' characterization of Foucault, *Renaissance Fictions*, p. 127, n. 12; See Michel Foucault, *Discipline and Punish: The Birth of the Prison*, trans. Alan Sheridan (New York: Pantheon, 1977).
29. Sawday, *Body Emblazoned*, p. 1.

30. Bacon, *Advancement of Learning*, in *Works*, vol. 3, p. 374; elaborated in *De Augmentis*, vol. 4, pp. 385–6. Here Bacon laments that bodily dissections are performed only on dead bodies: "Of that other defect in anatomy (that it has not been practiced on live bodies) what need to speak? For it is a thing hateful and inhuman, and has been justly reproved by Celsus. But yet it is no less true (as was anciently noted) that many of the more subtle passages, pores, and pertusions appear in dead bodies, though they be open and manifest in live. Wherefore that utility may be considered as well as humanity, the anatomy of the living subject is not to be relinquished altogether, nor referred (as it was by Celsus) to the casual practices of surgery; since it may be well discharged by the dissection of beasts alive, which, notwithstanding the dissimilitude of their parts to human, may, with the help of a little judgment, sufficiently satisfy this inquiry" (p. 286).
31. Sawday, *Body Emblazoned*, pp. 94–5, 139, quotation on p. 109.
32. Bacon, *Novum Organum*, in *Works*, vol. 4, Bk. I, Aphorism 124, p. 110; Hodges, *Renaissance Fictions*, p. 91. See also Jardine and Silverthorne, *New Organon*, Bk. I, Aphorism 124, p. 96: "For we are laying the foundations in the human understanding of a true model of the world, as it is and not as any man's own reason tells him it is. But this can be done only by performing a most careful dissection and anatomy of the world."
33. Quoting Hodges, *Renaissance Fictions*, p. 95, with reference to Timothy Reiss, *Discourse of Modernism* (Ithaca: Cornell University Press, 1982), p. 189.
34. Sawday, *Body Emblazoned*, quotation on pp. 222–3. For the illustrations, see figures 25–31. A series of human figures in erotic poses with dissected wombs was produced by Charles Estienne, *De dissectione partium corporis humani* (Paris, 1545). See Talvacchia, *Taking Positions*, Figs. 58, 60, 66–7, pp. 167–78. See also Figure 68, "Anatomical Study," woodcut from Walter Hermann Ryff, *Anatomi* (Strasbourg, 1541), Talvacchia, p. 185.
35. For an illustration, see Robert Fludd, *Utriusque Cosmi Maioris Scilicet et Minoris Metaphysica* (Oppenheim: Theodore de Bry, 1617), title page. Bacon criticized the microcosm theory: "The ancient opinion that man was Microcosmus, an abstract or model of the world, hath been fantastically strained by Paracelsus and the alchemists, as if there were to be found in man's body certain correspondences and parallels, which should have respect to all varieties of things, as stars, planets, minerals, which are extant in the great world." Bacon, *Advancement of Learning*, in *Works*, vol. 3, p. 370.
36. Sawday, *Body Emblazoned*, "View of Leiden Anatomy Theater, c. 1609," Figure 6. For a discussion, see pp. 72–6. The professor is Peter Pauw, chair of anatomy (appointed in 1589) and the theater is modeled after that at Padua. William Harvey, physician to both Francis Bacon and James I of England, studied anatomy at Padua. We may presume that Bacon was fully cognizant of advances in anatomy and dissection.
37. Bacon, *De Dignitate*, in *Works*, vol. 4, pp. 287, 294, 296, 298.
38. Bruno Latour, "Visualization and Cognition," in Henrika Kuklick and Elizabeth Long, eds., *Knowledge and Society: Studies in the Sociology of Culture Past and Present* (Greenwich, CT: JAI Press, 1986), vol. 6, pp. 22, 29.
39. Carolyn Merchant, "The Scientific Revolution and the Death of Nature," *Isis* 97 (2006): 513–33.
40. Merchant, *Death of Nature*, pp. 171–2; Bacon, *Novum Organum*, in *Works*, vol. 4, p. 246; *The Great Instauration*, in *Works*, vol. 4, p. 29; *Novum Organum*, in *Works*, vol. 4, p. 247.
41. Francis Bacon, "Thoughts and Conclusions on the Interpretation of Nature or A Science of Productive Works," in Benjamin Farrington, ed. and trans., *The Philosophy of Francis Bacon* (Liverpool, England: Liverpool University Press, 1964), pp. 93, 96, 99.

FIGURE 3.1 "Isis Conducting Queen Nefretere to her Tomb" (ca. 1297–1185 B.C.E.). Valley of the Queens, Thebes, Egypt.

Source: Nina de Garis Davies, *Ancient Egyptian Paintings, Selected, Copied and Described*, 3 vols. Chicago: University of Chicago Press, 1936, Vol. II, Plate XCI, courtesy of the Oriental Institute of the University of Chicago.

3

ISIS CONSCIOUSNESS RAISED*

When George Sarton, founding father of the History of Science Society, published the Society's first journal in 1913, he named it *Isis* after the Egyptian mother goddess associated with the annual flooding of the Nile. Isis, according to Sarton in his *History of Science*, "began her foreign conquests in the seventh century, if not before. Herodotus says that . . . the women of Cyrene worshipped her. . . . Temples and inscriptions to Isis and other Egyptian gods can be found in many of the Islands, even in the sacred Delos." In Greece, she was celebrated at the mysteries of Eleusis as "Demeter, the glorification of motherly love (cf. Isis)." For Sarton, Isis is symbolic of nature, and her robe conceals nature's secrets. She "says of herself," he wrote, quoting a passage from Plutarch on Isis and Osiris, "'I am everything which existed, which is now and will ever be, no mortal has ever disclosed my robe.'" Only those initiated through the mysteries (later through science) could glimpse the reality "which is now and will ever be."[1]

Sarton's own image of Isis seems to have derived from an Egyptian wall painting showing her leading Queen Nefretere to her tomb. He refers the reader to a painting, with which "the author (Sarton) is very familiar," of Isis with Queen Nefretere. In the accompanying text, Isis is described as "clad in a sheath-like red dress with a network of beads." In contrast to Isis, Queen Nefretere "wears a flowing robe, the transparency of which is well indicated."[2]

For Sarton, the goal of positivist science was to solve the mysteries of nature by disclosing the secrets "she" harbors within. The real meaning attached to Isis as patron of the history of science was to be found within the tradition of the conquest of nature by the "great men" of science. "I have been deeply moved time after time," he wrote, "while I was contemplating my fellow men wrestling not with other men but with nature herself, trying to solve her mysteries, to decode her message."[3]

Wrestling with nature to extract "her" secrets was the method that led to "positive knowledge" and hence to progress in understanding the natural world. Sarton formulated it as follows:

> Definition: Science is systematized positive knowledge, or what has been taken as such at different ages and at different places.
> Theorem: The acquisition and systematization of positive knowledge are the only human activities which are truly cumulative and progressive.
> Corollary: The history of science is the only history which can illustrate the progress of mankind. In fact, progress has no definite and unquestionable meaning in other fields than the field of science.[4]

The study of the history of science, he believed, was rooted in the purity of past texts. The texts were repositories of knowledge that withstood tests and trials, accumulating evidence of their validity over time and shedding the extraneous tainted clutter of particular ages.[5] The historian of science had to study the false starts of the ages in order to remain a true historian, but the task was not so much to understand the age on its own terms as to divine the process by which it shed its false consciousness and remained on the track of the truth.[6]

Writing the history of science was to construct an emerging scientific knowledge out of textual nuggets, while eliminating false pretensions to truth arising from the social context of each age. The underlying true, positive, cumulative knowledge was set free, while the messy inexact encumbrances of imperfect "men" in imperfect societies were cut off and tossed on the junk piles of the past.[7]

The image of science as positive knowledge, its construction out of atomistic textual nuggets, and the methodology of "wrestling with nature" to decode "her" secrets are all deeply imbedded in the history of Western culture. These assumptions about science, nature, and method pervade the texts of scientists and historians alike. They are challenged by new approaches to the study of science and its history put forward by critical theorists, postmodernists, and feminists.

Critical theory emerging from the Frankfurt School during the mid-twentieth century analyzes the implications of the Enlightenment for the domination of nature and human beings. Postmodernists offer approaches that deconstruct the meanings of textual representations of nature, especially those that conflate women with nature. Feminists reveal hidden biases in the science of the past, in methods of studying nature, and in the texts of scientists and historians of science. Beyond this, they offer alternatives to the domination of women and nature that could lead to liberation.

AN IDEOLOGY OF OBJECTIVITY

At the level of ideology, the philosophy of nature that has guided the work of many modern scientists, as well as historians such as George Sarton, has been logical positivism. Positivism assumes that valid, verifiable, and hence positive knowledge of the world derives ultimately from experience obtained through the senses or experiments and is interpreted via the conventions and rules of mathematical language and logic. Scientific knowledge is rule-governed, context-free, and empirically verifiable and, as such, claims to be objective; that is, independent of the influence of particular historical times and places. Yet the positivist approach to the study of both nature and history relies on a historically associated, interlocking structure of dualities: subject and object, activity and passivity, male and female, and culture and nature.

The basic dichotomy is that between subject and object, and indeed objectivity, the hallmark of logical positivism, depends on it. The objectification of nature is rooted in Aristotle's locus of reality in the objects of the natural world and made explicit in Descartes' separation of mind from matter; that is, of thinking subject from external object. The dualism between activity and passivity hypothesizes an active subject—man—who receives, interprets, and reacts to sense data supplied by a passive object—nature. Nature as object, whether conceived as things (in the Aristotelian framework) or as corpuscles (in the Cartesian) is composed of dead passive matter set in motion by efficient or final causes (Aristotle) or the transfer of motion (Descartes). Stemming from the same Aristotelian roots as the ideology of objectivity is the association of passivity with femaleness and activity with maleness. As Aristotle put it, "the female, as female, is passive and the male, as male, is active, and the principle of movement comes from him."[8] The male semen contributes power and motion—the active principle—to the embryo; the female supplies the matter, or passive principle. Finally, culture is identified with the active subject and thus with the male, as a passage from the philosopher Georg Simmel makes clear:

> The requirement of . . . correctness in practical judgments and objectivity in theoretical knowledge . . . belong as it were in their form and their claims to humanity in general, but in their actual historical configuration they are masculine throughout. Supposing that we describe these things, viewed as absolute ideas, by the single word "objective," we find that in the history of our race the equation objective = masculine is a valid one.[9]

The Aristotelian identification of the female principle with passivity and the further association of passivity with object and the natural world have furnished the basic philosophical framework of Western culture.

Critical theorists of the Frankfurt school have pointed out that the subject-object and attendant dualities of mainstream Western thought entail a philosophy of domination. Because an active controlling subject is separate from and dominant over a passive controlled object, the scientific rationale of objectivity can legitimate control over whatever has been assigned by culture to a lower place in the "natural" order of things.[10] It thus maintains a hierarchical domination of subject over object, male over female, and culture over nature. In particular, this conceptual system can be used to justify the subordination of women when compounded by the separation of productive (public, male) and reproductive (private, female) spheres in modern industrialized society. Historically, nature and the female have been conflated, and cultural ideology has legitimated the domination of both. This identification appears in the science of such "fathers" of modern science as Francis Bacon, William Harvey, Thomas Hobbes, Joseph Glanvill, and Robert Boyle and has permeated the work of scientists since the Scientific Revolution.

But feminism challenges these linkages. A feminist critique undermines the authority of modern science to make universal claims about knowledge, bodies, emotions, female "nature," and transcendent reality—claims that reinforce domination. First of all, feminists expose scientific images that gender both science and nature. Scientists, argues Londa Schiebinger, have used both male and female images to represent science to the public. A substantial number of texts from the early modern period through the 1790s depicted science as a woman, mediating between male scientists and female nature. But by the twentieth century, the image of science as female had been replaced by that of the scientist as efficient male, working in a modern laboratory, usually wearing a white laboratory coat. "Absent . . . are the patrons or politicians influencing his work. . . . The fact that he is white and male is both descriptive and prescriptive; the image cultivates its own clientele," thus legitimating male domination in the sciences.[11]

Second, feminists expose the language of dominance used by science. Ruth Bleier's *Science and Gender*, a critique of biological theories about women, uses Michel Foucault's analysis of knowledge as a discourse to argue that the very tools of scientific discourse—mathematics, observation, and experimentation—are permeated by the principle of domination. Scientists in power set the terms of the debate and determine the concepts that define reality. Scientific truth is actually produced through a gender-dichotomized social and scientific world, not revealed, as for Sarton and the positivists, through an objective mirror. Because women have historically been excluded from power, they have not participated in the debates and discourses that defined their own "nature" as emotional, passive, and untamed. The identification of male nature as rational, active, and scientific reinforces the principle of the domination of men over both women and nature. The concept of Cartesian dualism itself therefore maintains male hegemony.[12]

Third, feminism exposes certain postmodernist approaches to the study of science and its history that entail domination. Male critics of their intellectual fathers' stories fail to deconstruct the assumptions behind their own postmodernist terms such as "master narrative," "representations," and "witnessing." The "master narratives" being questioned are male stories about great men told by male historians of science.[13] The term "master narrative" is itself an example of colonizing language that looks at the "body of knowledge" from above rather than below. The narratives of the Scientific Revolution being criticized are not those of women (for whom there was no revolution), blacks (for whom white Enlightenment meant enslavement), or Nature (for which the Scientific Revolution meant domination). The male reappraisals conveniently ignore feminist reappraisals, failing to challenge the ways women are dominated through narrative devices.[14]

Similarly, vision is a dominating way of knowing—a male "enlightenment" category that tells "God's stories" from a transcendent "view from above," replacing participatory (use of all the senses), oral, and tactile modes of knowing with the "perspective" of the "witness." The distancing from nature (as object) inherent in the term "representations" is made possible by sixteenth-century perspective art, the Copernican view of the earth from above, and the voyeurism inherent in scientific instruments such as the microscope, telescope, camera, and space satellite. Through witnessing, Science can know Nature.[15]

Moreover, the very act of witnessing creates a gendered reality and sets standards about male and female credibility as observers. When Steven Shapin and Simon Schaffer in *Leviathan and the Airpump* (1985) set up witnessing as the key to the acceptance of scientific facts, they fail to analyze the significance of male and female witnessing of the scientific events they describe. In discussing the Duchess of Newcastle's visit, for example, they focus on male witnessing of the Duchess.[16] By contrast, Yaakov Garb has problematized the issue of male witnessing in a reading of an eighteenth-century painting by Joseph Wright of Derby (1734–1797), entitled "Experiment with the Air Pump." Here in public space, men and women display completely different responses to the sight of a pigeon dying as an air pump evacuates its glass container. The men examine the experiment with open curiosity, staring directly at the bird trapped in the glass globe, while the women and children cry, hide their eyes, or look only at the men, viewing the result vicariously. The men "witness" a scientific truth revealed by the experiment; the women "experience" a dying dove. The male painter has appropriated the power to gender both science and reality, forcing social norms about male and female intellectual and emotional responses onto nature and its study.[17]

Logical positivism, as the epitome of Enlightenment scientific method, is thus rooted in and dependent on the dualistic separation of a thinking subject from a passive object known through narrative, vision, and witnessing. This method makes possible the knowing of nature and simultaneously its domination. Positivism as Science's way of knowing Nature, however, is codified in textual representations that are equally problematic.

THE PROBLEM OF REPRESENTATIONS

Problems of domination inherent in dualism, narrative, and witnessing at the core of positivism and Enlightenment scientific method move to a new level in the concept of representation. Nature is represented by science through written texts, illustrations, metaphors, and symbols. A feminist perspective offers a critique of interpretations about science and its history in the realm of representations of nature. A representation is a likeness, image, picture, or written text that is presented to a viewer or reader again and again. As a likeness or sign, it stands in for the object in the field of a viewer located in a different place and subsequent time from the initial act or object. A representation is a sign or narrative account intended to influence, persuade, or be interpreted by a viewer or hearer. Of particular significance are visual and written representations of Nature as female because they reveal problems in the very concept of representation itself.

Representations, such as that of Nature as female, mediate between a society's ideological structure (ideas held by a dominant social group or class) and its daily activities (its behaviors and actions) through their inscription into scientific and historical texts. The texts convey meaning to daily life through images, myths, metaphors, and descriptions. Such representations can either legitimate a dominant conceptual system or offer alternatives to the mainstream view. They play a normative role, mediating between a society's conceptual ideology and people's daily lives, reinforcing individual behaviors. Representations reveal meanings and biases in the stories Science tells about Nature.[18]

The meanings conveyed by scientific images and metaphors are tied to historical contexts. Context sheds light on verbal and visual images for a given society at a given historical moment. The verbal fabric inscribed into the text by the author is given meaning by the reader, both of whom are situated in and informed by particular kinds of social arrangements.[19] Knowledge is constructed through the power of social groups to claim privileged access to reality and that power is revealed through the rhetoric of language.

In postmodern approaches to science and its history, the traditional meaning of the text as a written document is expanded. The new texts include illustrations, photographs, films, factories, laboratories, field stations, visitor centers, museum displays, research proposals, memos, equipment, artifacts, computer messages, printouts, television programs, video tapes, advertisements, and data collections. As texts they contain a dense network of multi-leveled, coded meanings about science and society. They are studied not for their nuggets of truth or positive knowledge, but for what they reveal about relations between language, "forms of life," and the distribution of power in the world.

These texts, however, are predominantly visual. Western culture's love affair with occularcentrism is fundamental to the power conveyed by these images. Evelyn Fox Keller and Christine Grontkowski, following Eric Havelock, point to the power of the "Mind's Eye" in the transformation from the oral culture of the Homeric era to the visual culture of Plato and beyond. The change from mythos to logos inherent in the rise of written texts and visual symbols meant that illumination, light, and seeing were associated with truth and power. Moreover, the mind's eye of cognitive, mathematical reasoning coupled with the empirical eye of observation and experimentation forms the core of the positivist scientific method. Through the centrality given to vision in Western culture, science and power fuse. But occularcentrism comes under attack from cultures that are more participatory in their reliance on all the senses and from feminists such as Luce Irigary, Hélène Cixous, and Monique Whittig who link occularcentrism with phallocentrism and point to the importance of touch and smell over vision in female relationships.[20]

Illustrative of the evolution of occularcentric, voyeuristic representations of nature is the portrayal of nature as a female harboring secrets, such as George Sarton's image of Isis. As these images changed their textual meanings over time, they eventually became an integral part of the scientific method eulogized by Sarton and the positivists. The symbolism associated with Nature deified that began with Isis' refusal to disclose her robe in the passage from Plutarch that Sarton quotes underwent significant changes in the Middle Ages and after.

In Alain de Lille's allegory *Nature's Complaint* (1160), *Natura* (the lower form of the Platonic world soul) laments her exposure to the view of the vulgar. Her "garments of modesty," she complains, are torn by the "unlawful assaults" of men aggressively penetrating the secrets of heaven. *Natura*, whose face is "bedewed with a shower of weeping," is questioned about her torn robe. She replies:

> As we have said before, many men have taken arms against their mother in evil and violence, they thereupon . . . tear apart my garments piece by piece, and . . . force me, stripped of dress, whom they ought to clothe with reverential honor, to come to shame like a harlot.[21]

Such imagery suggests the rape or sexual conquest of both women and nature. And just as nature aggressively investigated is depicted as a woman molested, so femininity is symbolized as an enclosure—often one associated with nature's bounty—that can be breached. Thus medieval artists depict the goddess Venus or the Virgin Mary in enclosed gardens or stone circles symbolic of the female womb and of love, fruitfulness, and pleasure. Chaucer set comic stories in enclosed gardens in which the lover in gaining access to the garden symbolically penetrates the female womb. In *The Merchant's Tale*, based on the biblical "Song of Solomon," Damyan fashions a key to unlock the circular garden and subsequently makes love to a maiden situated in a fruit-bearing tree.[22]

In the seventeenth century, the disclosure of Isis is carried beyond her robe into the interior of her body as Francis Bacon advises his new "man of science" to wrest from nature the secrets harbored in her womb, to search into the bowels of nature for "the truth that lies hid in deep mines and caves" and "to shape her on the anvil." "Nature must be taken by the forelock, being bald behind," he asserted. "Nor ought a man to make scruple of entering and penetrating into these holes and corners, when the inquisition of truth is his whole object."[23]

The problems of witnessing and voyeurism become apparent in Joseph Glanvill's use of instruments such as the microscope as the means by which Science can know Nature. Nature, he said, must be "mastered" and "managed" by "searching out the depths . . . and intrigues of remoter nature." In this project, nothing was more helpful than the microscope, for "the secrets of nature are not in the greater masses, but in those little threads and springs which are too subtle for the grossness of our unhelped senses." In the *Vanity of Dogmatizing*, Glanvill pointed out that "Nature's coarser wares" are "exposed to the transient view of every common eye; her choicer riches are locked up only for the sight of them that will buy at the expense of sweat and oil." In achieving such insights, however, true understanding is often misled by the emotions, for "the woman in us, still prosecutes a deceit, like that begun in the Garden: and our understandings are wedded to an Eve, as fatal as the mother of our miseries."[24]

By the nineteenth century, nature is represented as removing her own veil and voluntarily exposing her own secrets. A sculpture by Louis Ernest Barrias, "La Nature se devoilant devant la Science" ("Nature Revealing Herself to Science"), is appropriately located in the entry to the School of Medicine in Paris (above, Fig. 2.2, p. 34.). In Edouard Manet's "Le Dejeuner sur l'herbe" (1863), a naked woman (based on the nymph or nature goddess in a sixteenth-century engraving) picnics on the grass with two fully clothed gentlemen.[25]

In the twentieth century, we find scientists themselves fervently hoping that the veil of nature, like Isis' robe, can be lifted from matter itself (traditionally

feminine) so that all may view the hidden secrets of the atom—the mysteries that Isis' robe or Nature's veil conceals. One may hope, announced the
inaugural editorial from *Le Radium* in 1904, "to be able to lift a corner of
the veil that conceals creation. . . . Each of us hopes that . . . a sensational
application of radium will completely tear away the veil and that truth will
appear before everyone's eyes." "The notion of impenetrable mysteries has
been dismissed," wrote Sir William Crookes in 1903; "A mystery is a thing
to be solved—and 'man alone can master the impossible.'" The editors of
Harper's (1924) applauded the "laying bare" of the atom's structure, while
Hans Reichenbach in 1933 charged nuclear physicists with the task of the
"unveiling of the secrets surrounding the inner structure of matter."[26]

Such textual representations are suggestive of both voyeurism and sexual
assaults on nature and can be so interpreted when science and its history
are placed within the context of the historical evolution of the language and
metaphor of science. But they go beyond the goal that Science simply wishes
to know Nature to the idea of the domination and control of nature through
discovery of "her" secrets. The empirical eye of experimentation and observation coupled with the mind's eye of the disembodied calculating intellect
form the basis of logical positivism as the scientific method. Positivism and
occularcentrism thus combine knowledge with power over nature.

EPISTEMOLOGIES OF GENDER AND RACE

The method of knowing nature through positivism and occularcentric representations leads to a third problematic—the ways in which scientific knowing
is linked to gender and race. George Sarton associated the progress of science,
the rise of the "human race," and the fulfillment of human destiny with men:

> We have some degree of interest in every *man and woman* whom we approach
> near enough. Should we not be even more interested in those *men* who accom-
> plish more fully the destiny of the race? . . . The same instinct which causes
> sport-lovers to be insatiably curious about their heroes causes the scientific
> humanist to ask one question after another about the *great men* to whom he
> owes his heritage of knowledge and culture. In order to satisfy that sound
> instinct it will be necessary to prepare detailed and reliable biographies of the
> *men* who distinguished themselves in the search for truth.[27]
>
> *(Italics added)*

Sarton's passage not only makes it clear that it is men who set the standards
for knowing and culture, but it is men who also fulfill "the destiny of the
race." While Sarton apparently means the destiny of the human race, the

question arises as to the extent to which the human race and the white race are conflated in accounts of the rise of modern science. Does the history of science give undo weight to Greek and European roots and accomplishments in relation to those of other races and cultures? Just below the surface of many texts lies a Eurocentric implication that it is primarily the white race that has discovered the "truths of nature."

Although Sarton was eager to establish the pre-Hellenic roots of science among the Egyptians, Babylonians, and Hindus, he saw them as precursors to what he called the "Greek miracle." He pays tribute to specific achievements of the Egyptians and Sumerians whose work made possible Euclidean geometry and to Alexandria for keeping the Greek achievement alive after the decline of Greece. In his *History of Science*, he states, "There is no privileged 'race' or community in any absolute way, but for each task and for each time some people or some nations may excel all others." Yet he goes on to note that his concern in that volume was "with the ancient peoples whose cultural dawn was only the prelude to the greatest achievements of the third and second millennia before Christ." And in his *Study of the History of Mathematics*, he writes, "In reality the way for Euclidean mathematics was very gradually and thoroughly prepared, not only by the millenary efforts of Africans and Asiatics, but by three centuries of persistent investigations by the most gifted people among our ancestors, the Greeks of the Golden Age."[28]

Important nevertheless is the debate about the black roots of Egyptian science after which Sarton named the journals and guides to the history of science—Isis, Osiris, and Horus. His famous illustration of "Isis Conducting Queen Nefretere to her Tomb," reveals that Isis herself is brown or dark yellow. Herodotus, whom Sarton cites as an authority on Isis, described the Egyptians as having black skin and curly hair. Statues of Isis suckling her son Horus reveal her with dark skin and black, plaited or curled hair. Historians Danita Redd, Monica Sjöo, and Barbara Mor see such statues as prototypes of the black Madonnas found throughout Europe in the Christian era.[29] As historian of science David Kubrin noted in 1972, "Greece is European, white; Egypt is African, non-white. Yet these non-white roots of Western science have been nearly completely obfuscated, at least until recently." Science in China, India, and Egypt that preceded its development in Greece originated with men and women whose races were other than white.[30]

The idea that the body of Nature, concealed beneath the robe of Isis, might be brown or black raises additional questions about the "rape of nature," as well as about science as a method for revealing Nature's secrets. By the seventeenth century, matter at the base of the great chain of being was associated with putrefaction, black magic, witchcraft, and black African slaves, hence with the need for rational, scientific, and technological control over nature.[31] At the same time, Isis herself was becoming white, losing her brown Egyptian origins. Athenasius Kircher's depiction of Isis in his *Oedipus Aegypticus* (1652–54) shows her with European features and lightened skin and hair, while his replica of the ancient Egyptian "Bembine Table of Isis" (originally made of bronze and decorated with enamel and silver), in the same book, reveals her as having dark or black skin, the same color as the dark background.[32]

The black or brown woman's body as the object of scientific investigation and experimentation has been exposed by feminist historians of science in recent literature. In *Nature's Body* (1993), Londa Schiebinger investigates theories of gender and race at the root of modern science. By the eighteenth century, black women's bodies, especially their skulls, breasts, and genitalia, were being described by scientists and anthropologists as part of a broader "scientific" investigation of African and European anatomical and sexual differences. The prejudice that blacks were not capable of abstract thought because their skulls allegedly resembled those of apes threw into question early modern ideas held by Ambroise Paré, Galileo, and Newton that the Egyptians had invented science and mathematics. In the 1820s, Schiebinger notes, physician William Lawrence questioned the view that Egypt was a "birthplace of the arts" and asked whether the sciences, religion, and laws could have been "discovered and framed by men with black skin, woolly hairs, and slanting forehead?" Scientists and anthropologists examined mummies, murals, and sarcophagi for evidence as to the Negro, Hindu, or Caucasian origins of the Egyptians themselves.[33] While some authorities continued to assert that the Egyptians were black or that Egypt represented a crossroads of Ethiopian, Hindu, and Caucasian cultures and that science, language, and the arts originated there, the predominant trend was to deny the black and Egyptian origins of European culture.

Martin Bernal's *Black Athena: The Afroasiatic Roots of Classical Civilization* (1987) argues that in the late eighteenth century, the Egyptian origins of modern science were replaced with a white model that attributed the origins of science and civilization to the Greeks and Indo-Europeans. Bernal himself challenges this Aryan interpretation of Ancient Greece, seen as the result of an invasion from the north by Indo-Europeans who mingled with pre-Hellenic Greeks, and replaces it with a revised version of the Greeks own Ancient Model that they were colonized by Egyptians and Phoenicians around 1500 B.C.: "If I am right in urging the overthrow of the Aryan Model and its replacement by the Revised Ancient one, it will be necessary not only to rethink the fundamental bases of 'Western Civilization' but also to recognize the penetration of racism and 'continential chauvinism' into all our historiography, or philosophy of writing history."[34]

Bernal accepts the ancient testimony that the Greek fertility mysteries at Eleusis featuring the grain goddess Demeter (Ceres in Rome) and her daughter Persephone (Proserpina in Rome) arose from similar Egyptian mysteries surrounding Isis and Osiris that were transmitted into Attica possibly as early as the fifteenth century B.C., but still celebrated in classical times. The myth of Demeter searching for her daughter Persephone in the underworld of Hades was the Greek version of Isis' search for her husband/brother Osiris, her reassembly of his dismembered body, and their son Horus' victory over Seth, his murderer. Both were celebrations by agricultural societies of the renewal of nature's fertility in the spring planting time.

Like Sarton, Bernal examines the transmission of Egyptian cultural influences into ancient Greece. But unlike Sarton, Bernal is self-consciously promoting a muticultural, multiracial account of the origins of "Western" culture and science by calling Athena "black." Neither author, however, is concerned about the racial *and* sexual implications of Isis' body as simultaneously non-white and the object of investigation of the secrets of nature. Both issues are of importance if science is to transcend its treatment of women and nature as merely experimental objects, acknowledge its debt to other cultures, and realize its potential for a liberatory, democratic future.

Sandra Harding's edited collection *The "Racial" Economy of Science* (1993) is part of a new historiography about race, gender, and science that seeks to move toward a more democratic science in the future. Its authors analyze history and historians for their privileging of concepts associated with Western and First World societies, question the roots of social hierarchy and class, and look at non-Western contributions to the theory and practice of science.[35]

CONCLUSION

I have argued that science and its history have in the past shared, and to a large extent still do share, a methodological approach to the study of nature that leads to its domination. Logical positivism, which privileges mathematical and empirically verifiable statements as true, is reinforced by occularcentrism, based on the supremacy of the mind's eye and the empirical eye, and by Eurocentric assumptions of the supremacy of Western science since the "Greek miracle." The three prongs taken together fuse what counts as knowledge of nature with power over it. These deeply held assumptions, however, have been challenged by feminists, postmodernists, and critical theorists.

These new approaches to science and its history utilize the standpoints of feminist scholars who have uncovered patriarchal and racist elements in science, postmodernists who have studied texts, contexts, and discourses as representations of nature and science, and the Frankfurt school, which has raised the problematic of ideologies of domination over society and nature. They expose universalizing tendencies in Western culture that have been prevalent since the Enlightenment of the eighteenth century. They criticize the idea that history is linear and evolutionary and that reason reveals transcendent truths. They question whether reason can be separated from the body and from particular times and places, while challenging the authority of science to make universal claims about the body, particularly female bodies.[36]

These approaches to the history of science have:

1. destabilized the assumption that Science (whether the outcome of internal or external influences) can indeed know Nature (the problem of relativism). See Epilogue to this book;

2. linked power and knowledge at the levels of both epistemology and practice, so that what counts as scientific knowledge necessarily reflects the relations of domination (the problem of the dominated object);

3. questioned the possibility of a scientific knowledge system independent of the culture-bound influences of sex, race, and ethnocentrism (the problem of the independence of the knowing subject); and

4. challenged the assumption that the nature behind human representations changed only through its own evolutionary and physical laws, asserting instead that human practices give rise to new objects, such as chemically induced or genetically engineered mutants (the question of nature as actor).

All four linkages pose problems for the historian who in the very act of writing science's history may be participating in a project of cultural domination, from which she or he seeks emancipation. While the positivist approach of Sarton generally assumed that science (whether externally or internally produced) was objective, value-free, context-free knowledge of an external world, the new history has tended implicitly to accept Martin Heidegger's observation that all philosophy (including science and technology) since Descartes has been fundamentally concerned with power.[37]

The new history not only challenges the older authority of science, but also raises new problems. If reality itself is gendered by social relations, are we, either as men or women, necessarily bound to participate in the project of dominating nature, women, and underprivileged human groups? Does the social construction of science lead to a relativist historicism? Does society always mediate access to objects and processes? Is all knowledge bound by time, place, and culture?

Donna Haraway's *Primate Visions* struggles with the temptation to see science and its history through any single lens that implies that the answer to these questions is yes. Haraway's four compelling temptations are:

1. Science as a social construct suggests the rejection of scientific reality.
2. Marxism suggests that social and economic institutions structure the production of knowledge about the world.
3. Feminist and ethnic studies suggest that we should see science through the lens of domination.
4. Scientists suggest that organisms are real and that science can discover real relations about them.

To write the history of primate science from any one position, all of which are persuasive, would create a single but false narrative.

Haraway's book tells many stories from many perspectives, each contributing its own partial mix of fact and fiction about the natural world. The resulting book is written by and about people who have emotional, political, and scientific stakes in the outcome. She writes, "I want this book to be responsible to primatologists, to historians of science, to cultural theorists, to the broad left, anti-racist, anti-colonial, and women's movements, to animals, and to lovers of serious stories. It is perhaps not always possible to be accountable to those contending audiences, but they have all made this book possible."[38]

However compelling the politics of social constructivism may have been in the 1980s, a synthesis between social constructivism and realism seems to be the direction of the future. Jan Golinski points out that social constructivists have been criticized for ignoring the constraints posed by nature to the production of scientific knowledge: "Granted that observations are indeed shaped by prior expectations and by beliefs about the capacities of instruments . . . this does not open the way to indefinite interpretive flexibility."[39]

Feminism, postmodernism, and critical theory all suggest alternatives to totalizing histories, while attempting to move beyond problems of the domination of nature and people. Liberation entails recognizing that nature is a real autonomous actor rather than a passive object of experimentation and utility—Isis as active bringer of the renewal of life rather than harborer of Nature's secrets. It likewise means that women and minorities should also be accorded recognition as autonomous real beings. Finally, it means writing multilayered, sensitive, but perhaps at best partial perspectives on the past, recognizing that we too are but real bodies produced by real social relations reflecting imperfectly on a naturally and culturally constructed real world.

NOTES

* From Carolyn Merchant, "Isis Consciousness Raised," *Isis* 72, no. 268 (September 1982): 398–409. Copyright 1982 by the History of Science Society, University of Chicago Press. All rights reserved. Reprinted in Carolyn Merchant, Earthcare (New York: Routledge, 1996).

1. George Sarton, *A History of Science*, 2 vols. (Cambridge, MA: Harvard University Press, 1959), vol. 1, pp. 125, 152. Sarton cites Herodotus, IV, 186 and quotes Plutarch, "Isis and Osiris," (1–2) in *Moralia* (Loeb Classical Library), vol. 5, inscription on 354c. Herodotus, *The History of Herodotus* (New York: Tudor, 1928) writes: "Even at Cyrene, the women think it wrong to eat the flesh of the cow, honoring in this Isis, the Egyptian goddess, whom they worship both with fasts and festivals" (p. 260). Herodotus also writes: "the females [i.e., cows] they are not allowed to sacrifice, since they are sacred to Isis. The statue of this goddess has the form of a woman, but with horns like a cow, resembling thus the Greek representations of Io; and the Egyptians, one and all, venerate cows much more highly than any other animal. . . . The Egyptians do not all worship the same gods, excepting Isis and Osiris, the latter of whom they say is the Grecian Bacchus" (p. 95). Also, "The Egyptians tell the following story: 'Latona, one of the eight gods of the first order, who dwelt in the city of Buto, where now she has her oracle, received Apollo as a sacred charge from Isis, and saved him by hiding him in what is now called the floating island. Typhon meanwhile was searching everywhere in hopes of finding the child of Osiris.' According to the Egyptians, Apollo and Diana are the children of Bacchus and Isis; while Latona is their nurse and their preserver. They call Apollo, in their language Horus; Ceres they call Isis; Diana Bubastis" (p. 137).

2. Painting of "Isis Conducts Queen Nefretere to her Tomb," as reproduced by Nina de Garis Davies in *Ancient Egyptian Paintings, Selected, Copied, and Described*, 3 vols. (Chicago, IL: University of Chicago Press, 1936), vol. 2, Plate XCI. Description by Davies quoted from vol. 3, p. 177.

3. George Sarton, *The Study of the History of Science* (New York: Dover, 1936), pp. 41–2.

4. Ibid., p. 5. On historiography in the *History of Science*, see Tore Frängsmyr, "Science or History: George Sarton and the Positivist Tradition in the History of Science," *Lychnos* 37 (1973–4): 104–44.

5. George Sarton, *Introduction to the History of Science* (Baltimore: Williams and Wilkins, Co., 1927), p. 6. See Frängsmyr, "Science or History," p. 115.

6. Sarton, *Introduction to the History of Science*, p. 19.

7. Sarton, *A History of Science*, vol. 1, p. xii.

8. Aristotle, *De Generatione Animalium*, trans. Arthur Platt (Oxford, England: Clarendon Press, 1910), Bk.1, Ch.19, lines 279b13.

9. See Georg Simmel (1858–1918), *Philosophische Kultur*, as quoted in Karen Horney, "The Flight from Womanhood," in Jean Strouse, ed., *Women and Analysis* (New York: Grossman, 1974), p. 172. See also Evelyn Fox Keller, "Gender and Science," *Psychoanalysis and Contemporary Thought* 1 (1978): 409–33, on p. 409.

10. Vincent di Norcia, "From Critical Theory to Critical Ecology," *Telos*, no. 22 (1974/75): 85–95, on pp. 88–9; Max Horkheimer and Theodor Adorno, *Dialectic of Enlightment*, trans. John Cumming (New York: Herder and Herder, 1972); Max Horkheimer, *The Eclipse of Reason* (New York: Oxford University Press, 1947); Jürgen Habermas, *Toward a Rational Society* (London: Heineman, 1971), pp. 81–122; William Leiss, *The Domination of Nature* (New York: George Braziller, 1972); Theodor Adorno, Hans Albert, Ralf Dahrendorf, Jürgen Habermas, Harald Pilot, and Karl R. Popper, *The Positivist Dispute in German Sociology*, trans. Glyn Adey and David Frisby (New York: Harper & Row, 1976). For a feminist extension of the Frankfurt school's critique of objectivity, see Marcia Westkott, "Feminist Criticism of the Social Sciences," *Harvard Educational Review* 49 (November 1979): 422–30. See also Dorothy Smith, "Women's Perspective as a Radical Critique of Sociology," *Sociological Inquiry* 44 (1974): 7–13.

11. Londa Schiebinger, "Feminine Icons: The Face of Early Modern Science," *Critical Inquiry* 14, no. 4 (Summer 1988): 661–91, see pp. 663, 688. See also Londa Schiebinger, *The Mind Has No Sex? Women in the Origins of Modern Science* (Cambridge, MA: Harvard University Press, 1989), pp. 119–59.

12. Ruth Bleier, *Science and Gender: A Critique of Biology and Its Theories on Women* (New York: Pergamon, 1984), pp. 193–200. For other feminist critiques of science, see Sandra Harding, *The Science Question in Feminism* (Ithaca: Cornell University Press, 1986); Nancy Tuana, ed., *Feminism & Science* (Bloomington, IN: Indiana University Press, 1989); Evelyn Fox Keller, *Reflections on Gender and Science* (New Haven, CT: Yale University Press, 1985); Brian Easlea, *Science and Sexual Oppression: Patriarchy's Confrontation with Woman and Nature* (London: Weidenfeld and Nicholson, 1981); and Carolyn Merchant, *The Death of Nature: Women, Ecology, and the Scientific Revolution* (San Francisco: Harper & Row, 1980).

13. John A. Schuster, "(New) Master Narrative(s), Yes: 'Scientific Revolution,' No Thanks," paper presented to the annual meeting of the History of Science Society, Seattle, October 26, 1990; Robert Westman, ibid., comment.

14. For feminist reappraisals of the Scientific Revolution, see Merchant, *The Death of Nature*; Schiebinger, *The Mind Has No Sex?*; Keller, *Reflections on Gender and Science*; and Brian Easlea, *Witch-Hunting, Magic, and the New Philosophy* (Sussex: Harvester, 1980).

15. Elizabeth Ann R. Bird, "The Social Construction of Nature: Theoretical Approaches to the History of Environmental Problems," *Environmental Review* 11, no. 4 (Winter 1987): 255–64. Bird argues that the concept of representation implies an independently existing, evolving nature behind the representation that is accessible and knowable by science. Yet human social practice, not just "Natural" evolution, changes nature. Applications of pesticides and antibiotics, for example, create the conditions through which nature resists human technologies and mutates to new life forms. On perspective versus participatory ways of knowing, see Thomas Merriam, "The Disenchantment of Science," *The Ecologist* 7, no. 1 (1977): 23–8; and Morris Berman, *The Reenchantment of the World* (Ithaca: Cornell University Press, 1981). On the distancing process created by perspective art and satellite images, see Yaakov Garb, "The Use and Misuse of the Whole Earth Image," *Whole Earth Review*, no. 45 (March 1985): 18–25.

16. Stephen Shapin and Simon Schaffer, *Leviathan and the Airpump* (Princeton, NJ: Princeton University Press, 1985).

17. I thank Yaakov Garb for his analysis of the painting by Joseph Wright of Derby.

18. On the philosophy of metaphor, see George Lakoff and Mark Johnson, *Metaphors We Live By* (Chicago: University of Chicago Press, 1980); and Robin Lakoff, *Language and Woman's Place* (New York: Harper & Row, 1975).

19. On contextualism, see Robert F. Berkhofer, Jr., "A New Context for a New American Studies?" *American Quarterly* 41, no. 4 (December 1989): 588–613; and AHR Forum, "The Old History and the New," *The American Historical Review* 94, no. 3 (June 1989): 581–698.

20. Evelyn Fox Keller and Christine R. Grontkowski, "The Mind's Eye," in Sandra Harding and Merril B. Hintikka, eds., *Discovering Reality* (Dordrecht, Holland: D. Reidel, 1983), pp. 207–24; Martin Jay, *Downcast Eyes: The Denigration of Vision in Twentieth Century French Thought* (Berkeley, CA: University of California Press, 1993), pp. 526–42. On participatory consciousness, see Morris Berman, *The Reenchantment of the World* (Ithaca, NY: Cornell University Press, 1981).

21. Alain de Lille, *The Complaint of Nature*, trans. Douglas Moffat (New York: Henry Holt, 1908), pp. 15, 33, 41. For the original, see Alanus de Insulis, "De Planctu Naturae," in Thomas Wright, ed., *The Anglo-Latin Satirical Poets and Epigrammatists of the Twelfth Century* (London: Longman & Trubner, 1892), vol. 2, pp. 429–522, esp. pp. 441, 467. On the proper role of nature as teacher in revealing her truths to mankind, see p. 457 (Alain, *Complaint*, p. 31). For a commentary, see George Economou, *The Goddess Natura in Medieval Literature* (Cambridge, MA: Harvard University Press, 1972), esp. pp. 72–80;

and Carolyn Merchant, *The Death of Nature: Women, Ecology, and the Scientific Revolution* (San Francisco, CA: Harper & Row, 1980), pp. 10–20, 31–3.

22. See the French painting *St. Genevieve with Her Flock* (16th century), depicting the virgin with her flock of sheep within a protective stone circle on a hillside of trees and blooming flowers, reproduced in John Michell, *The Earth Spirit* (New York: Avon, 1975). Geoffrey, "The Merchant's Tale," in F. N. Robinson, ed., *Works* (Boston, MA: Houghton Mifflin, 1933), pp. 612-627, see lines 2044–6; 2143–6. On garden symbolism, see Stanley Stewart, *The Enclosed Garden: The Tradition and Image in Seventeenth Century Poetry* (Madison, WI: University of Wisconsin Press, 1966).

23. Francis Bacon, "De Dignitate et Augmentis Scientarum," James Spedding, Robert Ellis, and Douglas Heath, eds., *Works*, 14 vols. (London: Longmans Green 1857–1874), vol. 4, pp. 287, 343; Francis Bacon, "The Refutation of Philosophies," in Benjamin Farrington, ed. and trans., *The Philosophy of Francis Bacon* (Liverpool: Liverpool University Press, 1964), p. 130; Bacon, "De dignitate et Augmentis Scientarum," *Works*, vol. 4, pp. 294, 296.

24. Joseph Glanvill, *Plus Ultra* (Gainesville, FL: Scholar's Facsimile reprints, 1958; originally published, 1668), pp. 10, 56, 87; Joseph Glanvill, *The Vanity of Dogmatizing* (New York: Columbia University Press, 1931; originally published, 1661), pp. 118, 247.

25. For the illustration of "Nature Revealing Herself to Science," see Merchant, *Death of Nature*, p. 191. For the illustration of "Le Dejeuner sur l'Herbe," see George Mauner, *Manet: Peintre-philosophe* (University Park, PA: Pennsylvania State University Press, 1975), pp. 11–17, 34.

26. Inaugural editorial, *Le Radium*, 1 (January 1904): 2. Quotation translated by Spencer Weart (I thank Dr. Weart for this and the following three quotations); Sir William Crookes, "Modern Views on Matter," *Science* 26, vol. 17, no. 443 (June 1903): 993–1003; Hans Reichenbach, *Atom and Cosmos: The World of Modern Physics*, trans. and rev. Edward S. Allen (New York: MacMillan, 1933), p. 222; editor's note in *Harper's*, 149 (July 1924): 251, as quoted in Daniel Kevles, *The Physicists* (New York: Knopf, 1978), p. 174.

27. Sarton, *The Study of the History of Science*, pp. 41–2.

28. Sarton, *A History of Science*, vol. 1, quotation on p. 18; George Sarton, *The Study of the History of Mathematics* (New York: Dover, 1936), pp. 8–9, quotation on p. 9.

29. Davies in *Ancient Egyptian Paintings*, vol. 3, writes: "Her [Isis'] yellow complexion, contrasting markedly with the rosy flesh-tint of the queen, is traditional; the appearance of deities did not change with the times like that of mortals" (p. 177). She also notes, "Hair is very often modelled [with] the blobs being arranged. . . so as to create the appearance of short curls; these break up the surface pleasantly when the entire wig is painted black or grey" (vol. 3, p. xlii). On Isis as the prototype of the black Madonna, see Danita Redd, "Black Madonnas of Europe: Diffusion of the African Isis," in Ivan Van Sertima, ed., *African Presence in Early Europe* (1985; New Brunswick, NJ: Transaction Publishers, Rutgers–The State University, 1993), pp. 106–33, illustration of Isis with Horus on p. 109. See also Monica Sjöo and Barbara Mor, "The Original Black Mother," in Monica Sjöo and Barbara Mor, eds., *The Great Cosmic Mother: Rediscovering the Religion of the Earth* (San Francisco: Harper & Row, 1987), pp. 21–32, illustration of Isis with Horus, on p. 158. On Isis as exemplar of fertility and matriarchy in black Africa, see Cheikh Anta Diop, *The Cultural Unity of Black Africa* (Chicago, IL: World Press, 1990; originally published 1959), pp. 58–62.

30. David Kubrin, "How Sir Isaac Newton Helped Restore Law 'n' Order to the West," *Liberation* 16, no. 10 (March 1972): 32–41, quotation on p. 38. See also Londa Schiebinger, *Nature's Body: Gender in the Making of Modern Science* (Boston: Beacon Press, 1993), chap. 6. Schiebinger points out that Constantin-François Volney in 1787 cited Herodotus on the blackness of Egyptians in his defense of the Egyptian roots of Greek science. See Constantin-François Volney, *Voyage en Syrie et Egypte* (Paris: Mouton & Co., 1959; first published, 1787), pp. 62–4.

31. Winthrop Jordan, *White over Black: American Attitudes toward the Negro, 1550–1812* (Chapel Hill, NC: University of North Carolina Press, 1968); Ronald Takaki, *Iron Cages* (New York: Alfred Knopf, 1979).

32. Athenasius Kircher, *Oedipus Aegypticus*, 3 vols., in Latin (Rome: V. Mascardi, 1652–54).
33. Schiebinger, *Nature's Body*, chap. 6. Schiebinger points out that the Egyptian roots of
    modern science had been celebrated in the sixteenth and seventeenth centuries by such
    commentators as Ambroise Paré (1575), who stated that "Ethiopians, Egyptians, Africans,
    Jews, Phoenicians, Persians, Assyrians, and Indians have invented many curious sciences,
    revealed, the mysteries and secrets of Nature, ordered mathematics, observed the motions
    of the heavens, and introduced the worship of the gods" (Paré quoted in chap. 6, headnote).
    Galileo noted that the ancients had mapped the heavens and Newton was fascinated by the
    sacred cubit of the Egyptians as the underlying unit of the great pyramid of Cheops. See also
    Kubrin, "How Sir Isaac Newton Helped Restore Law 'n' Order to the West," p. 38: "Most
    historians of science today, it is true, trace the roots of ancient science back to the thinkers in
    pre-Socratic Ionia, in sixth century B.C. Greece. Yet, certainly during the scientific revolu-
    tion, this was not the opinion of the scientists themselves. Rather, many of them agreed that
    their knowledge and discipline was more properly traced back to Egypt. To take merely one
    example, Isaac Newton wrote in his *Chronology of Ancient Kingdoms Amended* that it was
    after 655 B.C. when Psamminticus became king of all Egypt, that the Greek Ionians had
    'access into Egypt; and thence came the Ionian Philosophy, Astronomy, and Geometry.'"
    Isaac Newton, *Chronology of Ancient Kingdoms* (London: Printed for J. Tonson, J. Osborn,
    and T. Longman, 1728), p. 37. On racism in English science, see Nancy Leys Stepan, *The
    Idea of Race in Science: Great Britain, 1800–1960* (Hamden, CT: Archon Books, 1982).
34. Martin Bernal, *Black Athena* (New Brunswick, NJ: Rutgers University Press, 1987, 1991),
    p. 2. For other reappraisals of science from a racial perspective, see Londa Schiebinger,
    "The Anatomy of Difference: Race and Sex in Eighteenth Century Science," *Eighteenth
    Century Studies* 23 (1990): 387–406; and Anne Fausto-Sterling, "The Dissection of Race
    and Gender in the Nineteenth Century," paper presented to the annual meeting of the His-
    tory of Science Society, Seattle, October 26, 1990.
35. Sandra Harding, ed., *The "Racial" Economy of Science: Toward a Democratic Future*
    (Bloomington, IN: University of Indiana Press, 1993).
36. See Linda Nicholson, ed., *Feminism/Postmodernism* (New York: Routledge, 1990); Irene
    Diamond and Lee Quinby, eds., *Feminism & Foucault: Reflections on Resistance* (Bos-
    ton: Northeastern University Press, 1988); Robert Young, ed., *Untying the Text: A Post-
    Structuralist Reader* (Boston: Routledge & Kegan Paul, 1981); Mark Poster, *Critical
    Theory and Poststructuralism: In Search of a Context* (Ithaca, NY: Cornell University
    Press, 1989); William Leiss, *The Domination of Nature* (New York: George Braziller,
    1972); Jürgen Habermas, *The Philosophical Discourse of Modernity* (Cambridge, MA:
    MIT Press, 1990); and Michel Foucault, *Power/Knowledge* (New York: Pantheon, 1980).
37. Martin Heidegger, "The Age of the World Picture," in Heidegger, *The Question Concerning
    Technology*, trans. William Lovitt (New York: Harper & Row, 1977), pp. 115–154; Martin
    Heidegger, *Der Satz vom Grund*, quoted in Hubert Dreyfus, *What Computers Can't Do*
    (New York: Harper & Row, 1972), p. 242, n. 16.
38. Donna Haraway, *Primate Visions: Gender, Race, and Nature in the History of Modern Sci-
    ence* (New York: Routledge, 1989), pp. 1–15, quotation on p. 3. See also Donna Haraway,
    "Situated Knowledges: The Science Question in Feminism and the Privilege of Partial
    Perspective," *Feminist Studies* 14, no. 3 (Fall 1988): 575–99.
39. Jan Golinski, "The Theory of Practice and the Practice of Theory: Sociological Approaches
    in the History of Science," *Isis* 81, no. 308 (September 1990): 492–505, quotation on
    p. 503.

Part II

ON ENERGY AND MOMENTUM

In November 1715, just a year before his death, Gottfried Wilhelm Leibniz (July 1, 1646–November 14, 1716) set down a fundamental challenge to his British rival Isaac Newton (1642–1727):

> Sir Isaac Newton and his followers have . . . a very odd opinion concerning the work of God. According to their doctrine, God Almighty [needs] to wind up his watch from time to time; otherwise it would cease to move. He had not, it seems, sufficient foresight to make it a perpetual motion. . . . [He] is obliged to clean it now and then by an extraordinary concourse, and even to mend it as a clockmaker mends his work.[1]

For Leibniz, Newton's God was a clockmaker, engineer, and mathematician who lacked the foresight to create a perfectly functioning machine at the creation of the world and had to use his power to repair a clock that ran down and whose planetary orbits could be disrupted by passing comets.

This colorful statement, which initiated the famous Leibniz-Clarke debate of 1716 on the nature of God (with Samuel Clarke speaking for Newton), was actually the apex of one of the most profound and divisive debates in the history of physics—the controversy over living force (*vis viva*), or conservation of energy. Leibniz had started the whole matter in 1686 with a paper arguing that "force" should be measured by mv^2 (living force) now known as kinetic energy ($\frac{1}{2}mv^2$) and not by the "quantity of motion" $m|v|$ (or when direction is considered as mv, mass times velocity—now known as momentum). In Part II, I present the interlinking physical and metaphysical arguments of

Leibniz, Newton, and d'Alembert, the third of whom allegedly resolved the debate in 1743, although as I show in Chapter 6, it lingered on for many years afterward.

In Chapter 4 on Leibniz, I argue that Leibniz's early insight into a universe that is fundamentally alive, vitalistic, and energistic underlay his efforts to define force as *vis viva* and describe it as mv^2. "Force" for Leibniz is a momentary state that carries within it a tendency toward a future state—what in 1714 he christened as the monad. Force is a striving, a *conatus* that has direction and is future-oriented. What is real in nature is activity, not extension as Descartes had argued. It is living force—mv^2—that is conserved in the universe. Leibniz's insight was later incorporated into the general law of the conservation of energy, also known as the first law of thermodynamics, which posits that the total energy in the universe (considered as a closed system) can neither be created nor destroyed; it is only changed in form.

In Chapter 5 on Newton, I place the *vis viva* controversy within the opposing views of Newton and Leibniz on natural philosophy, including the nature of God, matter, and force as represented by mv versus mv^2 and show that adherents to the two systems developed such intense loyalties to the two founders that they were blinded from seeing that both laws and both systems had validity. I ground their differing ideologies within the intellectualist versus voluntarist theological frameworks of the medieval period; the opposition between views of matter as dead, lifeless, and inert versus matter as point sources of force, alive, and energetic; and differing views as to whether the total "force" (energy) in the universe was constant and conserved or whether the universe could run down, requiring God's intervention to "rewind his clock." Indeed just as Leibniz's insight about the conservation of *vis viva* anticipated the first law of thermodynamics or general law of the conservation of energy, so Newton's intuition about the universe running down anticipated the second law of thermodynamics that order moves to disorder as the entropy of the universe (the energy unavailable to do work) increases, resulting in what was then considered to be a cosmic heat death.

Chapter 6 on d'Alembert argues that although the controversy over living force has often been considered to be resolved in 1743 when d'Alembert said that both mv and mv^2 were correct measures of "force," for a number of reasons, this date has little meaning. Scientists continued to prefer either mv or mv^2 when trying to solve problems of the interaction of bodies. It was not until the late nineteenth century that equal status was given to both the conservation of kinetic energy and momentum.

Together, these three chapters show that the controversy over living force was at the root of some of the most complex physical and metaphysical issues of early modern science. They demonstrate that critical linkages exist among assumptions about the nature of matter, energy, causality, order, disorder, and the properties and even existence of an ultimate deity. Science does not exist as an "objective," orderly system of discovering and demonstrating the truths of nature. Rather it is often a messy process, driven by chance, by assumptions that later prove incorrect, by intense loyalties, and by failures to recognize valid arguments and experiments. As these chapters demonstrate, science, in the process of reaching agreement and ultimately getting to "yes," can at times appear muddled, chaotic, disorganized, and confused even as it carves out pathways toward the laws of nature.

NOTE

1. Gottfried Wilhelm Leibniz, "The Controversy between Leibniz and Clarke, (1715–16)," in Leroy Loemker, ed., *Philosophical Papers and Letters*, vol. 2 (Dordrecht, The Netherlands: Kluwer Academic Publishers, 1989), pp. 675–721, quotation on p. 676.

FIGURE 4.1 Gottfried Wilhelm Leibniz (1646–1716). Copper engraving, 1775, by Johann Friedrich Bause (1738–1814), after a 1703 painting by Andreas Scheits (ca. 1655–1735).

4

LEIBNIZ*

In 1686, Gottfried Wilhelm Leibniz (1646–1716) publically set down some thoughts on René Descartes' mechanics. In so doing, he initiated the famous dispute concerning the "force" of a moving body known as the *vis viva* controversy. Two concepts, now called momentum (mv) and kinetic energy ($\frac{1}{2}mv^2$), were discussed as a single concept, "force," each differing from Newton's idea of force. One of the many underlying problems of the controversy was clarified by Roger Boscovich in 1745 and Jean d'Alembert in 1758, both of whom pointed out that *vis viva* (mv^2) and momentum (mv) were equally valid.[1]

The momentum of a body is actually the Newtonian force F acting through a time, since $v = at$ and $mv = mat = Ft$. The kinetic energy is the Newtonian force acting over a space, since $v^2 = 2as$ and $mv^2 = 2mas$ or $\frac{1}{2}mv^2 = Fs$. Although confusion over these two definitions is apparent in the various arguments of the contenders, many other sources of confusion entered into the debates. Some of these factors are clarified in the following discussion of the early years of the *vis viva* controversy.

The controversy had its roots in Descartes' law of the quantity of motion, as discussed in his *Principia philosophiae* of 1644.[2] It was Descartes' belief that God, the general cause of all motion in the universe, preserves the same quantity of motion and rest put into the world at the time of creation. The measurement of this quantity is mv, implied in the statement "we must reckon the quantity of motion in two pieces of matter as equal if one moves twice as fast as the other, and this in turn is twice as big as the first."[3] The conservation of quantity of motion is derived from God's perfection, for He is in Himself unchangeable and all His operations are performed in a perfectly constant and unchangeable manner. There thus exists an absolute quantity of motion that for the universe remains constant. When the motion in one part is diminished, that in another is increased by a like amount. Motion, like matter, once created cannot be destroyed because the same amount of motion has remained in the universe since creation. It is evident from Descartes' application of the principle in his rules governing the collision of bodies that this quantity mv conserves only the magnitude of the quantity of motion and not its direction; that is, velocity is always treated as a positive quantity, $|v|$ rather than as a vector quantity whose direction is variable. Beginning in 1686, Leibniz wrote a series of papers objecting that the quantity that remains absolute and indestructible in nature is not quantity of motion $m|v|$ but *vis viva*, or living force, mv^2.

Shortly before this, in 1668, John Wallis, Christopher Wren, and Christiaan Huygens had presented papers to the Royal Society showing that the quantity conserved in one-dimensional collisions was not $m|v|$ but mv, where the sign of the velocity is taken into consideration.[4] Wallis discussed hard-body inelastic collisions and Wren described elastic collisions. Huygens used rules equivalent to conservation of mv and mv^2 for elastic impacts. Leibniz was well acquainted with these contributions; he had discussed them in his own notes as early as 1669 and mentioned them in his *Discours de metaphysique*[5] published in 1686. He was thus aware of the distinction between quantity of motion $m|v|$ and the quantity later called momentum, mv. Leibniz referred to momentum conservation as conservation of total progress (1691).[6] His arguments against Descartes beginning in 1686 were thus designed to establish the superiority of mv^2 over $m|v|$, not over mv.

During the ensuing *vis viva* controversy, several concepts were confused in the arguments between Leibniz and the Cartesians. The concepts under discussion included force, quantity of motion, momentum, quantity of progress, *vis mortua* (dead force), and *vis viva* (living force). In addition to delineating the use of these concepts in the physical examples of the contenders, I wish to make the following points:

1. Confusion existed over the use of momentum (mv) and *vis mortua*, the mass times the virtual velocity increment (mdv), in the arguments of the Cartesians.

2. The controversy was not only a dispute over the measure of "force" but also over the conservation of "force." On metaphysical grounds, Leibniz was convinced that "force" was conserved in nature. He then successfully argued that mv^2 not $m|v|$ was the measure of this "force." But he implied without adequate empirical proof (except for elastic collisions) that mv^2 was also conserved in his examples. He did not use

isolated interacting mechanical systems in his discussions of conservation of "force."

3. Leibniz's arguments are directed against the inadequacy with which Descartes' measure of matter in motion, $m|v|$, described the physical world. Living force, measured by mv^2, was the essence of nature for Leibniz, an encompassing principle, basic to his whole philosophy. Thus the early *vis viva* controversy is not a pointless controversy over momentum versus kinetic energy, but a skillful attack by Leibniz against an inadequate concept, $m|v|$, and its description of the world.

LEIBNIZ'S INITIAL PAPER, 1686

Leibniz's controversy with the Cartesians over living force began in March 1686 with the publication in the *Acta Eruditorum* of his "Brevis demonstratio," or "Brief Demonstration of a Notable Error of Descartes and Others Concerning a Natural Law, According to which God is Said Always to Conserve the Same Quantity of Motion; A Law Which They Also Misuse in Mechanics."[7] In this paper and in a similar discussion in the *Discours de metaphysique* of the same year, Leibniz stated that there was a difference between the concepts motive force (*motricis potentiae*) and quantity of motion $m|v|$ (*quantitas motus*) and that one cannot be estimated by the other. Leibniz, like many others, did not distinguish between mass and weight. He interchanged the Latin terms *mole*, *corpus*, and *libra* and the French terms *masse*, *pesanteur*, and *poids*. Motive force should be designated *mgs* or *ws* (weight times height) because it is this that is equivalent (except for a factor of ½) to mv^2, which Leibniz called *vis viva*, or living force. Leibniz however did not use different words for the *m* in motive force and the *m* in *mv* and mv^2. Leibniz's motive force is a rudimentary form of our concept of potential energy. In modern terms, his proof establishes the idea of the conversion of potential energy to kinetic energy, or more generally, the basis for the work-energy theorem: $F \cdot s = \frac{1}{2}mv^2$.

Leibniz argued:

It is reasonable that the sum of motive force [*motricis potentiae*] should be conserved [*conservari*] in nature and not be diminished—since we never see force lost by one body without being transferred to another—or augmented; a perpetual motion machine can never be successful because no machine, not even the world as a whole, can increase its force without a new impulse from without. This led Descartes, who held motive force [*vis matrix*] and quantity of motion [*quantitatem motus*] to be equivalent, to assert that God conserves [*conservari*] the same quantity of motion in the world.[8]

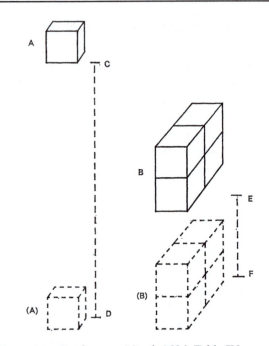

DIAGRAM 4.1 From *Acta Eruditorum*, March 1686, Table IV

Leibniz's argument is based on two assumptions, both of which he claims are accepted by the Cartesians (see Diagram 4.1).

1. "A body falling from a certain height [*altitudine*] acquires the same force [*vis*] necessary to lift it back to its original height if its direction were to carry it back and if nothing external interfered with it." "Motive force" is thus taken to be the product of the body's weight and the height from which it falls. This statement is the idea of the impossibility of a perpetual motion machine. If force is neither removed (by friction) nor added to the system, it will return to its initial height. Because it cannot rise to a greater height without an external force, a perpetual motion machine cannot be constructed.[9]

2. "The same force is necessary to raise body *A* of 1 pound [*libra*] to a height of 4 yards [*ulnae*] as is necessary to raise body *B* of 4 pounds to a height of 1 yard." In modern terms, the work done on bodies *A* and *B* will be equal: $Fs = mgs$.[10] From these two assumptions, Leibniz inferred that body *A* of 1 pound in falling a distance $s = 4$ will acquire the same force as body *B* of 4 pounds falling $s = 1$:

   For in falling from *C* and reaching *D*, the body *A* will have there the force required to rise again to *C* by the first assumption; that is, it will have the force needed to raise a body of 1 pound (namely itself) to the height of 4 yards. Similarly the body B after falling from E to F will there have the force required to rise again to E, by the first assumption; that is, it will have the force sufficient to raise a body of 4 pounds (itself namely) to a height of 1 yard. Therefore, by the second assumption, the force of the body A when it arrives at D and that of the body B at F are equal.[11]

On the other hand, argued Leibniz, the Cartesian quantities of motion are not equal. For, as Galileo showed, body A in its fall will acquire twice the velocity of body B (this is now written $2gs = v^2 - v_0^2$). Body A, 1 pound, falling from $s = 4$, will arrive at D with a velocity 2; hence its quantity of motion mv is 2. Body B of 4 pounds falling from $s = 1$ arrives at F with velocity 1, its mv thereby being 4. Thus the quantities of motion are unequal, but the "motive forces" (*vis motrix*), mgs, as proved previously, are equal.[12] Therefore, says Leibniz, the force of a body cannot be calculated by finding its quantity of motion but rather "is to be estimated from the quantity of the effect [*quantitate effectus*] it can produce, that is from the height to which it can elevate a body of given magnitude [*magnitudinus*]."

Several points are to be noted about the "Brevis demonstratio," the first paper in a long series of discussions between Leibniz and his opponents on the subject of "living force."

First, Leibniz has not yet introduced the term *vis viva*, that is, "living force," or its mathematical equivalent, mv^2. He does not publically speak of living force until 1695 in the well-known "Specimen dynamicum," though he uses the term in his unpublished "Essay de dynamique" in 1691.[13] In these earlier papers, the discussion involves the term "motive force" (*vis motrix*), ws, the equivalent mv^2 being only implied by the use of the square root of the distance of fall in calculating the mv of bodies A and B.

Second, he asserts that the Cartesians were led into error by confusing the force of motion, which they estimated by the quantity of motion, with the quantity used in statics in the case of the five simple machines. In statics, the tendency toward motion is estimated by the mass times the (virtual) velocity:

> Seeing that velocity and mass compensate for each other in the five common machines [*mdv*], a number of mathematicians have estimated the force of motion [*vim motricem*] by the quantity of motion, or by the product of the body and its velocity [*producto ex multiplicatione corporis in celeritatem suam*] [*mv*]. Or to speak rather in geometrical terms the forces of two bodies (of the same kind) set in motion, and acting by their mass [*mole*] as well as by their motion are said to be proportional jointly to their bodies [*corporum*] or masses [*molium*] and to their velocities [*velocitatem*].[14]

This accusation Leibniz also makes in later papers. There is no evidence that Descartes himself made this error,[15] although his followers certainly did. Quantity of motion, later known as momentum, is not the same as the quantity formed by the product of the mass and the virtual velocity as applied to static situations. This confusion will be seen in the contributions of Abbé Catalan and Denis Papin.

Third, there is a lack of clarity over what constitutes empirical proof of the conservation of "force" mv^2 over and above establishing mv^2 as a measure of "force."

Were it not for the title and the introduction quoted previously, one would consider Leibniz's presentation simply to have established "motive force," or its equivalent, mv^2, as a measure of force, for he succeeds in showing that force, defined by him as ws, is to be estimated by the height to which it can raise a body of a given magnitude. Thus he has established a rudimentary expression for the conversion of potential energy to kinetic energy. Quantity of motion $m|v|$ is not the measure of a force so defined. However, the title states that the Cartesians have made an error in asserting that quantity of motion is conserved. Similarly, in the first paragraph, it is stated that "it is reasonable that the sum of motive force should be conserved in nature," and Descartes "asserted that God conserves the same quantity of motion in the world." These statements imply—although Leibniz does not state this as a conclusion—that the "Brevis demonstratio" has shown that quantity of motion $m|v|$ is not conserved, whereas motive force, measured by ws, is conserved. The only basis for these implications concerning conservation is that the quantities of motion of bodies A and B were found to be unequal, while the motive forces ws of the two bodies were equal.

Three separate aspects of the establishment of conservation laws such as that of kinetic energy may be distinguished: (1) a metaphysical belief that some entity is conserved in the universe, (2) the mathematical expression or measure of the conserved entity, and (3) the empirical proof that this particular entity is conserved in physically interacting systems. Like many other natural philosophers, Leibniz was convinced on metaphysical grounds that something was conserved in nature. This conserved entity was taken by him to be living force, *vis viva*. If living force were not conserved, the world would either lose force and run down or a perpetual motion machine would be possible.

Such a philosophical conviction is not unusual and is important in the development of other conservation laws. For example, Parmenides and the pluralists argued that "being" could neither be created nor destroyed—long before it was possible for A.-L. Lavoisier to empirically establish conservation of matter. Descartes was convinced that motion $m|v|$ was conserved in the universe before the correct empirical law was given as mv conservation.

The caloric theory depended on the conservation of heat, before empirical evidence disproved it. Julius Robert Mayer[16] and Hermann von Helmholtz were convinced of the general law of conservation of energy before compiling empirical evidence.[17] James Joule, while supplying much empirical data for the law, generalized from values so widely divergent as to be scientifically unconvincing without prior metaphysical certainty.[18] Indeed the general conservation law that states that the total energy of the universe is conserved is a theoretical statement that cannot be verified empirically except in isolated closed systems.

Leibniz presented important mathematical arguments that mv^2 and not $m|v|$ was a correct measure of something conserved in nature. He did not however present convincing arguments that his measure of force was also conserved in the physical instances he claimed for it, with the exception of elastic collisions. In many of his other arguments, Leibniz does not adequately specify a closed conservative system because the mechanisms for transferring "force" among the parts of the system are not specified.

In the "Brevis demonstratio," if Leibniz were to establish conservation of mv^2, he would need a closed conservative system where there is a collision or a mechanical connection between the two bodies. This is not necessary for the mere establishment of the mathematical measure of a force, or the conversion of potential to kinetic energy. To establish conservation of mv^2, a mechanical method of transferring the motive force from body A to body B, such as an ideal spring, would be necessary. However, in Leibniz's example, the bodies fall to the ground side by side and the forces of the two falling bodies are compared merely as to equality. The effect of the ground and the possibility of a mechanical connection are ignored. Thus the implication of the title and of the introduction that the demonstration will yield information about conservation is not justified. The demonstration does successfully establish a mathematical measure of force. Leibniz's implicit identification of measure and conservation is not valid. He seems to have assumed conservation of motive force on the basis of the impossibility of perpetual motion, but his empirical demonstration of conservation is incomplete. The confounding of measure and conservation and the inattention to mechanical connections were two of the sources of confusion in the controversy with the Cartesians.[19]

THE CONTROVERSY WITH ABBÉ CATALAN

Leibniz's "Brevis demonstratio" was translated into French, and by September of the same year, 1686, it appeared in the *Nouvelles de la république des lettres*. Leibniz was immediately answered by the Cartesian Abbé Catalan in a "Courte Remarque."[20]

It has been shown, writes Catalan, that two moving bodies (*mobiles*) that are unequal in volume (for example, 1 to 4) but equal in quantity of motion (that is, 4) have velocities proportional to the reciprocal ratio of their masses (*masses*) (that is, 4 to 1). Consequently, they traverse (*parcourent*), in the same time, spaces proportional to these velocities.[21] Now Galileo, he says, showed the spaces described by falling bodies to be as the squares of the times (now written $s = \frac{1}{2}gt^2$). Therefore, in the example given by Leibniz, the body of 1 pound (*livre*) ascends to the height 4 in time 2 and the body of 4 pounds ascends to the height 1 in time 1. If the times are unequal, it is not surprising to find the quantities of motion unequal. But, says Catalan, if the times are made equal by suspending them to the same balance at distances reciprocal to their bulk (*grosseur*), the quantities formed by the products of their masses and distances, or masses and velocities, are equal.

Catalan here has lumped together three separate problems as one: a body's uniform traversal of space (momentum), free fall (*vis viva*), and the problem of the lever (virtual velocities). In the free-fall problem, if the times were equal, the *mv* would be equal only for bodies of equal weight. If the times for unequal bodies were made equal by use of a lever, the problem would be changed to a problem in statics, where virtual work or mass times the distance increment *mds* describes the situation. This is not the same as quantity of motion *mv*.

By the following February, Leibniz issued a reply to Catalan,[22] answering the objection that because the two falling bodies acquire their forces in unequal times, the forces ought to be different. If the force of a body of 4 pounds having a velocity of 1 degree is transferred (*transferer*) to a body of 1 pound, according to the Cartesians, the second will receive a velocity of 4 degrees to preserve (*garder*) the same quantity of motion. But, argues Leibniz, this second body should receive only a velocity of 2. And in estimating the forces that the bodies have acquired, no one (except the Abbé Catalan) will measure whether they have acquired these forces in times long or short, equal or unequal. Time has nothing to do with the measure of force (that is, *vis viva*). One can judge the present state without knowing the past. If there are two perfectly equal and identical bodies having the same velocity—the first acquiring its velocity in a collision, the second in a descent—can their forces be said to be different? This would be like saying a man is wealthier for taking more time to earn his money.[23]

Furthermore, one can change at will the time of descent by changing the line of inclination of the descent; and in an infinite number of ways, two bodies can be made to descend from different heights in equal times. But a body descending from a certain height acquires the same velocity whether that descent is perpendicular and faster, or inclined and slower. Thus the distinction of time has nothing to do with the argument.[24] This was countered by

Catalan in June 1687 with the observation that on an inclined plane, the force necessary to lift a body is less than that necessary to lift it perpendicularly to the same height.[25]

Here again two concepts are confused. Leibniz is discussing the fall of a weight through a vertical distance (*mgs*), or potential energy, where the time is irrelevant. Catalan's argument is based on the idea that the applied or Newtonian force needed to push a body up an inclined plane is less than that needed to lift the body perpendicularly to the same vertical height.

In addition to the argument that force should be defined as acting through distance rather than time, Leibniz employed another tactic in the argument with Catalan.[26] He attacked Descartes' invalid third rule of motion that stated: "If [hard] body *B* and [hard] body *C* are equal in heaviness, but *B* moves [toward *C*] with slightly greater speed than *C*, not only do both move to the left afterwards, but *B* also imparts to *C* half the difference of their initial speeds." Considering this third rule of motion, suppose that two bodies *B* and *C*, each 1 pound, move toward each other, *B* with a velocity of 100 degrees and *C* with a velocity of 1 degree. Together, their quantity of motion will be 101. Now *C* with its velocity of 1 can rise to 1 foot while *B* can rise to 10,000 feet. Thus the force of the two together before colliding would elevate 1 pound to 10,001 feet. According to Descartes' rule of motion, after the impact, both move together with a speed of 50½. By multiplying this speed by the combined weight of the two bodies, the quantity of motion 101 is retained. However, in this case, the force of the 2 pounds together can raise 1 pound to only $2(50½)^2 = 5,100½$ feet. Thus, says Leibniz, almost half the force is lost without any reason and without being used elsewhere; Descartes' third rule, therefore, is wrong and with it the principle upon which it is based—conservation of $m|v|$.

Now this example employs an actual collision of two bodies, not a mere proportionality of forces as in the first example, and again it attempts to show that $m|v|$ is not conserved. Here there is no leap from measure of force to conservation of force. Leibniz's argument seems to succeed not because of inattention to the mechanism, but because Descartes' third rule, based on $m|v|$, is itself in error. Here Leibniz is initiating a new line of argument upon which he relies in subsequent papers: that is, if Descartes' rules for colliding bodies are shown to be false, then the principle upon which they are based— conservation of quantity of motion—must also be false.[27]

THE CONTROVERSY WITH DENIS PAPIN

Another line of argument that was based on the impossibility of perpetual motion and upon the equipollence of cause and effect was followed in the discussion with Denis Papin during the period 1689–1691. In reply to Papin's paper showing that the quantities of motion in freely falling bodies are in the direct ratio of the times of motion,[28] Leibniz declares that the issue must be decided by whether or not perpetual motion can arise from the acceptance of either of the two definitions of force.[29]

He begins by clarifying the issue at stake in order, he says, to exclude all verbal misunderstanding. Anyone is at liberty to define force as he wishes, whether as quantity of motion or as motive force. The issue is to decide which is conserved (*conservare*), whether it be the product of weight (*pondus*) and speed or the product of weight and height. This will be decided by whether or not perpetual motion can arise from the acceptance of either definition.

Taking again balls of weight 1 and 4, he allows the larger to descend from a height of 1 by means of an inclined plane (see Diagram 4.2). When it reaches the horizontal and is moving with a velocity of 1, it meets the smaller body at rest. All of its force of 4 is now transferred to the smaller body of weight 1. Now if this body were to receive a velocity of 4, as the Cartesians would maintain in order to conserve quantity of motion, then, argues Leibniz, perpetual motion would arise, for this smaller body by virtue of its velocity of 4 could ascend an inclined plane to a height of 16 feet. Perpetual motion or an effect more powerful than its cause can arise because in falling again to the horizontal plane, it can elevate, by means of a lever, the first body of weight 4 to a height of 4 feet. Thus in the final state, the first body rests at height 4 rather than height 1 as in its initial state, while the second body has been returned to its original position in the horizontal plane. No new force has been contributed or absorbed by other agents or patients. "We conclude," writes Leibniz, "against the Cartesians that quantity of motion should not always be conserved."

Denis Papin's second paper shrewdly attacks Leibniz's argument.[30] He concedes that perpetual motion is absurd and that if it could actually be demonstrated by the previous example, the Cartesian measure of force would be reduced to an absurdity. But he denies the possibility of actually transferring

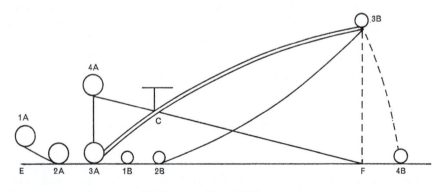

DIAGRAM 4.2 From *Acta Eruditorum*, May 1690

in nature all the "power" of body A to body B. He promises publicly that if any method can be indicated by which all the moving forces of the greater body can be transferred to the smaller body at rest without the occurrence of a miracle, he will concede the victory to Leibniz. Leibniz's final reply offers some methods for transferring the "force," none of which is physically feasible.[31]

In analyzing this example, several points of confusion become apparent. The purpose of Leibniz's argument is to show that $m|v|$, or quantity of motion, is not conserved. He is discussing the conservation of "force," not merely the measure of "force" in a physical experiment where the mechanism of transferring the "force" (whether defined as $m|v|$ or mv^2) is not specified. Suppose the apparatus for this thought experiment could be set up under idealized conditions. If the bodies were allowed to collide in order to transfer the force, body A would rebound slightly. Momentum mv would be conserved, but quantity of motion in $m|v|$ would not because it is not valid for such a collision. But the use of collisions as a method of transferring the force does not fulfill Leibniz's conditions because body A will retain some mv and mv^2. Papin's objection that all the force cannot be transferred is therefore a realistic one.

Leibniz would need to transfer the mv^2 of body A to body B by a method such as an ideal spring that does not dissipate the *vis viva*. The energy of the spring could be transferred to body B by releasing a catch on the spring. If such an external force is used, both quantity of motion and momentum conservation will be violated. *Vis viva* if not dissipated would be conserved. The point of Leibniz's argument is to show that neither quantity of motion nor momentum are conservation principles that are as general as *vis viva*. Later in 1691, Leibniz argued that any dissipated *vis viva* went into the small parts of a body's matter and was not lost for the universe; he had no empirical proof of this, however. The argument with Papin serves to illustrate the view that Leibniz's main effort was directed toward establishing the superiority of *vis viva* over quantity of motion $m|v|$ as a universal conservation principle. Conservation of living force encompasses a wider range of phenomena than quantity of motion.[32]

VIS VIVA AS A PHILOSOPHICAL PRINCIPLE

Leibniz was anxious to establish a broad and absolute conservation principle that would form a basis for his philosophical system. At the root of his controversy with Descartes and his followers lies not a mere mathematical dispute as to the measure of "force," $m|v|$, or mv^2 but a fundamental disagreement as to the very nature of force itself. As early as 1686 in the *Discours de metaphysique,* Leibniz first elaborated on the content of the difference between motive force, equivalent to *vis viva,* and quantity of motion.[33] Here he presented an argument that was to become the spearhead of his attack on Cartesianism and to become the basis of his own philosophy of monadology:

> Force is something different from size, from form, or from motion, and the whole meaning of body is not exhausted in its extension together with its modifications. Motion, if we regard only its exact and formal meaning, is not something entirely real. . . . But the force or the proximate cause of these changes [in the places of bodies] is something more real, and there are sufficient grounds for attributing it to one body rather than to another.[34]

What is real in nature for Leibniz is primitive force or striving, and this was developed by him in the succeeding years as the essence of the monad. Motion and extension, the essence of nature for Descartes, are to Leibniz merely relations and not realities at all.

A significant statement of the problem of the controversy is given in his "Essay de dynamique," written about 1691 but not published until 1860.[35] Here the problem is given as a search for an estimate of force as a mathematically absolute or positive quantity that can never be taken as null or negative in the impact of elastic bodies. This paper draws together the principle of conservation of relative velocity, conservation of momentum mv, which Leibniz calls quantity of progress and which does take into account the sign of the velocity, and conservation of living force mv^2. It presents the solution of elastic impact problems as the simultaneous solution of any two of these equations: "Although I put together these three equations for the sake of beauty and harmony, nevertheless two of them might suffice for our needs. For taking any two of these equations we can infer the remaining one."[36]

Although this paper remained unpublished until 1860, its ideas appeared in a paper of Leibniz's follower Jean Bernoulli (1727).[37] Leibniz wrote in his "Essay de dynamique" that after some philosophers abandoned the opinion that quantity of motion is preserved in the concourse of bodies, they did not recognize the conservation of anything absolute to hold in its place. However, our minds look for such a conservation and many find themselves unable to give up the axiom without finding another to which to subscribe.[38] He continues, "It is . . . plain that [the] conservation [of quantity of progress] does not correspond to that which is demanded of something absolute. For it may happen that the velocity, quantity of motion and force of bodies being very considerable, their progress is null. This occurs when the two opposed bodies have their quantities of motion equal."[39] But in the equation for the conservation of living force, the negative and positive velocities have the same square, and, writes Leibniz, these different directions produce nothing more. And it is also for that reason that this equation gives something absolute, independent of the progressions from a certain side. The question here concerns only the estimating of masses and velocities, without troubling ourselves from what side these velocities arise. And it is this which satisfies at the same time the rigor of the mathematicians and the wish of the philosophers—the experiments and reasons drawn from different principles.[40]

Leibniz knew that the conservation of *vis viva* did not hold for inelastic and semi-elastic collisions: "But this loss of the total force . . . or this failure of the third equation, does not detract from the inviolable truth of the law of the conservation of the same force in the world. For that which is absorbed by the minute parts is not absolutely lost for the universe, although it is lost for the total force of the concurrent bodies."[41] Although Leibniz argues on philosophical grounds that the dissipated *vis viva* is conserved for the universe, he gives no empirical proof and does not recognize the heat changes that accompany this phenomenon.[42]

In "Specimen dynamicum" (1695), Leibniz presents a mature synthesis of his concept of force, drawing together the observations and opinions expressed since 1686 in his paper on dynamics and incorporating philosophical views developed concurrently with his work in physics.[43] It summarizes his attack on the foundation of Descartes' explanation of the universe as extended matter in motion. He gives an interpretation of force as the very foundation for an understanding of both the physical and spiritual universe. What is real in the universe is activity; the essence of substance is action, not extension as Descartes had insisted. This activity is constituted as a primitive force or a striving toward change; it is the innermost nature of a body. The basic indivisible substances whose essence is a continual tendency toward action were later, in 1714, called monads by Leibniz.[44] These units of primitive force can neither be created nor destroyed naturally, and all must begin simultaneously and be annihilated at once.

Thus the conservation of substance and force form the basis of Leibniz's philosophical viewpoint. Because time and space are neither realities nor substances, but merely relations, motion, which is the continuous change in both space and time, is likewise only a relation.[45] What is real in motion is force, a momentary state that carries with it a striving toward a future state. It is therefore clear why motion and extension cannot be the essence of reality for Leibniz, as they were for Descartes.

We are thus able to view Leibniz's attack on the Cartesian measure of force as primarily an attempt to establish his own philosophical system based on the conservation of "force" and to place less emphasis on a simple attempt to substitute the mathematical formula mv^2 for the formula $m|v|$. This latter aim is encompassed in the more general purpose of the former. Perhaps his insight into a universe that was fundamentally energistic led him to make assumptions about the possibility of transferring that energy and to identify implicitly the conservation and the measure of force, the establishment of both being an integral part of his ultimate aim.

NOTES

* From Carolyn [Merchant] Iltis, "Leibniz and the *Vis Viva* Controversy," *Isis* 62, no. 1 (Spring 1971): 21–35. Copyright 1971 by the History of Science Society, University of Chicago Press. All rights reserved.

1. See Carolyn [Merchant] Iltis, "D'Alembert and the Vis Viva Controversy," *Studies in History and Philosophy of Science* 1, no. 2 (1970): 135–44; Carolyn [Merchant] Iltis, "The Controversy over Living Force: Leibniz to D'Alembert," doctoral dissertation, University of Wisconsin, 1967.

2. René Descartes, "Principia philosophiae," in Charles Adam and Paul Tannery, eds., *Oeuvres de Descartes*, 13 vols. (Paris: Cerf, 1897–1913), vol. 8, p. 61. On Leibniz and Cartesianism, see Richard A. Watson, *The Downfall of Cartesianism, 1673–1712: A Study of Epistemological Issues in Late 17th Century Cartesianism* (The Hague: Martinus Nijhoff, 1966), pp. 123–42.

3. Ibid.; Iltis, "The Decline of Cartesianism in Mechanics," *Isis 64*, no. 3 (Fall 1973): 356–73.

4. John Wallis, "A Summary Account of the General Laws of Motion," *Philosophical Transactions of the Royal Society* 3 (1669): 864–6; Christopher Wren, "Lex Naturae de Collisione Corporum," *Philosophical Transactions* 3 (1669): 867–8; Christiaan Huygens, "Regles du mouvement dans la rencontre des corps," *Journal de sçavans* 18 (March 1669): 22–24; Christiaan Huygens, "A Summary Account of the Laws of Motion," *Philosophical Transactions* 4 (1669): 925–8. Huygens enunciated the mv^2 law prior to Leibniz as rule 6 in the previous papers: "The sum of the products of the size of each hard body multiplied by the square of its velocity is always the same before and after impact."

5. Gottfried Wilhelm Leibniz, "Essay de dynamique sur les loix du mouvement, où il est monstré, qu'il ne se conserve pas la même quantité de mouvement, mais la méme force absolue, ou bien la même quantité de l'action motrice," in C. I. Gerhardt, ed., *Mathematische Schriften*, 9 vols. in 5 (Halle, Germany: H.W. Schmidt, 1860), ser. 2, vol. 2, pp. 215–31. English translation in Gottfried Wilhelm Leibniz, *New Essays Concerning Human Understanding*, appendix, ed. and trans. Alfred G. Langley (La Salle: Open Court, 1949), pp. 657–70.

6. Gottfried Wilhelm Leibniz, "Brevis demonstratio erroris memorabilis Cartesii et aliorum circa legem naturalem, secundum quam volunt a Deo eandem semper quantitatem motus conservari; qua et in re mechanica abutuntur," *Acta Eruditorum* (1686): 161–3. A translation appears in Gottfried Wilhelm Leibniz, *Philosophical Papers and Letters*, trans. Leroy E. Loemker, 2 vols. (Chicago: University of Chicago Press, 1956), vol. 1, pp. 455–63.

7. Gottfried Wilhelm Leibniz, "Discours de metaphysique," in C. I. Gerhardt, ed., *Die Philosophische Schriften von Gottfried Wilhelm Leibniz*, 7 vols. (Berlin, Germany: Weidmann, 1875–1890), vol. 4, pp. 442–3. English translation in Leroy E. Loemker, 1: 464–506.

8. Leibniz, "Brevis demonstratio," p. 161; Loemker, 1: 455.

9. This assumption had its beginnings in Jordanus de Nemore's (fl. ca. 1220) notion of *gravitas secundum situm* (gravity according to position). It is found in the writings of early seventeenth-century authors as the experimental observation that no system of falling weights will produce perpetual motion in any of its parts. Galileo showed that no series of inclined planes will impart to a descending body a velocity sufficient to carry it to a vertical height greater than its initial height. See Erwin Hiebert, *Historical Roots of the Conservation of Energy* (Madison: State Historical Society of Wisconsin, 1962), pp. 60–1.

10. The second assumption was stated by Descartes in a letter to Marin Mersenne in 1638 (*Oeuvres*, vol. 2, p. 228):

> The proof of this depends solely on the principle which is the general foundation of all statics, that no more or less force [force] is needed to lift a heavy body to a certain height [hauteur] than to lift another less heavy to a height as much greater as it is less heavy or to lift one heavier to a height as much less. As for example, that force which can lift a weight [*poids*] of 100 pounds to the height of 2 feet, can also lift one of 200 pounds to the height of 1 foot, or one of 50 to the height of 4 feet and thus of others if it is so applied to them.

11. Leibniz, "Brevis demonstratio," *Acta Eruditorum*, 162; Loemker, 1: 457.
12. For the relationship $mgs = \frac{1}{2}mv^2$ implied here, Leibniz is indebted chiefly to Christiaan Huygens, who used it in his derivation of the law of the compound pendulum in his *Horologium oscillatorium sive de motu pendulorum ad horologia aptato demonstrationes geometricae* (Paris: F. Muguet, 1673). Huygens also related the heights of fall of a body to the velocities acquired in proposition 8 of his *De Motu corporum ex percussione*, largely complete by 1656, but published posthumously in 1703. See Christiaan Huygens, *Oeuvres complètes de Christiaan Huygens*, 22 vols. (La Haye, France: Martinus Nijhoff, 1888–1950), vol. 16, pp. 30–91, see p. 35.
13. Leibniz first speaks of living force in his "Essay de dynamique" (1691), which was unpublished until discovered by Gerhardt in the papers at Hanover and included in the *Mathematische Schriften* (see note 5). He also uses the term in an essay recently discovered by Pierre Costabel, described in his *Leibniz et la dynamique: Les textes de 1692* (Paris: Hermann, 1960), p. 104.
14. Leibniz, "Brevis demonstratio," p. 162; Loemker, vol. 1, p. 455.
15. Descartes, *Oeuvres*, vol. 2, pp. 222–46. Descartes knew that it was the commencement of movement that must be taken into account at each instant; he says, "notez que [je] dis commencer à descendre, non pas simplement descendre." For a discussion of the history of the virtual velocity concept, see Hiebert, *Historical Roots*, chap. 1. Neither Leibniz nor the Cartesians used the term "virtual velocity." This was first used by Jean Bernoulli in 1717. The virtual velocity dv of a body is the ratio of the virtual displacement ds to the time element dt, i.e., ds/dt. Virtual displacement ds is the distance through which a body in equilibrium or under constraint would move if acted upon by a force that disturbs the equilibrium. Virtual velocity is the velocity the body would acquire in moving through the distance ds. On the use of the term, Hiebert writes (p. 53):

> Prior to the time of Varignon's *Nouvelle mecanique* of 1725, no name was attached to the principle we have been discussing [virtual work]. John Bernoulli (1667–1748) of Basel supplied an expression in 1717 in an off-hand suggestion in a letter addressed to Varignon. In this letter Bernoulli introduced the term virtual velocity [*vitesse virtuelle*]. . . . He had used the term . . . to designate the velocity which is associated with any infinitesimal displacement which is compatible with the constraints imposed upon a system in the state of equilibrium where neither the constraints nor the displacements need be actualized.

I am indebted to Professor Hiebert for his clarification of the way in which the Cartesians misused and misunderstood the use of mv and mdv throughout the controversy.

The virtual velocity principle in modern notation for the case of the lever is (see Diagram 4.3): $F_1 l_1 = F_2 l_2$ or $F_1 s_1 = F_2 s_2$. But $F = mg$ and $ds = dv\,dt$. Thus $m_1 g dv_1 \cdot dt_1 = m_2 g dv_2 \cdot dv_2$. For the case of the lever in equilibrium, the times are equal, $dt_1 = dt_2$; hence $m_1 dv_1 = m_2 dv_2$, or dead force. But the dv's are virtual velocities and not the actual velocities in the momentum expression mv for moving bodies (example mine; Leibniz's figure—Loemker, vol. 1, p. 459—with notation l, m, and s added). Leibniz stated the dead force idea in relation to the lever in a supplement to the "Brevis demonstratio" written in 1695. See Loemker, vol. 1, pp. 459–460:

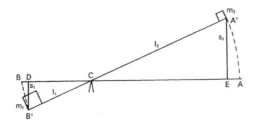

DIAGRAM 4.3 From "Supplement" to the *Brevis Demonstratio*, 1695, in Loemker, vol. 1, p. 459

> The same proposition is confirmed also by the five commonly recognized mechanical powers—the lever, windlass, pulley, wedge and screw; for in all these our proposition seems to be true. For the sake of brevity, however, it will suffice to show this in the single case of the lever, or what amounts to the same thing to deduce from our rule that the distances and weights of bodies in equilibrium are in reciprocal proportion. Let us assume AC [see figure] to be double BC, and the weight B double the weight A; then I say A and B are in equilibrium. For if we assume either one to preponderate, B for example, and so to sink to $B^{\prime}$ and A to rise to $A^{\prime}$ and drop perpendiculars $A^{\prime}E$ and $B^{\prime}D$ from $A^{\prime}$ and $B^{\prime}$ to AB, it is clear that if $DB^{\prime}$ is 1 foot, $A^{\prime}E$ will be 2 feet and therefore that, if 2 pounds descend the distance of 1 foot, 1 pound will ascend to the height of 2 feet, and thus that, since these two are equivalent nothing is gained and the descent becomes useless, everything remaining in equilibrium as before. . . .
> Even if some of these seem reconcilable with that hypothesis which estimates the product of mass by velocity, this is only accidental since the two hypotheses coincide in the case of dead forces (*potentia mortuus*) in which only the beginning or end of conatuses is actualized.

16. Julius Robert Mayer, "Bemerkungen über die Kräfte der unbelebten Natur," *Annalen der Chemie und Pharmacie* 42, no. 2 (1842): 41–2. See also translated excerpts in William F. Magie, *A Source Book in Physics* (New York: McGraw Hill, 1935), p. 196.
17. Thomas Kuhn, "Energy Conservation as an Example of Simultaneous Discovery," in Marshall Clagett, ed., *Critical Problems in the History of Science* (Madison: University of Wisconsin Press, 1959), pp. 321–56, see pp. 336–9 on the influence of *Naturphilosophie* in enunciating the general law of energy conservation: "In the cases of Colding, Helmholtz, Liebig, Mayer, Mohr and Seguin, the notion of an underlying imperishable force seems prior to research and almost unrelated to it. Put bluntly these pioneers seem to have held an idea capable of becoming conservation of energy for some time before they found evidence for it" (quotation on p. 336).
18. Emil Meyerson, *Identity and Reality* (New York: Dover, 1962), pp. 194–5:

> The numbers of the English physicist [Joule] vary within extraordinarily large limits; the average at which he arrives is 838 foot-pounds (for the quantity of heat capable of increasing the temperature of a pound of water by 1 °F . . .); but the different experiments from which this average is drawn furnish results varying from 742 to 1,040 foot-pounds—that is by more than a third of the lowest value—and he even notes an experiment which gives 587 lbs. without seeing in it any source of particularly grave experimental errors. . . it becomes really difficult to suppose that a conscientious scientist relying solely on experimental data could have been able to arrive at the conclusion that the equivalent must constitute, under all conditions, an invariable datum.

19. In another work of the year 1686, the *Discours de metaphysique*, Leibniz again refers to Descartes' error, giving the same proof and implying conservation of force in the following

statements: "Our new philosophers commonly make use of the famous rule that God always conserves the same quantity of motion in the world. . . . Now it is reasonable that the same force should be conserved in the universe. . . . So these mathematicians have thought that what can be said of force can also be said of the quantity of motion" (Loemker, vol. 1, pp. 482–3).

20. Abbé Catalan, "Courte Remarque de M. l'Abbé D. C. où l'on montre à M. G. G. Leibnits le paralogisme contenu dans l'objection précédente," *Nouvelles de la Republique des Lettres* 8 (September 1686): 1000–5.

21. Ibid., p. 1002.

22. Gottfried Wilhelm Leibniz, "Réplique à M. l'Abbé D. C. contenue dans une lettre écrite a l'auteur de ces nouvelles le 9. de Janr. 1687, touchant ce qu'a dit M. Descartes que Dieu conserve toujours dans la nature la même quantité de mouvement," *Nouv. Répub. Lett.* 9 (February 1687): 131–44.

23. Ibid., p. 133.

24. Ibid., p. 134.

25. Abbé Catalan, "Remarque sur la réplique de M. L. touchant le principe mechanique de M. Descartes, contenue dans l'article VII de ces nouvelles, mois de Février, 1687," *Nouv. Répub. Lett.* 10 (June 1687): 577–90; see pp. 586–7.

26. Leibniz, "Réplique a M. l'Abbé D. C.," p. 138.

27. If, as Descartes supposes, the bodies stick together, the collision is inelastic and mv^2 is not conserved. Five years later in 1691, Leibniz stated that mv^2 was not conserved in inelastic impacts. Thus both Descartes and Leibniz are wrong from a modern point of view. If the sign of the velocity is taken into account, the final speed is 49½: $mv + MV = 1(100) + 1(-1) = 99 = (m + M)vf = 2vf$; $vf = 49½$.

28. Denis Papin, "De Gravitatis causa et proprietatibus observationes," *Acta Eruditorum* (April 1689): 183–8. In this paper, Papin argues, as does Catalan, that the "force" mv of a falling body depends on the time of fall. Because falling bodies add equal increments of velocity in equal times, they also add equal quantities of motion in equal times: $v = at$; $mv = mat = F^t$ (modern terminology). Like Catalan, Papin argues incorrectly that in Leibniz's 1686 paper, if the times of fall are equal, the forces will be equal: "If the times are equal no more or no less force can be added or subtracted by making the space traversed longer or shorter. Thus a measure of force estimated by the spaces cannot be correct." The mv actually would be equal only for equal bodies falling in equal times. If balanced by a lever, it is an mdv problem. See p. 187.

29. Gottfried Wilhelm Leibniz, "De Causa gravitatis et defensio sententiae sua veris naturae legibus contra Cartesianos," *Acta Eruditorum* (May 1690): 228–39.

30. Denis Papin, "Mechanicorum de viribus motricibus sententia, asserta adversus cl. GGL. objectiones," *Acta Eruditorum* (January 1691): 6–13.

31. Gottfried Wilhelm Leibniz, "De Legibus naturae et vera aestimatione virium motricium contra Cartesianos. Responsio ad rationes a Dn. Papino mense Januarii proxima in *Actis* hisce p. 6. propositas," *Acta Eruditorum* (September 1691): 439–47; p. 443. Leibniz offers two methods of transferring all the "force" from a larger body to a smaller one at rest, claiming that additional demonstrations have been left with a friend in Florence. The first method is to divide body A into 4 parts, all equal to the size of body B, the totality retaining the velocity of body A, i.e., 1.

The "power" of each of these smaller bodies is then transferred successively onto body B at rest. (If this occurs, the first collision will set body B in motion with the velocity of the first small part. But thereafter, body B and the second small part of body A will be in motion with equal velocities.) Leibniz's second method is to connect bodies A and B by a sufficiently long rigid line. On this is assumed an immovable point H around which the compound is to be rotated. Point H is close enough to A and sufficiently removed from B that when A rests, B is unbound. (The details of this method are obscure, and it is not at all clear how such a device could be physically operated and still fulfill the conditions of A having an initial velocity of I and B having zero initial velocity.)

32. A text of Leibniz written in 1691 has been discovered, edited, and discussed by Pierre Costabel (*Leibniz et la dynamique*; n. 13). In regard to content, this Leibniz text is very similar to
the two papers written against the ideas of Papin but presents the argument in the form of logical definitions, axioms, and propositions. Proposition 4 is the same as discussed previously,
and the principles upon which the conclusions are based are the impossibility of perpetual
mechanical motion and the requirement that the total cause equal the complete effect and the
same quantity of force be conserved. Again, all transfer of force is by substitution of a body in
one state of motion and position for a body of a force, equal to that of the first. The possibility of physical transfer is not discussed except to say that one can imagine certain techniques
for the execution of these transfers. Propositions identical to the conclusions in the other two
papers are proved by use of the axioms and definitions. Proposition 8 reads: "When the forces
are equal the quantities of motion are not always equal and vice versa." While this proposition
is valid, the mechanical conservative system for the validity of proposition 9 is not specified:
"The same quantity of motion is not always conserved." The similarity of this 1692 paper to
Leibniz's 1690 paper against Papin is not mentioned by Costabel.

33. Leibniz, "Discours de metaphysique," Loemker, vol. 1, p. 487:

> If there were nothing in bodies but extended mass, and nothing in motion but change
> of place, and if everything should and could be deduced solely from the definitions
> by geometric necessity, it would follow, as I have elsewhere shown, that the smallest
> body in colliding with the greatest body at rest, would impart to it its own velocity,
> without losing any of this velocity itself; and it would be necessary to accept a num-
> ber of other such rules which are entirely contrary to the formation of a system. But
> the decree of the divine wisdom to conserve always the same total force and the same
> total direction has provided for this.

34. Ibid., p. 484.
35. Leibniz, "Essay de dynamique," ed. and trans. Langley (see note 5).
36. Ibid., p. 668.
37. Jean Bernoulli, "Discours sur les loix de la communication du mouvement," *Recueil des
pieces qui a remporté les prix de l'Académie royale des sciences* 2 (1727): 1–108; see p. 29.
38. Leibniz, "Essay de dynamique," ed. and trans. Langley (see note 5), pp. 657, 658.
39. Ibid., p. 658.
40. Ibid., p. 668.
41. Ibid., p. 670. The complete argument reads:

> Now when the parts of the bodies absorb the force of the impact as a whole as when
> two pieces of rich earth or clay come into collision, or in part as when two wooden
> balls meet, which are much less elastic than two globes of jasper or tempered steel;
> when I say some force is absorbed in the parts, it is as good as lost for the absolute
> force and for the respective velocity, that is to say for the third and the first equation
> which do not succeed, since that which remains after the impact has become less
> than what it was before the impact, by reason of a part of the force being turned else-
> where. But the quantity of progress or rather the second equation is not concerned
> therein. . . . But in the semi-elastics, as two wooden balls, it happens still further that
> the bodies mutually depart after the impact, although with a weakening of the first
> equation, following this force of the impact which has not been absorbed. . . . But this
> loss of the total force, or this failure of the third equation, does not detract from the
> inviolable truth of the law of the conservation of the same force in the world. For that
> which is absorbed by the minute parts is not absolutely lost for the universe, although
> it is lost for the total force of the concurrent bodies.

42. For an evaluation of Leibniz's statement, see Hiebert, *Historical Roots*, pp. 88–90:

> In these passages Leibniz apparently postulated an inner force of motion for the
> invisible smallest parts of bodies. These smallest parts were thought to acquire the

kinetic force lost by bodies for inelastic deformable collisions. Leibniz also assumed this inner force to be equivalent to the external force of motion, since he stated that the total force remains unchanged for the universe even for inelastic collisions. There is I believe no statement in Leibniz which would lead one to credit him with either observation or knowledge of the fact that this phenomenon is accompanied by heat changes. Nevertheless by this time it was common belief especially among philosophers that heat was due to or synonymous with the motion of the smallest parts of matter.

43. Gottfried Wilhelm Leibniz, "Specimen dynamicum," Loemker, vol. 2, pp. 711–38. In "Specimen dynamicum," Leibniz again attempts refutation of the Cartesian principle of "force." In an argument based on the $m|v|$ and mv^2 acquired by two pendula of equal length but different mass, Leibniz argues that perpetual motion could arise if Descartes' measure of "force" is accepted. To achieve a mechanical perpetual motion machine, an interacting mechanical system would be necessary. Again, no such system is specified by Leibniz. The argument is based on the mental substitution of an equipollent body. See pp. 724–7.

44. Gottfried Wilhelm Leibniz, "The Monadology" and "The Principles of Nature and of Grace," Loemker, vol. 2, pp. 1044–6, 1033–4. In his discussions on physics, Leibniz conformed the language of his philosophical system to that of ordinary speaking. Thus all these points on the level of physics have a counterpart in Leibniz's system of monads, or souls, in which there is no real space or motion and in which there is no real communication of motion. For each case of impact in the world of phenomena, there is a counterpart in the real world of monads that consists in the heightening and diminution of the states of perception of infinite numbers of monads. All of this takes place in accordance with the system of pre-established harmony. For Leibniz's discussion of this problem, see Gottfried Wilhelm Leibniz, *Discourse on Metaphysics and Correspondence with Arnauld* (La Salle: Open Court, 1957):

> Thus the souls change nothing in the ordering of the body nor do the bodies effect changes in the ordering of souls (and it is for this reason that forms should not be employed to explain the phenomena of nature). One soul changes nothing in the sequence of thought of another soul, and in general one particular substance has no physical influence upon another; such influence would besides be useless since each substance is a complete being which suffices of itself to determine by virtue of its own nature all that must happen to it (p. 153).

> [A]ll the phenomena of the body can be explained mechanically or by the corpuscular philosophy in accordance with certain assumed mechanical principles without troubling oneself whether there are souls or not. In the ultimate analysis of the principles of physics and mechanics, however, it is found that these assumed principles cannot be explained solely by the modifications of extension, and the very nature of force calls for something else (p. 163).

> Nevertheless, we have the right to say that one body pushes another; that is to say, that one body never begins to have a certain tendency excepting when another which touches it loses proportionally, according to the constant laws which we observe in phenomena; and since movements are rather real phenomena than beings, a movement as a phenomenon is in my mind the immediate consequence of effect of another phenomenon, and the same is true in the mind of others. The condition of one substance, however, is not the immediate consequence of the condition of another particular substance (p. 183).

45. Gottfried Wilhelm Leibniz, "Clarification of Bayles' Difficulties," Loemker, vol. 2, p. 806.

FIGURE 5.1 Isaac Newton (1643–1727) in 1689 (age 46). Portrait by Godfrey Kneller, 1689.

Source: By the kind permission of the Trustees of the Portsmouth Estates, UK, and Jeremy Whitaker.

5

NEWTON*

By the time of the Leibniz-Clarke correspondence of 1716, the Newtonian and Leibnizian systems of natural philosophy had reached maturity. Each system consisted of different physical as well as metaphysical principles which, taken together, formed a worldview. At the time of their famous debates, Leibniz at 70 and Newton at 74, the founders of two highly developed scientific philosophies were struggling to establish and defend the ontological and mechanical bases of differing bodies of organized knowledge.

One aspect of this clash of philosophies was the famous *vis viva* controversy which revealed metaphysical as well as physical disagreements.[1] In this chapter, I discuss the mechanical arguments between the Leibnizians and Newtonians, showing how these arguments were related to the scientific metaphysics of the two systems. The positions of the two great thinkers, Leibniz and Newton, were set forth in the Leibniz-Clarke correspondence of 1716 with Samuel Clarke representing Newton.[2] The followers of the two men carried on debates in mechanics during the 1720s through the communication channels of the Royal Society and certain continental journals.

In the following analysis, I make three main points:

1. The Leibnizian-Newtonian controversy was fundamentally a clash of philosophical worldviews on the nature of God, matter, and force. The two systems of natural philosophy were very different organizations of knowledge based on metaphysical and mechanical principles.

2. The adherents to a scientific system also function as a social system. The Newtonian and Leibnizian groups of the 1720s developed a commitment to the mother scheme and took on the task of defending that system against the perceived threats of outside attacks. These attacks were implicit in the mechanical problems and experiments posed by adherents to the opposing system, challenging fundamental presuppositions and principles.

3. The followers defended their respective worldviews by reinterpreting the challenging experiments so that they supported their own mechanical philosophy. They were unwilling and unable to see that the other side had valid arguments. The early *vis viva* controversy of the 1720s was therefore the result of a problem in communication brought about by the inability of the participants to cross the boundary lines of their particular natural philosophies. The recognition that both viewpoints could be valid began to take place by the 1740s, when integrations between the two schemes began to occur.

In attempting to substantiate these claims I shall discuss first the social psychology of the Newtonian and Leibnizian groups, then the Newtonian and Leibnizian natural philosophies, and finally the mechanics of the *vis viva* debates of the 1720s. In these arguments the challenging Leibnizian experiments were performed by William 's Gravesande, a convert from the Newtonian camp, and Giovanni Poleni. The Newtonian case was defended by Henry Pemberton, John Theophilus Desaguliers, John Eames, and Samuel Clarke.

SOCIAL PSYCHOLOGY OF THE NEWTONIAN AND LEIBNIZIAN GROUPS

It has often been stated that the *vis viva* controversy was the result of a communication problem. Contemporary participants as well as historians have considered it "a mere question of words."[3] However, the communication barriers were more than matters of definition; they were the results of social and psychological considerations.

It has been thought that the controversy was a result of inadequate communication over the meaning of words, that if the participants had been better able to define their terms, the controversy would not have arisen, or at least would have been quickly resolved. Although an abundance of information was repeatedly stated by many individuals, constant repetitions continually failed to resolve the controversy. With the recognition that the adherents to a scientific system also function as a social system, the course that the controversy took can be explained better. The transmission of ideas and the production of results depend upon communication among people working within a given system of natural philosophy and between systems.

Although a scientific system is a structure of knowledge, it always has associated with it an informal organization of scientists. The Newtonian group concerned with the *vis viva* controversy in the 1720s consisted of Samuel Clarke, Henry Pemberton, John Theophilus Desaguliers, and John Eames.[4] These men were involved in the task of expounding Newton's ideas, translating them into popular language, devising demonstrations and experiments for explicating Newtonian principles, and teaching Newtonian concepts to the general public through lecture demonstrations and textbooks. They were in close physical proximity to Newton, now in old age, relating to him by direct communication or through correspondence. Intellectually they related directly through the implications and applications of the Newtonian metaphysics and concept of force. Because they functioned in this close satellite relationship to Newton, they formed a scientific bureaucracy devoted to the exposition and explanation of Newtonian principles.

We may argue that the followers of a particular scientific system identify with the central ideas of the system, developing a loyalty to it and its originator. The metaphysical and theoretical presuppositions of the system become imprinted on them. The scientists become functioning members of an informal group, perceiving and communicating from within the assumptions, objectives, and principles of the system. As a cohesive group they feel a strong sense of responsibility to the ideals of the conceptual scheme and their leader. There may also be a tendency to exclude outsiders.

The Newtonian and Leibnizian followers developed a commitment to the systems of natural philosophy developed by Newton and Leibniz. As a result of this commitment, they became wedded to the goals, methods, concepts, and analysis of nature afforded by each of these scientific schemes. Theology, metaphysics, and mechanics formed aspects of the systems to which they adhered.

Newtonian followers, operating under this commitment, viewed problems and competing theories with a different perception from those operating outside the group. The writings and experiments of adherents to other systems were perceived by them as a threat to the legitimacy of Newtonian natural philosophy. Their psychological reaction to these outside disruptive factors was to try to restore the Newtonian scheme to its original validity, by explaining the threatening data in their own terms. This prevented them from seeing the validity of supposedly "objective factual" experimental results from another equally legitimate perspective.[5]

This analysis can serve to explain the violent reactions of both the Newtonians and Leibnizians to outside attacks on the systems of the masters. It also helps to undermine the notion of objectivity in the sciences, by showing how social factors can influence a scientist's perception.

One of the challenges to the Newtonian scheme took the form of mechanical free-fall experiments conducted by the Leibnizians, William 's Gravesande and Giovanni Poleni, supporting the measure of force, mv^2. The Newtonian group in explaining the experiments from within the Newtonian framework attempted to restore the system to its established state by demonstrating the successful handling of mechanical problems using momentum (mv) consider-ations. In regard to these free-fall experiments, they adequately demonstrated their ability to apply and translate the concept of Newtonian force so as to explain the externally imposed Leibnizian problem. They also discussed the previously established problems of the lever and impact from the point of view of momentum conservation. But in the early years of the controversy they were unable to perceive any validity in the arguments of the opposition.

The Leibnizians responded to these defenses by further explicating the mv^2 interpretation of the free-fall experiments from their own particular per-spective. 's Gravesande, who had crossed the boundaries between the two schemes through his conversion to the Leibnizian concept of force, was now unable to accept the adequacy of the Newtonian arguments.

Theological and metaphysical commitments on the part of these experi-menters caused them to interpret the mechanical experiments in a manner consistent with their natural philosophies. I shall show that although their experimental results were unconvincing and fraught with experimental error, their positions were unchanged and their loyalties were not undermined.

THE NEWTONIAN AND LEIBNIZIAN WORLDVIEWS

The Newtonian and Leibnizian views of nature were radically different. Con-cepts of God, matter, force, and causality formed fundamental metaphysical dichotomies. It is insufficient to argue that Newton and Leibniz both added differently defined concepts of force to the mechanical philosophy's ontology of matter in motion.[6] The metaphysics behind these concepts of force had developed from widely differing intellectual traditions.

Theology

Newton's and Leibniz's opinions on the nature of God may be examined against the background of the intellectualist-voluntarist debates of the medi-eval period.[7] The intellectualist tradition, going back to Thomas Aquinas, with which Leibniz can be associated assigned primary importance to God's intellect, logic, and rationality. The voluntarists, stemming from St. Augustine, who included Newton, made the divine will prior to divine intelligence.

Aquinas had considered the essence of God to be identical with his infi-nite intellect. The logical consistency of his properties was primary; from these followed his power to act. Intellect gave rise to the will and from this proceeded God's love. The *potentia anima* was uppermost in man and likewise in God. If the will was stressed too much, God became unintelligible. For the Thomists, omniscience regulates omnipotence.

The Augustinian voluntarist tradition emphasized the will, power, and love of God in his active creation and intervention in the world. God could create everything immediately, spontaneously, and directly, out of nothing. This manifestation of infinite power and will guarded God's freedom. The divine will was prior to and motivated the intellect's interests. Following in the voluntarist philosophy were the Franciscans and nominalists, Duns Scotus and William of Ockham.

The intellectualist-voluntarist argument was of primary importance in initiating the Leibniz-Clarke correspondence. Leibniz considered the necessity of God's intervention in the Newtonian machine of the universe to be a limitation on his wisdom and foresight.[8] Newton and Clarke argued that God's glory and power were manifested in his providential care and interposition.[9] The world as Newton and Clarke viewed it could have been otherwise, for it depended on the free exercise of God's will and its continued sustenance.

For Leibniz, the actual world was the best of all possible worlds since God operated rationally within the laws of logic to create it. The possibility for the existence of the natural world must be consistent with the principle of non-contradiction; its beings must exhibit nothing mutually destructive or incompatible.[10] However, such a possible world may not actually exist; the principle of sufficient reason explains the existence of this world and no other.[11] This principle is necessary in proceeding from the laws of logic to those of natural philosophy. God's sufficient reason unites his logic with his power.[12] The creation of the world by will alone might result in an ill-constructed, inferior world.

At the root of the intellectualist-voluntarist debate was the fear that God's nature would be limited. The Newtonians feared that Leibniz's concept of God would lead to atheism, for if God could not intervene in his creation, it was only one more step to say that the concept of a creator was unnecessary. The Leibnizians held that the necessity of God's intervention implied a limitation on his intelligence and foresight. These anxieties helped to program the positions that individual "scientists" took in the *vis viva* controversy over the concept of "force."

Philosophy of Matter

A related but equally fundamental difference between the two philosophies of nature was the issue of a mechanistic versus a vitalistic view of the relationship between matter and force. The mechanical philosophy expressed in Newton's *Queries to the Optics* presupposed dead, static, unchanging, extended particles of matter.[13] From his correspondence and private papers it is clear that he considered the ultimate source of force and motion to be God himself, externally superimposed upon bodies.[14] Matter itself was lifeless; the machine of the world inert without its operator.

On the other hand, Leibniz viewed the world as an organic whole in which all parts were interconnected and interrelated. Matter was alive and contained a force or a principle of change within it. Nothing in nature was fixed or static, but was in constant dynamic change. In "The Monadology" of 1714, Leibniz had explained that natural changes in the lives of the simple unextended substances called monads came from an internal principle.[15]

External causes could not influence the interior actions of these window-less monads. Each monad mirrored the universe in its own way, its life unfolding simultaneously with the lives of all other monads in an organically related, pre-established harmony. As Leibniz put it,

> There is a world of creatures, living beings, animals, entelechies, souls in the smallest particle of matter. Each part of matter can be thought of as a garden full of plants or as a pond full of fish. But each branch of the plant, each member of the animal, each drop of its humors, is also such a garden or such a pond.[16]

It is important to explore briefly the intellectual traditions that gave rise to these dichotomous views of matter. Frances Yates and Allen Debus have discussed the increased interest in Renaissance Hermeticism and neoplatonism which paralleled the rise of the mechanical philosophy.[17] Walter Pagel has shown that Leibniz's monadology stemmed from the Helmontian aspect of this tradition and has suggested that Leibnizian vitalism can be pushed back to Paracelsus, who was an important influence on van Helmont.[18] Newton, however, was influenced by another strand of Renaissance neoplatonism, as has been demonstrated by James McGuire, Piyo M. Rattansi, and Richard Westfall.[19]

Leibniz's theory of matter may be analyzed in the light of a Paracelsian dynamism, emphasizing the interconnectedness of all things. Paracelsus, in his "Hermetic philosophy," held a vitalistic view of matter.[20] All created things consisted of the four elements.[21] "An element," he said, "is really neither more nor less than a soul." "An element is spirit and lives and flourishes in those things as the soul in the body. . . . For the first matter of the elements is nothing else than life which all created things possess."[22] Like Leibniz's monads, the four elements contain a principle of change within them. The monads, like the elements, are souls in their simplest state.[23]

The Paracelsian elements exist independently of one another. Things are not compounded of several elements in conjunction, but four worlds develop separately from each element:[24] "The doctrine of the elements does not lay it down that the world must be sustained by the four elements but rather that everything is conserved by one element, namely that from which it sprang. . . . Neither is the world going to perish by itself but suffices for its own sustentation. . . . Nothing decays, nothing perishes", Paracelsus stated.[25] Leibniz's monads are likewise simple substances, whose lives unfold separately, conserving within them the total "force" of the universe. They cannot be destroyed naturally nor can they have a natural beginning; instead all are created or annihilated at once. The monads are "the elements of things."[26]

From the four elements of Paracelsus flow four worlds, each separate and self-contained, yet co-existing. Each element puts forth its own different species and essences.[27] For example, the element of fire gives forth the firmament, the sun and stars. The fire which burns is not the element fire, but its soul, the life of which can be present in all things.[28] So as roots, stems, filaments and flowers emerge from a single seed, the elements produce their own worlds. "Every element nourishes itself."[29] "So in water a special world is to be recognized together with its mystery, even to the end of the world. There is no beginning in these save that which is in the other elements; nor is there any other end than is found in the other elements. . . . Thus we must understand the four worlds according to the four elements."[30] The flowing out of four worlds from the four elements of Paracelsus became the unfolding of a plurality of worlds in the philosophy of Leibniz. Each monad, its life unfolding from within, contains a world within itself. It reflects the larger world from its own point of view.[31]

Paracelsus, like Leibniz, emphasized the relations between the concurrent processes in the four worlds:

One element . . . gives sign of its course and its advent which are easily recognized by the stars, not because these rule or influence us but only because they run concurrently with us and imitate the inner movement of our body. . . . If anything suffers from the error of the elements, other things grow uncertain too. All ought to proceed with a perfect and unimpeded motion. . . . And the defects and errors of the firmament can be observed by us, no less than the firmament observes our defects.[32]

Leibniz expressed a similar idea of the interconnectedness of all things when he wrote:

This mutual connection or accommodation of all created things to each other and of each to all the rest causes each simple substance to have relations which express all the others and consequently to be a perpetual living mirror of the universe.[33]

"Every body responds to everything which happens in the universe so that he who sees all could read in each everything that happens everywhere."[34]

Pagel has pointed out that the repercussions of particular changes on the rest of the world implied a "consensus" of individual actions in the philosophies of both Paracelsus and Leibniz.[35]

Leibniz carefully dissociated himself from the philosophy of Robert Fludd, which denied "a proper activity to created things" and Henry More whose doctrine of a universal spirit external to matter negated an activity of particular souls within it.[36]

Pagel has demonstrated further important connections between van Helmont (who was influenced by Paraeelsus) and Leibniz's "Monadology." Van Helmont created a vitalistic pluralism of seeds, unifying spirit and matter. His dynamic principles like those of Leibniz were immanent in matter. The dynamic principle in matter, or the *archeus* of van Helmont, "acts by its own spontaneity according to its own innate schedule, which runs down to its destined end," unalterable from without.[37]

Newton, in sharp contrast with Leibniz, was concerned with demonstrating the passivity and non-activity of matter. The active principles which provide the source of motion in bodies were external to matter. He held that matter depended ultimately on the will of God for its existence and motion.[38] The conception of matter as self-active led to atheism.

Newton's belief in the passivity of matter with its external source of activity developed from another strand of the Hermetic tradition. This conception emphasized the idea of spirit as the source of activity infusing matter with life and vital processes. The *spiritus* notion played an important role in the natural magic of Ficino, and the "philosopher's mercury" of alchemists such as Elias Ashmole and Robert Fludd. Ashmole held that

> The power and vertue is not in Plants, Stones, Minerals, etc. . . . but 'tis that universal and all-piercing Spirit, the One operative vertue and immortal Seede of Worldly things that God in the beginning infused into the Chaos, which is everywhere active and still flows through the world in all kindes of things by universal extension.[39]

For Fludd, matter was never the first cause but was transformed by the action of winds and ultimately influenced by the angels whose activity was an instrument of God's eternal wisdom.[40]

The chemist Stahl believed motion to be an immaterial substance which was superimposed on a body from the outside, an active external influence of the *anima* or soul on matter.[41]

Henry More, an early influence on Newton, stated that "The Notion and Idea of a Spirit . . . is plainly distinguished from a Body whose parts cannot penetrate one another, is not Self-moveable, nor can contract nor dilate itself; is divisible, and separable one part from another."[42] The active properties of spirit were thus opposed to the attributes of dead matter.

In the natural philosophies of Descartes and Boyle, the active-passive polarities of the alchemists and Hermetic philosophers became a dualism of mind and matter. Descartes reduced nature to passive, inert, extended matter, and translated the *spiritus* into a fine, subtle ether which provided the external source of the motion of bodies.[43]

Newton's mechanical aether of the 1670s, his belief in an immaterial cause of gravity of the 1690s, his active principles and repulsive aether of the 1706–17 *Optics* all reflect this tendency toward external sources of activity in nature. We can see therefore that Renaissance Hermeticism and neoplatonism were important influences on the philosophies of both Newton and Leibniz, but diverging trends led to their differing mechanistic and vitalistic philosophies of matter.

Causality

A third but also logically related difference between the Newtonian and Leibnizian philosophies of nature brought out by the Leibniz-Clarke correspondence was the problem of causality. It related directly to the previous theological positions and views of matter. For Leibniz the equality of cause and effect relationships in nature was synonymous with a general metaphysical principle of conservation. The "same force and vigor" was always present in the world passing from one particle of matter to another.[44] In contrast, Newton held to no such principle of strict causality. In his philosophy, the world could decay and run down owing to loss of motion between colliding hard atoms.[45] God's power and providential care could be manifested in supplying new motion to the unwinding clockwork mechanism. His intervention in the universe was therefore guaranteed.

Leibniz's principle that total cause equals total effect in mechanical interactions was consistent with his view of the primacy of God's rational omniscience and a manifestation of the principles of identity, and non-contradiction: A is A and cannot be non-A.[46] Since matter was held to be elastic, force could be stored in the small parts and released, conserving "force," mv^2, between the macroscopic and microscopic realms.

Newton's concern with the ontology of causation was directed toward the relationship between the hidden forces and invisible atoms of the microscopic world and the manifest quantifiable forces and laws of the macrocosm.[47] By the "analogy of nature" similar laws could be hypothesized to operate in both realms. But since the underlying hard atoms of the invisible realm could dissipate macroscopic motion one could not assume causal conservation relationships between the two levels of reality.

In the Leibniz-Clarke correspondence Clarke, speaking for Newton, discussed the question of conservation of motion between hard colliding atoms. In his fourth reply he stated that two inelastic bodies colliding with equal forces lost all their motion, implying that this was an example of the diminution as opposed to the conservation of force in the universe.[48] Leibniz had answered that in the collision of two soft or inelastic bodies, the "forces" (meaning mv^2) were lost only in appearance. For "the wholes lose it with respect to their total motion, but their parts receive it, being shaken internally by the force of the concourse. . . . The bodies do not lose their forces, but the case here is the same as when men change great money into small."[49]

To this Clarke had replied that the problem lay not with *soft* inelastic bodies but with hard inelastic bodies, as were Newton's atoms:

> But the question is: when two perfectly HARD unelastic bodies lose their whole motion by meeting together, what then becomes of the motion or active impulsive force. It cannot be dispersed among the parts, because the parts are capable of no tremulous motion for want of elasticity.[50]

Although the death of Leibniz in 1716 cut short the correspondence before he had answered Clarke's fifth reply, his approach would have been to deny the existence of absolutely hard bodies in nature. Leibniz had argued often on the basis of the law of continuity that the diminution of motion cannot take place in leaps.

In his "Fifth Reply" Clarke elaborated on the diminution of motion and the role of God in preventing blind mechanism:

> And if God, or Man, or Any Living or Active Power, ever influences any thing in the material world; and everything be not absolute mechanism; there must be a continual Increase and decrease of the whole Quantity of Motion in the Universe. Which this Learned Man frequently denies.[51]

The argument between Clarke and Leibniz emphasized fundamental differences for the role of force, F, and causality in hard and elastic matter mechanics. Motion in the mechanics of Newton and Clarke was inertial, a state of being. A body, mass m, continued its constant velocity, v, because of its inertia or resistance to change of motion. This was expressed as a quantity of motion, or momentum, mv. If the momentum changed, the action of an impressed external force was indicated. If the total motion in the universe decreased, owing to head-on hard-body collisions between equal atoms, the universe could run down. New motion must be supplied by God, an instance of his providential care. In Leibniz's energy mechanics the action was internal. Force was measured by mv^2, the mass multiplied by the square of the velocity. Activity and the tendency toward motion were inherent within matter. These tendencies and motions stored in the small parts of matter could be changed to the motions of the entire body when dead force changed to living force. The energy of matter was thus fundamental to Leibniz's view. The elastic parts of matter were a storehouse where energy and motion were conserved. For Newton, the infinite storehouse of new motion was God because matter itself was composed of hard unchanging inelastic atoms.

In section 2, I have tried to characterize certain aspects of the fundamentally dichotomous views of nature held by Leibniz and Newton. These radically different systems of natural philosophy were related to intellectual traditions and placed within a historical framework. That these deep differences existed is important in understanding the psychology of the emotional ties and loyalties developed by the followers of the two systems. The heated arguments over mechanics to which we now turn are better comprehended within such an intellectual and socio-psychological framework.

MECHANICS AND THE FREE-FALL DEBATES: 1718–1728

Adherents to the Newtonian and Leibnizian systems of natural philosophy devised mechanical arguments in support of the extremely different concepts of force, mv and mv^2. In the period 1718 to 1728, a lively debate occurred concerning the problem of the "force" acquired by freely falling bodies. The debate was triggered by free-fall experiments performed by Giovanni Poleni and William 's Gravesande in support of the *vis viva* principle. Counterarguments and experiments were presented by the Newtonians Henry Pemberton, John T. Desaguliers, John Eames, and Samuel Clarke.

In my discussion of these mechanical problems I wish to show that the two groups reacted to the externally imposed threats by strengthening their own analyses of force and by reinterpreting the experiments to fit their respective conceptual schemes. Secondly, I hope to demonstrate that the experiments in themselves were unconvincing and hence that the insistence of the practitioners that these experiments supported concepts of either mv or mv^2 were colored by loyalties and preconditioned adherence to the mother philosophies. Thirdly, wherever possible I shall indicate the extent to which the various participants adhered to the systems of natural philosophy outlined in section 2.

The Leibnizian Free-Fall Experiments

In the "Brevis Demonstratio" of 1686 Leibniz had presented logical arguments concerning the force of two unequal bodies (of weights or masses 1
and 4) falling from heights inversely proportional to their masses.[52] "Force,"
he said, should be measured by its effect, i.e., by the height to which a given
force can elevate a body of a given magnitude. The mathematical measure of
force was later expressed by Leibniz as *vis viva*, mv^2, or the body's mass multiplied by the square of its velocity. (If bodies having masses, m, or weights
in the ratio 1 to 4 fall from heights, s, of 4 and 1, their "forces" or *vires vivae*,
mv^2, will be equal because s α v^2; see Diagram 5.1.)

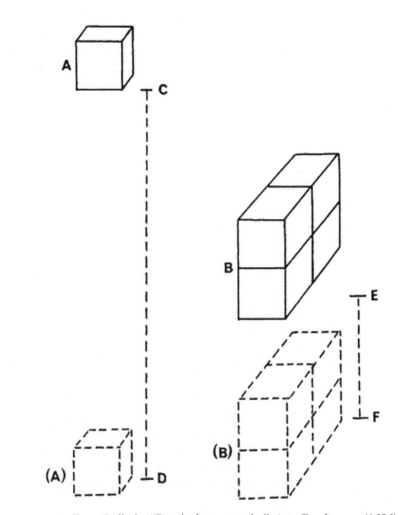

DIAGRAM 5.1 From Leibniz, "Brevis demonstratio," *Acta Eruditorum* (1686)

It was not until after Leibniz's death in 1716 that the thought experiment described in the "Brevis Demonstratio" was empirically tested. A work by Giovanni Poleni of Padua, *De Castellis per quae derivantur fluxiomru latera convergentia* (1718), summarized the arguments for *vis viva* which had appeared prior to 1718 and described experimental support for the principle.[53] In this treatise Poleni discussed the forces produced by water pressures in several vessels resembling castles, hence the title, *De Castellis*. In the concluding pages of his book he presented a theory for the "force" of bodies in motion based upon his work on the flow of water in which he distinguished between the momentum and *vis viva*.

He described the loss of motion of a body in impact, in which a body experienced a pressure (*pressio*) brought about by the thrust (*impressio*) of another body.[54] The change brought about by the completion of the pressure was the *momentum pressionis*. If a body used up all its motion in the interaction, the cause of this complete effect could be measured as *vis viva* or living force. He described free-fall experiments in which a moving body lost all motion in impact with a soft medium. His experiments were designed to show that this concept of "force" should be measured by the "body" multiplied by the square of the velocity:

> I took a Vessel, that had in it congeal'd Tallow six Inches deep, and fix'd it to a level floor, in such manner that the surface of the Tallow, which was flat, should every where be equally distant from the Floor. I had caused to be made two Balls of equal Bigness, the one of Lead, the other of Brass, the last of which was a little hollow in the middle, that it might weigh but one Pound, whilst the other weigh'd two. Suspending these Balls from the Ceiling by Threads, in such manner, that the lighter Ball hung over the Surface of the Tallow, from twice the Height that the Heavier Ball did, I cut the Threads, and the Balls falling perpendicularly upon the Tallow, by their Fall made Pits in the Tallow, that were precisely equal; the Ball of one Pound, from the Beginning of its Fall, till it came to rest, going through a Space express'd by the Number two, produced an effect equal to that which the two Pound Ball did produce, in falling thro' a Space express'd by the Number one. It follows therefore that we may look upon it as a settled truth, That the active Forces (*vires vivae*) of falling Bodies are in a reciprocal Ratio of the Spaces which the said Bodies describe by their Fall. And because these Spaces are in the same Ratio, as the Squares of the Numbers expressing the Velocities; it appears by the Experiment that the active Force (*vis viva*) of the Falling Body, is that which is made up of the Body itself; multiplied into the Space described in the Fall, or into the Square of the Number that expresses the Velocity of the Body, at the end of the Motion. This Experiment I did not only make once, but several times, changing the Balls, the Distances, and the Body on which they fell; as for example making use of Clay,

or of soft Wax: and notwithstanding these various ways of trying the Experiments, the Effects were constantly the same; which made me easily conclude, that there was always the same Reason in Nature for this Phenomenon.[55]

$$\frac{ws}{w's'} = \frac{mv^2}{m'v'^2} = \frac{1(2)}{2(1)}$$

In attempting to repeat and evaluate the procedure of this eighteenth-century experiment today, several experimental difficulties should be noted. The falling objects must be uniformly round so that, after falling, the impressions formed will be uniform. An increase in the volume of the balls results in a shallower impression. The balls must be made of a dense substance such as lead in order to make impressions of a measurable depth in a substance such as clay or fat, from heights of the order of 6 to 12 feet, presumably the height of Poleni's ceiling. The clay into which the objects fall must be homogeneous and as soft as possible to produce the deepest impressions, but not so soft as to stick to the balls after falling. If a fatty medium is used, it must be kept cold to prevent the fat from sticking and heaping up. Care must be taken to achieve a level surface for the medium. The balls must be rigid so that the energy will not be dissipated upon striking the surface. With lead balls falling from a few feet, air resistance, which depends on v, is not an important contribution to the errors. With lead balls of 1 and 2 lb (446.0 g and 892.3 g) falling from heights of 6 feet and 3 feet, I found that rather shallow impressions of the order of 7/8" ± 1/16" were obtained in soft clay, and 1 5/8" ± 1/8" in vegetable shortening. Considering the difficulties in maintaining a level surface and the shallowness of the impression, errors of about 8 per cent are inherent in the experiment. Whereas Newton, in the percussion experiments described in the *Principia*, is careful to discuss and estimate the errors involved, the free-fall experimenters do not do so.[56]

Poleni concluded that regard should be paid to the *effects* of the "forces" of the bodies in motion. These "forces" are seen to be composed of the ratio of the simple power of the body and the square of its speed.[57] The "forces" are of the same nature, irrespective of the causes which produced the motions.

Poleni's experiment is an actual physical experiment set up to demonstrate empirically the logic of Leibniz's "Brevis demonstratio." The results seemed to Poleni to confirm the theory that mv^2 is the measure of a force acting through a distance. The shallow, seemingly equal, impressions caused him to conclude that the "forces" with which the two bodies hit the ground were equal. Poleni thus accepted Leibniz's measure of "force". However, he did not indicate adherence to the metaphysics of monads, the philosophical basis of the Leibnizian "force" concept.

In 1729 Poleni published a rebuttal of his critics, among whom were the Newtonians Pemberton and Desaguliers.[58] He analyzed their objections and attempted to refute the theoretical basis of their arguments. He reinforced his own viewpoint, while pointing to errors in his opponents' assumptions.

William 's Gravesande, who had presented a Newtonian analysis of collision problems in his *Mathematical elements of natural philosophy* (1719), became converted to the Leibnizian camp after performing some experiments similar to those of Poleni. It is interesting to note the ways in which his intellectual framework changed after he declared allegiance to the Leibnizian concept of "force".

In the preface to his 1719 Newtonian textbook he had adhered to certain theological views shared by Newton:

> That the world was created by God is a position wherein Reason so perfectly agrees with Scripture, that the least Examination of Nature will show plain footsteps of Supreme Wisdom. It is confounding and over-setting all our clearest notions to assert that the World may have taken its Rise from some general laws of motion. . . . This assertion . . . overthrows all our clearest Notions as has been fully proved by many learned Men; and is indeed so unreasonable and so injurious to the Deity that it will seem unworthy of an answer to anyone who does not know that it has been maintained by many ancient and modern philosophers and some of them of the first rank and far removed from any suspicion of atheism.[59]

He held that the properties of matter depended on the free power of God and that there were many "reasonings" other than mathematical ones which followed from the predetermined will of God.[60]

Following his conversion to Leibniz's concept of force, 's Gravesande took on other philosophical notions consistent with the new framework. According to his biographer Jean Allemand, this conversion occurred at the time when he became interested in the possibility of using experimental methods to refute Leibniz's measure of the "force" of bodies in motion, having already convinced himself that Leibniz was in error on rational grounds.[61] His prior conviction that the experiment would successfully refute Leibniz's theory guided the experimental work. His brother-in-law J. Sacrelaire, who happened to be present when the first experiments were performed, reported his astonished cry, "It is I who am wrong". His subsequent experiments repeatedly convinced him of the truth of the Leibnizian position. He then proceeded to redevelop the mathematics of his percussion theory using the mv^2 principle. He discussed his conversion in "A New Theory on the Collision of Bodies", published in 1722.[62] There he wrote:

> The experiments I have made on collision have made me see demonstratively that the opinion of M. Leibniz is true, that is to say that the forces of different

bodies are in a ratio of the masses multiplied by the squares of the velocities; it appears to me that to determine the effects of collision one should never as has been done up to the present, consider the products of the masses by the velocities, as if these products were proportional to the quantities of motion in the bodies. Quantity of motion and force are not things that one can distinguish. This consideration involved me in pushing my experiments further and I have arrived at a completely new theory of collision which, as regards the collision of two bodies and the direct collision of several non-elastic bodies, does not lead to different rules from those already known, and which experience confirms; but here one will find these rules demonstrated in a manner different from that which they have been up to the present; and one will see how from a principle contrary to experience, philosophers have arrived at these rules, by an argument in which they have neglected to pay attention to all they should have considered; without which it is impossible to arrive at the truth by the path they have taken. . . . This new theory regards only collision and does not change anything which has been demonstrated regarding the projection of weights, central forces, centers of oscillation, the resistance of fluids, etc. The effects which in all these cases change the motion of bodies, are of a different nature from collision.[63]

In a supplement to this essay he wrote that, after his "New Theory" was printed, he saw the book, *De Castellis*, of Poleni. The experiments of Poleni, he said, differed from his own only in insignificant details. These experiments were performed prior to his, but his own method of demonstrating the rules of collision was new.[64]

In this same supplement he stated that, after the "New Theory" had been printed, many objections were raised concerning his reasoning and proofs of *vis viva*. In answering them he had not entered directly into dispute with those raising them as was inevitable if one replied directly to each objection. His method, he said, was to clarify the truth to the extent to which he was capable, and, for this, ordinary disputes were not proper.[65] 's Gravesande performed both collision and free fall experiments in order to verify the *vis viva* principle.

In the free fall experiment he took balls of copper, all 1½ inches in diameter.[66] One was solid, the other two were hollow and composed of two hemispheres joined together. Their masses were in ratio of 1, 2, and 3, with the heaviest referred to as ball 3, and the lightest as ball 1. A tray, 1 inch in depth, was filled with soft homogeneous potter's clay. The balls were allowed to fall into this clay from different heights. Precautions were taken so that the balls would fall from rest, receiving no motion from the hands of the experimenter. Since the balls he used were smaller than Poleni's, they would make deeper impressions and could be dropped from lower heights. The experimental difficulties were similar to those in Poleni's experiment. In my repetitions of this experiment, I used balls weighing 892.3 g for ball 3, 595.0 g for ball 2, and 297.0 g for ball 1. Since the balls measured 2½ inches instead of 1½ inches in diameter, I doubled the heights in order to obtain measurable impressions.

's Gravesande allowed ball 3 to fall from 9 inches and ball 1 from 27 inches. The impressions in the clay, he said, were equal. [mv^2 = (3) (9) = 1(27)]. I obtained impressions of 5/8" ± 1/16".

Ball 2 was allowed to fall from 9 inches and ball 1 from 36 inches. [2(9) ≠ 1(36)]. The impressions in the clay were different. I obtained impressions of 5/8" ± 1/16" for ball 2 and 7/16" ± 1/16" for ball 1.

When ball 3 fell from a height of 18 inches and ball 2 from a height of 27 inches, the impressions were exactly equal. [3(18) = 54 = 2(27)]. I obtained impressions of 7/8" ± 1/16". The error range of 7–10 per cent for the experiment was quite high.

The cavities which the balls make in falling in the clay, said 's Gravesande, represent the entire actions of the "forces" which the bodies have at the end of their falls.[67] The "forces", mv^2, which would be acquired by balls 1 and 3 in falling from a height of one inch would be 1 to 3; hence the action of ball 1 in falling from the height of 27 inches is triple that which it has in falling from a height of 9 inches. It therefore appears that the "force" of a ball is proportional to the height from which it falls. But this height is as the square of the velocity acquired in falling and with which the body strikes the clay. *Vis viva* could be measured only through its effects or the total action which consumed it. This measure was mv^2.

It is significant that 's Gravesande's expectations had been determined by rational considerations. Furthermore, the results of the experiment did not suggest to him that both viewpoints could be valid. An "objective" evaluation leading to the legitimacy of both interpretations was not open to him. The only option was to choose one system or the other. Following his conversion, he spent much effort strengthening his Leibnizian position with mathematical and metaphysical arguments.

He now felt compelled to alter his mathematical solution to impact problems in order to remain consistent with his new Leibnizian interpretation. Inelastic collisions, however, presented a great difficulty since *vis viva* was not conserved. For these cases he derived an expression for the "force", mv^2, lost in the collision and subtracted it from the total initial "force" in order to find the common velocity of the two bodies together. This gave the "force" remaining after the collision which, when divided by the sum of the masses, yielded the final velocity.[68] For the elastic case the change in the velocity of each body was twice that for the inelastic case, and relative velocities were conserved.[69]

's Gravesande's concept of "force" was also altered to make it consistent with the Leibnizian interpretation. He now defined "force" as inherent within a moving body by means of which it was transported from place to place, something altogether different from inertia.[70] A pressure or Leibnizian "dead force" was a continuous "effort" acting over a time without causing motion. If not destroyed by a contrary pressure it would produce "living force". When a body hit a mass of soft clay, part of the pressure was destroyed by the contrary pressure of the clay but the impression was formed by that part of the pressure due to the "living force" acquired in falling. There were therefore two possible effects of pressure. In the first case the effect was destroyed in each instant as in dead force; in the second the effect of pressure produced *vis viva*.

In reaction to criticism made by the Newtonian Samuel Clarke, 's Gravesande in 1729 further strengthened his metaphysics of "force" by developing it along the lines of Leibniz's 1695 "Specimen dynamicum".[71] He pointed out that the mere transportation of a body from place to place was often confused with the ability to act. A body in motion can act only because it has a force. *Vis viva* is the measure of a body's inherent power to act.[72]

In a motion carried out over a period of time two things must be considered: first, the instantaneous action or pressure exerted by acting bodies and, second, the total action or sum of all the small actions.[73] Following Leibniz, he appealed to causality arguments, as already discussed in section 2. The total action is proportional to the total effect. If the definition of force is taken as the "total capacity to act" or to produce an effect, then the capacity to produce a certain effect is proportional to that effect and thus to mv^2.[74]

He attempted to resolve the controversy by arguing that the momentum proponents were really talking about instantaneous action, $mvdt$. If the instantaneous action is summed up over a time interval the sum represents the total action or force, mv^2.[75]

$$m \int_0^t v\,dt = m \int_0^s \frac{ds}{dt}\,dt = ms = mv^2$$

's Gravesande did not use the concept of an integral, but it seems clear that he was following Leibniz's analysis of the integral of momentaneous impetuses, mv, over an interval of time, as presented in "Specimen Dynamicum".

's Gravesande developed his ideas on causality more completely in his *Introduction to philosophy* in 1736–37.[76] He argued that there was a necessary chain of causes and effects in nature.[77] It is necessary that a wise Deity acts wisely and a contradiction that He should not do so. Moral necessity is comprehended within physical necessity.[78] In spite of a chain of necessary connexions, that which exists does not exist in and of itself because nothing cannot be the cause of an effect. Hence created things could not have come from nothing and religion is therefore not a mere chimera.[79] In this way 's Gravesande sought to dispel the arguments that a necessary order in the physical world could lead to atheism. In addition, he held that any system in which the essences of things depended on the volition of God confined the divine power within limits too narrow.[80] This represented a change from his earlier supposition that the properties of matter depended upon the free power of God. 's Gravesande's natural philosophy therefore changed as his intellectual development gradually assumed more aspects of the Leibnizian system of philosophy and concept of force.

The Newtonian Reaction

's Gravesande's "New Theory of Collision" with his new opinion concerning *vis viva* caused a great stir in the intellectual world of the 1720s. His conversion was greeted with astonishment and disbelief. Desaguliers, translator of 's Gravesande's Newtonian textbook, considered him to be an ingenious professor who had been wholly overcome and led into error by his experiments.[81] Needless to say, the new experimental evidence of 's Gravesande and Poleni was not sufficient to convince the adversaries that *vis viva* had anything of value to offer to physics. Their discussions sparked a series of counter experiments and arguments by British Newtonians in the years 1722–28. Their response was to analyze and refute the validity of the experiments in terms of Newtonian mechanics. A counter-experiment of questionable adequacy was offered by Desaguliers.

The free-fall problem interpreted in terms of Newtonian mechanics required the use of either Newton's third law, stating that action and reaction are equal and opposite, or his definition that the accelerative quantity of the centripetal force is proportional to the velocity generated in a given time.[82] The second law of motion, as stated by Newton, concerned impulses or instantaneous changes of motion applicable to billiard ball collisions: $F \propto \Delta mv$.[83] For the case of gravitational free-fall involving continuous constant accelerative forces, the rate of change of momentum was the appropriate modification of Newton's statement of his second law. Whereas Newton concerned himself with its application to planetary motions, his followers in the *vis viva* controversy used rates of change to determine the increased momentum of falling bodies over a time interval.

The first of these Newtonian contributions, by Henry Pemberton dating from 1722, gained for its author recognition and association with Isaac Newton. Pemberton, who was well versed in the mathematical details of Newton's *Principia*, made Newton's acquaintance when his refutation of

Poleni's experiment was shown to Newton by Dr. Mead.[84] It was said that Newton was so pleased with it that he condescended to visit Pemberton at his "lodgings bringing along a confutation of his own based on other principles".[85] Both Pemberton's paper and Newton's anonymous postscript were published in the *Philosophical transactions of the Royal Society* for 1722.[86] Pemberton's association with the Newtonian group and the friendship that arose between Pemberton and Newton resulted in his superintendence of the third edition of the *Principia*, which appeared in 1726. In preparing this edition, he showed his support for Newton's theological belief in God's Providence, as outlined in section 2 of this paper, and his opposition to the eternity of the world. Like Bentley, who had edited the second edition, he altered and struck from Halley's "Ode to Newton" the word eternal in the lines:

> until, the origin of things
>> He established, the omnipresent Creator, unwilling the laws
>> To violate, he fixed the eternal foundations of His work.[87]

In 1728 he published one of the well known popular introductions to Newtonian science, a non-technical *View of Sir Isaac Newton's philosophy*. Although published after Newton's death (1727), this account, written during his close association with Newton in old age, was authorized by Newton himself. In this work he again mentioned "a very strong philosophical argument against the eternity of the world". He implied that the Leibnizian position cast "a reflection upon the wisdom of the author of nature for framing a perishable work".[88] In addition he repudiated the Leibnizian view of matter as self-active:

> For suppose a body by the structure or disposition of its part, or by any circumstance in its make was imbued with a power of moving itself, the self-moving principle which should be thus inherent in the body and not depend on anything external must change the direction wherein it would act, as often as the position of the body was changed.[89]

Pemberton's 1722 contribution to the *vis viva* controversy reflected his commitment to the Newtonian system. Pemberton stated to Dr Mead his contention that Poleni's conclusions were wrong and that Leibniz's opinion concerning force was unreasonable. If Newton's third law was applied to the experiment, it was consistent with the concept of force, *mv*.

> Perusing the Learned Polenus" Tract, *De Castellis* you were pleased to send me, I have found in it several curious experiments among which I reckon that of letting globes of equal Magnitude but of different weights fall upon a yielding substance as Tallow, Wax, Clay or the like from . . . heights reciprocally proportional to the weights of the globes. This experiment engaged in

particular my attention as it is brought with design to overturn one of the First Principles established in Natural Philosophy . . . I cannot by any means admit of the Deduction that is drawn from thence, that because the globes make in this experiment equal impressions in the yielding substance, therefore they strike upon it with equal force. . . . On the contrary I think this very experiment proves the great unreasonableness of Mr. Leibniz's notion.[90]

The experiment of Poleni, he wrote, "better informs us of the law by which these yielding substances resist the motion of bodies striking them, than to shew the forces with which Bodies strike".[91] Using the Newtonian law that action equals reaction, Pemberton changed the problem of free fall from a *vis viva* problem to a momentum problem. He treated Poleni's experiment in terms of the action-reaction forces between the falling globe and the tallow rather than measuring the distance the globe travels in the tallow. Since the impact was inelastic, it could not be considered instantaneous, and the time for the action to occur had to be considered. Pemberton thus used Newtonian force as a rate of change of motion in the yielding material.

He argued that the opposition of the yielding substance to the globes of different weight entering equal distances into the substances was reciprocally proportional to the time it took them to move through the substance. (In modern terms $mv = Ft$, where F is the Newtonian force of the globe on the yielding substance as well as the reaction of that substance to the globe. The force, F, must be assumed constant in Pemberton's analysis. The distance to which the globe penetrates the tallow would be given by $s = \frac{1}{2}vt$.) The resistance of the tallow, $(-F)$, is therefore proportional to the velocity of each globe (since $F = mv/t$). The "force" of motion of the falling globe, mv, is likewise proportional to the velocity of each globe. The globes while penetrating equal distances into the substance lost parts of their force, ($\Delta\,mv$), which bear the same proportion to the whole force, mv. Hence, even if the velocities are proportional to the square root of the weights (masses), as in the case of living forces (mv^2), they are still proportional to the "forces" (mv) with which they press into the substance and will make equal indentations in it. "And therefore upon the Theory of Resistance here supposed, when the whole Force and Motion of both these Globes is entirely lost, they will be plunged into the substance at equal depths."[92] Pemberton concluded:

But as I have asserted in the beginning of this letter that the very experiment of Polenus is not only reconcilable to the common Doctrine of Motion, as I have now demonstrated; but even that it does itself make manifest the great unreasonableness if not the absolute absurdity of Mr. Leibniz's opinion.[93]

Although Pemberton considered himself to have disproven the Leibnizian analysis of the experiment, he had merely shown another way to explain the result by using momentum considerations. He was unable to see the validity in the *vis viva* interpretation.

In Newton's anonymous postscript to the article there appeared an argument that soon became the basis for an experiment devised by another of Newton's followers, John Theophilus Desaguliers.[94] Newton supposed that fine pieces of silk or other thin substance could be stretched in parallel planes at small intervals. If a globe could strike the middle of the outermost silk sheet perpendicularly, it would lose some of its motion in breaking through it. If the resistances of the pieces of silk are all equal, then equal forces (F) will be required to break each one. But the faster the ball is moving when it hits the silk, the shorter the time required to break through it. The loss of motion ($\Delta\ mv$) of the globe is therefore proportional to the time during which the silk opposes itself to the globe. Again force, F, is being used as a rate of change of motion, rather than an instantaneous change.

Desaguliers, known for his translation of 's Gravesande's work on physics, entered the discussion in 1723 with a paper entitled "An account of some experiments made to prove that the force of moving bodies is proportionable to their velocities: (Or rather that the momentum of moving bodies is to be found by multiplying the masses into the velocities.) In answer to such who have sometime ago affirmed that force is proportionable to the square of the velocity and to those who still defend the same opinion."[95] His work reflected the Newtonian natural philosophy.

Upon the revocation of the Edict of Nantes in 1685, Desaguliers, who had been born in France, fled with his Protestant father to England.[96] He succeeded John Keill as lecturer on experimental philosophy at Oxford's Hart Hall in 1710, and eventually became intimately acquainted with Isaac Newton and the group surrounding him. Appointed curator of experiments at the Royal Society in 1713, he attained a reputation for skillful demonstration experiments which he used in public lectures and courses on Newtonian science.

Desaguliers's commitment to a natural religion in which God as creator was the "Great Architect of the Universe" and his rejection of the tendency toward atheism which could be implied as a consequence of the Leibnizian position were expressed in *The constitutions of the Freemasons*. This work was revised by James Anderson in the years 1717–22, under the influence of Desaguliers as Grand Master (c. 1720–21) of the Westminster Lodge. It stated:

> A Mason is oblig'd by his Tenure to obey the Moral law; and if he rightly understands the Art, he will never be a stupid Atheist nor an irreligious Libertine.[97]

Anderson and Desaguliers's changes conceived of a natural religion, apprehended by human reason and binding all men who rejected atheists and agnostics.

As a result of Desaguliers's influence, other members of the Royal Society joined the fraternity of Freemasons. Through him "Freemasonry emerged from its original lowly station and became a fashionable cult".[98]

Corroboration of his commitment to the Newtonian worldview can be obtained from the second edition (1719) of the initially unauthorized transcription of Desaguliers's *Lectures of experimental philosophy*, prepared by Paul Dawson.[99] In the preface Desaguliers stated that he had looked over the whole book and corrected every error because he was unwilling that those who bought it should find it in any way imperfect. The transcription of the first lecture stated:

> And tho' it is manifest to sense that there is a local Motion in Matter; yet Motion is not included in the Nature of Matter or Coeval with it. . . . And though it be wholly disputed, how Matter came by that Motion, by those who acknowledge not an Author of the Universe; yet since a Man is not the worse Naturalist for not being an Atheist; we allow that the origin of Motion in Matter, as well as of Matter itself, is from God.[100]

Although Desaguliers, in the second volume of his *Course of Experimental Philosophy* (1744), finally came to the conclusion that both measures of "force" were correct, in the 1723 paper, as a committed Newtonian, he was very opposed to the Leibnizian opinion. He based his analysis in this paper on the Newtonian accelerative force of a falling body and used the term momentum to designate the mv of the falling body, a term that had been introduced by his predecessor John Keill in 1700. Keill had used the term momentum to mean the same thing as quantity of motion: "A momentum (which is often called the quantity of motion, and also simply motion) is that Power or Force incident to moving Bodies whereby they continually tend to change their present places.[101] If a body is in motion, it has a moving force, hence a momentum; the force to stop the body or change its motion is an impressed force.

By the time Desaguliers wrote the first volume of his *Course of experimental philosophy* in 1734, he stated Newton's second law, as had Keill, in the form: "the change of motion is proportional to the moving force impressed", but deemed it necessary in defining quantity of motion to refer to Newton's definitions 2 and 8.[102] "The Quantity of motion may be increased by applying more force; for here Force and Motion mean the same thing. (See Sir Isaac Newton in the first book of his *Principia*. Def. 2 and 8)."[103] Force is thus quantity of motion by definition 2, and by definition 8 is proportional to the motion generated in a given time. Hence Desaguliers took a step in the direction of defining force as a rate of change of motion. He used the concept of the motion generated in a given time implicitly in his analysis of Poleni's experiment (1723).

He began this "Account of some experiments" which were to answer the Leibnizian argument with a summary of his view of the controversy:

> As far as I can learn Monsieur Leibniz was the first that opposed the received opinion concerning the Quantity of the Force of moving Bodies by saying that it was to be estimated by multiplying the Mass of the Bodies not by their velocity but by the square of it. But instead of shewing any Paralogism in the mathematical Demonstrations which are made up to Prove the Proposition of any mistakes in the Reasonings from the Experiment made to confirm it, he uses other Mediums to prove his assertions; and without any Regard to what others had said on that subject brings new Arguments which the Reverend and Learned Dr. Clarke has fully answered in his fifth letter to him. Messieurs John Bernoulli, Wolfius, Hermannus and others have followed and defended Mr. Leibniz's opinion and in the same manner so that what is answer to him is so to them. Polenus (Prof. at Padua) has acted after the same manner in the experimental way making some experiments to defend Mr. Leibniz's Opinion, without having shown those to be false which are made use of to prove the contrary.[104]

Desaguliers argued, as had Catalan and Papin, that the time of descent and the momenta rather than the spaces should be considered. But in this case the argument was drawn from Newtonian rather than Cartesian physics. "As the Time of the fall through a space of four Foot [s_2] is twice the Time of a fall through one Foot [s_1 where $s \propto t^2$], the Velocity in the latter Case [i.e., the four foot space] is double that of the first and consequently the Blow, [$Ft = mv$] that the Body will give, will be double."[105]

$$if \; \frac{s_1}{s_2} = \frac{1}{4}, then \frac{t_1}{t_2} = \frac{v_1}{v_2} = \frac{1}{2}$$

This defines the "Blow" as the body's momentum, mv. Desaguliers, in attempting to refute Leibniz by referring to the times of fall rather than the distances, altered the problem by describing the momentum acquired by a falling body. Leibniz's "Brevis demonstratio" had analyzed the *vis viva*, mv^2, acquired in falling, an equally valid concept.

A second paper by Desaguliers in the succeeding issue of the *Philosophical Transactions* criticized Poleni's experiment using bodies falling from different heights into soft clay.[106] According to Desaguliers, the mistake made by Poleni was in estimating the force of the stroke of the falling balls by the depth of the impression in the yielding substance. Instead one must consider "That when two Bodies (of different weights) move with equal Forces [mv] but different velocities, that which moves the swiftest must make the deepest Impression."[107]

He designed an experiment along the same lines as Newton's postscript to Pemberton's paper, in which the depth of the impression could be "stretched out" and presumably measured more precisely (Diagram 5.2). An apparatus was constructed which consisted of a horizontal base on which stood two vertical parallel boards four inches apart. Between these boards, placed as

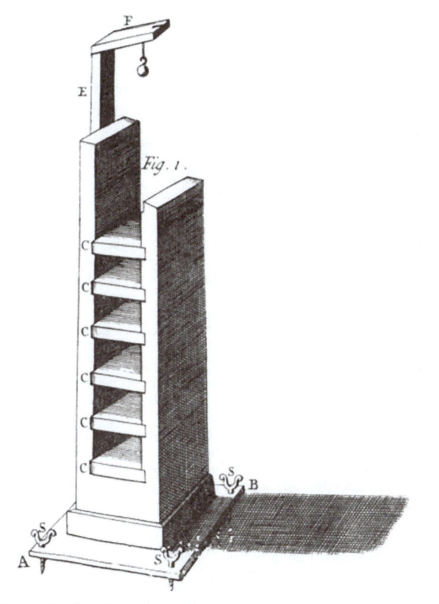

DIAGRAM 5.2 From Desaguliers, "Animadversions upon some experiments relating to the force of moving bodies," *Philosophical Transactions*, 32 (1723)

horizontal shelves, were six evenly spaced wooden frames across each of which a paper diaphragm (C) was extended. The papers were similar to the pieces of fine silk suggested by Newton in his postscript and served the same function as the soft clay of Poleni. Like Leibniz, Desaguliers used heights in the ratio 4 : 1, but, unlike Leibniz, used weights in the ratio 1 : 2, rather than 1 : 4. Thus the momenta rather than *vires vivae* were equal. From a support (F) a hollow ivory ball weighing 1½ ounces was suspended by a thread four feet above the first diaphragm. When the thread was cut, the falling ball broke through four of the paper diaphragms. [$ws = (1½)(4) = 6$]. The hollow ball was then filled with lead such that it weighed twice as much as before and was allowed to fall from a height of 1 foot. This time it broke only two diaphragms. [$ws = 3 (1) = 3$]. Since the velocities are in the ratio 2 : 1, the forces, or *mv*'s are equal:

$$\frac{m_1 v_1}{m_2 v_2} = \frac{(1\frac{1}{2})(2)}{(3)(1)} = \frac{3}{3}$$

Upon repetition of the experiment using different heights whose proportion was always 4 to 1, it was found that whenever the weight of the balls was in the ratio 1 : 2, the heavier, slower ball broke through but half the number of papers.

Although Desaguliers' language indicated no variation in the number of diaphragms broken in these trials, this was not the case when the actual experiment was reconstructed and repeated. I found that when balls of 1½ ounces and 3 ounces were allowed to fall from heights of four feet and one foot the ratio of tissue paper diaphragms broken was not always 4 : 2. In approximately one out of three trials the ball falling from four feet went through either three or five diaphragms. In this experiment much depends upon achieving a uniform tension in the diaphragms as well as the thickness of the tissue. The proper thickness of tissue must be found such that the falling ball does not stop at the first tissue or plunge through all the tissues. In my experiments this turned out to be two thickness of ordinary tissue paper. Hence if the ball falls through 4 ± 1 diaphragms, the number of papers per frame can themselves introduce an error.

Desaguliers interpreted the experiment on the basis of Newtonian mechanics. Both balls, of weights in the ratio 1 : 2 falling through heights in the ratio of 4 : 1, with velocities in the ratio of 2 : 1 hit the diaphragms with equal momenta [$mv = (1) (2) = (2) (1)$]. The *vis viva* of the lighter [$w = 1$; $mv^2 = 1 (2)^2 = 4$] is twice that of the heavier [$w = 2$; $mv^2 = 2 (1)^2 = 2$] and it breaks twice as many diaphragms, which would seem to confirm the predictions of Leibniz. However, Desaguliers argued that the time of fall ($s \propto t^2$) of the lighter, falling through $s = 4$ is double that of the heavier falling through $s = 1$. The faster-falling ball moves through the papers faster, each diaphragm having half the time to offer resistance to the faster ball. Since the force of resistance, F, varies with the time, each diaphragm offers half the resistance to the ball with the greater velocity. The faster ball will therefore break more diaphragms.

Desaguliers concluded as follows:

> Now tho' this Experiment does at first seem to confirm Polenus' Theory; yet; when duly weigh'd, it proves no such thing. For the lighter Ball does not break thro' more Papers, because it has more Force, or a greater Quantity of Motion, but because each Diaphragm has but half the time to resist the Ball that falls with a double Velocity, and therefore their Resistance being as the time, as many more of them must be broken by the swift Ball as by the slow one.[108]

Although the ball having the greater *vis viva* breaks more diaphragms and thus seems to confirm Poleni's conclusion that it will make a deeper impression, Desaguliers interpreted the experiment on the basis of momentum: if mv is the correct measure, and if the mv of two falling bodies are equal, the depth of the impressions or the number of diaphragms broken are unequal. Therefore the depth of the impression cannot be used as a measure of the body's force.

Here, then, the problem is one of definition. If force is defined as mv^2 (Leibniz) then the depth of the impressions are equal for equal forces because mv^2 depends on the height. But if mv is the measure of motion (Desaguliers) then for equal mv the impressions are not equal.

A third member of the Newtonian group, John Eames, tutor in theology, science, and classics, contributed to the controversy in 1726. Through the friendship and influence of Newton, he had been elected to the Royal Society and was engaged in preparing an abridgement of its *Philosophical Transactions*. His theological writings have all been lost, but we know that he was trained for the dissenting ministry in 1696, though never ordained.[109] He was the only layman who held a theological chair in the non-conformist Fund Academy in Moorfields.

In 1735 he joined the liberal divines Jeremiah Hunt and Samuel Chandler in a debate with Roman Catholic priests. Both Hunt and Chandler were non-conformist moderate Calvinist dissenters.[110] These facts would indicate that the three men held theological positions supporting the primacy of God's will and the manifestation of his providential care in the world. There would be a strong tendency to reject any intellectualist position which reduced God's role to that of a mere creator.

In his "Remark upon the New Opinion Relating to the Force of Moving Bodies", Eames reiterated the conclusions of Pemberton (1722) and Desaguliers (1723) that the proper use of an experiment such as Poleni's was to discover the laws of resistance which soft or yielding substances make to bodies moving in them and not to discover the "force" itself of the moving bodies.[111] Here the resistance was equivalent to the Newtonian impressed force, F. The latest experiments made on soft and yielding substances, said Eames, are "a little complicated and improper for (their) purpose." To discover the "forces" by which bodies move, some simple experiments are "more fit to determine the matter." Eames's statement was an attempt to use Newton's third law to interpret the free-fall experiment as an action-reaction problem in which the resistance of the substance is the reaction to the Newtonian force, F, impressed on the clay by the falling body. Hence "force" means mv, and resistance is equivalent to F. His paper thus represented another attempt to strengthen the Newtonian scheme by showing that its concepts could adequately explain problems or experiments offered by competing systems of natural philosophy.

Samuel Clarke formed a fourth member of the group of intimate and devoted acquaintances surrounding Isaac Newton in old age, who were determined to apply the Newtonian conceptual scheme to all possible physical problems. In comparison to the foregoing men, we see in Clarke's contributions the most intense loyalty and the strongest imprinting of the Newtonian worldview. It was said that Clarke as a young university student of 22 in 1697 knew "so much about those sublime discoveries (of Sir Isaac Newton) which then were almost a secret to all but a few mathematicians" that it was most amazing.[112] He was then engaged in a translation of the Cartesian Jacques Rohault's *System of Natural Philosophy* which he used as a vehicle to explain Newtonian ideas.[113]

His contribution of 1728 to the controversy appearing after the death of both Newton and Leibniz was one of the bitterest attacks the controversy produced.[114] His fanatical devotion to Newton led him to make outrageous insults to those who opposed Newtonian ideas. An interesting illustration of this purely polemical aspect of the controversy is provided by the following statement from the pen of Dr. Clarke (1728):

It has often been observed in *general* that Learning does not give men Understanding; and that the absurdest things in the world have been asserted and maintained by persons whose education and studies should seem to have furnished them with the greatest extent of Science.

   That knowledge in many *languages* and *Terms* of *Art* and in the History of *Opinions* and *Romantick* Hypotheses of Philosophers, should sometimes be of no effect in correcting Man's *Judgment*, is not so much to be wondered at. But that in *Mathematicks* themselves, which are a *real Science*, and founded in the *Necessary Nature* of *Things*; men of very great abilities in abstract computations, when they come to apply those computations to the *Nature* of *Things*, should persist in maintaining the most palpable absurdities, and in refusing to see some of the most evident and obvious truths; is very strange.

An extraordinary instance of this, we have had of late years in very eminent Mathematicians, Mr. *Leibniz*, Mr. *Herman*, Mr. *'s Gravesande*, and Mr. *Bernoulli*; (who in order to raise a *Dust* of Opposition against Sir *Isaac Newton's* philosophy, the glory of which is the *application* of *abstract Mathematics* to the real *phenomena* of *Nature*,) have for some years insisted with great Eagerness, upon a principle which subverts all Science, and which may easily be made to appear . . . to be contrary to the *necessary and essential Nature of Things*.

What they contend for is, That the *Force* of a *Body in Motion* is proportional, not to its Velocity, but to the Square of its Velocity.

The Absurdity of which Notion I shall first make appear and then shew what it is that had led these gentlemen into Error.[115]

Clarke's free-fall arguments were taken directly from Newton, who had chosen to remain in the background of the controversy.[116] The arguments in his "Fifth Reply" in the correspondence of 1716 with Leibniz were very close to those made in his later 1728 "Letter to Mr. Benjamin Hoadly". Clarke presented four main refutations of *vis viva* drawn from the free-fall case. The first argument attacked Leibniz' concept of "force" and *monads* from a philosophical viewpoint. The second presented a Newtonian interpretation of the free fall experiments of 's Gravesande and Poleni. The third utilized the concept of gravitational force. The final argument was based on Newton's accelerative concept of "force" applied to bodies projected upwards.

1. Clarke disagreed with the philosophical basis behind Leibniz's concept of "force". He considered the question of what could possibly produce the "force" of motion of a falling body if this "force" was measured by mv^2, since he did not agree with Leibniz that living force was an essential property of monads. He argued that "In the Nature of Things . . . every Effect must necessarily be proportionate to the cause of that Effect; that is to the Action of the Cause of the Power exerted at the Time when the Effect is produced. To suppose any Effect proportional to the Square or Cube of its Cause, is to suppose that an Effect arises partly from its Cause and partly from Nothing."[117]

With regard to a body in motion, Clarke believed that the portion of the force arising from the quantity of matter as its cause is necessarily proportional to its quantity of matter, and the force arising from the velocity is proportional to its velocity. "If the *Forces* were as the *Square* of the velocity, all that *part* of the *Force* which was *above* the (simple) *Proportion* of the *Velocity* would arise either out of *Nothing* or (according to Mr. Leibniz's Philosophy) out of some *living soul* essentially belonging to every Particle of Matter.[118] This pointed up the fundamental differences between the philosophical interpretations of "force" in the dynamics of Newton and Leibniz. For Leibniz "force" was a substance, an inherent internal principle of matter, a tendency or striving toward motion. For Newton and his followers impressed forces were external, acted to change a body's state of rest or uniform motion and afterwards no longer remained in the body.

2. In his 1729 paper, Clarke answered the experimental arguments of Poleni and 's Gravesande:

When a Body projected with a double Velocity, enters deeper into snow or soft clay or into a heap of springy or elastic parts, than in proportion to its Velocity; t'is not because the Force is more proportional to the Velocity; but because the Depth it penetrates into a soft Medium, arises partly from the Degree of the Force or Velocity, and partly from the Time wherein the Force operates before it be spent [$s = \frac{1}{2} vt$].[119]

Like Pemberton, Desaguliers, and Eames, Clarke interpreted the fall of bodies through soft substances in terms of the duration of the motion through them. The impression can be explained by considering the momentum, dependent on the velocity, with which the body hits the soft clay. The Newtonian force impressed on the clay is to be measured by this momentum in proportion to the time during which it acts while moving through the clay.

3. Clarke's third argument, taken directly from Newton, was based on the concept of gravitational force or weight and appeared in the "Fifth Reply" of his correspondence with Leibniz.[120] In the case of a single falling, accelerating body the uniform action of gravity generates equal velocities in equal times hence equal amounts of momentum in equal times. But in the case of *vis viva* the force is measured by the space. In the first part of a series of equal times, the body will gain one part of *vis viva*, ($v_1^2 = 1$). During the second moment it gains three parts of *vis viva*, ($v_2^2 - v_1^2 = 4-1 = 3$); in the third moment it gains five parts, ($v_3^2 - v_2^2 = 9-4 = 5$), in the fourth it gains seven parts ($v_4^2 - v_3^2 = 16-9 = 7$), etc. So unequal increments of *vis viva* are added, depending on the velocity the body has at the beginning of each instant. Newton and Clarke argued that the gravitational force, hence the body's weight which produces the motion would have to vary to produce this result. The force of gravity:

will be proportional to the time and to the velocity acquired. And by Consequence in the Beginning of the Time it [the action of gravity] will be none at
all and so the body for want of gravity [weight] will not fall down. And by the
same way of arguing when a body is thrown upwards its gravity will decrease
as its velocity decreases and cease when the body ceases to ascend, and then for
want of gravity, it will rest in the Air, and fall down no more. So full of absurdities is the Notion of the Learned Author in this particular.[121]

The *vis viva* hypothesis thus implied to Clarke that the body's weight which
produced its force of motion in free fall would increase, and this was clearly
absurd. Near the surface of the earth, where gravity can be assumed uniform,
$F = mg = mv/t$, hence the body's weight does not vary. But $mg \neq mv^2$ since on
such a hypothesis the weight would vary in equal increments of time.

$$F = \frac{mv}{t} = \frac{1(1)}{1} = \frac{1(2)}{2} = \frac{1(3)}{3} = \frac{1(4)}{4}; \text{or} 1 = 1 = 1 = 1$$

$$F = mg \neq \frac{mv^2}{t}; \frac{1(1)^2}{1} \neq \frac{1(2)^2}{2} \neq \frac{1(3)^2}{3} \neq \frac{1(4)^2}{4}; \text{or} 1 \neq 2 \neq 3 \neq 4$$

4. In a fourth argument in the 1729 "Letter to Hoadly" Clarke related the time
    of fall to the concept of "force", mv. Clarke discussed the inverse prob-
    lem of throwing bodies upward until they came to rest under the action
    of gravity. He cited the importance of considering the time by saying that
    the space described by a body in motion is not as the "force" alone but as
    the "force" and the time taken together.[122] "A body thrown upwards with
    double force [$2mv$] will be carried *four times* as high, before its motion be
    stopped by the uniform Resistance of Gravity; because the *double Force*
    will carry it *twice as high* in the same Time and moreover require *twice
    the Time* for the uniform Resistance to destroy the Motion."[123] That is, if
    a body is thrown upward with velocity v rising to height s in time t, then
    when the "force", mv, is doubled, $v = 2$, and $t = 2$, since $v \propto t$; but because
    $s \propto t^2$, when $t = 2$, s will equal 4, i.e., "four times as high".

Samuel Clarke's analysis of the problem of free fall echoed that of Newton
and his other followers. The scientific bureaucracy which had formed around
Isaac Newton was epitomized by Clarke's devotion to and his dependence
on Newton's ideas, notes, and manuscript drafts. The Newtonians, however,
were a far more cohesive group than the Leibnizians, at least until Newton's death in 1727. The free-fall experiments which formed the basis of the
debates between the two groups were discussed by many, but repeated by

hardly anyone. Without evaluating the inherent adequacy of the experiments for establishing the conclusions drawn, the followers saw in them support for their prior commitments. The repetition of the experiments was not the method by which converts to either system were produced.

CONCLUSION

In the preceding analysis I have tried to show how intellectual and metaphysical positions taken by scientists can provide emotional psychological commitments which determine supposedly "objective" analyses of elements as fundamental to science as experiments. Strong loyalties on the part of scientists to systems of nature prevented communication from taking place among adherents to opposing philosophies. Experiments have often been held to be the basis for objectivity and consensus among scientists. Yet the same experiment can be interpreted in a number of equally valid ways depending on the scientific metaphysics within which it is analyzed. Observers can easily be convinced that what they are seeing verifies a certain interpretation of nature.

It is commonly taught that all sides of a problem must be analyzed objectively before a conclusion is made, an opinion is formed, or a position taken, in accordance with the so-called scientific method. But because of the emotional commitments of social groups to certain views of nature, such objectivity is rarely, if ever possible.

The previous study has shown that instead of communicating, each group used the same data to strengthen its own analysis of nature. In the 1720s two strong opposing schemes of knowledge developed simultaneously, each using the other in its process of self-definition. It was not until the 1740s that integrations between the two systems of nature began to occur, as a few natural philosophers recognized the validity of both interpretations of "force". Yet the dichotomies between the underlying views of nature remained unresolved. Processes which contributed to the partial resolution of the *vis viva* controversy will be analyzed in a future paper. (See this book, Ch. 6)

For the present, it may be suggested that the previous analysis of the Leibnizian-Newtonian debates may be useful in interpreting other controversies which have occurred in the history of science. Furthermore, in the social and political ferment of the modern crisis over nature, it can be seen that individuals develop loyalties to organizations holding mechanistic or organic views of nature, both legacies of the Newtonian and Leibnizian philosophies. The imprinting of these contradictory philosophies causes the members of social groups to interpret data and experiments from within their own perspective. Because of socio-psychological considerations such as those developed in section 1 above, objective analysis of and communication between these deeply divergent worldviews may not be possible.

NOTES

* From Carolyn [Merchant] Iltis, "The Leibnizian-Newtonian Debates: Natural Philosophy and Social Psychology," British Journal for the History of Science 6, no. 4 (Dec. 1973): 343–377 © Cambridge University Press, used by permission. Thanks expressed to Peter Heimann, David Kubrin, and Charles Weiner. Repetitions of the experiments of Poleni, 's Gravesande, and Desaguliers were presented to the H.M. Evans History of Science Dinner Club, Berkeley, California, May 1975.

1. This paper forms one of a series of discussions by myself and others concerning various aspects of the *vis viva* (living force) controversy over the measure of the "force" of a body in motion. Carolyn [Merchant] Iltis, "Leibniz and the *Vis Viva* Controversy," *Isis* 62, no. 1 (Spring 1971): 25–35; Carolyn [Merchant] Iltis, "The Decline of Cartesianism in Mechanics: The Leibnizian-Cartesian Debates," *Isis* 64, no. 3 (Fall 1973): 356–73; Carolyn [Merchant] Iltis, "D'Alembert and the *Vis Viva* Controversy," *Studies in History and Philosophy of Science* 1, no. 2 (August 1970): 135–44. Thomas Hankins, "Eighteenth Century Attempts to Resolve the *Vis Viva* Controversy," *Isis* 56 no. 3 (Fall 1965): 281–97. Lawrence L. Laudan, "The *Vis Viva* Controversy, a Post-Mortem," *Isis* 59, no. 2 (Summer 1968): 131–43. On Cartesianism see also Richard A. Watson, *The Downfall of Cartesianism 1673–1712: A Study of Epistemological Issues in Late 17th Century Cartesianism* (The Hague: Martinus Nijhoff, 1966).

2. Samuel Clarke, *A Collection of Papers Which Passed between the Late Learned Mr. Leibniz and Dr. Clarke* (London, 1717).

3. William Whewell, *A History of the Inductive Sciences*, 3rd ed. (New York, 1872), vol. 1, p. 361: "Finally d'Alembert in 1743 declared it to be, as it truly was, a mere question of words," Jean d'Alembert, *Traité de Dynamique*, 1st ed. (Paris, 1743), p. xxi: "The entire question cannot consist in more than a very futile metaphysical discussion or in a dispute of words unworthy of still occupying philosophers." William 's Gravesande, "Remarques sur la Force des Corps," *Journal Littéraire de La Haye* 13 (1729), Pt. 1: 196: "I will pass to impact where it will be seen that what was at first a dispute over words becomes a dispute on the thing itself." Max Jammer, *Concepts of Force* (Cambridge, MA: Harvard University Press, 1957), p. 165: "Without going into details and discussing the various arguments of the participants in this discussion, it may be stated that it was a mere battle of words, since the disputants discussed different concepts under the same name."

4. On the concept of a Newtonian group see Frank Manuel, *A Portrait of Sir Isaac Newton* (Cambridge, MA: Harvard University Press, 1968), Ch. 13; and Walter George Hiscock, *David Gregory, Isaac Newton, and Their Circle* (Oxford: Oxford University Press, 1937).

5. For an account of the psychological dynamics of social groups see Daniel Katz and Robert L. Kahn, *The Social Psychology of Organizations* (New York: Wiley, 1966), esp. pp. 233–8.

6. Richard S. Westfall, *Force in Newton's Physics* (London: Macdonald, 1971), p. 283.

7. On the voluntarist background to Boyle's philosophy, see James E. McGuire, "Boyle's Conception of Nature," *Journal of the History of Ideas* 33 (1972): 523–42.

8. Gottfried Wilhelm Leibniz, *Philosophical Papers and Letters*, ed. Leroy E. Loemker, 2 vols. (Chicago: Chicago Univeristy Press, 1956), vol. 2, p. 1096.

9. Loemker, Ibid., p. 1098. See also David Kubrin, "Newton and the Cyclical Cosmos: Providence and the Mechanical Philosophy," *Journal of the History of Ideas* 28 (1967): 326–46.

10. Loemker, vol. 2, p. 1099.

11. Ibid., p. 1100.

12. Ibid., p. 1102.

13. Isaac Newton, *Opticks*, (based on the 4th ed., London, 1730; New York: Dover Publications, 1952), p. 400.

14. James E. McGuire, "Force, Active Principles, and Newton's Invisible Realm," *Ambix* 15 (1968): 154–208. P. M. Heimann, "Nature Is a Perpetual Worker," *Ambix* 20 (1973): 1–25.

15. Loemker, op. cit. (8), vol. 2, p. 1045. The first published version of the "Monadology" appeared in German translation in 1720.

16. Ibid., p. 1056. This passage bears striking resemblance to Far Eastern views of the universe as an organic whole whose parts are interrelated. Although the purpose of this paper is to place Leibniz's view of nature within a Western intellectual tradition, it should be pointed out that Leibniz was in close contact with Jesuit missionaries bringing back ideas and texts from China to Western Europe (see Loemker, Ibid., vol. 1, p. 11). Joseph Needham, *Science and Civilization in China*, 7 vols. (Cambridge, England: Cambridge University Press, 1956), vol. 2, pp. 291–2, 498–500, has suggested a strong influence of Chinese philosophical thought on Leibniz: "Against the Cartesian view of the world as a vast machine, Leibniz proposed the alternative view of it as a vast living organism, every part of which was also an organism. This picture was finally presented (in 1714 at the very end of his life) in the short but brilliant treatise posthumously published, the "Monadology." The hierarchy or monads and their "pre-established harmony" resembled the innumerable individual manifestations of the Neo-Confucian Li in every pattern and organism. Each monad mirrored the universe like the nodes of Indra's Net" (499).

17. Frances A. Yates, "The Hermetic Tradition in Renaissance Science," in Charles S. Singleton, ed., *Art, Science, and History in the Renaissance* (Baltimore: Johns Hopkins Press, 1968); Frances A. Yates, *Giordano Bruno and the Hermetic Tradition* (Chicago: University of Chicago Press, 1964). Allen Debus, *The English Paracelsians* (London: Oldbourne, 1965).

18. Walter Pagel, "The Religious and Philosophical Aspects of van Helmont's Science and Medicine," *Bulletin of the History of Medicine*, supp. no. 2 (1944): 1–43; Walter Pagel, *Paracelsus :An Introduction to Philosophical Medicine in the Era of the Renaissance* (New York: Karger, 1958), pp. 36, 108.

19. James E. McGuire and Piyo M. Rattansi, "Newton and the 'Pipes of Pan'," *Notes and Records of the Royal Society of London* 21 (1966): 108–43; Piyo M. Rattansi, "Newton's Alchemical Studies," in Allen G. Debus, ed., *Science, Medicine and Society: Essays to Honor Walter Pagel* (New York, 1972), pp. 167–82; and Richard S. Westfall, "Newton and the Hermetic Tradition," in Allen G. Debus, ed., *Science, Medicine and Society: Essays to Honor Walter Pagel* (New York, 1972), pp. 183–98.

20. Paracelsus, *Hermetic and Alchemical Writings*, ed. A. E. Waite, 2 vols. (London, 1894), vol. 2, pp. 249–81.

21. Ibid., p. 263.

22. Ibid., p. 266.

23. Loemker, op. cit. (8), vol. 2, p. 1047.

24. Paracelsus, op. cit. (20), vol. 2, p. 270.

25. Ibid., p. 264.

26. Loemker, op. cit. (8), vol. 2, p. 1044.

27. Paracelsus, op. cit. (20), vol. 2, p. 267.

28. Ibid., p. 266.

29. Ibid., p. 271.

30. Ibid., p. 268.

31. Loemker, op. cit. (8), vol. 2, p. 1053.

32. Paracelsus, op. cit. (20), vol. 2, p. 268.

33. Loemker, op. cit. (8), vol. 2, p. 1053.

34. Ibid., pp. 1054–55.

35. Pagel, *Paracelsus*, op, cit. (18), p. 38.

36. Loemker, op. cit. (8), vol. 2, pp. 816, 901.

37. Pagel, "Religious Aspects," op. cit. (18), p. 34.

38. McGuire and Rattansi, op. cit. (19), p. 119.

39. Quoted in Rattansi, "Newton's Alchemical Studies," op. cit. (19), p. 174.

40. Walter Pagel, "Religious Motives in the Medical Biology of the XVIIth Century," *Bulletin of the Institute of the History of Medicine* 3 (1935): 270.

41. Pagel, "Religious attitudes," op. cit. (18), p. 33.

42. Alexandre Koyré, *From the Closed World to the Infinite Universe* (New York: Harper and Row, 1958), p. 128.
43. Westfall, op. cit. (19), pp. 186–7.
44. Loemker, op. cit. (8), vol. 2, p. 1096.
45. Newton, *Opticks*, op. cit. (13), pp. 397–9.
46. Loemker, op. cit. (8), vol. 2, p. 1099.
47. James E. McGuire and P. M. Rattansi, op. cit. (19), p. 125, McGuire, op. cit. (14), pp. 194–7; J. E. McGuire, "Atoms and the 'analogy of nature'," *Studies in History and Philosophy of Science* 1 (1970): 4–6.
48. Loemker, op. cit. (8), vol. 2, p. 1131.
49. Ibid., pp. 1161–2.
50. Clarke, op. cit. (2), p. 111, sec. 99.
51. Ibid., footnote to sec. 99, pp. 111–12.
52. Gottfried Wilhelm Leibniz, "Brevis Demonstratio Erroris Memorabilis Cartesii et Aliorum circa Legem naturalem, secundum quam volunt a Deo eandem semper Quantitatem Motus conservari; qua et in re mechanica abutuntur," *Acta Eruditorum* (1686): 161–3. Translation in Loemker, op. cit. (8), vol. 2, pp. 445–63.
53. Johannis Marchionis Poleni, *De Castellis per quae derivantur fluviorum latera convergentia* (Padua, 1718), pp. 47–54. The title was also a play on the name of Benedetto Castelli.
54. Ibid., pp. 45–6.
55. Ibid., pp. 56–7. The above translation of Poleni's experiment made from the Latin by J. T. Desaguliers appeared as "Animadversions Upon Some Experiments Relating to the Force of Moving Bodies; with Two Experiments on the Same Subject," *Philosophical Transactions of the Royal Society* 32 (1723): 285–6.
56. Isaac Newton, *Mathematical Principles of Natural Philosophy*, trans. Andrew Motte and Florian Montucla (Berkeley, CA: University of California Press, 1960), pp. 22–3.
57. Poleni, op. cit. (53), p. 57, sec. 119.
58. Giovanni Poleni, *Epistolarum mathematicarum fasciculus* (Padua, 1729), p. 114. Excerpts in Giovanni Poleni, "Recueil de Lettres sur divers Sujets de mathématique, second Extrait," *Journal Historique de la République des Lettres* (March/April, 1733): 220–9.
59. William 's Gravesande, *Mathematical Elements of Natural Philosophy*, trans. J. T. Desaguliers, 5th ed. (London, 1737), pp. ix–x.
60. Ibid., pp. xi, xiv.
61. Jean Allemand, "Histoire de la vie et des ouvrages de M 's Gravesande," in William 's Gravesande, ed., *Oeuvres philosophiques et mathématiques* (Amsterdam, 1774), vol. 1, pp. xiv–xv.
62. William 's Gravesande, "Essai d'une nouvelle théorie sur le choc des corps," *Journal Litteraire, de La Haye* 12 (1722): 1–54 and supplement, pp. 190–7.
63. Ibid., pp. 2, 3. Italics added.
64. Ibid., p. 190.
65. Ibid.
66. Ibid., pp. 21–2.
67. Ibid., pp. 408–11.
68. Ibid., pp. 31–8. For inelastic collisions 's Gravesande derived an expression which said that the lost force was proportional to the square of the relative velocity multiplied by the product of the masses, divided by the sum of the masses: $F \propto ABdd/A+B$ (p. 38).
69. Ibid., pp. 47–52.
70. Ibid., pp. 19–20.
71. William 's Gravesande, "Remarques sur la Force des Corps en Mouvement et sur Choc; précédées de quelques Réflexions sur la Maniere d'Ecrire, de Monsieur le Docteur Samuel Clarke," *Journal Litteraire, de La Haye* 13 (1729): Pt. 1: 189–97 and Pt. 2, 407–32.
72. Ibid., pp. 407–9.
73. Ibid., p. 413.

74. Ibid., pp. 413–14.
75. Ibid., p. 417.
76. 's Gravesande, "Introduction a la Philosophie," in *Oeuvres*, op. cit. (61), vol. 2, p. 179.
77. Ibid., p. 178.
78. Ibid., p. 179.
79. Ibid.
80. Ibid., vol. 2, pp. 2, 3.
81. John Theophilus Desaguliers, "An Account of Some Experiments Made to Prove That the Force of Moving Bodies Is Proportionable to Their Velocities," *Philosophical Transactions* 32 (1723): 269–79.
82. Newton, *Mathematical Principles*, op. cit. (56), p. 4.
83. J. Bernard Cohen, "Newton's Second Law and the Concept of Force in the *Principia*," *Texas Quarterly* 10 (1967): 127–57.
84. James Wilson, *A Course of Chemistry, Formerly Given by the Late and Learned Dr. Henry Pemberton* (London, 1771), preface, "A Biographical Sketch of Pemberton's Life," pp. iii–xxv.
85. Ibid., p. xiii. Evidence for Newton's anonymous postscript was first given in Henry Pemberton, *A View of Sir Isaac Newton's Philosophy* (London, 1728), preface.
86. Henry Pemberton, "A letter to Dr. Mead. . . Concerning an Experiment, Whereby It Has Been Attempted to Shew the Falsity of the Common Opinion in Relation to the Force of Bodies in Motion," *Philosophical Transactions* 32 (1722): 57–66.
87. Quoted in Kubrin, op. cit. (9), p. 328.
88. Ibid., p. 329.
89. Pemberton, op. cit. (85), p. 34.
90. Ibid. (86), p. 57.
91. Ibid.
92. Ibid., p. 60.
93. Ibid., p. 62.
94. Ibid., p. 66.
95. Desaguliers, op. cit. (81).
96. Wilfred Reginald Hurst, *An Outline of the Career of John Theophilus Desaguliers* (London: Edson, 1928).
97. "Freemasonry," *Encyclopedia Britannica* (Chicago, 1954), vol. 9, p. 735.
98. Alfred Rupert Hall, "Desaguliers," in Charles Gillispie, ed., *Dictionary of Scientific Biography*, 8 vols. (New York: Charles Scribner, 1971), vol. 4, p. 43.
99. John Theophilus Desaguliers, *Lectures of Experimental Philosophy*, 2nd ed. (London, 1789).
100. Ibid., pp. 7, 8.
101. John Keill, *An Introduction to Natural Philosophy*, 4th ed., trans. from 3rd Latin ed. (London, 1745), p. 84.
102. John Theophilus Desaguliers, *A Course of Experimental Philosophy*, 2 vols. (London, 1734), vol. 1, pp. 317, 63.
103. Ibid., pp. 43, 63.
104. Desaguliers, "An Account of Some Experiments. . . ," op. cit. (81), pp. 269–71.
105. Ibid., p. 272. In this paper Desaguliers also described his repetition of 's Gravesande's initial collision experiments from the *Mathematical Elements of Natural Philosophy* as confirmation that the "congress of elastic bodies" shows that the "momentum of bodies is in proportion to the mass multiplied into the velocity. . . as demonstrated by Isaac Newton in his *Principia*," ibid., pp. 275–8.
106. John Theophilus Desaguliers, "Animadversions Upon Some Experiments Relating to the Force of Moving Bodies; with Two New Experiments on the Same Subject," *Philosophical Transactions* 32 (1723): 285–90.
107. Ibid., p. 286.
108. Ibid., p. 288.

109. "John Eames," in *Dictionary of National Biography*, ed. Leslie Stephen and Sidney Lee, 63 vols. (London: Smith Elder, and Co., 1917), vol. 6, p. 313.
110. "Samuel Chandler," ibid., vol. 4, p. 42, and "Jeremiah Hunt," ibid., vol. 10, p. 274.
111. John Eames, "A Remark upon the New Opinion Relating to the Forces of Moving Bodies, in the Case of the Collision of Non-Elastic Bodies," *Philosophical Transactions* 34 (1726): 183–7. In this paper Eames also showed the *vires vivae* of non-elastic colliding bodies were not the same before and after the collision. A second paper by Eames in the same issue was a discussion of a proof by John Bernoulli based on the composition and resolution of forces showing that forces are as the squares of the velocities; see John Eames, "Remarks upon a Supposed Demonstration, That the Moving Forces of the Same Body Are Not as the Velocities, but as the Squares of the Velocities," *Philosophical Transactions*, 34 (1726): 188–91.
112. William Whiston, *Historical Memoirs of the Life of Dr Samuel Clarke* (London, 1730), pp. 5–7.
113. Jacques Rohault, *System of Natural Philosophy, Illustrated with Dr. Samuel Clarke's Notes Taken Mostly Out of Sir Isaac Newton's Philosophy* (London, 1733).
114. Samuel Clarke, "A Letter from the Rev. Dr. Samuel Clarke to Mr. Benjamin Hoadly, F.S.R. Occasion'd by the Present Controversy among Mathematicians, Concerning the Proportion of Velocity and Force in Bodies in Motion," *Philosophical Transactions* 35 (1728): 381–9.
115. Ibid., pp. 381–2. Clarke's italics.
116. Alexandre Koyré and Ierome Bernard Cohen, "Newton and the Leibniz-Clarke Correspondence," *Archives Internationales d'Histoire des Sciences* 15 (1962): 63–126.
117. Clarke, op. cit. (114), p. 383.
118. Ibid., pp. 383–4.
119. Ibid., p. 387.
120. Clarke, "Fifth reply," *Leibniz-Clarke Correspondence*, op. cit. (2), pp. 338–9, footnote.
121. Ibid. For comparison see the following two fragments written by Newton and quoted in Koyré and Cohen, op. cit. (116), p. 118; inserts are Koyré's and Cohen's.

"And upon these rules of ascending and descending, Galileo demonstrated that projections would, in spaces void of resistance, describe Parabolas. And all Mathematicians (not excepting Mr. Leibniz himself) unanimously agree that he was in the right. And yet Mr. Leibniz would have us measure the force imprest, not by the velocity generated to which it is proportional, but by the space of ascent to which it is not proportional."

In a second fragment Newton wrote (Ibid., p. 119):

"The [weight or] gravity of the body which by its action impresses these impulsive forces upon the body acts with three times more force in the second part of [the] time than in the first and with five times more force in the third part of the time than in the first and with seven times more force in the fourth part of the time than in the first and so on. Which is as much as to say that the falling body grows heavier and heavier as it falls, and becomes three times heavier in the [middle of the] second part of the time than in the [middle of the] first and so on. Or that the weight of the body is proportional to the time of its falling. And by consequence that in the beginning of the first part of the time the body hath no weight at all. Which is contrary to the hypothesis of uniform gravity and to experience itself."
122. Clarke, op. cit. (114), p. 384.
123. Ibid., p. 385.

FIGURE 6.1 Jean-Baptiste le Rond d'Alembert (1717–1783). French mathematician, physicist, and philosopher.

Source: Portrait by Maurice Quentin de la Tour (1705–1788), Welcome Library, London, Creative Commons.

6

D'ALEMBERT*

The usual date cited for the conclusion of the controversy over the measure of force is 1743, the year of publication of Jean d'Alembert's *Traité de Dynamique*.[1] The controversy, however, lingered on for many years after this date. A study by L. L. Laudan has documented its existence through the remainder of the eighteenth century.[2] This and other articles have questioned the priority of d'Alembert's solution of the controversy.[3] However, none of these analyses has pointed out that there are significant differences between d'Alembert's discussions of the controversy in the first edition of the *Traité de Dynamique* of 1743 and in the revised second edition of 1758. The crucial argument that *vis viva* is the measure of a force acting through a distance while momentum is the measure of a force acting through a time was not given until 1758. As Pierre Costabel has shown, this argument had already been presented by Roger Boscovich in 1745.[4] The 1743 edition of the *Traité* goes only as far as distinguishing dead from living forces and characterizing the controversy as a dispute over words. As Thomas Hankins has pointed out, 's Gravesande called it a verbal debate as early as 1729.[5] The intention of this paper is to discuss the differences between the two editions of d'Alembert's *Traité* as regards the controversy over living force.

The first edition of 1743 accepts two valid measures of force: (a) the measure mdv for the case of equilibrium (i.e., dead force), which d'Alembert equates misleadingly with quantity of motion, and (b) the measure mv^2 (living force) for the case of retarded motion where the "number of obstacles overcome" is as the square of the velocity. Here force is defined as "a term used to express an effect:"

> Nevertheless as we have only the precise and distinct idea of the word force, in restricting this term to express an effect, I believe that the matter should be left to each to decide for himself as he wishes. The entire question cannot consist in more than a very futile metaphysical discussion or in a dispute of words unworthy of still occupying philosophers.[6]

To the second edition is added a section in which a third meaning is given to the measure of force. Here the valid measures of force are described as being (1) dead force, (2) the space traversed up to the total extinction of motion (mv^2), and (3) the space traversed uniformly in a given time (mv). Let us discuss the details of each of the two editions.

In his preface to the 1743 edition of the *Traité de Dynamique*, d'Alembert stated that he would consider the motion of a body only as the traversal of a certain space for which it uses a certain time. He rejected a discussion of the causes of motion and the inherent forces of moving bodies as being obscure, metaphysical and useless to mechanics. It was for this reason, he said, that he refused to enter into an examination of the question of living forces. Mentioning in passing the part played by Leibniz, Bernoulli, Maclaurin and a lady 'famous for her spirit' (Emilie du Châtelet), d'Alembert proposed to expose succinctly the principles necessary to resolve the question.[7]

It is not the space uniformly traversed by a body, nor the time needed to traverse it, nor the simple consideration of the abstract mass and velocity, by which force should be estimated. Force should be estimated solely by the obstacles which a body encounters and by the resistance it offers to these obstacles. The greater the obstacles it can overcome or resist, the greater is its force, provided that by "force" one does not mean something residing in the body.

One can oppose to the motion of a body three kinds of obstacle.[8] First, obstacles that can completely annihilate its motion; second, obstacles that have exactly the resistance necessary to halt its motion, annihilating it for an instant, as in the case of equilibrium; and third, obstacles that annihilate its motion little by little, as in the case of retarded motion. Since the insurmountable obstacles annihilate all motion they cannot serve to make the force known. "One must look for the measure of the force either in the case of (a) equilibrium or (b) in that of retarded motion." Concerning these two possibilities for a measure:

> Everyone agrees that there is equilibrium between two bodies, when the products of their masses by their virtual velocities, that is the velocities by which they *tend* to move, are equal. Thus in equilibrium the product of the mass by its velocity, or, what is the same thing, the quantity of motion, can represent the

force.[9] Everyone agrees also that in retarded motion, the number of obstacles overcome is as the square of the velocity. For example, a body which compresses one spring with a certain velocity can with a double velocity compress, all together or successively, not two but four springs similar to the first, nine with a triple velocity, etc.[10]

In this second case, continues d'Alembert, the force of a body is as the product of the mass by the square of the velocity. Should not then "force" mean only the effect produced in surmounting an obstacle or resisting it? Force should be "measured by the absolute quantity of the obstacles or by the sum of their resistances." Hence we have the precise and distinct idea of "force" as a term to express an effect.

In the previous quotation, d'Alembert incorrectly identifies the product of the mass and the virtual velocity with quantity of motion. In the case of equilibrium the measure of force is the product of the mass of the body and its virtual velocity, mdv.[11] This measure of force was what Leibniz had called dead force, or *vis mortua*, although he did not use the term virtual velocity or the expression mdv. For the case of moving bodies the measure of force was given by mv or quantity of motion, later called momentum. In the early years of the controversy, according to Leibniz the erroneous identification of mdv and mv was made by Cartesians such as Father Honoratius Fabri, Father Ignatius Pardies, Father Malebranche, Marcus Marci and Claude Deschales.[12] The error was also made by Abbé Catalan[13] and later by the British scientist J. T. Desaguliers.[14] D'Alembert does not make the distinction clear in the previous paragraph, but in the 1758 edition, an added section distinguishes between them. From this misleading use of the term quantity of motion may have arisen the idea that d'Alembert resolved the controversy in 1743.[15]

In summary, the 1743 edition of the *Traité* distinguishes two meanings of force. *Vis viva* is defined by the effect it can produce and is proportional to the square of the velocity. Secondly, force is defined for the case of equilibrium as the product of the mass and the virtual velocity, mdv.

D'Alembert's discussion concluded with the much quoted statement that "the question cannot consist in more than a completely futile metaphysical question, or a dispute over words unworthy of still occupying philosophers."[16] At this point in the 1758 edition of the *Traité de Dynamique*[17] are inserted what the foreword to that edition describes as "several reflections on the question of living forces," "added to the preliminary discourse." In this insert, three, rather than two, meanings of force are described.

The three cases are: (1) [dead force], where a body has a tendency to move itself with a certain velocity, but the tendency is arrested by some obstacle; (2) [quantity of motion], in which the body actually moves uniformly with this certain velocity; and (3) [living force], where the body moves with a velocity which is consumed and annihilated little by little by some cause. The effect produced in each case is different because in each, the action of the same cause is differently applied. The body in itself however, possesses nothing more in one case than the other. "In the first case, the effect is reduced to a simple tendency which is not properly a measure since no motion is produced; in the second *the effect is the space traversed uniformly in the given time* and this effect is proportional to the velocity; in the third case, *the effect is the space traversed up to the total extinction of motion*, and this effect is as the square of the velocity."[18]

The two parties, d'Alembert added in 1758, are entirely in accord over the fundamental principles of equilibrium and motion, and their solutions are in perfect agreement. Thus the question is a "dispute over words" and is "entirely futile for mechanics." Thus, although the 1743 edition of d'Alembert's *Traité* had been cited by many authors as resolving the dispute, it provided little more clarification than contrasting dead with living forces and calling the argument a "dispute over words." 's Gravesande in 1729 had also called it a dispute over words but neither he nor d'Alembert (in 1743) really defined in what way this was true.[19]

Although the 1758 edition of the *Traité* did point out that momentum could be considered as a force acting during a given time, and *vis viva* as a force acting over the space traversed, d'Alembert likewise was anticipated in this insight by Roger Boscovich. Pierre Costabel has shown that Boscovich's *De Viribus Vivis* (Rome, 1745) suggested a separate graphical representation for each of the two measures of force.[20] The *De Viribus Vivis* is a fifty-page work of difficult Latin dealing with two separate subjects involving living force. According to Costabel it shows that Boscovich possessed a very thorough understanding of the history of the quarrel before his own intervention, from Leibniz and Bernoulli to Voltaire, de Mairan and du Châtelet. Boscovich does not cite d'Alembert's *Traité de Dynamique*, but this had been published only two years earlier.[21] He did not meet d'Alembert until a visit to Paris in 1759. Nor does he mention Euler, whose *Mechanica* of 1736 contained ideas suggestive of a general treatment of mechanics. The reflections of Euler on the nature of forces did not take form until 1749–50. For comparative purposes certain aspects of Costabel's discussion will be summarized here with additional interpretations.

Employing both the ancient scholastic categories and the new mathematical methods of his time, Boscovich discussed the graphical representation of a pressure applied through a time and a force applied over a distance. *Vis activa*, for Boscovich, was the "instantaneous action" by which a pressure (*pression*) passes into action and engenders a new velocity. He said that it corresponded to Leibniz's dead force (*vis mortua*).[22] This instantaneous pressure passes to a velocity, not by multiplication of effects in the course of an instant, but only by continuous application. In the same way a line produces a surface not by its own multiplication but by its continual motion along a path. Thus a pressure is related to the velocity produced as a straight line to the surface engendered. The pressure, an active presence (*puissance*), passes into action not by multiplication of effects but by generating a two-dimensional image adequately rendered only by geometry.

Without taking a position on the definition of force, Boscovich measured the velocity acquired as a ratio composed of the pressure and its duration. A geometrical image is generated by the line representing the pressure with time as the second dimension of the diagram. The pressure is thus a function of time.[23] Interpreting this in modern terminology, the momentum mv would be represented as the integral of these instantaneous pressures (or impulses) over a time, or $\int m dv = \int p dt$.[24]

Boscovich suggested that, if the time coordinate is replaced by the space traversed and the pressure coordinate by the force which at any instant produces the velocity proportional to it, a second aspect of the phenomenon is represented. Boscovich, however, explained neither this substitution nor the introduction of the concept of force. The new term "force" must be interpreted as an entity proportional to the velocity engendered at any instant. If the pressure coordinate is changed to the force and the time coordinate to the space then the new geometrical image producing the velocity would be represented in modern notation as $\int F ds$. We would then interpret *vis viva* as $\int mv dv = \int F ds$ (where $ds = v dt$).[25] Boscovich does not bring the mass into his analysis.

Although not explicitly stated, Boscovich's analysis contains the necessary elements for distinguishing force, mv, as a time-dependent function and mv^2 as a space-dependent function. It brings together aspects of force analyzed previously by Bernoulli, Louville, and others (see Notes 24 and 25). On the question of elastic and inelastic collisions briefly discussed in his paper, Boscovich used the principle of action and reaction and its equivalent, the conservation of quantity of motion taken in an algebraic sense. In verifying the conservation of living force in the sense of Leibniz, he said that living force, being formed as it is by the square of the velocity, destroys the sign of that velocity, whereas the quantity of motion conserves all its characteristic elements. Boscovich concludes in paragraph 39 of *De Viribus Vivis* that the question of living force is a question of language and completely useless.[26] In spite of this analysis of "force," however, Boscovich believed that momentum was the true measure of force, *vis viva* being valid only as a method of calculation. In his *De Viribus Vivis* as well as in his later *Philosophiae Naturalis Theoria* (1758), he argued that there were no living forces in nature.[27]

Thus Boscovich, while providing an insight which theoretically helped to resolve the *vis viva* controversy, did not claim equal status for the two principles in treating physical problems. Since d'Alembert also preferred momentum to *vis viva*,[28] it is of interest to inquire when equal status was given to both principles by practicing scientists in the solution of mechanical problems, particularly in cases of elastic impact. A sampling of textbooks through the eighteenth and nineteenth centuries shows that most authors who treated the problem of collision employed the two principles, conservation of momentum and conservation of relative velocities.[29]

A small number of scientists in the eighteenth and early nineteenth centuries accepted the use of both momentum and *vis viva* for problems of elastic collisions. The mutual acceptance of both principles had to await the fuller understanding and development of energy relations which took place in the 1840s. The simultaneous use of both momentum and kinetic energy was advocated in textbooks at least by the 1860s.[30]

It seems, therefore, that d'Alembert had very little to do with the termination of the *vis viva* controversy either theoretically, practically, or historically. He was not the first to call it a "dispute over words." He was not the first to contrast momentum as a force acting through a time interval with *vis viva* as a force acting over the space traversed. He did not advocate the simultaneous use of momentum and *vis viva* to solve impact problems. He did not give a complete discussion of the uses of *vis viva* in solving problems relating to compressed springs and falling bodies. Nor did he deal with some of the important philosophical and theological issues regarding conservation of *vis viva* which were basic to the arguments of some participants. Finally, in the year 1743 d'Alembert did not present the argument which had heretofore been cited as resolving the controversy. The date 1743 is therefore of no significance as a terminus for the *vis viva* controversy.

NOTES

* Reprinted from Carolyn [Merchant] Iltis, "D'Alembert and the *Vis Viva* Controversy," *Studies in History and Philosophy of Science*, 1, no. 2 (1970): 135–44. Copyright 1970 Elsevier, all rights reserved. Used by permission.
1. Jean d'Alembert, *Traité de Dynamique*, 1st ed. (Paris: David l'Aîné, 1743), preface. References to the date 1743 are made in the following works: Ernst Mach, *Science of Mechanics*, 6th ed. (La Salle, IL: Open Court, 1960), p. 365; William Whewell, *History of the Inductive Sciences*, 3rd ed., 2 vols. (New York, 1872), vol. 1, p. 361; John Bernard Stallo, *The Concepts and Theories of Modern Physics* (New York: Appleton, 1884), p. 72; Jean-Etienne Montucla, *Histoire des Mathématiques*, 3 vols. (Paris, 1799–1802), vol. 3, p. 641.
2. L. L. Laudan, "The *Vis Viva* Controversy, a Post-Mortem," *Isis* 59 (1968): 131–43.
3. Thomas Hankins, "Eighteenth-Century Attempts to Resolve the Vis Viva Controversy," *Isis* 56, no. 3 (1965): 281–97; Pierre Costabel, "Le De Viribus Vives de R. Boscovich ou de la Vertu des Querrelles de Mot," *Archives Internationales d'Histoire des Sciences* 14 (1961): 54–7.
4. Costabel, op. cit. (3).
5. Hankins, op. cit. (3).

6. D'Alembert, op. cit. (1), p. xxi.

7. Ibid., pp. xvi, xvii.

8. Ibid., pp. xix, xx: "Ceci bien entendu, il est clair qu'on peut opposer au Mouvement d'un Corps trois sortes d'obstacles; on des obstacles invincibles qui anéantissent tout-a-fait son Mouvement, quel qu'il puisse être; ou des obstacles qui n'ayent précisément que la résistance néccssaire pour anéantir le Mouvement du Corps, et qui l'anéantissent dans un instant, c'est le cas de l'équilibre; ou enfin des obstacles qui anéantissent le Mouvement peu à peu, c'est le cas du Mouvement retardé. Comme les obstacles insurmontables ané-antissent également toutes metes de Mouvements, ils ne peuvent servir a faire connoître la force: ce n'est donc que dans l'équilibre, ou dans le Mouvement retardé qu'on doit en chercher la mesure. Or tout le monde convient qu'il a équilibre entre deux Corps, quand les produits de leurs masses par leurs vitesses virtuelles, c'est-à-dire par les vitesses avec lesquelles ils tendent à se mouvoir, sont égaux de part et d'autre. Donc dans l' équilibre le produit de la masse par la vitesse, ou, cc qui est la même chose, la quantité de Mouvement, peut représenter la force. Tout le monde convient aussi que dans le Mouvement retardé, le nombre des obstacles vaincus cot eomme le quarré de la vitesse; ensorte qu'un Corps qui a fermé un ressort, par exemple, avee une certaine vitesse, pourra avec une vitesse double fermer, ou tout á la fois, ou successivement, non pas deux, mais quatre ressorts semblables au premier, neuf avec une vitesse triple, et ainsi du reste. D'où les partisans des forces vives concluent que la force des Corps qui se meuvent actuellement, est en général comme le produit de la masse par le quarré de la vitesse."

9. Italics mine. The case of equilibrium was not equivalent to the quantity of motion. This was pointed out by Leibniz in 1686: "We need not wonder that in the common machines the lever, windlass, pulley, wedge, screw and the like there exists an equilibrium since the mass of one body is compensated for by the velocity of the other. . . . For in this special case the quantity of the effect or the height risen or fallen will be the same on both sides no matter to which side of the balance the motion is applied. It is therefore merely accidental here that the force can be estimated from the quantity of motion." (Gottfried Wilhelm Leibniz, "Brevis Demonstratio Erroris Memorabilis Cartesii," *Acta Eruditorum* (1686): 161–3). In a supplement to the above, written in 1695, Leibniz says "Even if some of these [i.e., the laws of the inclined plane and acceleration of falling bodies] seem reconcilable with that hypothesis which estimates power by the product of mass by velocity, this is only acciden-tally, since the two hypotheses coincide in the case of dead forces [*potentia mortuus*] in which only the beginning or end of conatuses is actualized. But in living forces, or those acting with an actually completed impetus, there arises a difference just as the example shows which I have given above in the published paper. For living power is to dead power or impetus (actual velocity) is to conatus, as a line is to a point or as a plane is to a line.' (Gottfried Wilhelm Leibniz, *Philosophical Papers and Letters*, trans. and ed. Leroy F. Loemker, 2 vols. (Chicago, 1956), vol. 1, p. 460.

10. D'Alembert, op. cit., (1), pp. xix–xx. The idea of moving balls compressing elastic springs (res-sorts) and thus surmounting an obstacle was used by Jean Bernoulli in 1727 in a paper support-ing *vis viva* submitted for a contest on the communication of motion sponsored by the Académie des Sciences (Paris). Subsequently these springs were used in the arguments of many other participants in the controversy, among them Jean Jacques de Mairan (1728), Camus (1728), Louville (1729), Abbé Deidier (1741) Madame du Châtelet (1740). For a detailed discussion of this problem see Carolyn [Merchant] Iltis, "The Controversy Over Living Force: Leibniz to d'Alembert," Doctoral Dissertation, The University of Wisconsin, Madison, 1967, 403 pp.

11. In the ease of the lever, for example, $F_1 l_1 = F_2 l_2$ or $F_1 s_1 = F_2 s_2$. But $F = mg$ and $ds = dv \cdot dt$. Thus $m_1 g dv_1 \cdot dt = m_2 g dv_2 \cdot dt_2$. For the case of the lever in equilibrium the times are equal $(dt_1 = dt_2)$ and hence $m_1 dv_1 = m_2 dv_2$, dead force. But the dv's are virtual velocities and not the actual velocities in the momentum expression mv for moving bodies. (Example mine.) The term "virtual velocity" was first used by John Bernoulli in 1717 in a letter to Varignon, dated January 26, 1717 (See Pierre Varignon, *Nouvelle mécanique ou statique* [Paris, 1725], vol. 2, p. 174; Erwin Hiebert, *Historical Roots of the Principle of Conservation of*

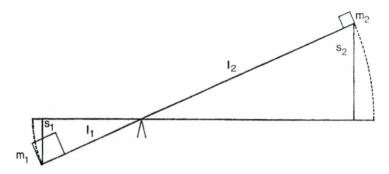

DIAGRAM 6.1 D'Alembert Diagram

Energy [Madison, WI, 1962], pp. 53, 82, 97). Then Bernoulli in his "Discours sur les Loix de la Communication du Mouvement," *Recueil des Pièces qui a Remporté les Prix de l'Académie Royale des Sciences* 2 (1727): 1–108, see p. 19, stated: "the fundamental principle of statics lies in the equilibrium of 'powers', the moments being composed of absolute forces and their virtual velocities." He argued that by extending this principle to the forces of bodies which have actual velocities, philosophers had gone too far. Here Bernoulli gave a definition of virtual velocities: "I call virtual velocities [*vitesses virtuelles*] those acquired by two or more forces taken in equilibrium when a small movement is imprinted upon them. . . . The virtual velocity is the element of velocity already acquired that each body gains or loses in an infinitely small time along its direction." For a history of the virtual velocity concept, see Hiebert, *Historical Roots*, pp. 53–6, 82–5.

12. Leibniz, "Brevis Demonstratio," op. cit. (9), p. 162.
13. Abbé Catalan, "Courte Remarque de M. l'Abbé D. C. où l'on montre à M. G. G. Leibnits le paralogisme contenu dans l'objection précédente," *Nouvelles de la republique des lettres* 8 (September 1686): 1000–5, see 1002.
14. John Theophilus Desaguliers, "An Account of Some Experiments Made to Prove That the Force of Moving Bodies Is Proportionable to Their Velocities," *Philosophical Transactions* 32 (1723): 269–79; John Theophilus Desaguliers, "Animadversions Upon Some Experiments Relating to the Force of Moving Bodies with Two New Experiments on the Same Subject," *Philosophical Transactions* 32 (1723): 285–90.
15. Although d'Alembert in 1758 distinguished *mv* and *mdv* he did not delete the misidentification in the previous quotation from the 1758 edition.
16. D'Alembert, op. cit. (1), p. xxi.
17. Jean d'Alembert, *Traité de Dynamique*, 1758 ed. (Paris: Gauthier-Villars, 1921), p. xxx. This second edition was expanded and revised by d'Alembert. The three definitions of force discussed later were added to this edition.
18. Ibid., p. xxx. My italics.
19. Jean d'Alembert, *Traité de Dynamique*, 1st ed., 1743, preface. William 's Gravesande, "Remarques sur la Force des Corps en Mouvement et sur Choc; précédées de quelques Réflexions sur la Maniere d'Ecrire, de Monsieur le Docteur Samuel Clarke," *Journal Litteraire de La Haye* 13 (1729): 989–7, 407–30, see 407–8, 432.
20. Pierre Costabel, op. cit. (3), p. 3.
21. Here Costabel recognizes that d'Alembert's own contribution to the controversy did not really occur until the 1758 edition of the *Traité*. However, he does not specify that here d'Alembert added the section to the preface concerning the difference between a force acting through a time and a force acting over a distance. He indicates rather that this was due to d'Alembert's addition of a section generalizing the principle of living force to the main body of the *Traité*. See Costabel, op. cit. (3), p. 4.

22. Costabel, op. cit. (3), p. 6. In his *Specimen Dynamicum* Leibniz said that in dead force "motion does not yet exist . . . but only a solicitation to motion." It is a pressure or a tension. Loemker, op. cit. (9), vol. 2, p. 717.

23. Costabel, op. cit. (3), pp. 6, 7.

24. In 1729 Jacques de Louville somewhat confusedly presented a definition with reference to compressed springs of what we would interpret as the impulse of a Newtonian force. He defined the force of each impulsion, f_1 communicated in an instant as the "instantaneous force." "Actual force" is the "product of the force of each impulsion by the number [i.e., the sum] of impulsions the moving body receives in equal times [or $_{t2}\int^{t1} f_t \, dt$]. To Louville this meant that mv and not mv^2 was the measure of force. Since the impulse, f_1 is equivalent to the pressure, p (and to the Newtonian force), Boscovich's analysis is similar to Louville's. Boscovich, however, also recognized the usefulness of mv^2 in calculations whereas Louville did not. (Jacque Eugène de Louville, "Sur la théorie des Mouvements varies," *Histoire de l'Académie Royale des Sciences* [1729], 154).

25. In 1727 Jean Bernoulli presented an analysis of *vis viva* in terms of balls moved by releasing compressed springs. The velocity increment is represented by the pressure of the spring, p, or dead force, and the increment of time. Thus $dv = pdt$. Since $v = dx/dt$, dt dx/v. Therefore $dv = pdx/v$ or $vdv = pdx$. The integral is $v^2/2 = \int pdx$. Bernoulli then adds the concept of mass showing that living force, mv^2, is as the square of the velocity. Since pressure and Newtonian force are equivalent, this can be interpreted as $mv^2/2 = \int Fdx$. This is essentially Boscovich's argument (Jean Bernoulli, "Discours sur les Loix de la Communication du Mouvement," *The Recueil des Pièces qui a Remporté les Prix de l'Académie Royale des Sciences* 2 [1727], pp. 1–108, separate pagination.)

26. Ibid., p. 9.

27. Roger Boscovich, *A Theory of Natural Philosophy*, trans. James M. Child, from the second edition of 1763 (London: Open Court, 1922), section 293, p. 223: "it will be sufficiently evident, both from what has already been proved as well as from what is to follow, that there is nowhere any sign of such living forces nor is this necessary. For all the phenomena of Nature depend upon motions and equilibrium, and thus from dead forces and the velocities induced by the action of such forces. For this reason, in the dissertation *De Viribus Vivis*, which was what led me to this theory thirteen years ago, I asserted that there are no living forces in Nature, and that many things which were usually brought forward to prove their existence, I explained clearly enough by velocities derived solely from forces that were not living forces." For a discussion of Boscovich's views on living force and on momentum, see Hankins, op. cit. (3), p. 291.

28. See Hankins, op. cit., p. 284.

29. The standard approach utilizing momentum and relative velocities followed the lines of Wallis's and Wren's solution to the problem in 1668. See John Wallis, "A Summary Account of the General Laws of Motion," *Philosophical Transactions* (1669): 864; John Wallis, *Mechanica sive de Motu*, 2 vols. (London, 1669–71), vol. 1, p. 660; Christopher Wren, 'Lex Naturae de Collisione Corporum,' *Philosophical Transactions of the Royal Society* 3 (1669): 867–8. Examples of textbooks using conservation of momentum and conservation of relative velocities, but not *vis viva*, are as follows: Richard Helsham, *A Course of Lectures in Natural Philosophy* (London, 1743), vol. 8, p. 68; Anonymous, *La Physique Experimentale et Raisonnée* (Paris, 1756), p. 16; Abbé Para du Phanjas, *Théorie des Etres sensibles ou Cours complet de Physique* (Paris, 1772), p. 304; Denison Olmsted, *A Compendium of Natural Philosophy* (New Haven, CT, 1833), p. 25; James Renwick, *First Principles of Natural Philosophy* (New York, 1842), 68.

30. For example see James Wylde, *The Circle of the Sciences*, 4 vols. (London, 1862–69), vol. 1, p. 745. This second approach, using both momentum and kinetic energy in the solution of elastic impact problems, had its origins in Christian Huygens's paper of 1668 "Extract d'une Lettre de M. Huygens," *Journal de sçavans* (March 18, 1669): 22-24 and Christian Huygens, "A Summary Account of the Laws of Motion," *Philosophical Transactions of the Royal Society* 4 (1669): 925–8. A general solution to the problem of impact was presented

by Leibniz in 1692. Leibniz set down three equations equivalent to conservation of relative velocities, conservation of momentum, and conservation of *vis viva*. Any two of these used simultaneously, he said, would be sufficient for elastic imparts. For inelastic impacts conservation of *vis viva* does not hold "but this loss of the total force, or this failure of the third equation does not detract from the inviolable truth of the law of the conservation of the same force in the world. For that which is absorbed by the minute parts is not absolutely lost for the total force of the concurrent bodies." (Gottfried Wilhelm Leibniz, "Essay de Dynamique sur let Loix du Mouvement," *Mathematische Schriften*, ed. C. I. Gerhardt, 9 vols. in 5 (Halle, 1860), ser. 2, vol. 2, p. 215). The manuscript containing these equations was not published until 1860 when Leibniz's works were collected and published by Gerhardt. The three equations, however, did appear in the work of Leibniz's follower Jean Bernoulli in an essay submitted to the *Academie des Sciences* in 1727. (Jean Bernoulli, "Discours sur les Loix de la Communication du Mouvement," *Recueil des Pièces qui a Remporté Prix de l'Académie Royale des Sciences* 2 (1727): 1–108; see p. 29.); L. L. Laudan, op. cit. (2), p. 137, has pointed out that Desaguliers in 1744 was convinced that 'the phaenomena of the Congress of Bodies may be equally solv'd according to the Principles of the Defenders of the new [mv^2], as well as those of the old [mv] Opinion." (Desaguliers, *Course of Experimental Philosophy*, 2 vols. (London, 1735–44), vol. 2, p. 63.) Thomas Young in a chapter "On Collision" from his book, *A Course of Lectures on Natural Philosophy and the Mechanical Arts*, 2 vols. (London, 1807), vol. 1, p. 78), admits the utility of both the momentum and energy principles, but he does not suggest their simultaneous application as the most general method of attacking elastic collision problems. In 1824, William Whewell mentioned the validity of both mv and mv^2 in his discussion of impact. See William Whewell, *Elementary Treatise on Mechanics* (Cambridge, 1824), 258.

Part III

WOMEN AND THE SCIENTIFIC REVOLUTION

As women, proclaimed Margaret Cavendish, Duchess of Newcastle, in her *Philosophical and Physical Opinions* (1655), "we are kept like birds in cages to hop up and down in our houses."[1] Indeed women who had both the education and the means to write and publish on science at the turn of the seventeenth century were relatively few. Most were members of the nobility who with the support of their husbands and mentors were able to move in learned circles that studied and discussed the "new science." These "scientific ladies" drew support from men such as Henry Cornelius Agrippa who in 1525 had written a treatise *On the Nobility and Excellency of the Female Sex* and mentors such as philosophers Ralph Cudworth, John Locke, and Gottfried Wilhelm Leibniz. In Part III on "Women and the Scientific Revolution" I discuss the contributions of three noteworthy women who contributed to early modern science.

Margaret Cavendish (1623–1673), subject of Chapter 7, was a colorful, prolific, energetic noblewoman and foundational feminist who wrote fiction, poetry, plays, and natural philosophy. The author of some twenty-three books, including her own memoirs, she gained notoriety for insisting in 1667 on being the first woman to visit the Royal Society of London and to view experiments and demonstrations staged especially for her. Incredibly, women were subsequently banned from the society for the following three centuries until 1945. In the *Grounds of Natural Philosophy* (1668), discussed here, she took the materialist stance that motion was inherent in matter and that nature was self-knowing and perceptive. A "first cause" was non-sensical because the immaterial could not have material motion. Matter might be motionless but all motion must be attended by matter. Corporeal bodies could not have incorporeal perceptions; thoughts were corporeal motions united by conjunction.

Chapter 8 analyzes the work of Anne Conway (1631–1679), whose *Principles of the Most Ancient and Modern Philosophy* (published anonymously in 1690), on the unity of matter and spirit, was a major influence on Leibniz's concept of the monad. The term monad as Conway employed it was introduced to Leibniz by Francis Mercury van Helmont who had stayed at her home for several years while trying to treat her terrible, incessant headaches and who then visited Leibniz in Hanover. As Leibniz later wrote, "my ideas approach somewhat closely the ideas of the late Countess of Conway."[2] Conway, an avid reader of philosophy and a lively conversationalist, benefitted both from her own family connections and her marriage to Edward Conway by engaging with Cambridge Platonists Henry More, Ralph Cudworth, and Joseph Glanvill. Her ideas helped to establish the vitalistic tradition in late seventeenth century philosophy, which treated the entire world as active, alive, and a unity of matter and spirit in opposition to Descartes' dualism of mind and body.

A third prominent woman who wrote during the Scientific Revolution was Gabrielle Emilie du Châtelet (1706–1749). As discussed in Chapter 9, Du Châtelet translated what is still the only existing French version of Isaac Newton's *Principia mathematica* (published in 1756). In 1740 she published the *Institutions de Physique*, meant as a textbook for her son's use, in which she featured the ideas of Newton on mechanics and Leibniz on dynamics. In the process she engaged with ideas such as God's power and free will, along with the nature of matter, space, and force, while attempting to integrate and reconcile Cartesian, Newtonian, and Leibnizian physics and philosophy.

The three chapters in Part III help to give educated women who were beginning to study and write about natural philosophy and scientific ideas at the turn of the seventeenth century some of the recognition they deserve.

NOTES

1. Margaret Cavendish, *The Philosophical and Physical Opinions* (London, 1655), preface.
2. Gottfried Wilhelm Leibniz, *Philosophische Schriften*, ed. C. I. Gerhardt, 7 vols. (Berlin: Akademie-Verlag, 1875–1890), vol. 3, p. 217.

FIGURE 7.1 Margaret Cavendish, Duchess of Newcastle (1623–1673). In portrait of Margaret and William Cavendish by Gonzales Coques, 1662.

Source: Used with permission from Staatliche Museen, Berlin. Copyright Gemäldegalerie, Berlin, Germany.

7

MARGARET CAVENDISH*

At the turn of the seventeenth century, numerous upper class "learned ladies" began studying and contributing to the "new science" by attending and discussing its advances in salons, by writing treatises, novels, and articles and by exchanging letters. This cluster of women, supported by the men of their class, contributed to the philosophy, science, and educational literature of the Scientific Revolution and enlightenment. These women and their achievements deserve more detailed study and evaluation than has been accorded them. Women with great intellectual gifts were taken seriously by philosophers such as John Locke, Ralph Cudworth, and Gottfried Wilhelm Leibniz and the writer and philosopher Voltaire. They comprized Margaret Cavendish, Duchess of Newcastle (1623–1673), subject of this chapter, Lady Anne Conway (1631–1679), who was a major influence on Leibniz's philosophy (Chapter 8), and Gabrielle Emilie du Châtelet (1706–1749), Voltaire's mistress, who was a principal expounder of Leibniz's system and translator of Newton's *Principia Mathematica* into French (Chapter 9).

WOMEN AND THE "NEW SCIENCE"

Women who were educated in the "new science" of the seventeenth century included Sophie, the Electress of Hanover; her daughter Sophia Charlotte, queen of Prussia after 1701; the latter's ward, Princess Caroline (1683–1737), later queen of Great Britain, in answer to whose questions the entire Leibniz-Clarke correspondence of 1716 was directed; and Lady Damaris Masham

(1658–1708), daughter of Ralph Cudworth (who educated her), friend and student of John Locke, and a theological writer with whom Leibniz carried on an extensive correspondence.[1] During this period, an expanding group of educated women began to participate in the philosophical and intellectual life of the period.

By the late seventeenth century, upper-class English women were noticing and reacting to the economic and educational advances men had made, while their own opportunities were by comparison significantly constricted. They argued that differences in male and female achievement stemmed not from female intellectual inferiority, but from differences in childrearing practices, educational opportunities, and social position. Hannah Wooley, writing in 1655, Bathsua Makin, writing in 1673, and Mary Astell, writing in 1694, deplored women's lack of education and advocated the study of philosophy, foreign languages, medical care, household accounts, and writing. Their ideal went far beyond the emphasis on morals, Christian virtue, chastity, and the reading of the scriptures that had characterized women's education in the Renaissance.[2]

Translations were made of Henry Cornelius Agrippa's 1525 essay *On the Nobility and the Excellency of the Female Sex*, and François Poulain de la Barre's French treatise, *The Woman as Good as the Man* (written in 1673), which argued for the equality of the sexes. Agrippa's treatise had been presented to Margaret of Austria in 1509. Although not printed until 1525, it was subsequently reprinted many times before its English translations were published in 1652 and 1670. Agrippa marshaled numerous arguments to make a case for the superiority of women over men. Eve, whose name meant life, was created last in the chain of creatures and was therefore more perfect. Her body was more beautiful, her face unspoiled by a beard. As a mother, the woman contributed more in material and intellect to the embryo than the man. A female could conceive without a man: witness the Virgin Mary. In the 1677 English translation of *The Woman as Good as the Man*," Poulain de la Barre asserted, "we have found that both Sexes are equal; that is to say, that Women are as noble, as perfect, and as capable as men." The problem is that "Women have been Subjected, and excluded from Sciences, and Employments."[3]

MARGARET CAVENDISH, DUCHESS OF NEWCASTLE

While learned ladies had always been present among the educated nobility, and women had contributed to science and mathematics from earliest times, the "scientific lady" was a product of the Scientific Revolution. Leading the way toward recognition of women as students of the new philosophy was

Margaret Cavendish, Duchess of Newcastle (1623–1673), a member of the famous Newcastle circle which in the mid-seventeenth century played a major role in the formation of the mechanical philosophy. She was educated at home along with her six siblings and then during the English Civil War was exiled to France where she met and married William Cavendish, Duke of Newcastle. There she studied and discussed philosophy with her husband and his brother in the salons they held in Paris that included such luminaries as Thomas Hobbes, René Descartes, Pierre Gassendi, Marin Mersenne, and Kenelm Digby. She later engaged with the ideas of the Cambridge Platonists such as Henry More and Ralph Cudworth. In her *Philosophical Letters*, published in 1664, she began: "You have been pleased to send me the Works of four Famous and Learned Authors, to wit, of two most Famous Philosophers of our Age, Descartes, and Hobbs, and of that Learned Philosopher and Divine Dr. More, as also of that Famous Physician and Chymist Van Helmont." Throughout her work however, she rarely mentioned names and only occasionally used initials when referring to individuals.[4]

A feminist who between 1653 and 1671 wrote some twenty-six works, including fourteen scientific books about atoms, matter and motion, butterflies, fleas, magnifying glasses, distant worlds, and infinity, Cavendish's ideas and theories are at times inconsistent, contradictory, and eclectic, which is attributable at least in part to her lack of formal education—a lack she herself deplored. She was acutely aware of the problems of leisured ladies who were made "like birds in cages to hop up and down in their houses." "We are shut out of all power and authority by reason, we are never employed either in civil nor marshall affairs, our counsels are despised and laughed at, the best of our actions are trodden down with scorn by the overweaning conceit men have of themselves and through a despisement of us."[5] An epistle in her book *Poems and Fancies* (1653), written to Mistress Toppe, a now unknown lady, lamented the "truth" that "our sex hath so much waste time, having but little employments, which makes our thoughts run wildly about, having nothing to fix them upon, which wild thoughts do not only produce unprofitable, but indiscreet actions, winding up the thread of our lives in snarls."[6]

Another epistle in the same book, addressed "To All Writing Ladies," noted that in different ages different types of spirits rule and have power; sometimes they are masculine, sometimes feminine. The present age had produced many feminine writers, rulers, actors, and preachers and was perhaps a feminine reign. "Let us take advantage, and make the best of our time . . . in any thing that [might] bring honor to our sex."[7]

Cavendish's preface to "Poems and Fancies" requested the support of her own sex for a work "belonging most properly to themselves." "All I desire," she said, "is fame . . . but I imagine I shall be censured by my own sex and men will cast a smile of scorn upon my book, because they think thereby, women encroach too much upon their prerogatives; for they hold books as their crown, and the sword as their scepter, by which they rule and govern."[8]

Poems and Fancies begins with Nature calling a council consisting of the female principles, Motion, Figure, Matter, and Life, to advise her on creating the world. Life, Figure, and Motion all agree that Death is the "great enemy" who does not obey Nature's laws, undoes Form, and corrupts Matter.

First Matter she brought the Materials in,
And Motion cut, and carv'd out everything.
And Figure she did draw the Formes and Plots,
And Life divided all out into Lots.
And Nature she survey'd, directed all,
With the foure Elements built the World's Ball.

Though Death finally submits, he continues his attempt to obstruct and hinder Nature in all her efforts. Nevertheless, Nature creates a world made up of atoms—square, round, long, sharp, and so on—which form the vegetables, minerals, and animals of the everyday world. By their combinations atoms make heat and cold, life and death, and cause illnesses such as dropsy, consumption, and colic.

Small Atomes of themselves a World may make,
A being subtle, and of every shape:
And as they dance about, fit places finde,
Such formes as best agree, make every kinde.

In an attempt to gain recognition for her achievements, Margaret Cavendish insisted on a visit to the all-male scientific society, the Royal Society of London in 1667, where scientific experiments and instruments were displayed for her surveillance. Samuel Pepys, the London gossip and journalist, "did not like her at all," but John Evelyn was "pleased with her fanciful habit, garb, and discourse."[9] Excluded from membership in the Royal Society because of her sex, she invented her own scientific community in *The Blazing World* (1666), which would bring her the fame and recognition for which she hungered. "I am not covetous, but as ambitious as ever any of my sex is, or can be; which though I cannot be Henry the Fifth or Charles II, yet I endeavor to be Margaret the First." The sole survivor of a shipwreck, in which all the men have been killed, a lady finds herself on an island where she marries the Emperor and becomes an Empress who resembles Margaret I. She founds schools and societies and receives scientific instruction from beast-men who walk upright. Bear-men and bird-men are her experimental philosophers, who bring telescopes and microscopes for her investigations. Fish-men and worm-men answer her questions about the sea and earth, while the ape-men, her chemists, give an account of transmutations. Fox-men are her politicians, and spider- and lice-men teach her mathematics. Thus the Duchess, in her fantasies, poems, and many prefaces to her voluminous writings presented one of the earliest explicitly feminist perspectives on science.[10]

Cavendish's *Grounds of Natural Philosophy*

Margaret Cavendish's *Grounds of Natural Philosophy* (1668) represented the culmination of her writing career as a feminist natural philosopher. The *Grounds* was the second edition of her earlier book, *Philosophical and Physical Opinions*, published in 1655, but in her own words, "much altered." The updated *Grounds of Natural Philosophy*, published in London in 1668, was "written by the thrice Noble, Illustrious, and excellent Princess, the Duchess of Newcastle." Indeed this book was a substantial revision of many of her earlier writings and can be considered an innovative revision and synthesis of her life work that now expressed a vitalist-materialist philosophy.[11]

Cavendish, like many writers of the period, did not often identify her sources of information although she engaged with and often opposed the assumptions of many of the philosophers she met in the salons of Paris where she and her husband had lived in exile. In her *Observations upon Experimental* Philosophy (1666) she included a chapter titled "Observations upon the Opinions of Some Ancient Philosophers." Here she drew on the summary of ancient and modern philosophers discussed by "that learned author Mr. Stanley, wherein he describes the lives and opinions of the ancient philosophers; in which I found so much difference betwixt their conceptions and my own, in natural philosophy that were it allowable or usual for our sex, I might set up a sect or school for myself." And in *The Blazing World*, also of 1666, she mentions "Aristotle, Pythagoras, Plato, and Epicurus" along with "modern writers" including "Galileo, Gassendus, Des Cartes, Helmont, Hobbes, H. More, etc."[12]

We can nevertheless make some assumptions about her sources based on the ideas she pulled together to create her own unique philosophy and also identify philosophers whose ideas she anticipated. She wrote within "substance theory" or the "theory of being" (ontology) that was prevalent during the seventeenth century. Her perspective stemmed from Aristotle's concept of substantial forms (or form within matter). In the previously mentioned chapter, "Observations upon the Opinions of Some Ancient Philosophers," in opposition to Plato, she wrote: "Form and matter are but one thing; for it is impossible to separate matter from form, or form from matter." Yet in opposition to Aristotle, she stated, "nature and all her parts are perpetually self-moving." She also opposed the idea of occult powers prevalent in the Aristotelianism of the medieval Scholastics. She accepted Heraclitus's theory of change that, "there are not only real, but also apparent or seeming contraries in nature, which are her irregularities." She opposed Descartes' dualism of mind and body, while assuming Hobbes's monist position that all substance was material and that only matter existed. But unlike Hobbes, in her later work she held a vitalist-materialist view that all of nature was self-moving, perceptive, and animate.[13]

While many of her early writings emphasized the empirical methodology of the telescope and the microscope, Cavendish's later works shifted toward a rationalist critique of empiricism and developed a materialist ontology. In the *Grounds of Natural Philosophy* (1668), she engaged with the most fundamental questions of philosophy: (1) How was the world created? What is it made of? (the ontological question, or theory of being); (2) What is knowing? How do we know? (the epistemological question, or theory of knowledge); and (3) How does change occur? (the theory of process). In examining the underlying assumptions in her *Grounds of Natural Philosophy*, we can discern her approaches to these ultimate philosophical questions.[14]

(1) The Ontological Question: How was the world created and what is it made of? In her 1655 *Philosophical Opinions*, Cavendish had argued that both God and Nature were eternal, a version of "pantheism" that by 1668 she now denied. In the 1655 *Philosophical Opinions*, she began Chapter 1 with the statement: "There is no first matter nor first motion for matter and motion are infinite, and being infinite, must consequently be Eternal." In Chapter 3, she had written, "Nature is infinite and eternal," and in Chapter 17 on "The Order of Nature," she stated, "Eternal matter is always one and the same." These statements implied that Nature was an eternally existing substance like God—statements that she later came to repudiate.[15]

In the *Grounds of Natural Philosophy* (her revision of the *Philosophical Opinions*), Nature (although still infinite) was no longer eternal. Here she moved away from an atheistic pantheism and toward the view that an incorporeal God created a separate corporeal Nature. In her chapter "Of the Differences between God and Nature," she differentiated between the two. Although God was an infinite creator, nature was separate from God and was his infinite creature. "God is an Infinite and Eternal Immaterial Being: Nature, an Infinite Corporeal Being," she wrote. "God is Immovable, and Immutable: Nature, Moving, and Mutable." God is without error while nature is full of irregularities. God is Infinitely and Eternally Worshipped: Nature is the Eternal and Infinite Worshipper."[16]

The second part of the ontological question is: What is the world made of? As philosopher Eugene Marshall argues, her ontology was a vitalistic materialism in which the world consisted of a plenum of material, self-living, self-moving parts. In Chapter 1 of *The Grounds of Natural Philosophy*, she set out the proposition that all substance was material and that matter and body were one and the same thing. There could be no motion that was not attached to matter. She denied the existence of spirits, arguing that there were no spirits or minds that somehow existed in the realm between body and not-body. Moreover, something immaterial could not have material motion. Matter might be motionless, but all motion must be the motion of matter. Corporeal bodies (matter) could not have incorporeal (mental) perceptions; thoughts were actually corporeal motions united by conjunction.[17]

Consistent with a materialist view, the universe was full of matter. There could be no vacuum or empty spaces in nature; no pores or void space between the parts. All parts therefore influence each other. Chance was merely an effect produced by an invisible cause.[18]

(2) The Epistemological Question: What is knowing and how do we know? Cavendish's epistemology was one in which all parts of the world were not only alive, but knowing and perceptive, a view identified by Eugene Marshall as pan-psychism. In her 1666 *Observations Upon Experimental Philosophy*, she held that "there can be no regular motion without knowledge, sense, and reason."[19]

In the *Grounds of Natural Philosophy*, she elaborated further that "all the self-moving parts are perceptive." "Nature," she stated, "is self-knowing, self-living and also perceptive." Everything is alive; all parts of nature have life and knowledge. "And though all her parts, even the inanimate parts are self-knowing and self-living; yet only her self-moving parts have an active life, and a perceptive knowledge."[20]

Nature was thus a material whole comprising infinite self-knowing parts united in one infinite material body. Moreover, Nature knows herself. "She" has unified knowledge and unified power. But although God has given her self-knowledge and power, that power is limited, "for she cannot move beyond her nature" or "create or annihilate any part." And although she is infinite, Nature has an "exact figure"—an exact frame and form. Each being is unique. Nature cannot give the knowledge, life, motion, or perception embedded in one part to another part. "[O]ne creature cannot have the properties or faculties of another; they may have the like, but not the same."[21]

Consistent with pan-psychism, the living creatures of the world are individual beings comprising self-moving parts all of which have the ability to perceive. "All Creatures being composed of these sorts of parts must have a sensitive and rational knowledge and perception as animals, vegetables, minerals, elements, or what else there is in Nature." Nevertheless individual creatures have "different lives, knowledges, and perceptions." The self-moving parts when united in an individual creature move according to the nature of that particular individual as a whole; it is the "whole creature" that comprises the individual within it. But individual creatures cannot perceive the mind and thoughts that are within the body of another individual or even the information shared by the parts within its own body. Information can, nevertheless, be communicated between creatures.[22]

The second part of the epistemological question is: How do we know? In her writings, Cavendish demonstrated a dialectical, or Socratic, method of knowing and reasoning. In her *Philosophical* Letters (1664), she used the device of two women debating each other as "Madam."[23] In other writings, she introduced chapters as a debate between parts of her own self. Thus in *The Grounds*, in a chapter on irregular and regular worlds, she began: "Some parts of my mind were of [the] opinion, that there might be a world composed only of irregularities; and another only of regularities, and some that were partly composed of the one and the other." She then gave the "minor part's opinion" followed by the "major part's opinion," concluding "after which discourse they generally agreed, there might be regular and irregular worlds."[24]

(3) **The Theory of Process:** How does change occur? In answer to this question, Cavendish offered a dialectical theory of change. Drawing on assumptions going as far back as Heraclitus's idea that all is in flux and constantly changing and anticipating the dialectical theories of Friedrich Engels and Karl Marx, she argued that Nature operated in a series of opposed, but balanced actions. Nature acted both by dividing and composing, dilating and contracting, and with regularity and irregularity. Oppositions included life and death, peace and war, hot and cold, light and dark, wet and dry, soft and hard, heavy and light, etc. Matter, she said, was divided into three parts—the rational, the sensitive, and the inanimate (which although it did not move in space, was nevertheless composed of self-moving parts). Human beings were the rational; other animals and vegetables the sensitive; and minerals and the elements the inanimate.[25]

The elements—fire, air, water, and earth—divided and joined, changed and re-changed, while retaining their own innate properties. The four elements acted and interacted through such means as flames, lightning, thunder, tides, floods, ice, snow, wind, smoke, and clouds. Metals could be transformed by melting, burning, boiling, and evaporating, vegetables by dividing and growing down into the earth or above its surface. Both natural and artificially created productions came from the composing, joining, and mixing of similar or "foreign" parts. Concerning artificial things, Cavendish asked, do they have "sense, reason, and perception?" Her answer was "if all the rational and sensitive parts of nature are perceptive and . . . no part is without perception then all artificial productions are perceptive." These answers buttressed her vitalism and pan-psychism.[26]

Cavendish identified the process of change as "production." The self-moving parts of nature, or corporeal motions, produced the creatures of the world (animals, vegetables, minerals, and elements). Consistent with her theory of opposed, but balanced actions, corporeal motions were the "laboring parts" through which individual beings were produced and then dissociated. "Matter is a perpetual motion that is always dividing and composing." Individual productions are compositions of parts. Through the process of production, creatures are composed and then dissolved, they live and then die. Creatures are produced by creatures. All creatures are produced and then in turn become producers, some in a few hours, others in a few years. Productions are both natural and artificial.[27]

The production of individual creatures, however, takes time. Creatures are not produced in a single act or moment, but by degrees. The production of a "human creature," for example, takes nine months. Cavendish described human gestation as a process taking place over a specific period of time. "The reason that a woman or such like animal, doth not feel her child so soon as it is produced is, that the child cannot have an animal nature . . . until it be perfectly an animal creature; and as soon as it is a perfect child, she feels it to move." However when the child moves, the mother only feels the sensitive or moving parts of the child. She cannot perceive the child's rational parts as they are unique to that individual. But consistent with her theory of change, nature acts both regularly and irregularly. The gestation process can proceed with regularity and result in a perfect child at the end of the nine-month period or irregularly, resulting in a miscarriage or a deformed child.[28]

The tension (or dialectic) between regularity and irregularity was an important aspect of Cavendish's theory of change. In her 1666 *Observations upon Experimental Philosophy*, she wrote: "all her actions are balanced by their opposites . . . there is no animate without inanimate; no regularity without irregularity: all [of] which produces a peaceable, orderly and wise government in Nature's kingdoms." In the *Grounds of Natural Philosophy*, she stated: "'Nature being poised, there must of necessity be Irregularities, as well as Regularities." And in her chapter "Of the Irregularity of Nature's Parts," she asserted: "Nature's fundamental actions are so poised, that irregular actions are as natural as regular." And later, "Infinite self-moving matter hath infinite varieties of actions." In fact, irregularity was necessary in order to account for diseases, deformities, disasters, and disorder. Regularity and irregularity operated in tension with each other to produce the ordered world of nature in which we live.[29]

Having dealt with these three fundamental questions of philosophy, Cavendish culminated her *Grounds of Natural Philosophy* by speculating about the existence of other worlds. There were other kinds of worlds, she believed, with other kinds of creatures. All such worlds, however, were material and self-moving. The creatures of these other worlds might respond differently to different properties such as light and dark, hot and cold, wet and dry. Or, they might not need them at all. "The properties of a human creature are quite different from other kinds of creatures . . . but in all material worlds, there are self-moving parts." In these worlds "there is perception amongst the parts or creatures of nature; and what worlds or creatures soever are in nature, they have sense and reason, life and knowledge." Yet in all these worlds, the same "dialectical" processes of change exist. There are regularities and irregularities, uniting and dividing, composing and dissolving. She thus held to her firm belief in a vitalistic, dialectical form of materialism.[30]

Writing during the 1650s to 1670s in England, Margaret Cavendish was indeed a pioneer, both as a feminist and a natural philosopher. While not only standing up for the rights and intellectual abilities of women, she attempted to address the most fundamental ontological and epistemological questions of philosophy. Over the course of her career she drew on elements of systems that went back as far as those of Greek philosophers Heraclitus, Plato, and Aristotle, while engaging with and differing from contemporaries such as Descartes, Hobbes, Gassendi, and Digby and later with the Cambridge Platonists such as Henry More and Ralph Cudworth. At various points in her writings, she also anticipated and articulated ideas associated with future philosophers, such as Spinoza's pantheism, Leibniz's vitalism, Hegel's dialectics, and Marx and Engels's dialectical materialism. In synthesizing ideas into her own system of a vitalistic dialectical form of materialism, she paved the way both for the "new science" and the "new philosophy" that emerged during the seventeenth-century Scientific Revolution.

WOMEN AS AN AUDIENCE FOR SCIENCE

Not only were women such as Margaret Cavendish innovative thinkers in an age when women's intellectual talents were beginning to be recognized, they were also an eager audience for learning. Seizing on these opportunities, men began to participate in the project of teaching science to women. Among the early teachers was Bernard Fontenelle (1657–1757) although at times he did so in a somewhat condescending tone. In his *Conversations on the Plurality of Worlds* (1686), writing before the publication and acceptance of Isaac Newton's 1687 *Principia Mathematica*, Fontenelle attempted to educate women in the intricacies of the Cartesian universe through the device of a bright and beautiful young lady who is instructed in the mysteries of vortex motion and other worlds. His Marchioness of G "without tincture of learning understands what is said to her, and without confusion rightly apprehends." Although a woman might not have the application of the mind "for scientific discovery, she can approach it as many do a romance or novel when they would retain the plot." On six successive evenings the marchioness walks with her philosopher lover through formal French gardens as he instructs her in scientific matters. Throughout the discourse the Marchioness is praised for her agreeableness and acuity in understanding the philosopher's teachings. "And yet were her company but half so agreeable, I am persuaded all the world would run mad after wisdom."[31]

Significantly, in this new age when God becomes an engineer and mathematician, nature in Fontenelle's fantasia had, however, become a housewife. "Nature is a great housewife, she always makes use of what costs least. . . and yet this frugality is accompanied with an extraordinary magnificence, which shines through all her works; that is, she is magnificent in the design, but frugal in the execution."

Fontenelle's book was translated into English in 1688 by playwright Aphra Behn. Although she approved of the idea of instructing women in science, Behn found the Marchioness somewhat less than convincing because, for a student, her comments vacillated between silly and excessively profound.

As capitalist forms of economic life displaced women from household production, creating more leisure time, noble and bourgeois ladies became audiences for the new scientific discoveries. One step in the long process of institutionalizing and integrating classical physics and philosophy into Western consciousness was scientific popularization. A tradition of textbooks for the lay person, popular lectures, museums, and itinerant scientific demonstrators, as well as the foundation of professional societies for the more learned, began to emerge by the late seventeenth century. Part of this effort was directed specifically toward the female.

The attempt by bourgeois entrepreneurs to capture a wider female audience lay behind the publication of scientific serials for city and country ladies of all social levels. Pamphleteer John Dunton began including in 1691 a "Ladies Day" section in his twice-weekly serial, the *Athenian Mercury*. The annual *Ladies Diary* begun in 1704 by John Tipper taught science and posed difficult mathematical and astronomical questions for its audience to solve. The semiweekly *Free Thinker*, published from 1718 to 1721 and later bound into permanent three-volume sets, featured articles on natural history for the "philosophical girl" who "did not aspire to masculine virtues" but was above female capriciousness.[32]

Whereas Fontenelle had explained the Cartesian vortex heavens to his female audience, eighteenth century popularizers appropriated his method and format to educate women in Newtonian science and to enhance their abilities as salon conversationalists. Francesco Algarotti (1718–1764) consulted with Emilie du Châtelet, translator of the French edition of Isaac Newton's *Principia Mathematica*, in preparing his *Newtonianism for the Ladies* (1737), and then to her disappointment dedicated it to Fontenelle. In six dialogues, a learned lady was instructed in Newtonian physics and optics.

The theory of light and color as produced by prisms and lenses and the use and construction of telescopes and microscopes prepared her and her readers for their own experimentation. An English translation of Algarotti's book was made two years later by Elizabeth Carter at the age of twenty-two—*Sir Isaac Newton's Philosophy Explained for the Use of the Ladies.*[33]

In the mid-eighteenth century, scientific entrepreneurs Benjamin Martin and James Ferguson manufactured telescopes and microscopes, wrote scientific books for well-informed middle-class ladies and gentlemen, and invited women to attend popular lectures. In Martin's *Young Gentlemen and Lady's Philosophy* (1750s) and Ferguson's *Easy Introduction to Astronomy, for Young Gentlemen and Ladies* (1768) the authors' device was an Oxford-educated brother who returned home to teach his eager sister the secrets of the new science, with the expectation that the newly converted sister would purchase her own scientific instruments. Even children were recruited into the ever-expanding scientific market by John Newberry's best-seller, *The Newtonian System of Philosophy Adapted to the Capacities of Young Gentlemen and Ladies . . . Being the Substance of Six Lectures Read to the Lilliputian Society, by Tom Telescope* (1766). Tom Telescope interrupts the frivolous games of the Lilliputian boys and girls with lectures on astronomy, natural history, air pressure experiments, and geography.[34]

Because the Scientific Revolution itself was not isolated from social, economic, and intellectual changes, its meaning for women was directly tied to these developments. The women who contributed to the intellectual life of late seventeenth century England were not only reacting against the constriction of women's roles into the domestic sphere and to the slow pace of women's educational advancement, but, as in the Reformation, were responding to opportunities for women made possible within the more radical and traditionally more egalitarian religious sects. Caught up by the excitement of the "new science," educated women, along with men, became an eager audience for the new ideas. The dissemination of the new learning facilitated its spread into other spheres of human life, where it was becoming institutionalized as a problem-solving methodology and as the dominant conceptual framework, reshaping the older Renaissance organic image of the cosmos and society into a new mechanistic philosophy of science and society.

NOTES

* From Carolyn Merchant, *The Death of Nature: Women, Ecology, and the Scientific Revolution* (San Francisco: HarperCollins, 1980), pp. 268–74, used by permission of HarperCollins, and from Carolyn Merchant, Keynote Address to the Margaret Cavendish Society, June 2017. Revised and updated for this volume.

1. On Princess Caroline of Wales, pupil of Leibniz at Hanover, see Leibniz, "The Controversy between Leibniz and Clarke," in Leroy E. Loemker, ed. and trans., *Philosophical Papers and Letters*, 2 vols. (Chicago: University of Chicago Press, 1956), vol. 2, pp. 1095–169; Leibniz, *Philosophische Schriften*, ed. C. I. Gerhardt (Berlin, 1875–1890), vol. 7, pp. 345–440. Leibniz's correspondence with Lady Masham is collected in Leibniz, *Philosophische Schriften*, vol. 3, pp. 336–75. On Gabrielle Émelie du Châtelet as an exponent of Leibnizian thought, see Carolyn [Merchant] Iltis, "Madame du Châtelet's Metaphysics and Mechanics," *Studies in History and Philosophy of Science* 8 (1977): 29–48 (see this volume Ch. 10), and W. H. Barber, "Mme. du Châtelet and Leibnizianism: The Genesis of the *Institutions de Physique*," in William Henry Barber [and others] eds., *The Age of the Enlightenment: Studies Presented to Theodore Besterman* (Edinburgh and London: Oliver & Boyd, 1967), pp. 200–22.
2. Hannah Wooley, *The Gentlewomen's Companion* (London, 1673; first published, 1655); Bathsua Makin, *An Essay to Revive the Antient Education of Gentlewomen, in Religion, Manners, Arts, and Tongues* (London, 1673); Mary Astell, *A Serious Proposal to the Ladies for the Advancement of Their True and Greatest interest...* (London, 1694). On seventeenth-century feminist ideas concerning women's education, see Hilda Smith, *Reason's Disciples: Seventeenth Century English Feminists* (Urbana: University of Illinois Press, 1982), pp. 75–95. On women's learning see Myra Reynolds, *The Learned Lady in England, 1650–1760* (Boston: Houghton Mifflin, 1920).
3. Feminist books reprinted in England included Henry Cornelius Agrippa, *De Nobilitate et Praecellentia foeminei sexus* (1529). English translations: Henry Cornelius Agrippa, *The Glory of Women: Or a Looking-Glasse for Ladies* (London, 1652); Henry Cornelius Agrippa, *Female Pre-Eminence; or the Dignity and Excellency of That Sex, Above the Male* (London, 1670). François Poulain de la Barre, *The Woman as Good as the Man; or the Equality of Both Sexes*, trans. A. L. (London: N. Brooks, 1677; first published, 1673), Preface, p. A5. On Poulain de la Barre see Michael A. Seidel, "The Woman as Good as the Man," *Journal of the History of Ideas* 35 (July–September 1974): 499–508.
4. Eugene Marshall, "Margaret Cavendish (1623–1673)," *Internet Encyclopedia of Philosophy*, www.iep.utm.edu/cavend-m/. See Marshall's discussion of Cavendish's engagement with the philosophy of contemporaries such as Descartes, Hobbes, Gassendi, and others and later with Cambridge Platonism. Quotation from: Margaret Cavendish, *Philosophical Letters, or, Modest Reflections upon Some Opinions in Natural Philosophy Maintained by Several Famous and Learned Authors of This Age, Expressed by Way of Letters / by the Thrice Noble, Illustrious, and Excellent Princess the Lady Marchioness of Newcastle* (London, 1664), section 1.1, p. 1 (spelling of Descartes modernized).
5. Margaret Cavendish, *The Philosophical and Physical Opinions* (London: Martin and Allestrye, 1655), preface, "To the Two Universities." Discussions of Margaret Cavendish's feminism and scientific work include Smith, *Reason's Disciples*, pp. 75–95; Douglass Grant, *Margaret the First: A Biography of Margaret Cavendish, Duchess of Newcastle, 1623–1673* (London: Hart-Davis, 1957); Gerald Dennis Meyer, *The Scientific Lady in England* (Berkeley and Los Angeles: University of California Press, 1955), pp. 1–15; Robert H. Kargon, *Atomism in England from Hariot to Newton* (Oxford, England: Clarendon Press, 1966), pp. 73–6. Recent works on Cavendish include: Anna Battigelli, *Margaret Cavendish and the Exiles of the Mind* (Lexington, KY: University Press of Kentucky, 1998); Line Cottegnies and Nancy Weitz, eds., *Authorial Conquests: Essays on Genre in the Writings of Margaret Cavendish* (Madison, NJ: Fairleigh Dickinson University Press, 2003); Emma L. E. Rees, *Margaret Cavendish: Gender, Genre, Exile* (Manchester, UK: Manchester University Press, 2003); Brandie R. Siegfried and Lisa T. Sarasohn, eds., *God and Nature in the Thought of Margaret Cavendish* (Burlington, VT: Ashgate, 2014); Lisa Walters, *Margaret Cavendish: Gender, Science, and Politics* (Cambridge, UK: Cambridge University Press, 2014).
6. Margaret Cavendish, *Poems and Fancies* (London: Martin and Allestrye, 1653), "An Epistle to Mistris Toppe," p. A4.

7. Cavendish, *Poems and Fancies*, Preface, "To All Writing Ladies," p. A.
8. Cavendish, *Poems and Fancies*, Preface, "To All Noble and Worthy Ladies," p. A3. Poetry quotations on pp. 3, 5.
9. Emma Wilkins, "Margaret Cavendish and the Royal Society," *Notes and Records, the Royal Society Journal of the History of Science*, 2014, http://rsnr.royalsocietypublishing.org.
10. Meyer, op. cit., note 4, pp. 10–11; Margaret Cavendish, *The Description of a New World Called the Blazing-World* (London, 1668), preface, "To the Reader," and pp. 4, 15, and passim.
11. Margaret Cavendish, *Grounds of Natural Philosophy* (London: A. Maxwell, 1668). On Cavendish's vitalistic materialism, see Eugene Marshall, "Margaret Cavendish (1623–1673)," *Internet Encyclopedia of Philosophy*, www.iep.utm.edu/cavend-m/. On her early vitalism, see Walters, Margaret Cavendish, pp. 18–19, 37, 119; see also, Ch. 1 on gender in her theory of matter. On Cavendish, see also David Cunning, "Margaret Lucas Cavendish," https://plato.stanford.edu/entries/margaret-cavendish/.
12. Margaret Cavendish, "Observations upon the Opinions of Some Ancient Philosophers," *Observations Upon Experimental Philosophy*, ed. Eileen O'Neill (New York: Cambridge University Press, 2001; originally published, London, 1666), pp. 249–75. Cavendish, *The Blazing World*, pp. 37, 39–41.
13. On substance theory see Edward N. Zalta, ed., *Stanford Encyclopedia of Philosophy*, https://plato.stanford.edu/entries/substance/#DesSpiLei, see section 2.2: "Substances for Aristotle are individuals, but it is much debated whether they are individualized forms or composites of form and matter." Cavendish, "Observations upon the Opinions of Some Ancient Philosophers," in *Observations Upon Experimental Philosophy*, quotation in opposition to Plato, p. 252; in opposition to Aristotle, p. 268, see also, p. 270; on Heraclitus, see p. 273. On Cavendish's differences with her contemporary philosophers, see Eugene Marshall, "Margaret Cavendish (1623–1673)," *Internet Encyclopedia of Philosophy*, www.iep.utm.edu/cavend-m/: "Against Descartes, however, she rejected dualism and incorporeal substance of any kind. Against Hobbes, on the other hand, she argued for a vitalist materialism, according to which all things in nature were composed of self-moving, animate matter. Specifically, she argued that the variety and orderliness of natural phenomena cannot be explained by blind mechanism and atomism, but instead require the parts of nature to move themselves in regular ways, according to their distinctive motions. And in order to explain that, she argued for panpsychism, the view that all things in nature possess minds or mental properties. . . . In several ways, Cavendish can be seen as one of the first philosophers to take up several interesting positions against the mechanism of the modern scientific worldview of her time. Thus it is possible to add that she presages thinkers such as Spinoza and Leibniz."
14. Cavendish, *Grounds of Natural Philosophy*, pp. 1–3; Smith, *Reason's Disciples*, pp. 75–95, 110–12.
15. Cavendish, *Philosophical Opinions*, pp. 1, 3, 5. See also p. 59: "As I said before in my first part of my Book, that there is no first Matter, nor no first Motion, because Eternal, and Infinite. . . . " (p. 30) Lisa Sarasohnin *God and Nature in the Thought of Margaret Cavendish*, ed., Siegfried and Sarasohn, chap. 7, writes: "Cavendish's most detailed analysis of specific Christian beliefs appear in Letter 3 of *Philosophical Letters* addressed to an unidentified "Madam"—who, Cavendish says, is offended at my Opinion that Nature is Eternal without beginning, which you say is to make her God, or at least coequal with God.". . . "Cavendish realized that her belief in the eternity of nature was suspect, particularly in relation to the scriptural account of creation." (Sarasohn, p. 102).
16. Cavendish, *Grounds of Natural Philosophy*, p. 241. See also Appendix I to the *Grounds of Natural Philosophy*, p. 239: "I cannot conceive how an Immaterial can be in Nature: for, first, an Immaterial cannot, in my opinion, be naturally created. . . . an Immaterial in my opinion, must be some uncreated Being; which can be no other than God alone."
17. Cavendish, *Grounds of Natural Philosophy*, Ch. I, "Of Matter," p. 1, Ch. II, "Of Motion," p. 2.
18. Cavendish, *Grounds of Natural Philosophy*, pp. 3, 4, 16. See Cavendish, *Grounds*, Ch. 4, "Of Vacuum" p. 4: "In my opinion, there cannot possibly be any vacuum: for though Nature

being material, is divisible and compoundable; and having self-motion, is in perpetual action: yet Nature cannot divide or compose from her self."

19. Eugene Marshall, "Margaret Cavendish (1623–1673)," *Internet Encyclopedia of Philosophy*, see section 2c, www.iep.utm.edu/cavend-m/#SH2c.

20. Cavendish, *Grounds of Natural Philosophy*, pp. 6–7.

21. Ibid., pp. 11–12, quotations on pp. 11 and 12.

22. Ibid., pp. 17–21, quotations on p. 18.

23. Stephen Clucas, "A Double Perception in All Creatures: Margaret Cavendish's *Philosophical Letters* and Seventeenth-Century Natural Philosophy," in Brandie R. Siegfried and Lisa T. Sarasohn, eds., *God and Nature in the Thought of Margaret Cavendish* (Farnham, UK: Ashgate, 2015), p. 125.

24. Cavendish, *Grounds of Natural Philosophy*, quotations on p. 254.

25. Ibid., pp. 9, 12–13, 235.

26. Ibid., pp. 163–4, 181, 185, 181–96, 229–32, quotations on pp. 163–4, 233.

27. Ibid., pp. 28, 31, 34–35, 163,180, quotation on p. 28.

28. Ibid., quotation on p. 41.

29. Cavendish, *Observations Upon Experimental Philosophy*, p. 232; *Grounds of Natural Philosophy*, quotations on pp. 60, 106, 177–8. See also Walters, *Margaret Cavendish*, p. 179.

30. Cavendish, *Grounds of Natural Philosophy*, pp. 234–6, quotations on p. 236.

31. Bernard de Fontenelle, *Entretiens sur la Pluralité des Mondes* (Paris, 1686); English trans.: Bernard de Fontenelle, *Week's Conversation on the Plurality of Worlds*, trans. William Gardiner (London, 1737), pp. iv–v, 16, xi–xii. Aphra Behn's translation was Bernard de Fontenelle, *A Discovery of New Worlds, from the French, Made English by Mrs. Aphra Behn . . . Wholly New* (London, 1688). For a discussion see Meyer, *Scientific Lady*, op. cit. [5], note 45, pp. 21–2.

32. Meyer, op. cit., note 4, pp. 49–70.

33. Francesco Algarotti, *Il Newtonianismo per le Dame* (Naples, 1737). For a discussion, see Meyer, pp. 29–32. Elizabeth Carter's translation was Francesco Algarotti, *Sir, Isaac Newton's Philosophy Explain'd for the Use of the Ladies: In Six Dialogues on Light and Colours: From the Italian of Sig. Algarotti* (London, 1739).

34. Meyer, op. cit.[5], note 4, pp. 36–48.

FIGURE 8.1 Anne Conway, Viscountess of Conway (1631–1679). By Samuel van Hoogstraten, c. 1662–1667.

Source: Duke University, Project Vox, Creative Commons.

8

ANNE CONWAY*

For those with no prior introduction to Anne Finch Conway (1631–1679), a few words concerning her background are in order before exploring her philosophy and its influence. Anne Conway was a seventeenth century philosopher whose ideas were praised and respected in her own day and who through scholarly error, has only recently begun to receive proper recognition for her important contributions to the philosophy of her period.

The youngest child of Heneage Finch, she was a member of the English nobility and upon her marriage to Edward Conway, she became a Viscountess. As a young girl, Anne was an avid reader of philosophy, literature, the classics, mathematics and astronomy. Her interest in philosophy was greatly inspired by her introduction to Henry More, who was the teacher of her brother, John Finch, and a respected professor at Christ College in Cambridge. Through this continued contact, Anne Conway became one of More's most brilliant and devoted pupils. Anne was an intelligent, vital conversationalist and had a charming personality. Her home at Ragley Hall in Warwickshire became an intellectual center which entertained some of the most exciting minds of her century including Henry More, Ralph Cudworth, Joseph Glanvill, Benjamin Whichcote and Francis Mercury Van Helmont, son of the renowned Jean Baptiste Van Helmont.[1]

The younger Van Helmont made her acquaintance due to her being afflicted by a life long bane. This bane came in the form of severe headaches which began at age fourteen and increased in frequency and severity throughout her life. Her headaches became a famous medical case. She was tormented by them and even journeyed to France at one point to have her skull opened up to relieve the pressure. Fortunately, circumstances prevented the operation from ever taking place. Anne Conway was treated by many of Europe's most noted physicians including William Harvey, the noted healer Valentine Greatrakes and Van Helmont. All failed.

It was quite fortuitous that Francis Mercury Van Helmont, the wandering "scholar gypsy," was introduced to Anne Conway in 1670. He had come to England in order to deliver to Henry More several letters from Princess Elizabeth of Bohemia and to discuss with him their mutual interest in the Cabala, an esoteric occult and mystical tradition stemming from the Middle Ages. He had only planned to remain in England one month, but through the joint efforts of More and Viscount Edward Conway he was finally persuaded to travel to Ragley to visit the learned Lady Anne Conway, in order to attempt a cure of her migraine headaches.[2]

Van Helmont's intended month in England turned into eight years during which he remained with Lady Conway, unsuccessful in treating her terrible headaches, but introducing stimulating new intellectual avenues for her mind. Henry More likewise spent much time there, experimenting with Van Helmont in the laboratory which the wandering alchemist had set up, and discussing Hebrew and cabalistic texts. Whenever Lady Conway was too ill to do so herself, Van Helmont read to her from a variety of books and pamphlets and reported on the activities of a group of Quakers meeting near Ragley. Under his influence, she began studying the texts of Quakers, Behmenists, Seekers, and Familists—religious sects that had flourished during the period of the Civil War.

In spite of her illness, Anne Conway carried on an active intellectual life. Her only book, *The Principles of the Most Ancient and Modern Philosophy*, continued the Cambridge school's interest in spiritualism, Platonism, and cabalism. Truer to the Platonic tradition than the writings of either of her colleagues, More or Cudworth, it was far more sweeping in its rejection of Cartesianism and embracement of vitalism.

Anne Conway developed a vitalistic philosophy which in many ways anticipated the philosophy of Leibniz. Her treatise was thought by Marjorie Nicolson to have been written early in the 1670's, perhaps in 1672 or 1673. But, in an edition published by Peter Loptson in 1982, its writing is placed somewhat later in her life and closer to her death, around 1677 and during her association with Van Helmont.[3] Both Nicolson and Loptson agree that her work bears the strong influence of Van Helmont and the Cabala. Her original edition, written in English, seems to have been lost very early on. The earliest edition we have is a Latin translation, edited and published in Holland in 1690 by Van Helmont in a volume containing several other works by him. It was republished and retranslated back to English in 1692. This edition, mentioned that it had been written by a certain English Countess, "a woman learned beyond her sex, being very well skilled in the Latin and Greek tongues and exceedingly well-versed in all kinds of philosophy."[4]

Because her name was withheld from the original Latin title page—the custom regarding female authors in that period—the book was attributed by modern scholars to its editor, Van Helmont. In 1853, the German historian of philosophy, Heinrich Ritter, erroneously based his analysis of the younger Van Helmont's philosophy almost entirely on Conway's book. His discussion became the basis for historian Ludwig Stein's theory (1890) that Van Helmont had transmitted to Leibniz the most fundamental term in his whole philosophy—the monad, Leibniz's infinitesimal vital active force.[5] Actually, Van Helmont did use the tern, but the book containing his discussion of it was apparently unknown to Ritter. Thus the major textual evidence for attributing Leibniz's appropriation of the term monad to Van Helmont, rather than including Anne Conway, was due to inaccurate scholarship. The withholding of Conway's name, as a woman writer, from the Latin edition of her book excluded from recognition her important role in the development of Leibniz's thought. Later scholarship has rightfully honored Anne Conway as author.

More than any other contemporary philosopher, Loptson has taken Anne Conway seriously as a philosopher in the essentialist tradition. In his recent edition which contains both the first published Latin treatise and the English re-translation, Loptson has included an introduction to her life and work. He has also spent much time analyzing the philosophical content of her work chapter by chapter providing an explication and summary of each section.

For me, the importance of Conway's ideas and work lies in the fact that she was a vitalist in direct contrast to the mechanistic philosophies which treat matter as dead and asserts that change comes from external forces acting upon matter. She was a critic of Hobbes, Descartes, Spinoza and others espousing mechanical philosophies. She saw herself as a vitalist and held that spirit and matter are one and the sane substance. Body is essentially spiritual and change and motion come from within.

The vitalists affirmed the life of all things through a reduction of Cartesian dualism to the monistic unity of matter and spirit. Among the proponents of a vitalist philosophy were Francis Glisson, Jean Baptiste Van Helmont and his son, Francis Mercury Van Helmont, Lady Anne Conway, and Gottfried Wilhelm von Leibniz.

As a philosophy of nature, vitalism in its monistic form was inherently anti-exploitative. Its emphasis on the life of all things as gradations of soul, its lack of separate distinction between matter and spirit, its principle of an immanent activity permeating nature, and its reverence for the nurturing power of the earth endowed it with an ethic of the inherent worth of everything alive. Contained within the conceptual structure of vitalism was a normative constraint. Perhaps it is not an accident to find among its advocates a woman philosopher, Anne Conway, and a wandering scholar-healer, Francis Mercury Van Helmont both of whom turned to Quakerism as a moral and religious alternative.

More and Conway discussed the philosophy of Jacob Boehme and the Familists in their letters during the years 1667–1670. More was skeptical of the neglect of the power of reason by the Behmenists and Familists, and deplored their tendency toward enthusiasm, but Anne Conway was sympathetic. Because the Quakers were "quiet people," she employed them as servants and also lent her home for their meetings. She made the acquaintance of Quaker leaders—George Fox, George Keith, Isaac Pennington, and Charles Lloyd—and corresponded with William Penn. To the despair of More, who identified the Quakers with Ranters, Seekers, Familists, and other enthusiasts of the Civil War years, both she and Van Helmont became Quakers—Van Helmont in the spring of 1676 and Conway at least by 1677.

The Quakers, far more than the other Protestant sects, gave both women and men full equality. Quakerism, growing out of discontent with Puritanism, began to spread in southern and eastern England around 1655, carried not only by men but also women preachers, such as Anne Blaykling, Mary Fisher, Dorothy Waugh, Jane Waugh, and Mary Pennington. Women, some of whom left their families behind, became traveling preachers, bearing the Quaker message not only all over England but as far as the Ottoman Empire. Under the leadership of George Fox, separate meetings for business were established, and administered and attended solely by women throughout England.[6]

The Quakers emphasized the inward presence of God, the living Christ within each individual, and the vitality of the living word, as opposed to the deadness of tradition and inertness of the written word. They distinguished between the historical figure of Christ, who had died, and the voice of the living, vital Christ within.

Van Helmont, George Keith, and Anne Conway saw much in common between the Cabala and the Quaker doctrines of the "inner light," "Christ within," and the Christian trinity. The three collaborated over a four-year period on a treatise entitled the "Two Hundred Queries . . . Concerning the Doctrine of the Revolution of Humane Souls" (1684). In subsequent years, this book became the bone of contention between the Quakers and Keith and Van Helmont because the latter two emphasized the transmigration of human souls and disputed the reality of the historical figure of Christ.[7]

Interest in cabalistic literature was keen among the members of the Cambridge school, and both More and Cudworth had at times viewed Descartes as the restorer of the true philosophy of Moses. One of More's works least appreciated by modern scholars, his *Conjectura Cabbalistica* (1653), written before he had read the Zohar and admitted to be the product of his own imagination, was nevertheless an important influence on John Milton.[8] More subsequently repudiated the Cabala in s treatise in the *Kabbalah Denudata* entitled "The Fundamentals of Philosophy." But the Cabala was an important source of validation to those philosophers who wished to restore life and spirit to the dead world of the mechanists. Cudworth, More, and Conway all used it to argue that the ancient wisdom that perceived a total unity and vitality in the universe was the true knowledge, whereas the dead mechanical world of the moderns was a distortion emphasizing only the atomistic aspect of old gnosis.

Anne Conway died in 1679 while her husband was away on business to the north. In order to preserve the body till her husband could return and see his wife one last time, Van Helmont used the rather bizarre method of keeping her body in a bath of wine. Her husband arrived back home some two months later. Her tombstone was simple and inscribed merely with "Quaker Lady." After her death, Van Helmont left for the continent where he continued to carry her writings and ideas with him for years to come.

In March 1696, Van Helmont arrived in Hanover, where he remained for several months, meeting with Leibniz each morning at nine for philosophical discussion. According to Leibniz, Van Helmont took the desk, while Leibniz became the pupil, interrupting frequently to ask for greater clarification. Van Helmont recounted to Leibniz the history of the "extraordinary woman," the Countess of "Kennaway," and his own relationship with Henry More and John Locke. From him, Leibniz learned of Anne Conway's metaphysics and her studies of the works of Plato, Plotinus, and the Cabala.[9] In a 1697 letter to English divine Thomas Burnet (1635–1715), Leihniz, having read her book, went so far as to state:

> My philosophical views approach somewhat closely those of the late Countess of Conway, and hold a middle position between Plato and Democritus, because I hold that all things take place mechanically as Democritus and Descartes contend against the views of Henry More and his followers, and hold too, nevertheless, that everything takes place according to a living principle and according to final causes—all things are full of life and consciousness, contrary to the views of the Atomists.[10]

Leibniz spoke subsequently with praise and approval of both Lady Anne Conway and Van Helmont, although the latter he often found puzzling and quixotic. In the *New Essays Concerning Hunan Understanding* begun in 1697 and published posthumously in 1765, Leibniz referred to both as explicating the doctrine of vitalism better than their Renaissance predecessors, writing that he saw:

> how it is necessary to explain rationally those who have lodged life and perception in all things, as Cardan, Campanella, and better than they, the late Countess

of Connaway, a Platonist, and our friend, with late M. François Mercure Van
Helmont (although elsewhere bristling with unintelligible paradoxes), with his
friend the late Mr. Henry More.[11]

The elements of Conway's system were a significant influence in the important period of Leibniz's thought leading up to the writing of his "Monadology" (1714).

A concern that dominated much of seventeenth-century philosophy was
the concept of substance. Different philosophers defined the term "substance"
in very different ways. For instance, Descartes held that there were two
fundamentally distinct substances underlying all reality: mind and matter.
To him, these two substances were separate and unrelated to each other in a
most absolute way. Hobbes, on the other band, took a more purely materialist
position and declared there to be only one substance, namely matter. But for
Conway and Leibniz substance was better understood as spiritual in nature,
something living and capable of movement.

Anne Conway's vitalism was based on the idea of the unity of spirit and
matter and was an influential reaction against the ideas of the mechanists. She
was well versed in and sharply critical of the ideas of her adversaries, Descartes, Hobbes, and the Dutch philosopher Benedictus Spinoza (1632–1677),
as well as her teachers and friends, More and Cudworth. Ritter, mistaking the
work of Conway for that of Van Helmont, saw the author of the *Principles* as
carrying out a wide-ranging battle against the Cartesian philosophy of dualism and against the basis of mechanical physics in general.[12] Whereas the
Cartesians and the Cambridge Platonists, More and Cudworth, were dualists,
Anne Conway was a monist. In her philosophy, there was no essential difference between spirit and body and, moreover, the two were interconvertible.
She distinguished her views sharply from those of Descartes and also from
More and Cudworth on these points. Body was condensed spirit and spirit
was subtle, volatile body. Body and spirit were not contrary entities, the first
impenetrable and divisible, the other penetrable and indivisible, as More had
held. Matter was not dead, "stupid," and devoid of life, as Descartes and the
Cambridge Platonists had thought. For Lady Conway, an intimate bond and
organic unity existed between the two. Body and soul were of the same substance and nature, but soul was more excellent in such respects as swiftness,
penetrability, and life.[13]

Matter and spirit were united as two different aspects of the same substance.
Division into parts, ordinarily attributed to bodies, was equally an attribute of
spirit. Just as bodies were composed of lesser bodies, the human spirit was
composed of several spirits under one governing spirit. Conversely, motion
and figure, which were supposed to be attributes of extended matter, applies
equally to spirit, for spirit was even more movable and figurable than body.[14]

Her break from Descartes and the other Cambridge Platonists was sharpest on the issue of dualism. She insisted that her philosophy was not Cartesianism in a new form, as she perceived that of her friends to have been, but fundamentally anti-Cartesian:

> For first, as touching the Cartesian Philosophy, this says that everybody is a mere dead mass, not only void of all kind of life and sense, but utterly uncapable thereof to all eternity; this grand error also is to be imputed to all those who affirm body and spirit to be contrary things, and inconvertible one into another, so as to deny a body all life and sense.[15]

Body and spirit were interconvertible because they were of the same substance and differed only as to mode. The distinctions made between the attributes of matter as impenetrable and extended, and spirit as penetrable and unextended, could not be assigned respectively to two separate substances. Body was simply the grosser part of a thing and spirit the subtler. The penetration of spirits within a body caused it to swell and puff up, an alteration that might or might not be visible to the senses. Just as spirit and body could interpenetrate, so a less gross body or spirit could penetrate a more gross one. Penetrability like other properties of objects (heat, weight, and solidity), was relative. The dualists had "not yet proved that body and spirit are distinct substances."[16]

Like other organicists of the period, Conway based her system of creation not on the machine but on the great, hierarchical chain of being, modified to incorporate an evolution or transmutation to higher forms, based on the acquisition of goodness and perfection. Conway denied that any created essences could reach God's essence, which was infinitely perfect, but within the creation there was an ascension up the scale of being. Dust and sand were capable of successive transmutation to stones, earth, grass, sheep, horses, humans, and the noblest spirits, so that after a long period of time they could achieve the perfections common to the highest creatures; that is, "feeling, sense, and knowledge, love, joy, and fruition, and all kind of power and virtue."[17]

Creation was like a ladder whose steps were species placed in finite, rather than infinite, distances from one another. Hence,

> stones are changed into metals, and one metal into another, but lest some should say these are only naked bodies and have no spirit, we shall observe the same not only in vegetables, but also in animals, like as barley and wheat are convertible the one into the other, and are in very deed often so changed. . . . And in animals worms are changed into flies and beasts, and fishes that feed on beasts, and fishes of a different kind do change them into their own nature, and species.[18]

This, she believed, was consistent with the biblical account that the waters brought forth birds and fishes and the earth, beasts and creeping things at the command of the Creator.

The transmutation of spirits into new bodies after death was effected by the soul's plastic nature, a concept obtained from More and Cudworth, hypothesizing a force capable of forming matter into new shapes:

> And when the said brutish spirit returns again into some body, and has now dominion over that body, so that its plastic faculty has the liberty of forming a body, after its own idea and inclination (which before in the humane body, it had not); it necessarily follows, that the body, which this vital spirit forms, will be brutal, and not humane. . . . Because its plastic faculty is governed of its imagination, which it doth most strongly imagine to itself, or conceive its own proper image; which therefore the external body is necessarily forced to assume.[19]

Leibniz, differing from Conway and Van Helmont on this point, not only argued against transmigration or metempsychosis in animals, but also against the idea of plastic natures. Plastic natures could not move, alter, or change the direction of a body, all motion being consonant with the system of preestablished harmony. In a letter of 1710, he called plastic natures an outmoded theory.[20]

Anne Conway radically opposed Hobbes and Spinoza, both of whom had reduced nature to a monistic materialism that denied any distinction between God and his creation. Like Conway, they accepted the interconvertibility of all things, but their materialism admitted no distinction between lower and higher forms and saw God as interconvertible with corporeal species.[21]

In much of her discussion of the essential spiritual vitality of the whole world, Anne Conway's thought converged with that of Leibniz, and she was for this reason held in high esteem by him. Like Leibniz, who believed that in each portion of matter there was a whole world of creatures each one containing within it also an entire world, Anne Conway wrote that "in every creature, whether the same be a spirit or a body, there is an infinity of creatures, each whereof contains an infinity, and again each of these, and so ad infinitum."[22]

Like Leibniz, who wrote that there was nothing dead or fallow in the universe, Conway asked, "How can it be, that any dead thing should proceed from him or be created by him, such as is mere body or matter. . . . It is truly said of one that God made not death, and it is true, that he made no dead thing: For how can a dead thing depend of him who is life and charity?" Death was not annihilation, but "a change from one kind of and degree of life to another." A dead body could not receive goodness nor perfect itself in any way; changes in motion or shape would not help it to attain life or improve itself intrinsically. This idea was echoed in Leibniz's statement that "Every possible thing has the right to aspire to existence in proportion to the amount of perfection it contains in germ."[23]

Like Leibniz, who stressed the interconnectedness of all spirits (or minds) in a "kind of fellowship with God," so that the totality composed the City of God, Lady Conway based her system on the interdependence of all creatures under God in a "certain society or fellowship . . . whereby they mutually subsist one by another, so that one cannot live without another." Each creature had a "central or governing spirit" having dominion over the other spirits which composed it. "The unity of spirits that compose or make up this center or governing spirit, is more firm and tenacious than that of all the other spirits; which are, as it were, the angels or ministering spirits of their prince or captain." Akin to this was Leibniz's dominant monad unifying the simple monads.[24]

But unlike Leibniz, who held to a system of preestablished harmony to solve the problem of the dualism between the body and the spirit, and unlike More and Cudwortb, who used plastic natures to unify the two worlds, Conway followed the *Kabbalah Denudata* and the ancient system of the Hebrews. She argued that the soul was of one nature and substance with the body, "although it is many degrees more excellent in regard of life and spirituality, as also in swiftness of motion, and penetrability, and divers other perfections." Between the two extremes of gross and subtle bodies were "middle spirits," which either joined body and soul or, if absent, dissolved its unity. Similarly, Jesus Christ functioned as a middle nature or medium uniting the soul of man to God.[25]

Yet Anne Conway's philosophy ultimately did not go beyond the limits of the categories of substance philosophy within which she worked. Her monistic resolution of the mind-body problem, although more parsimonious than the dualism of Descartes, was simply a reduction of all of reality to the idealist category of spirit. By denying the validity of body as an explanatory category, her philosophical framework was unable to provide a satisfactory description of empirical phenomena, Unlike Leibniz, whose system of preestablished harmony and "well-founded Phenomena" obeying mechanical laws also fell short of a solution, she did not even address herself to the issue of bodies and their interactions.

Furthermore her assumption of the transmigration of souls, and the concepts of "middle natures," plastic natures, and vital virtues that composed the core of her vitalism were based neither on rigid logical consistency nor on firm empirical evidence, a problem that continued to weaken the case for vitalists and holists of the nineteenth and twentieth centuries, such as German biologist Hans Driesh, French philosopher Henri Bergson, and South African statesman Jan Christiaan Smutts. Like other protagonists in the mechanist-vitalist debates that have continued ever since the rise of mechanism, her embracement of vitalism was based on metatheoretical commitments. Her philosophy falls within a post-Cartesian scientific tradition that operates on the assumption that the living and non-living constitute two fundamental categories of reality. Her commitment to spirit as the solution to the dualistic dilemma derived not only from the logic of philosophical alternatives, but from psychological needs connected to her physical health and her adoption of Quakerism as a spiritual refuge friendly to women.[26]

Despite its philosophical weaknesses, vitalism represented an important reaction to Cartesian mechanism and dualism. At a time when mechanism was turning all of nature into something dead, inanimate, and void of sensation thereby creating a subtle justification for the domination and control of nature, the vitalists along with the Cambridge Platonists raised voices of protest. They perceived the dangers in the reduction of matter to dead, inert atoms the motion of which stemmed from externally imposed forces rather than from the immanent spontaneity of vital principles. The older organic view of nature, however, was dying along with an inherent value system that paid recognition to the life and worth of all things, the concept of cyclical renewal, and the binding of nature into a close-knit holistic unity. In the light of our current ecological crisis, which stems in part from the loss of this organic value system, we might regret that the mechanists did not take their vitalistic critics more seriously.

Recent scholarship has emphasized not only the contributions of women such as Margaret Cavendish and Anne Conway to science and natural philosophy at the turn of the seventeenth century, but also their contributions to women's education. English women began to urge that women be educated in the same manner as men. Hannah Wooley in *The Gentlewoman's Companion* (written 1655, published, London, 1673) stated: "The right Education of the Female Sex, as it is in a manner everywhere neglected . . . ought to be generally lamented." She urged all women to make certain that their daughters were educated. "I . . . must condemn the great negligence of Parents, in letting the fertile ground of their Daughters lie sallow, yet send the barren Noddles of their Sons to the University."[27]

Bathsua Makin in *An Essay to Revive the Antient Education of Gentlewomen, in Religion, Manners, Arts, and Tongues* (1673) asserted, "it is verily believed (especially amongst a sort of debauched Sots) that Women are not endued with such Reason, as Men." "A Learned Woman is thought to be a Comet, that bodes Mischief." But, she argued, "Were Women thus Educated now, I am confident the advantage would be very great." Women, she stated, "have been good *Logicians, Philosophers, Mathematicians, Divines*, and *Poets*," and "have attained an extraordinary knowledge" in "Mathematicks." She took special note of "*Hyppatia* of *Alexandria*, Daughter of *Theon*, . . .

Professor in the School in Alexandria, where she was frequented by many worthy Scholars. Afterwards by such as envied her Fame for Learning, she was pitifully slain and massacred." In 1694 Mary Astell anonymously published, *A Serious Proposal to the Ladies for the Advancement of Their True and Greatest Interest, In Two Parts,* By a Lover of her Sex. She asked the ladies, "How can you be content to be in the World like Tulips in a Garden. . . ?" "Let us learn to pride ourselves in something more excellent than the invention of a Fashion." These goals for women's education reached new levels as the Scientific Revolution continued into the eighteenth century.[28]

NOTES

* From Carolyn Merchant, "Anne Conway, Quaker and Philosopher," *Perspectives on the Seventeenth Century World of Viscountess Anne Conway, Guilford Review* 23, no. 1 (Spring 1986): 2–13, reprinted by permission of *Guilford Review*. Portions of this article are drawn from Carolyn Merchant, "The Vitalism of Anne Conway: Its Impact on Leibniz's Concept of the Monad," *Journal of the History of Philosophy* 17, no. 3 (July 1979): 255–69. Copyright 1979 Journal of the History of Philosophy, Inc., reprinted with permission of Johns Hopkins University Press, and from Carolyn Merchant, "The Vitalism of Francis Mercury van Helmont: Its Influence on Leibniz," *Ambix* 26, no. 3 (November 1979): 170–82, used by permission of Taylor and Francis.

1. Marjorie Nicolson, *Conway Letters: The Correspondence of Anne, Viscountess Conway, Henry More, and Their Friends 1642–1684* (New Haven, CN: Yale University Press, 1930), pp. 1–9, 39–51, 116–18, 244–61, 316–18, 381–3, 407–8.

2. Marjorie Nicholson, "The Real Scholar Gipsy," *Yale Review* 18 (January 1929): 347–63, see p. 356. On Anne Conway's life and philosophy, see Gilbert Roy Owen, "The Famous Case of Lady Anne Conway," *Annals of Medical History* 9 (1937): 567–71: Alan Gabbey, "Anne Conway et Henri More, *Lettres sur Descartes*," *Archives de Philosophie* 40 (1977): 379–404; Alison Coudert, "A Quaker-Kabbalist Controversy," *Journal of the Warburg and Courtauld Institutes* 39 (1976): 171–89, and "A Cambridge Platonist's Kabbalist Nightmare," *Journal of the History of Ideas* 36 (1975): 633–52; Alison Gottesman (Coudert), "Francis Mercurius Van Helmont: His Life and Thought," Unpublished-Doctoral Dissertation, University of London, 1972; Joseph Politella, *Platonism, Aristotelianism, and Cabalism in the Philosophy of Leibniz* (Philadelphia: Politella, 1938), pp. 13–19, 55–7.

3. Anne Conway, *The Principles of the Most Ancient and Modern Philosophy*, ed. Peter Loptson (The Hague: Martinus Nijhoff, 1982).

4. Conway, *Principles* Loptson, ed. p. 147.

5. Ludwig Stein, *Leibniz and Spinoza* (Berlin: Reimer, 1890), p. 212, note 1; Heinrich Bitter, *Geschichte der Philosophie* (Hamburg, 1853), vol. 12, pp. 3–47, 7, note 1.

6. Richard T. Vann, "Toward a New Lifestyle: Women in Preindustrial Capitalism," in Renate Bridenthal and Claudia Koonz, eds., *Becoming Visible* (Boston: Houghton Mifflin, 1977), pp. 210–11; Richard T. Vann, *The Social Development of English Quakerism 1655–1755* (Cambridge, MA: Harvard University Press, 1969), pp. 1, 10, 15, 32.

7. Alison Gottesman [Coudert], "Francis Mercurius Van Helmont," Doctoral Dissertation, University of London, 1972, pp. 463, 584–5, 597.

8. Henry More, "Conjectura Cabbalistica: Or a Conjectural Essay of Interpreting the Mind of Moses in the Three First Chapters of Genesis According to a Threefold Cabbala: Viz. Literal Philosophical, Mystical, or, Divinely Moral (first published, 1653)," in *A Collection of Several Philosophical Writings of Dr. Henry More* (London, 1712). On this work, see Marjorie Nicolson, "Milton and the *Conjectura Cabbalistica*," *Philological Quarterly* 6 (1927): 1–18.

9. Gottfried Wilhelm von Leibniz, *Correspondance de Leibniz avec l'Electrice Sophie de Brunswicke-Lunebourg*, ed. Onno Klopp (Hanover: Klindworth, 1874), vol. 2, p. 8, letter of Sept. 1696; G. W. Leibniz, *Philosophischen Schriften*, ed. C. I. Gerhardt (Berlin, 1875–1890), vol. 3, pp. 176, 180; Politella, *Platonism, Aristotelianism*, p. 16; Nicolson, *Conway Letters*, p. 455.
10. Leibniz, *Philosophischen Schriften*, vol. 3, p. 217.
11. G. W. Leibniz, *New Essays Concerning Human Understanding* (written 1697), trans. Alfred G. Langley (Lasalle, IL: Open Court, 1949; first published, 1765), p. 67.
12. Ritter, vol. 12, pp. 26, 27, 30.
13. Conway, *Principles*, pp. 217, 221, 201, 211, 214.
14. Ibid., pp. 208, 210, 202.
15. Ibid., p. 221.
16. Ibid., pp. 191, 205, 206, 202, 204.
17. Ibid., pp. 224, 225, 285.
18. Ibid., pp. 182–3.
19. Ibid., p. 185.
20. G. W. Leibniz, "Considerations of Vital Principles and Plastic Natures, by the Author of the System of Pre-Established Harmony" (written 1705), *Philosophischen Schriften* vol. 6 (1885), p. 539; trans. in Leroy H. Loemker, ed. and trans. *Philosophical Papers and Letters*, 2 vols. (Chicago: University of Chicago Press, 1956), vol. 2, p. 954; William H. Hunter, Jr., "The Seventeenth Century Doctrine of Plastic Natures," *Harvard Theological Review* 43 (1950): 212; G. W. Leibniz, *Opera Omnia*, ed. Ludovici Datens (Geneva, 1768), vol. 5, p. 359.
21. Conway, *Principles*, pp. 222, 227.
22. Leibniz, *Philosophischen Schriften*, vol. 3 (1887), p. 217; Leibniz, "The Monadology," in *Philosophischen Schriften*, vol. 6 (1885), pp. 607–23, sec. 66, 67; Conway, *Principles*, p. 160.
23. Leibniz, "The Monadology," secs, 69, 54; Conway, *Principles*, pp. 196, 219, 197–8.
24. Leibniz, "The Monadology," secs. 84–84, 1, 2, 70; Conway, *Principles*, pp. 209, 210.
25. Conway, *Principles*, pp. 214, 168, 216.
26. On the mechanist-vitalist debates, see Hilda Hein, "Mechanism and Vitalism as Theoretical Commitments," *The Philosophical Forum* 1, no. 1, n.s. (Fall 1968): 185–205; Hilda Hein, "The Endurance of the Mechanism-Vitalism Controversy," *The Journal of the History of Biology* 5, no. 1 (Spring 1972): 159–88; Leonard R. Wheeler, *Vitalism: Its History and Validity* (London: Witherby, 1939).
27. Hannah Wooley, *The Gentlewoman's Companion* (London, 1673: first published, 1655), Introduction, pp. 1–2.
28. Bathsua Makin, *An Essay to Revive the Antient Education of Gentle-Women, in Religion, Manners, Arts, and Tongues* (London, 1673), pp. 3, 4, 13, 15; Mary Astell, *A Serious Proposal to the Ladies for the Advancement of Their True and Greatest Interest. . .* (London, 1694), pp. 9, 11. On seventeenth century feminist ideas concerning women's education, see Hilda Smith, *Reason's Disciples: Seventeenth Century Feminists* (Urbana: University of Illinois Press, 1982), pp. 75–114. On women's learning see Myra Reynolds, *The Learned Lady in England, 1650–1760* (Boston: Houghton Mifflin, 1920).

FIGURE 9.1 Emilie du Châtelet (1706–1749). After Maurice Quentin de la Tour (1704–1788).

Source: From Château Breteuil. Duke University, Project Vox, Creative Commons.

9

EMILIE DU CHÂTELET*

Gabrielle Emilie du Châtelet's historical identity has all too often centered on her role as the witty temperamental mistress of Voltaire.[1] Accounts of their life delight in relating the gossip of their relationship: Voltaire's anger when she remained closeted in her locked study with Clairaut, claiming difficulties with a mathematical proof; or his hysterical weeping causing his fall down a flight of stairs upon hearing of her death during childbirth, to be picked up at the foot by the young soldier Saint-Lambert who had made her pregnant.

In an age when marriage was a convenience and affairs—one at a time— the rule, when women unaided by aristocracy or money had little prospect of intellectual achievement, she recognized her worth and asked to be evaluated on her own grounds as a scholar:

> Judge me for my own merits or my lack of them but do not look upon me as an appendage to this great general or that renowned scholar. This star that shines at the court of France or that famed author. I am in my own right a whole person, responsible to myself alone, for all that I am, all that I say, all that I do.[2]

Recent scholarship has begun to produce evaluations of her contributions to science and philosophy which treat her own unique accomplishments. Her influence on Voltaire's thought, her mathematical achievements, her translation of Newton's *Principia Mathematica*, her dissemination of the Leibnizian philosophy in France, and her dissertation on the nature of fire have all been researched and discussed.[3]

In this chapter, I present an analysis of du Châtelet's natural philosophy and mechanics as it appeared in the anonymously published *Institutions de Physique* of 1740 (although some title pages say London, 1741).[4] The *Institutions* was meant as a textbook for her son's use. In part an attempt to popularize Leibniz's views, it was successful in creating immediate interest and excitement. Du Châtelet was probably introduced to Leibnizian ideas in 1736–1737 through manuscripts sent to Voltaire by Frederick of Prussia containing translations of Christian Wolff's Leibnizian metaphysics and from Voltaire's copy of Jean Jacques Mairan's "Dissertation sur l'estimation et la mesure des forces matrices du corps" (1728) against the Leibnizian concept of *vis viva*, mv^2.[5] Through Voltaire she was also familiar with the Leibniz-Clarke correspondence. In 1738 she read Jean Bernoulli's "Discours sur les lois de la communication du movement", and after an enquiry and a response from Maupertuis which favored Bernoulli over Mairan was converted to the Leibnizian position, at least in dynamics.[6] In a letter of April 30, 1738 to Maupertuis, she relates that she has read what Leibniz has written in the *Acta Eruditorum* on *vis viva*.[7]

Then in March 1739 Samuel Koenig was brought to Voltaire's chateau in Cirey, France by Maupertuis as a tutor for her and Voltaire in mathematics. By way of Koenig she became converted to Leibniz's philosophical views through their expression in the work of Christian Wolff. In the *Institutions* she states her indebtedness to Wolff's *Ontologia* of 1729, the author of which she had earlier called "*un grand bavard en metaphysique*".[8] As a result of Koenig's teachings she revised the philosophical chapters of the *Institutions de Physique* which had been written in secret and approved for publication by September 1738. Although Newtonian in its basic mechanical principles, the resulting work followed Leibniz on the subject of dynamics, while the natural philosophy of the early chapters presented an integration of elements from the thought of Leibniz, Descartes, and Newton.

It is this integrative character of Emilie du Châtelet's thought which sets her *Institutions* apart from other attempts to disseminate Newtonian mechanics. The metaphysical foundations of scientific theory, the place of physics in the context of a broader philosophy of nature, and the problem of the freedom of the will stimulated her intellectual imagination. Her attempts to integrate aspects of Cartesianism and Newtonianism with Leibnizian ideas reflected a need among natural philosophers of the 1740s to reconcile the conflicts among these systems. But these same integrative tendencies left her uncritical of logical inconsistencies in her account of the metaphysics underlying her system. In addition, her Leibnizian convictions in dynamics prevented her from achieving a full recognition of the validity of both measures of "force", mv and mv^2. The following is a discussion of her synthesis and its strengths and weaknesses.

A metaphysical question had first stimulated du Châtelet's interest in Leibniz's *vis viva* principle. In her correspondence with Maupertuis she exhibited great concern for the implications of the conservation of living force for free will. Stating early in 1738 that she had read much on the subject of *forces vives*, she asked whether the freedom of living beings to create motion must not be a violation of conservation. "I believe myself free", she wrote, "and I do not know whether the same quantity of force in the universe does not destroy freedom".[9] In the commencement of motion, she reasoned, is it not true that a force is produced which hitherto did not exist? If we do not have the power to produce motion, then there is no free will. But if there is free will then it is absolutely necessary that the will can initiate motion."[10]

The issue of the free will of individuals in initiating motion was related to the larger question of God's will in creating motion in the universe and in subsequently causing particular motions. One of the central issues of the *vis viva* controversy had been the question of God's role in the natural order. Was God's nature to be characterized by his power and volition or by his wisdom and foresight?[11] The distinction between the omnipotence of God's will and omniscience of his logic formed the framework within which Emilie du Châtelet formulated the natural philosophy of her *Institutions de Physique*.

A basic question discussed by Leibniz and Clarke in their famous letters on the nature of God, space, matter, and force was the kind of world God could create.[12] For Newton and Clarke the world could have been otherwise, for it depended on the free exercise of God's will and its continued sustenance through God's providence.[13] For Leibniz it was the best of all possible worlds since God operated rationally within the laws of logic to create the actual existing world.[14]

Rejecting the voluntarist theology of Newton and Clarke, Emilie du Châtelet held that the logical possibility for the existence of the natural world was to be explained by Leibniz's principle of non-contradiction, and its actual existence by the principle of sufficient reason which accounts for the existence of some things and not others.[15] A logically possible world is a non-contradictory world, whose beings could exhibit nothing, within themselves, mutually destructive or incompatible. However, such a world may not actually exist; the actual world is created by God's volition (*volonté*). "Thus the divine understanding is the eternal region of truths and the source of possibilities; the same as his volition is the source of actuality and existence".[16] God's understanding as the origin of all that is possible is thus prior to divine volition, the source of existence and actuality. "If the possibility of things depended on his volition, then it would be necessary to say that God had been without understanding while his volition was occupied in creating the possibles".[17]

In asserting that God's "understanding contains all that is possible [while] all that is not found is impossible",[18] she failed to give adequate consideration to the area lying between logical possibility and actual existence which had been stressed by Leibniz in his mature years. According to Leibniz that which does not actually exist is not logically impossible but it may not be part of the "best of all possible worlds", i.e., the most perfect. She did not argue, as had Leibniz, that the external possibilities must also be those which are the most perfect if they are to become actual.[19]

Criticizing the arbitrariness of natural explanation based on no other reason than God's volition, she rejected Malebranche's occasionalist doctrine of God's immediacy in the action of moving bodies.[20] In the occasionalist system, she said, natural law as expressed through secondary causation has no efficacy because bodies are never the causes of activity but only the receptors.[21] God's immediate concourse would be an immanent manifestation of Divine Causation external to nature. Such continual miracles are not consistent with the laws of motion and the essence of bodies.

Emilie du Châtelet's philosophy of nature in the *Institutions de Physique* was basically a Leibnizian exposition, yet it showed the influence of Cartesian substance philosophy—the position that whatever exists is a substance or a modification of a substance.[22] For Descartes the two substances, matter and mind, differed in essence. The essence of matter was extension, the essence of mind was thinking.[23] Material things could be modified by the attributes size, shape, and motion; minds by sensations and ideas.

Du Châtelet had schooled herself in the Cartesian distinctions between essences and their attributes and modes (or invariable and variable properties). When she came to treat these matters in her *Institutions*, her account revealed the influence of the Leibnizian view that attributes and properties are contained in the concept of each individual substance and not amenable to external influences.[24] She argued that the attributes of existing bodies are logically deduced from and harmoniously related to their essence in that they are possible, non-contradictory, and not mutually destructive, although they are not always found in actual existing beings.[25] When the essentials are posed, the attributes follow by the law of sufficient reason.[26] In any being, essence and attributes are constant; essences are invariable and attributes incommunicable. Modes, however, are variable properties; their existence is contingent. From the essence it can be understood why a mode is possible, but not why it becomes actual. Modes do not depend logically on attributes because attributes do not contain the reason for the existence of antecedent modes or external existing beings.[27]

In general, then, God's understanding was the source of what was possible, the essences themselves being founded on the principle of non-contradiction. If, on the other hand, essences depended on God's will, they would be arbitrary and would be possible or impossible simply because God willed it so.[28] Hence, to achieve a rational understanding of nature, it was necessary first to demonstrate the intrinsic possibility of a body from the principle of non-contradiction, secondly to establish its external possibility from the principle of sufficient reason, and then to deduce the attributes and the modes of which it was susceptible.[29] Placing the body within the order of nature it was finally necessary to show how it depended on its neighbors and which causes gave actuality to the many possible modes.[30] Relationships between bodies could thus be understood through internal relations within the order of nature not as externally imposed upon unrelated particulars.

In his analysis of nature, Leibniz had distinguished between primitive and derivative force (mv^2). The monads, or primitive active force, were true substances; derivative force was a *phenomenon bene fundatum*, not fully real, yet derived from primitive force and subject to the order and laws of nature. Derivative force, found in the impact of bodies, was attached to and was "like" the primitive force or true substance—it was "substantialized".[31] Leibniz had also assigned extension to the world of well-founded phenomena, arguing that extension and motion are only attributes of phenomenal bodies, whereas primitive force is a true substance.[32] He held that space was a relation: the order of simultaneous states in the unfolding lives of monads, and that extension was the magnitude of space. "It is wrong", said Leibniz, "to confuse extension with what is extended as is commonly done, and so to consider it a substance".[33]

Emilie du Châtelet maintained the Leibnizian distinction between primitive force and derivative force which "derives from the former but is only a phenomenon", grounding primitive force in the "simple unextended beings" Leibniz had called monads.[34] These simple beings consisted of a continual tendency to act, an indestructible tendency which constantly produced change when there was no sufficient reason to prevent the completion of the action.[35] Sensible changes were the result of a continued perpetual succession of internal states in the simple beings. That the internal action of each simple being differed from that of all others followed from Leibniz's principle of the identity of indiscernibles.[36]

She argued that extension could be grounded in non-extended beings and that extended beings existed because there were simple unextended beings. However, it was impossible to represent these simple unextended beings in the imagination or to detect them with the senses.[37] Mechanical phenomena discernible by the senses derive from higher metaphysical principles; the metaphysical union of elements produces the mechanical union of bodies which we see.[38]

The repugnance which one has at conceiving how simple non-extended beings can, by their own assemblage, compose extended beings is not a reason to reject them. This revolt of the imagination against simple beings comes simply from habit in which we represent our ideas as sensible images. . . . Perhaps someday there will be found a calculus of true metaphysics in which by the sole substitution of characters one can come to truths, as done in algebra. M. Leibniz believed he had found such a calculus but died before communicating his ideas on it.[39]

In attempting to relate extension to the non-extended she held that phenomenal extension is a composite of substances; both extension and force have their origin in the same simple beings.[40] The extension of matter arises from the aggregate of simple beings; force and resistance arise from the harmonious conspiring of active and passive principles within the aggregated elements.[41] Just as colors and the sensible phenomena of gross bodies result from confusion and the imperfection of our sense organs, the confusion decreases by degrees when the real origin of phenomena is found.[42] The gradation leads to simple beings or monads, the real substances which are the origin of what we see. Thus phenomena are born from the confusion of the several realities.[43] Abstraction allows us to focus our attention either on the whole confused aggregate or on the real elements of the aggregate.[44]

Although du Châtelet attempted to present a Leibnizian analysis of the relationship between the phenomenal and substantial levels of nature and between the parts of an aggregate, she did not really try to clarify the logic of these relations. This left her account incomplete and unconvincing. For Leibniz the elements of a composite whole were connected by ideal or external relations as opposed to the necessary intrinsic connections between substances. Thus physical connections such as those between a pile of stones did not provide a "true unity". The link between substances and *phenomena bene fundata* was for Leibniz ultimately explained in analogical language and while far more subtle than du Châtelet's account represented one of the weaknesses of his system.[45]

In her discussion of the phenomenal world Emilie du Châtelet argued that matter was to be described in terms of extension, force, and inertia. Extension combined with the passive force of inertia and the active moving force of *vis viva* (derivative force) is what we "call" matter. However, the terms of her analysis were often inconsistent. In some places she stated that the nature of body "consists" of these three principles, "subsisting together" and mutually independent.[46] In other places she wrote that force is "different from matter", but "inseparably attached to it".[47] Nevertheless, the main point of her philosophy was that force and matter must be placed on the same ontological level. Force is to be found in all matter; one is unknown without the other. Bodies cannot be described solely in terms of simple extension as Descartes and Malebranche had believed.[48] It was therefore necessary to join the "power to act" to extension.[49] In insisting on the activity of matter she contributed to a new synthesis emerging from the older Cartesian philosophy long held in France.

Another source of major confusion in her philosophy was her use of the term substance in describing the elements of her ontology. In some places she referred to extension, force, and inertia as *phenomes substantiés*, a term she attributed to Wolff, asserting that the three were only substantial phenomena, "which appear to us as substances but which are not".[50] But in other places she directly labeled them substances:

> At first it appears strange that bodies should be composed of two substances, extension and active force and to admit of a species of action of an immaterial substance such as active force on matter, (Sur la matière), but as on the one hand, the phenomena show the substantiality of active force the same as that of matter and on the other there are insurmountable difficulties which oppose if one should conclude that neither matter nor active force are true substances, it is necessary to mount higher and look for their source in something prior from which one can show why active force and matter should be substances.[51]

This left it unclear as to whether extension and active force were substantial phenomena or true substances. To further compound the problem, du Châtelet, like Descartes, sometimes referred to extension as a principal property of substance and sometimes as substance itself.[52] Force, inertia, and extension were likewise referred to sometimes as principles and other times as essences or essential properties of matter. Her failure to use terms carefully thus left considerable confusion as to the exact status of the components of her ontology.

In evaluating Emilie du Châtelet's philosophy of nature we may say that she did not claim originality for the philosophical ideas she expressed. She regarded herself as the disseminator and translator of the work of others. Philosophically her ideas were often confused and inconsistent. She did not grasp the subtleties of the full Leibnizian doctrine but this was due in part to the limited availability of texts, the failure of Leibniz himself to provide a systematic exposition of his own philosophy, and its dissemination through the second-hand accounts of Wolff and Koenig. In addition, substance philosophy, which formed her framework, was dying out as a viable mode of analysis. Yet the *Institutions de Physique* represented one of many attempts in the mid-eighteenth century to integrate the central ideas of the Cartesian, Leibnizian, and Newtonian systems of nature. In recognizing the activity of matter and in placing matter and force on the same ontological level, she contributed to an emerging view of nature which ultimately became important in the development of the general law of energy conservation.

DU CHÂTELET'S DYNAMICS

The *Institutions de Physique* also presented a Leibnizian interpretation of the dynamics of bodies in motion, or *vis viva*. It discussed the standard examples used by the participants in the *vis viva* controversy and defended the Leibnizian position. Du Châtelet began her analysis of dynamics with Leibniz's distinction between dead (or Newtonian) and living force. Living force can arise from dead force when a body is continually subject to a series of infinitely small forces or pressures (*pressions*). If a body yields to these dead forces, it conserves them and acquires a force which is the sum of all these accumulated pressures.[53]

She gave two examples of the relationship of dead to living force: elasticity and gravity. Following the elastic spring argument introduced by Jean Bernoulli (1727) she pictured a set of three similar sections of elastic springs (*ressorts*) "equally strong and equally tense" (see Figure 9.2).[54] If a body receives the force held in one of these elastic springs, a second body receiving the force held in two similar elastic springs equal to the first will acquire two times more force. A body receiving the force of three equal and similar springs will acquire three times the force.

An analogous example was the force of gravity.[55] Gravity presses uniformly on heavy bodies at each instant and at all points of their fall. Gravity can be considered as an infinite elastic spring NR pressing equally on body A in the space AB and acting at all points between A and B (see Figure 9.3). The forces that the bodies have received at A and R are as the lines AB and AR since the living forces are as the number of equal elastic springs communicating by expansion their forces to the bodies in motion. In a double space there are two times as many elastic coils as in a single space, and the number of coils are in the ratio of the spaces AB to AR. Thus the living forces of the body descending by gravity are as the spaces AB to AR. But these spaces are as the squares of the velocities, and thus the living forces of the bodies at B and R are as the squares of their velocities.

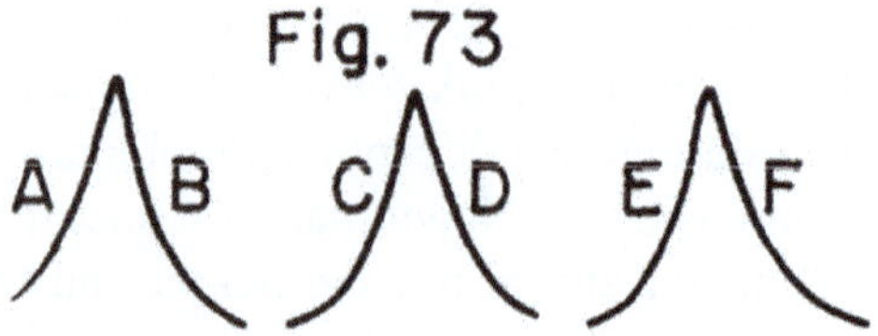

FIGURE 9.2 Du Châtelet's Figure 73

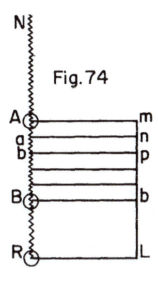

FIGURE 9.3 Du Châtelet's Figure 74

Space and not time, she argued, was the basis for the measure of "force":

Time should enter into the consideration of force no more than into the measure
of riches of a man, which are the same whether dispensed in a day, a year, or
a hundred years.[56]

For force to be real and not merely a metaphysical notion, therefore, a resistance was necessary by which its effects could be seen. If a body encountered
other bodies which it set in motion, or if it bent elastic springs or compressed
or transported other masses, then the presence of the force was known and
could be estimated by the quantity of the effects it produced.

Du Châtelet then proceeded to reduce the arguments of Jean Jacques Mairan
(1728), supporter of the Cartesian measure of force, $m|v|$, to nonsense.[57] The out-
cry which followed rekindled the famous *vis viva* controversy, inspiring Mairan,
Voltaire, Abbé Deidier, and d'Alembert to re-examine the issue.[58]

Mairan had followed the Cartesian definition of force, $m|v|$ (i.e., the quan-
tity of matter multiplied by the uniform velocity of the body). In his 1728
paper he attempted to reduce accelerated and retarded motion to cases of
uniform motion. In this way, force in the Newtonian sense, Δmv, could be
eliminated from the analysis of nature, a philosophical position which followed from Malebranche's rejection of the concept of force.[59] Mairan had
defined $m|v|$ in terms of the "elastic bands not lifted, the objects not flattened,

and in general the objects not overcome which would be under uniform motion." Force $m|v|$, was therefore proportional to the simple velocity, i.e., Cartesian force.

He had argued that the momentum of a moving body could be retarded by degrees by elastic bands placed at equal intervals in its path. Each one of these bands would offer a resistance equal to that of a body of mass 1, moving with velocity 1, so that the moving body lost momentum at each encounter. Mairan calculated the mv lost by the body in successive instants by the number of bent strips. He also calculated the number of bands the body would have passed if it were moving uniformly during the same time. He then measured the total mv by the difference or total number of bands not bent.[60]

Du Châtelet pointed out that Mairan was analyzing nature not as it was, but as it was not. He appealed to events which did not occur rather than those which did. In refuting his supposition that force is measured by the spaces not traversed which would be under uniform motion, du Châtelet argued that two contradictory ideas were being used simultaneously. If a body exhausted a part of its force in compressing three elastic springs in the first second of its retarded motion, and only had enough force remaining to compress one more in the next second, then it would have to take back some of its force if it could compress two springs in the second of uniform motion. It is contradictory to suppose that a force can remain constant and yet at the same time that it can produce a portion of the effects which consume it. A body cannot, at one and the same time, be considered as moving under uniform motion and retarded motion.[61]

In general, she said, the effects produced by uniform motion and retarded motion are different and cannot be compared. The effect of the first is only the space traversed, without obstacles encountered within it; that of the second consists in the displacement of these obstacles. In all those cases which are possible, the force of bodies should be evaluated by the obstacles which it is possible to overcome. As she put it in a later reply to Mairan, it is not permissible to substitute for real parts actually overcome or consumed, imaginary parts that cannot be surmounted, without supposing contradictions.[62]

Equally forcefully, Emilie du Châtelet also exposed the "error" in an argument contrived by James Jurin, who supported Descartes" quantity of motion $m|v|$ as the measure of "force".[63] Jurin had supposed a plane moving in a straight line with a velocity of 1. On this plane is a body of mass 1 acquiring its velocity from the moving plane and consequently having a "force" of 1. Now suppose that a spring capable of giving the body a velocity of 1 is fastened to the plane and in being released pushes the body in the same direction as the plane. In so doing it communicates one degree of velocity and consequently one degree of force to the body. Now, asks Jurin, what will be the total force of the body? The total force adds to 2, but the total velocity is

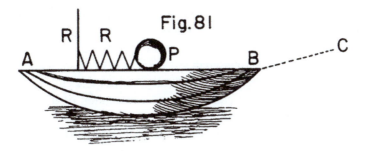

FIGURE 9.4 Du Châtelet's Figure 81

also 2. Thus the force of a body is proportional to the mass multiplied by the simple velocity.

The error that du Châtelet correctly and astutely finds in the previous reasoning is this: Suppose for greater ease that in place of the plane of Jurin, a boat AB moves on a river in the direction BC, with velocity 1 (see Figure 9.4). Body F is transported on the boat, acquiring thereby the same velocity as the boat. The elastic spring touching the ball is supported at the other end by an immobile support. When released it pushes toward both directions, A and B, and communicates to the body P not a velocity of 1 but this velocity minus a second quantity which depends on the proportion between the mass of the boat, AB, and the mass of body P. The quantity of living force residing in the coiled spring will, after its release, be found in the body and the boat taken together. Thus Jurin's case is founded on the false supposition that the elastic R will communicate to body P transported on a movable plane the same force that it communicated to it when the spring was supported by an immovable obstacle at rest.[64] In other words, this is a case in which one must consider the energy exchange ($\Delta E = \frac{1}{2}mv^2$) between the moving object and the moving plane or ship. In failing to recognize this, Jurin had made the same logical error as had Colin Maclaurin in an earlier argument (1724) comparing bodies released with equal velocities on a moving ship and on the shore.[65] Both had made calculations which supported the measure of "force", mv, and both had neglected the recoil energy supplied to the moving ship. Emilie du Châtelet was alone in recognizing the inconsistency in this type of argument.

Du Châtelet's *Institutions de Physiques* was sufficiently provocative and controversial that it caused Mairan, secretary of the Académie des Sciences in Paris, to respond to her criticisms in a *"Lettre a Madame sur la question des forces vives en reponse aux objections"*, in 1741.[66] She in turn submitted a reply later in the same year which was published with her *"Dissertation sur la nature et propagation du feu"*.[67]

The publication of the *Institutions* also brought to a head deep philosophical differences which existed between du Châtelet and Voltaire. Voltaire, who joined the controversy in 1741, was the author of the popular French presentation of the principles of Newtonianism and was in every way opposed to the Leibnizian way of thinking.[68] His sceptical, practical, and empirical approach to science led him to impatience with any explanation of the world which went beyond the strictly material. The philosophy of Leibniz and that of his follower Christian Wolff, from whom Voltaire learned Leibnizian metaphysics, left him with little respect for Leibniz's views.

A French translation of one of Wolff's books appearing in 1736 was Voltaire's first introduction to Leibniz. His and Emilie du Châtelet's association with Samuel Koenig in 1739 taught him more of Wolffian metaphysics and confirmed him in his opposition. His loyalty to Madame du Châtelet, however, caused him to restrain his attacks on Leibnizianism. Nevertheless, he regretted her conversion and made fun of her enthusiasm for Leibniz. In spite of this he seems to have appreciated the merits of the *Institutions de Physique*.[69] An article by Voltaire, presented to the *Académie des Sciences* in 1741 and entitled "Doubts on the Measure of Motive Force and Their Nature", took issue with Emilie du Châtelet and with Leibnizian dynamics:[70]

> Force is not . . . an internal principle [*un principe interne*] a substance which animates bodies and is distinguished from bodies as some philosophers have maintained [i.e., Leibniz]. Force is nothing but the action of bodies in motion and does not exist primitively in simple beings called monads which these philosophers say are without extension and yet constitute extended matter. They can no more produce moving force than zeros can form a number. If force is only a property it is subject to variation as are all modes of matter. And if it is in the same ratio as the quantity of motion, is it not obvious that its quantity alters if the motion augments or diminishes?[71]

In attempting to prove this point, Voltaire gave an interesting incorrect example which followed from Descartes' concept of the quantity of motion, $m|v|$. The quantity of motion is always *increased*, he said, when a small *elastic* body collides with a larger one at rest. For example, an elastic body A of mass 20, in motion with velocity 11 ($mv = 220$), hits B at rest whose mass is 200 ($mv = 0$). A rebounds with a quantity of motion of 180 ($mv = 180$) and B goes forward with $mv = 400$ (i.e., $220 + 0 = -180 + 400$). But Voltaire reasoned that A, which originally had a "force" of 200, had produced a total "force", $m|v|$ of 580. "On the other hand, as everyone agrees, a great deal of motion is lost in the collision of inelastic bodies. Thus force in particular parts of matter increases and decreases".[72]

In Leibniz's philosophy "force" (mv^2) was conserved in elastic collisions. Voltaire is arguing that "force" ($m|v|$) is not conserved either in this elastic case or in inelastic collisions; rather, it varies as do other properties of matter. "Force", therefore, cannot be a primary or invariant property of matter. Voltaire's disagreement with du Châtelet rested in part on a difference in the mathematical definition of force and in part on metaphysical differences within the context of substance philosophy. For du Châtelet force itself was a substance, while for Voltaire it was only a property of the universal substance, matter.

In his first published work, "Thoughts on the True Estimation of Living Forces" (1747), Immanuel Kant commented on Emilie du Châtelet's role in the long controversy.[73] He gave his own account of her objections to Mairan and Jurin, arguing that there was justification for both the Cartesian and Leibnizian positions.[74] For his own purposes he classified forces into two types: internal, or metaphysical, force which causes a body to move unless hindered but which, since it is not subject to the law of conservation of force, is for that reason not capable of mathematical treatment despite the fact that one can provide an "estimate" for its magnitude, namely, mv^2, in all of which it bears an uneasy resemblance to a mixture of Leibniz's "primitive active" and "derivative active" (*vis viva*) forces. The other type of force was externally produced, phenomenal, and subject to conservation, hence "mathematical", and expresses as mv, the Cartesian measure of "force".[75]

Moreover, in a section entitled "Vindication of the Thoughts of Mairan against Mme du Châtelet", Kant chastized the Marquise for failing to show more respect to such a great man as Mairan. But, he concluded, because she stood far above those of her own sex, and most of the opposite sex as well, it was understandable that she did not avail herself of the flattery and praise especially reserved for the fairer sex![76]

Although both Kant, in his own manner, and Voltaire, in his, paid tribute to Emilie du Châtelet's outstanding abilities, the limits of their own conceptual systems prevented either man from giving adequate recognition to her mechanical analysis of the *vis viva* controversy.

CONCLUSION

In Chapter 5 above on "The Leibnizian-Newtonian Debates", I argued that adherents to the Newtonian and Leibnizian measures of force in the 1720s were influenced by intellectual commitments to the Newtonian and Leibnizian worldviews and by social commitments to the groups and institutions surrounding the two scientists.[77] These commitments rendered it difficult or impossible to entertain the possibility that the opposing interpretations of the experiments and mechanical examples might have any validity. I suggested that such commitments would be weakened in the succeeding generation of scientists which had begun to integrate elements of the two philosophies of nature by the 1740s.

Emilie du Châtelet's *Institutions de Physique* represented such an integration. In her metaphysics she adopted and unified arguments from the Cartesian view that extension was the defining characteristic of matter and from the Leibnizian philosophy in which force was viewed as the primary substance. In her mechanics she presented the Leibnizian position in dynamics along with a Newtonian exposition of basic mechanics. Although her analysis of mechanical problems was of very high quality, she did not reach the conclusion that both Newtonian and Leibnizian measures of force were valid in the solution of problems.

However, other natural philosophers, namely, d'Alembert, Desaguliers, Boscovich, and Reid, writing during the 1740s, did arrive at integrations of various elements of the three worldviews such that it became possible for them to admit of the validity of both measures of force. Even so, it cannot be claimed that through these integrations they "resolved" the *vis viva* controversy. Thus d'Alembert in 1743 accepted as valid measures of force mdv, or dead force, for cases of equilibrium, and mv^2, or living force, while calling the controversy a "dispute over words".[78] Not until 1758 did he add to this the measure mv defined in terms of the space traversed uniformly in a given time. But his *Traité de dynamique* was basically a text in Cartesian kinematics. Forces were rejected as "obscure and metaphysical"; mechanics was properly the study of motion or "observed effects" only.[79]

In 1744, John Theophilus Desaguliers finally published the second volume of his *Course of Experimental Philosophy*, explaining the nine-year delay between the two volumes as due to his inability to resolve the "question about the Force of Bodies in Motion".[80] At the conclusion of his discussion of the opposing arguments, he stated: "I am now convinc'd that all the Phaenomena of the Congres of Bodies may be equally solv'd according to the Principles of the Defenders of the new [mv^2] as well as those of the old [mv] opinion".[81] In spite of this admission, however, Desaguliers was a committed Newtonian who accepted and operated within a conceptual framework which made force external to matter rather than an internal principle of activity.[82]

Boscovich, in his *De Viribus Vivis* of 1745, had analyzed mv as a time dependent function and mv^2 as a space dependent function using geometric diagrams.[83] But he did not claim equal status for the two measures of "force"; momentum was the true measure while *vis viva* was valid only as a calculating device. He could not accept Leibniz's philosophy of the internal activity of matter.[84]

Thomas Reid's *Essay on Quantity* of 1748 likewise stated acceptance of both mv and mv^2 as valid principles in mechanics.[85] An early adherent to momentum, over a period of several years he gradually came to the realization that the various problems and experiments discussed in the *vis viva* controversy could be explained equally as well by using the principle mv^2.

In spite of the fact that during the 1740s Desaguliers, Boscovich, Reid, and d'Alembert independently came to the conclusion that both mv^2 and mv were valid mechanical principles, this did not imply their equal acceptance philosophically and mechanically. Only a few scientists utilized both principles in the solution of mechanical problems until after the enunciation of the general law of energy conservation one hundred years later in the 1840s.[86]

While Emilie du Châtelet did not adopt the validity of both measures of force in her mechanics, her insistence on the equal status of matter and "force" contributed to a new view of nature. During the eighteenth century, the Newtonian-Cartesian dualism of passive matter and external mechanical forces was replaced by an ontology of active substances within extended matter.[87] The view that the essence of matter consisted not only of extension but also of attractive and repulsive forces was important in the emergence of the general law of the conservation of energy in the 1840s.[88] Thus a philosophical reorientation as well as a mechanical "solution" were both necessary before it could be said that the *vis viva* controversy had been "resolved."

NOTES

* From Carolyn Merchant, "Madame du Châtelet's Metaphysics and Mechanics," *Studies in History and Philosophy of Science* 8, no. 1 (May, 1977): 29–48. Copyright 1977 Elsevier, all rights reserved. Thanks are expressed to Dr. Dierdre LaPorte for sending me portions of her doctoral dissertation, "Theories of Fire and Heat in the First Half of the Eighteenth Century," Harvard, 1970, relating to du Châtelet and Voltaire; and to Keith Symon for reading and evaluating du Châtelet's contributions to mechanics as discussed in my dissertation, "The *Vis Viva* Controversy: Leibniz to d'Alembert," University of Wisconsin, 1967. I am indebted to Gerd Buchdahl for comments on du Châtelet's ideas in relation to the philosophy of Leibniz and Kant. I wish to thank the Frederick E. Brasch Collection on Sir Isaac Newton and the History of Scientific Thought, Special Collections, Stanford University Libraries, Stanford, California, for permission to reprint the accompanying plate from Mme Du Châtelet's Institutions de Physique, Paris, 1740. Section I of this paper was presented to the annual meeting of the History of Science Society, Washington, DC, December, 1972. A conference, "Emilie du Châtelet: 310th Anniversary," was held at Boston University, Nov. 18–19, 2016.

1. For accounts of the life of Gabrielle Emilie du Châtelet (1706–1749) and her relationship with Voltaire see Mme de Graffigny, *La vie privée de Voltaire et de Mme du Châtelet* (Paris: Treuttel and Wurtz, 1820); Frank Hamel, *An Eighteenth Century Marquise: A Study of Emile du Châtelet and Her Time* (London: Stanley Paul and Company, 1910); André Maurel, *La Marquise du Châtelet, Amie de Voltaire* (Paris: Librairie Hachette, 1930); Jean-Baptiste Capefigue, *La Marquise du Châtelet et les amies: des philosophes du XVIIIᵉ Siecle* (Paris: Amyot, 1868); and Nancy Mitford, *Voltaire in Love* (London: Hamilton, 1957).

2. Letter to Frederick of Prussia, quoted in Samuel Edwards [pseud. Noel Bertram Gerson], *The Divine Mistress* (New York: David McKay, 1970), p. 1. This popular account of her life fails to make a serious evaluation of her scientific achievements.

3. For evaluations of du Châtelet's intellectual achievements see Ira O. Wade, *Voltaire and Madame du Châtelet: An Essay on the Intellectual Activity at Cirey* (Princeton: Princeton University Press, 1941); W. H. Barber, "Mme. du Châtelet and Leibnizianism: The Genesis of the Institutions de Physique," in William H. Barber, et al., eds., *The Age of Enlightenment: Studies Presented to Theodore Besterman* (Edinburgh and London: Oliver & Boyd, 1967), pp. 200–22; William H. Barber, *Leibniz in France from Arnauld to Voltaire: A Study in French Reactions to Leibnizianism, 1670–1760* (Oxford: Clarendon Press, 1955), pp. 135–40, 182–6. On her work on chemistry and the nature of fire see Dierdre LaPorte, "Theories of Fire and Heat in the First Half of the Eighteenth Century," Doctoral Dissertation, Cambridge, MA: Harvard University, 1970, pp. 296–343; and Robert L. Walters, "Chemistry at Cirey," *Studies on Voltaire and the 18th Century* 58 (1967): 1807–27. On her French edition of Newton's *Principia* see I. Bernard Cohen, "The French Translation of Isaac Newton's *Philosophiae naturalis principia mathematica* (1756, 1759, 1966)," *Archives Internationales d'Histoire des Sciences* 21(1968): 261–90. On her mathematics see Julian L. Coolidge, "Six Female Mathematicians," *Scripta Mathematica* 17 (1951): 20–31; and Florian Cajori, "Madame du Châtelet on Fluxions," *Mathematical Gazette* 13 (1926): 252.

4. Gabrielle Emilie du Châtelet, *Institutions de Physique* (Paris, 1740).

5. Jean Jacques de Mairan, *Mémoires de l'Académie des Sciences de Paris* (1728): 1–49. On her Leibnizian background see Barber, "Mme. du Châtelet and Leibnizianism," pp. 205–6, and René Taton, article on "Gabrielle Emilie du Châtelet," in Charles Coulston Gillispie, ed., *Dictionary of Scientific Biography* (New York: Charles Scribner's Sons, 1970), vol. 3, pp. 215–17.

6. Theodore Besterman, ed., *Les Lettres de la Marquise du Châtelet* (Geneva: Institut et Musée Voltaire, Las Delices, 1958), vol. 1, lettres 1–231, 1733–9; vol. 2, lettres 232–486, 1740–9. See Lettre 118 à Maupertuis, 2 février 1738, vol. 1, p. 213. Jean Bernoulli, "Discours sur les lois de la communication du mouvement," in *Recueil des pièces qui a remporté les prix de l'Academie Royale des Sciences* (Paris, 1727), vol. 2, pp. 1–108 (separate pagination).

7. Besterman, *Lettres*, lettre 122, vol. 1, p. 220. Probably Leibniz's, "Brevis demonstratio," *Acta Eruditorum*, March, 1686; and "Specimen dynamicum," *Acta Erud.*, April, 1695.

8. Besterman, *Lettres*, lettre 146 "a Maupertuis, 29 September 1738, vol. I, p. 246. Barber, *Leibniz in France* [3], pp. 135–40; and "Mme. du Châtelet and Leibnizianism" [3], pp. 208–9. On her debt to Leibniz and Wolff see the *Institutions*, "avant-propos," pp. 12, 13. (Christian Wolff, *Philosophia Prima Sive Ontologia* [1st ed., Frankfurt, 1729], critical edition edn. Jean Ecole," in *Gesammelte Werke, Abt. II, Bd. 3* [Hidesheim: Georg Olms, 1962]). In a footnote, du Châtelet declared her indebtedness principally to the following chapters of the *Ontologia*; "De Principio Contradictionis, de Principio Rationis Sufficientis, de Possibili et Impossibili (1962 edn., pp. 15–87), de Necessario et Contingente (pp. 223–60); de Extensions, Continuitate, Spatio, Tempore etc. (pp. 425–492). On the relations of Wolff's philosophy to that of Leibniz see Jean Ecole, "Cosmologie wolffienne et dynamique leibnizienne," *Les Etudes philosophiques* 19 (1964): 3–10.

9. Besterman, *Lettres*, lettre 122 Maupertuis, 30 avr. 1738, vol. 1, p. 220.

10. Ibid., lettre 124 "a Maupertuis, 9 mai 1738, vol. 1, p. 226.

11. Carolyn [Merchant] Iltis, "The Leibnizian-Newtonian Debates: Natural Philosophy and Social Psychology," *British Journal for the History of Science* 6 (December 1973): 343–77, see Ch 5 above; David Kubrin, "Newton and the Cyclical Cosmos: Providence and the Mechanical Philosophy," *Journal of the History of Ideas* 28 (July–September 1967): 325–46.

12. Samuel Clarke, *A Collection of Papers Which Passed between the Late Learned Mr. Leibniz and Dr. Clarke* (London, 1717).

13. On voluntarism and 17th century natural philosophies see James E. McGuire, "Boyle's Conception of Nature," *Journal of the History of Ideas* 33 (1972): 523–42. On God's will

and direct action in Newton's natural philosophy see James E. McGuire, "Force, Active Principles, and Newton's Invisible Realm," *Ambix* 15 (1968): 154–68, esp. pp. 161–4. See also Peter M. Heimann, "Nature Is a Perpetual Worker," *Ambix* 20 (1973): 1–25.

14. Gottfried Wilhelm Leibniz, *Philosophical Papers and Letters*, ed. Leroy E. Loemker (Chicago: University of Chicago Press, 1956), vol. 2, pp. 1099, 1100.
15. Du Châtelet, *Institutions* [4], pp. 21–2 (section 7, 8); p. 55 (section 34). On Leibniz's principle of non-contradiction see Margaret D. Wilson, "Leibniz and Locke on First Truths," *Journal of the History of Ideas* 28 (1967): 847–66.
16. Du Châtelet, *Institutions*, p. 68 (section 48); see also p. 134 (section 121).
17. Ibid., p. 68 (section 48).
18. Ibid., p. 67 (section 49).
19. Gerd Buchdahl, *Metaphysics and the Philosophy of Science* (Oxford: Blackwell, 1969), pp. 399, 404, 454.
20. Du Châtelet, *Institutions*, p. 69 (section 49); p. 154 (section 138). On Malebranche see Eric J. Aiton, *The Vortex Theory of Planetary Motions* (New York: Elsevier, 1972), p. 71; Thomas L. Hankins, "The Influence of Malebranche on the Science of Mechanics During the Eighteenth Century," *Journal of the History of Ideas* 28 (1967): 193–210.
21. Du Châtelet, *Institutions*, p. 154 (section 138).
22. On Cartesianism and substance philosophy see Richard A. Watson, *The Downfall of Cartesianism, 1673–1712: A Study of Epistemological Issues in Late 17th Century Cartesianism* (The Hague: Martinus Nijhoff, 1966).
23. René Descartes, *The Meditations* (La Salle: Open Court, 1952), pp. 52, 53. On Descartes' physics and its reception in 18th century thought see Paul Mouy, *Le developpement de la physique cartesienne* (Paris: Vrin, 1934); Jean Ehrard, *L'Idée de nature en France dans la première moitié du XVIIIe siècle*, 2 vols. (Paris: S.E.V.P.E.N., 1963); Daniel Mornet, *Les sciences de la nature en France XVIIIe siècle* (Paris: Armand Cohn, 1911). On Descartes' philosophy see Gerd Buchdahl, *Metaphysics and the Philosophy* [19], chap. 3, pp. 79–180.
24. Gottfried Wilhelm Leibniz, *Discourse on Metaphysics and Correspondence with Arnauld* (La Salle: Open Court, 1957), pp. 103–36.
25. Du Châtelet, *Institutions*, pp. 59–60 (section 39, 41).
26. Ibid., p. 61 (section 42); p. 66 (section 47).
27. Ibid., p. 59 (section 40); p. 65 (section 47); p. 62 (section 44).
28. Ibid., p. 67 (section 48).
29. Ibid., p. 69 (section 50).
30. Ibid., p. 70 (Section 50).
31. Buchdahl *Metaphysics and the Philosophy* [19], pp. 410, 417, 420, 423. On Leibniz's dynamics see also Carolyn [Merchant] Iltis, "Leibniz and the Vis Viva Controversy," *Isis* 62 (1970): 21–35, see also Ch 4, this book; Wilson, "Leibniz's Dynamics and Contingency in Nature,"; and James E. McGuire, "*Labyrinthus continui*: Leibniz on Substance, Activity and Matter," in Peter K. Machamer and Robert G. Turnbull, eds., *Motion and Time, Space and Matter: Interrelations in the History of Philosophy and Science* (Columbus: Ohio State University Press, 1976): 290–326.
32. Leibniz, *Philosophical Papers*, ed., Loemker, vol. 1, pp. 13–14, 417; vol. 2, pp. 641, 843, 845, 978.
33. Ibid., vol. 2, p. 1084.
34. Du Châtelet, *Institutions*, p. 172 (section 158–159).
35. Ibid., pp. 137–8 (section 126).
36. Ibid., p. 139 (section 128); p. 155 (section 139).
37. Ibid., p. 136 (section 124); p. 132 (section 120); p. 135 (section 123); p. 170 (section 156).
38. Ibid., p. 148 (section 133).
39. Ibid., pp. 150–1 (section 135).
40. Ibid., p. 166 (section 152).
41. Ibid., p. 157 (section 142); p. 169 (section 155).
42. Ibid., pp. 166–8 (section 153).

43. Ibid., p. 169 (section 154).
44. Ibid., p. 171 (section 157).
45. See Buchdahl *Metaphysics and the Philosophy* [19], Ch. 7, esp. pp. 393, 414, 417, 420, 422.
46. Du Châtelet, *Institutions*, p. 159 (section 143, 144); p. 160 (section 145).
47. Ibid., pp. 164, 165 (section 149).
48. Ibid., p. 152 (section 137); p. 155 (section 139), "la force est done aussi nécessaire a l'essence du corps que l'étendre"; pp. 164–5 (section 149, 150, 151).
49. Ibid., p. 159 (section 143); p. 165 (section 150); p. 165 (section 151).
50. Ibid., p. 170 (section 156). See Christian Wolff, *Cosmologia generalis* (Francofurti et Lipsiae, 1737), p. 119 (section 138): "Per extensionem, vim inertiae, et vim activam omnes corporum mutationes explicari possunt"; p. 121 (section 141): "Materia est extensum vi inertiae praeditum"; p. 144 (section 178): "Materia igitur et vis activa substantiae non sunt quoniam tamen instar substantiarum concipi debent substantiae apparent".
51. Du Châtelet, *Institutions*, p. 165 (section 151).
52. See Buchdahl, *Metaphysics and the Philosophy* [19], pp. 89–91.
53. Du Châtelet, *Institutions*, p. 420 (section 567).
54. Bernoulli, "Discours sur les lois de la communication du mouvement" [61]. On Bernoulli's springs and their role in the *vis viva* controversy, see Carolyn [Merchant] Iltis, "The Decline of Cartesianism in Mechanics: The Leibnizian-Cartesian Debates," *Isis* 64 (1973): 356–73.
55. Du Châtelet, *Institutions*, pp. 420–2 (section 567).
56. Ibid., pp. 423–4 (section 568–9).
57. Jean Jacques de Mairan, "Dissertation sur l'estimation et la mesure des forces motrices des corps," in *Mémoires de l'Académie des Sciences de Paris* (Paris, 1728), pp. 1–49. For an analysis of Mairan's arguments see Carolyn [Merchant] Iltis, "The Decline of Cartesianism in Mechanics," *Isis* 54 (Fall 1973): 370–3.
58. Mairan, *Lettre à Madame [du Chastelet] sur la question des forces vives en réponse aux objections* (Paris: Jombart, 1741), pp. 1–37. François Voltaire, "Doutes sur la mesure des force motrices et sur leur nature, presentés à l'academie des sciences de Paris, en 1741," in *Oeuvres completes* (Paris, 1819–1825), vol. 28, p. 420. A summary of this essay appears in *Histoire de l'Academie Royale des Sciences* (1741), Hist., pp. 149–53. Abbé Deidier, *Nouvelle refutation de l'hypotheses des force vives* (Paris, 1741), p. 145. Jean d'Alembert, *Traité de dynamique*, 1st ed. (Paris, 1743), preface.
59. See Hankins, "The Influence of Malebranche" [20], pp. 205–7.
60. Mairan, "Dissertation sur l'estimation et la mesure des forces motrices des corps" [57] (section 40–41).
61. Du Châtelet, *Institutions*, p. 432 (section 574).
62. Gabrielle Emilie du Châtelet, "Réponse de Madame la Marquise du Châtelet à la lettre que M. de Mairan, secretaire perpetuel de l'académie royale des sciences, lui à écrite le 18. Février, 1741, sur la question des forces vives" (Brussels, 1741), p. 37, bound with *Dissertation sur la nature et propagation du feu* (Paris, 1744), p. 18.
63. Du Châtelet, *Institutions*, p. 441 (section 584).
64. Ibid.
65. Colin Maclaurin, "Démonstration des loix du choc des corps," *Recueil des pièces qui a remporté les prix de l'academie royale des sciences* 1 (1724): 1–24 (separate pagination). See pp. 7, 8. Maclaurin's argument was as follows: Suppose that two persons, one on a ship which advances with uniform motion with a velocity of 2 and the other at rest on the shore, throw two equal bodies A and B with equal efforts in the direction of motion of the ship. Suppose that the body B which was at rest gains a velocity of 8. Body A advances on the ship with a velocity of 10, the sum of the boat's velocity and its own. According to Leibniz the force of body A before it was thrown forward was 4, the square of the boat's velocity. Its increase of force after being thrown is 8 or 64, making its total force 64 + 4 = 68. But since its total velocity after being thrown is 8 + 2 = 10, its force ought to be 100. This is contradictory and therefore forces cannot be proportional to the squares of the velocities. I am indebted to Professor Keith Symon for pointing out to me the inadequacy of Maclaurin's argument and the correctness of Emilie du Châtelet's analysis of Jurin's

example. For a discussion of Maclaurin's role in the controversy see Wilson L. Scott, *The Conflict Between Atomism and Conservation Theory, 1644 to 1860* (London: MacDonald; New York: Elsevier, 1970), pp. 24–30.

66. See note [58].
67. See note [62].
68. Voltaire, *Lettres philosophiques*, 1794; and *Elements de la philosophic de Newton* (Amsterdam, 1738). On Voltaire see Ira O. Wade, *Studies on Voltaire* (Princeton: Princeton University Press, 1947). See also note [3].
69. Barber, *Leibniz in France* [31], pp. 174–83, 191. Du Châtelet apparently concealed the writing of the *Institutions* from Voltaire just as she had done with the dissertation on fire. See Barber, "Mme. du Châtelet and Leibnizianism" [3], p. 212.
70. See note [58].
71. Voltaire, *Oeuvres* [58], pp. 428–9. See Leibniz, "Correspondence with Arnauld" [24], p. 221: "For I think rather that everything is full of animated bodies, and in my opinion there are incomparably more souls than M. Cordemoy has atoms. His atoms are finite in number while I hold that the number of souls, or at least of forms is wholly infinite, and that matter being divisible without end, no portion can be obtained so small that there are not in it animated bodies, or at least such as are endowed with primitive entelechy, and (if you will permit to use the word life so generally), with vital principle, that is to say, with corporeal substances, of all of which it may be said in general that they are alive".
72. Voltaire, *Oeuvres*, pp. 428–9.
73. Immanuel Kant, "Gedanken von der wahren Schätzung der lebendigen Kräfte," in *Immanuel Kant's Werke* (Berlin: Bruno Cassirer Verlag, 1922), vol. 1, pp. 1–187.
74. Ibid., p. 55 (section 44); p. 67 (section 57); p. 127 (section 111); pp. 133–6.
75. Ibid., pp. 27–8 (section 16, 17); pp. 39–40 (section 28, 29). See Buchdahl, *Metaphysics and the Philosophy* [19], p. 553, and Max Jammer, *Concepts of Force* (Cambridge, MA: Harvard University Press, 1957), p. 179.
76. Kant, "Gedanken von der wahren Schätzung der lebendigen Kräfte" [73], p. 136. Although Kant argued philosophically for the equality of the sexes, especially on the issue of property rights, on an experimental level he fell back on the "fact" of the "natural superiority of the husband's faculties compared with those of the wife" (Immanuel Kant, *The Philosophy of Law*, trans. William Hastie [Edinburgh: T. & T. Clark, 1887], vol. 1, p. i (section 24–6), excerpts in Julia O'Faolain and Lauro Martines, eds., *Not in God's Image* [New York: Harper & Row 1973], pp. 284–6).
77. [Merchant] Iltis, "The Leibnizian-Newtonian Debates" [11].
78. Carolyn [Merchant] Iltis, "D'Alembert and the *Vis Viva* Controversy," *Studies in the History and Philosophy of Science* 1 (1970): 135–44; see pp. 135–8; see Ch 6, this book. Jean d'Alembert, *Traité de dynamique*, 2nd ed. (Paris, 1758 [1743]).
79. Thomas Hankins, *Jean d'Alembert: Science and the Enlightenment* (Oxford: Clarendon Press, 1970), p. 155. See also Thomas Hankins, "Eighteenth Century Attempts to Resolve the *Vis Viva* Controversy," *Isis* 56 (Fall 1965): 281–97; see pp. 284–5.
80. Lawrence L. Laudan, "The Vis Viva Controversy, a Post Mortem," *Isis* 59 (Summer 1968): 131–43; see p. 137; John Theophilus Desaguliers, *A Course of Experimental Philosophy* (London, 1734), 11, v.
81. Desaguliers, *Course of Experimental Philosophy*, vol. 2, p. 65.
82. [Merchant] Iltis, "Leibnizian-Newtonian Debates" [11], p. 367, see Ch 5, this book.
83. [Merchant] Iltis, "D'Alembert and the *Vis Viva* Controversy" [78], pp. 138–40, see Ch 6, this book. Pierre Costabel, "Le De Viribus Vivis de R. Boscovich ou de la vertue des querelles de mot," *Archives Internationales d'Histoire des Sciences* 14 (1961): 54–7. Roger Boscovich, *De Viribus Vivis* (Rome: Komarek, 1745).
84. Hankins, "Eighteenth Century Attempts" [79], p. 295.
85. Laudan, "The *Vis Viva* Controversy" [80], pp. 138–43. Thomas Reid, "An Essay on Quantity," *Philosophical Transactions of the Royal Society of London* 45 (1748): 505–20. Unabridged version in Laudan, "The *Vis Viva* Controversy," pp. 140–3.
86. [Merchant] Iltis, "D'Alembert and the *Vis Viva* Controversy," see Ch 6 above, notes 29, 30.

87. Peter M. Heimann and James E. McGuire, "Newtonian Forces and Lockean Powers: Concepts of Matter in Eighteenth-Century Thought," in Russell McCormmach, ed., *Historical Studies in the Physical Sciences* (Philadelphia: University of Pennsylvania Press, 1971), vol. 3, pp. 233–306; see pp. 236–7.

88. Charles Coulston Gillispie, *The Edge of Objectivity* (Princeton: Princeton University Press, 1960), p. 385. Thomas S. Kuhn, "Energy Conservation as Simultaneous Discovery," in Marshall Clagett, ed., *Critical Problems in the History of Science* (Madison, WI: University of Wisconsin Press, 1959), pp. 321–56; see pp. 336–9. On Helmholtz, see Yehuda Elkana, "Helmholtz's Kraft: An Illustration of Concepts in Flux," *Historical Studies in the Physical Sciences* 2 (1970): 263–98; esp. p. 264; Peter M. Heimann, "Helmholz and Kant: The Metaphysical Foundations of *Uber die Erhaltung der Kraft*," *Studies in the History and Philosophy of Science* 5 (1974): 205–38.

Part IV

ECOLOGY AND CONSERVATION

"Wherever man plants his foot," wrote George Perkins Marsh in 1864, "the harmonies of nature are turned to discords." He especially noted that new "vegetable forms and . . . alien tribes of animals" introduced by human settlement brought about major changes that "constitute indeed great revolutions."[1] What Marsh observed in 1864 with respect to ecological change was greatly amplified in the lives of indigenous peoples, colonial settlers, and industrial capitalists during the settlement of the New World. These changes constitute what I have called the colonial, capitalist, and global ecological revolutions.

Chapter 10 on "Ecological Revolutions" develops a theoretical framework for understanding major changes in land and life on the American continent and beyond. Drawing on approaches to revolutionary transformations at the intellectual level by Thomas Kuhn in his *Structure of Scientific Revolutions* (1962) and at the economic and social levels by Karl Marx, I develop a framework based on the concepts of ecology, production, reproduction, and consciousness as depicted in a diagram of interlinked circular levels. I especially integrate concepts of gender and the roles of women into the analysis and illustrate the framework with changes in the New England landscape.

Chapter 11, "Shades of Darkness," on race and environmental history carries the argument beyond gender to integrate race and class. I argue that there are deep seated linkages between environmental degradation and racial discrimination and that hidden and overt biases in language and policies call for historical analysis and for new liberatory policies. We also need to recognize environmental writers who wrote positively about people of color and who advocated change. In this chapter, I examine the writings of men such as Henry David Thoreau, John Muir, and Aldo Leopold and women such as Helen Hunt Jackson, Mary Austin, and Zora Neal Hurston. The interlinking of the environmental, civil rights, and environmental justice movements in the mid- to late twentieth centuries offer ideas for moving forward in healing the past and inspiring the future.

Chapter 12, "Restoring Nature," explores ways to restore the damage wrought by the colonial, capitalist, and global ecological revolutions. It asks not only how to rebuild the landscape using human tools but how to work within the laws of ecology to bring about biotic and abiotic changes that will ultimately benefit both humans and nature. In so doing it places restoration in the context of past philosophies about imitating nature that go back to native peoples and how imitation changed to analysis during the Scientific Revolution. In restoring the land much can be learned from traditional polycultures, biological control, agroecology, and agroforestry as practiced in the developing world and also from new philosophies rooted in participatory forms of consciousness that engage humans in partnership with the earth.

Together, the chapters of Part IV move my ideas about the Scientific Revolution in early modern Europe to the larger framework of Ecological Revolutions throughout the Americas and the wider world. They develop philosophical and historical analyses of the use and misuse of nature and human beings and offer solutions about restoring the land.

NOTE

1. George Perkins Marsh, *Man and Nature* (Cambridge, MA: Harvard University Press, 1965; originally published, 1864), p. 56.

FIGURE 10.1 The Advance of Civilization (1892)

Source: From Horace T. Mann, *Castorologia* (Montreal: W. Drysdale, 1892), p. 60. Public domain.

10

ECOLOGICAL REVOLUTIONS*

Environmental history has reached a point in its evolution in which explicit attention to the theories that underlie its various interpretations is required. Theories about the social construction of science and nature that have emerged over the past decades in the wake of Thomas Kuhn's *Structure of Scientific Revolutions* represent one such approach. They accept the relativist stance toward science set forth in the first edition of his book. (Kuhn backed away from that position toward a view of the progress of knowledge in a second edition.) Marxist theories that attempt to understand history as constructions of the material-social world existing in particular times and places provide a second influence. The theory of ecological revolutions that follows draws on both these approaches and uses New England as a case study.[1]

Two major transformations in New England land and life took place between 1600 and 1860. The first, a colonial ecological revolution, occurred during the seventeenth century and was externally generated. It resulted in the collapse of indigenous Indian ecologies and the incorporation of a European ecological complex of animals, plants, pathogens, and people. It was legitimated by a set of symbols that placed cultured European humans above wild nature, other animals, and "beastlike savages." It substituted a visual for an oral consciousness and an image of nature as female and subservient to a transcendent male God for the Indians' animistic fabric of symbolic exchanges between people and nature.

The second transformation, a capitalist ecological revolution, took place roughly between the American Revolution and about 1860. That second revolution was internally generated and resulted in the reintroduction of soil nutrients and native species. It was initiated by internal tensions within New England and by a dynamic market economy. Local factories imported natural resources and exported finished products. It demanded an economy of increased human labor, land management, and a legitimating mechanistic science. It split human consciousness into a disembodied analytic mind and a romantic emotional sensibility.

My thesis is that ecological revolutions are major transformations in human relations with non-human nature. They arise from changes, tensions, and contradictions that develop between a society's mode of production and its ecology and between its modes of production and reproduction. Those dynamics in turn support the acceptance of new forms of consciousness, ideas, images, and worldviews. The course of the colonial and capitalist ecological revolutions in New England may be understood through a description of each society's ecology, production, reproduction, and forms of consciousness; the processes by which they broke down; and an analysis of the new relations between the emergent colonial or capitalist society and non-human nature.

Two frameworks of analysis offer springboards for discussing the structure of such ecological revolutions. In *The Structure of Scientific Revolutions* (1962), Thomas Kuhn approached major transformations in scientific consciousness from a perspective internal to the workings of science and the community of scientists.

One of the strengths of Kuhn's provocative account is its recognition of stable worldviews in science that exist over relatively long periods of time, but are rapidly transformed during periods of crisis and stress. One of its limitations is its failure to incorporate an interpretation of social forces external to the daily activities of scientific practitioners in their laboratories and field stations. Internal developments in scientific theories are affected, at least indirectly, by social and economic circumstances. A viewpoint that incorporates social, economic, and ecological changes is required for a more complete understanding of scientific change.

A second approach to revolutionary transformations is that of Karl Marx and Friedrich Engels. Their base/superstructure theory of history viewed social revolutions as beginning in the economic base of a particular social formation and resulting in a fairly rapid transformation of the legal, political, and ideological superstructure. In the most succinct statement of his theory of history, in 1859, Marx wrote:

> At a certain stage of their development, the material productive forces of society come in conflict with the existing relations of production . . . Then begins an epoch of social revolution. With the change of the economic foundation the entire immense superstructure is more or less rapidly transformed.[2]

One weakness of this approach is in the determinism assigned to the economic base and the sharp demarcation between base and superstructure. But its strength lies in its view of society and change. If a society at a given time can be understood as a mutually supportive structure of dynamically interacting parts, then the process of its breakdown and transformation to a new whole can be described. Both Kuhn's theory of Scientific Revolution and Marx's theory of social revolution are starting points for a theory of ecology and history.

Science and history are both social constructions. Science is an ongoing negotiation with non-human nature for what counts as reality. Scientists socially construct nature, representing it differently in different historical epochs. These social constructions change during scientific revolutions. Similarly, historians socially construct the past in accordance with concepts relevant to the historian's present. History is thus an ongoing negotiation between the historian and the sources for what counts as history. Ecology is a particular twentieth-century construction of nature relevant to the concerns of environmental historians.

A scientific worldview answers three key questions:

(1) What is the world made of? (the ontological question)
(2) How does change occur? (the historical question)
(3) How do we know? (the epistemological question)

Worldviews such as animism, Aristotelianism, mechanism, and quantum field theory construct answers to these fundamental questions differently.

Environmental history poses similar questions:

(1) What concepts describe the world?
(2) What is the process by which change occurs?
(3) How does a society know the natural world?

The concepts most useful for this approach to environmental history are ecology, production, reproduction, and consciousness. Because of the differences in immediacy of impact of production, reproduction, and consciousness on non-human nature, a structured, leveled conceptual framework is needed. This framework provides the basis for an understanding of stability as well as evolutionary change and transformation. Although change may occur at any level, ecological revolutions are characterized by major alterations at all three levels. Widening tensions between the requirements of ecology and production in a given habitat and between production and reproduction initiate those changes. Those dynamics in turn lead to transformations in consciousness and legitimating worldviews. (See Diagram 10.1)

FIGURE I.1
ECOLOGICAL REVOLUTIONS

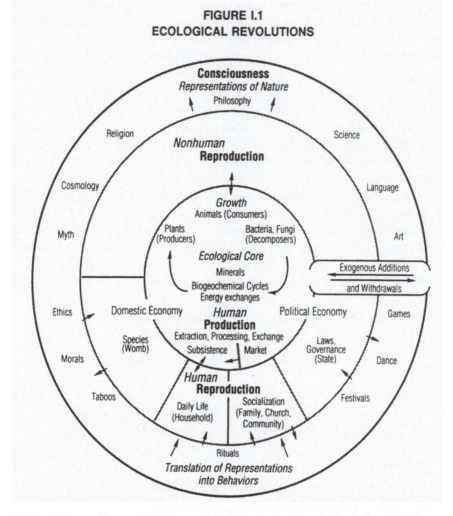

DIAGRAM 10.1 Conceptual Framework for Interpreting Ecological Revolutions. Ecology, production, reproduction, and consciousness interact over time to bring about ecological transformations. The innermost sphere represents the ecological core within the local habitat, the site of interactions between ecology and human production. Plants (producers), animals (consumers), bacteria and fungi (decomposers), and minerals exchange energy among themselves and with human producers in accordance with the laws of thermodynamics and the biogeochemical cycles. Introductions and withdrawals of organisms and resources from outside the local habitat can alter its ecology. Human production (the extraction, processing, and exchange of resources and commodities) is oriented toward immediate use as food, clothing, shelter, and energy for subsistence or toward profit in mercantile trade and industrial capitalism. With increasing industrialization, the subsistence-oriented sector declines and the market-oriented sector expands.

The middle sphere represents human and non-human reproduction. The intergenerational reproduction of species and intragenerational survival rates influence ecological interactions directly in the case of non-human individuals or as mediated by production in the case of humans. In subsistence (or use value) societies, production is oriented toward the reproduction of daily life in the household through the production of food, clothing, shelter, and energy. For humans, the reproduction of society also includes socialization (in the family, church, and community) and the establishment of laws and governance that maintain order in the tribe, town, state, or nation.

Human consciousness, symbolized by the outermost sphere, includes representations of "nature" reflected in myth, cosmology, religion, philosophy, science, language, and art, helping to maintain a given society over time and to influence change. Through ethics, morals, taboos, rituals, festivals, dance, and games, they are translated into actions and behaviors that both affect and are affected by the environment.

The "semi-permeable" membranes between the spheres symbolize possible interactions among them. Ecological revolutions are brought about through interactions between production and ecology and between production and reproduction. These changes in turn stimulate new representations of nature and forms of human consciousness.

Source: Carolyn Merchant, *Ecological Revolutions: Nature Gender, and Science in New England*. Chapel Hill, NC: The University of North Carolina Press, 1989, pp. 6–7, reprinted by permission.

Since the Scientific Revolution of the seventeenth century, the West has seen nature primarily through the spectacles of mechanistic science. Matter is dead and inert, remaining at rest or moving with uniform velocity in a straight line unless acted on by external forces. Change comes from outside as in the operation of a machine. The world itself is a clock, adjustable by human clockmakers. Nature is passive and manipulable.

An ecological approach to history asserts the idea of nature as historical actor. It challenges the mechanistic tradition by focusing on the interchange of energy, materials, and information among living and non-living things in the natural environment.

Non-human nature is not passive, but an active complex that participates in change over time and responds to human-induced change. Nature is a whole of which humans are only one part. We interact with plants, animals, and soils in ways that sustain or deplete local habitats, but through science and technology, we have great power to alter the whole in a short period of time.

But like the mechanistic paradigm, the ecological paradigm is a socially constructed theory. Although it differs from mechanism by taking relations, context, and networks into consideration, it has no greater or lesser claim to some ultimate truth status than do other scientific paradigms. Both mechanism and ecology construct their theories through a socially sanctioned process of problem identification, selection and deselection of particular "facts," inscription of the selected facts into texts, and the acceptance of a constructed order of nature by the scientific community. But laboratory ecology and field ecology merge through the replication of laboratory conditions in the field. The ecological approach of the twentieth century, like the mechanistic, has resulted from a socially constructed set of experiences sanctioned by scientific authority and a set of social practices and policies.[3]

Production is the human counterpart of "nature's" activity. The need to produce subsistence to reproduce human energy on a daily basis connects human communities with their local environments. Production of food and fiber for human subsistence (or use) from the elements (or resources) of nature and the production of surpluses for market exchange are the primary ways in which humans interact directly with the local habitat. An ecological perspective unites human and non-human processes of production through exchanges of energy. All animals, plants, bacteria, and minerals are energy niches involved in the mutual exchange of energy, materials, and information. The relation between human beings and the non-human world is reciprocal; when humans alter their surroundings, "nature" responds to those changes through ecological laws.

Production is the extraction, processing, and exchange of natural resources. In traditional cultures exchanges are often gifts or symbolic alliances, while in market societies they are exchanged as commodities. Over much of Western history, humans have produced and bartered food, clothing, and shelter primarily within the local community to reproduce daily life. When, instead, commodities are marketed for profit, as is the norm in capitalist societies, they are often removed from the local habitat to distant places and exchanged for money. Marx and Engels distinguished between use-value production (or production for subsistence) and production for profit. When people "exploit" non-human nature, they do so in one of two ways: they either make immediate or personal use of it for subsistence or they exchange its products as commodities for personal profit or gain.

New England is a significant historical example because several types of production evolved within the bounds of its present geographical area. Native Americans engaged primarily in gathering and hunting in the north and in horticulture in the south. Colonial Americans combined mercantile trade in natural resources with subsistence oriented agriculture. The market and transportation revolutions in the nineteenth century initiated the transition to capitalist production. Historical bifurcation points within the evolutionary process can be identified as occurring *roughly* between 1600 and 1675 (the colonial ecological revolution) and between 1775 and 1860 (the capitalist ecological revolution).[4]

To continue over time, life must be reproduced from generation to generation. The habitat is populated and repopulated with living organisms of all kinds. Biologically, all living things must reproduce themselves intergenerationally. For humans, reproduction is both biological and social. Each adult generation must maintain itself, its parents, and its offspring so that human life may continue. And each individual must also reproduce its own energy and that of its offspring (intragenerationally) on a daily basis through gathering, growing, or preparing food. Socially, humans must reproduce future laborers by passing on family and community norms. And they must reproduce and maintain the larger social order through the structures of governance and law (such as laws of property inheritance) and the ethical codes that reinforce behavior. Thus although production is twofold—oriented toward subsistence-use or market-exchange—reproduction is fourfold, having both biological and social articulations.[5]

Reproduction is the biological and social process through which humans are born, nurtured, socialized, and governed. Through reproduction sexual relations are legitimated, population sizes and family relationships are maintained, and property and inheritance practices are reinforced. In subsistence-oriented economies, production and reproduction are united in the maintenance of the local community. Under capitalism production and reproduction separate into two different spheres.

Claude Meillassoux's *Maidens, Meal, and Money* (1981) best explains the necessary connections between biological and social reproduction in subsistence economies. Production, he argues, exists for the sake of reproduction; the production and exchange of human energy are keys to the reproduction of human life. Food must be extracted or produced to maintain the daily energy of the producing adults, to maintain the energy of the children who will be the future producers, and to maintain that of the elders, the past producers. Reproducing life on a daily (intragenerational) basis through energy is thus directly linked to intergenerational reproduction of the human species.[6]

Although the biological reproduction of life itself is possible only through the necessary connections between inter- and intragenerational reproduction, the community itself is maintained by social reproduction. In addition, the political, legal, and governmental structures helped to maintain the mode of production and reproduce the social whole.[7]

Whereas Meillassoux was primarily interested in the concept of reproduction in subsistence societies, sociologist Abby Peterson formulated an analysis of reproduction in capitalist societies by looking at the gender-sex dimension in politics. Under capitalism, the division of labor between the

sexes results in a situation in which men bear the responsibility for and dominate the production of exchange commodities, while women bear responsibility for reproducing the work force and social relations. Peterson argues:

> "Women's responsibility for reproduction includes both the biological repro-
> duction of the species (intergenerational reproduction) and the intragenera-
> tional reproduction of the work force through unpaid labor in the home. Here
> too is included the reproduction of social relations—socialization." Under
> capitalist partiarchy, reproduction is subordinate to production.[8]

Meillassoux's and Peterson's work offers an approach through which the
analysis of reproduction can be advanced beyond demography to include
daily life and the community itself. The sphere of reproduction becomes
fourfold, having two biological and two social manifestations: (1) the intergenerational reproduction of the species (both human and non-human),
(2) the intragenerational reproduction of daily life, (3) the reproduction of
social norms within the family and community, and (4) the reproduction of
the legal-political structures that maintain social order within the community and the state. The fourfold sphere of reproduction exists in a dynamic
relationship with the twofold (subsistence or market oriented) sphere of
production (see Diagram 10.1).

Production and reproduction are in dynamic tension. When reproductive
patterns are altered, as in population growth or changes in property inheritance, production is affected. Conversely, when production changes, as in the
addition or depletion of resources or in technological innovation, social and
biological reproduction are altered. A dramatic change at the level of either
reproduction or production can alter the dynamic between them resulting in
a major transformation of the social whole.

Socialist-feminists have further elaborated the interaction between production and reproduction. In a 1976 article, "The Dialectics of Production
and Reproduction in History," Renatè Bridenthal argues that changes in
production give rise to changes in reproduction, creating tensions between
them. For example, the change from a preindustrial agrarian to an industrial
capitalist economy that characterized the capitalist ecological revolution
can be described with respect to tensions, contradictions, and synthesis
within the gender roles associated with production and reproduction. In
the agrarian economy of colonial America, production and reproduction
were symbiotic. Women participated in both spheres, since the production
and reproduction of daily life were centered in the household and domestic
communities. Likewise, men working in barns and fields and women working in farmyards and farmhouses socialized children into production. But
with industrialization, the production of items such as textiles and shoes

moved out of the home into the factory, while farms became specialized and mechanized. Production became more public, reproduction more private, leading to their social and structural separation. For working-class women, the split between production and reproduction imposed a double burden of wage labor and housework; for middle-class women, it led to an increase in domesticity and indoor housework or to enforced idleness as "ladies of leisure."[9]

In New England the additional tensions between the requirements of intergenerational reproduction and those of subsistence production in rural areas also stimulated the capitalist ecological revolution. A partible system of patriarchal inheritance meant that farm sizes deceased after three or four generations to the point that not all sons inherited enough land to reproduce the subsistence system. The tensions between the requirements of subsistence-oriented production (a large family labor force) helped create a supply of landless sons, wage laborers for the transition to capitalist agriculture. The requirement of reproduction in its fourfold sense, therefore came into conflict with the requirements of subsistence-oriented (use-value) production, stimulating a movement toward capital-intensive market production.

Consciousness is the totality of one's thoughts, feelings, and impressions, the awareness of one's acts and volitions. Group consciousness is a collective awareness by an aggregate of individuals. Individual and group consciousness are shaped by both environment and culture. In different historical epochs, a society's consciousness is dominated by particular characteristics. Those forms of consciousness, through which the world is perceived, understood, and interpreted, are socially constructed and subject to change.

A society's symbols and images of nature express its collective consciousness. They appear in mythology, cosmology, science, religion, philosophy, language, and art. Scientific, philosophical, and literary texts are sources of the ideas and images used by controlling elites, while rituals, festivals, songs, and myths provide clues to the consciousness of ordinary people. How are the ideas, images, and metaphors that legitimate human behaviors toward nature translated into ethics, morals, and taboos? Anthropologist Clifford Geertz holds that religious beliefs establish powerful moods and motivations that translate into social behaviors. Also, ideological frameworks or worldviews "secrete" behavioral norms. According to Charles Taylor, particular frameworks give rise to a certain range of normative variations and not others because their related values are not accidental. When sufficiently powerful, worldviews and their associated values can override social changes, but if weak or weakened they can be undermined. A tribe of New England Indians or a community of colonial Americans may have a religious worldview that holds it together for many decades while its economy is gradually changing. Eventually, however, with the acceleration of commercial change, ideas that had formerly existed on the periphery or among selected elites may become dominant if they support and legitimate the new economic directions.[10]

For Native American cultures, consciousness was an integration of all the senses with the body in sustaining life. In that mimetic consciousness, culture was transmitted intergenerationally through imitation in song, myth, dance, sport, gathering, hunting, and planting. Aural/oral transmission of tribal knowledge through myth and transactions between animals, Indians, and neighboring tribes produced sustainable relations between the human and the non-human worlds. The primal gaze of locking eyes between hunter and hunted initiated the moment of ordained killing when the animal gave itself up so that the Indian could survive. (The very meaning of the gaze stems from the intent look of expectancy when a deer first sees a fire, smells a scent, or looks into the eyes of a pursuing hunter.) For Indians engaged in an intimate survival relationship with nature, sight, smell, sound, taste, and touch were all of equal importance, integrated together in a total participatory consciousness.[11]

When Europeans took over Native American habitats during the colonial ecological revolution, vision became dominant within the mimetic fabric. Although daily life for most colonial settlers, as for Indians, was still guided by imitative, oral, face to face transactions, Puritan eyes turned upward toward a transcendent God who sent down his word in written form in the Bible. Individual Protestants learned to read so that they could interpret God's word for themselves. In turn the biblical word legitimated the imposition of agriculture and artifact in the new land. The primal gaze of the Indian was submerged by the objectifying scrutiny of fur trader, lumber merchant, and banker who viewed nature as resource and commodity. Treaties and property relations that extracted land from Indians were codified in writing. Alpha-numeric literacy became central to religious expression, social survival, and upward mobility.[12]

The Puritan imposition of a visually oriented consciousness by Puritans was shattering to the continuance of Indian animism and ways of life. With the commercializing of the fur trade and the missionary efforts of Jesuits and Puritans, a society in which animals, plants, and rocks were equal subjects changed to one dominated by transcendent vision in which individual human subjects were separate from resource objects. That change in consciousness imposed by dominant elites characterized the colonial ecological revolution.

The rise of an analytical, quantitative consciousness was a feature of the capitalist ecological revolution. Capitalist ecological relations emphasized efficient management and control of nature. With the development of mechanistic science and its use of perspective diagrams, visualization was integrated with numbering. The superposition of scientific, quantitative approaches to nature and its resources characterized the capitalist ecological revolution. Through education analytic consciousness expanded beyond that of dominant elites to include most ordinary New Englanders.

Viewed as a social construction, "nature" (as it was conceptualized in each social epoch—Indian, colonial, and capitalist) is not some ultimate truth that was gradually discovered through the scientific processes of observation, experiment, and mathematics. Rather it was a relative changing structure of human representations of "reality." Ecological revolutions are processes through which different societies change their relationship to nature. They arise from tensions between production and ecology and between production and reproduction. The results are new constructions of nature, both materially and in human consciousness.

NOTES

* From Carolyn Merchant, "The Theoretical Structure of Ecological Revolutions," *Environmental Review* 11, no. 4 (Winter 1987): 265–74 (notes 4 and 5 added to original). Reprinted by permission of Oxford University Press.

1. Thomas S. Kuhn, *The Structure of Scientific Revolutions* (Chicago: University of Chicago Press, 1962; 2nd ed. 1970).

2. Karl Marx, "Preface to *A Contribution to the Critique of Political Economy*" (1859) in Karl Marx and Friedrich Engels, eds., *Selected Works* (New York: International Publishers, 1968), pp. 182–3.

3. On ecology as a social construction see Elizabeth Ann R. Bird, "Social Construction of Nature: Theoretical Approaches to the History of Environmental Problems," *Environmental Review* 11 (Winter 1987): 255–64; Karen D. Knorr-Cetina and Michael Mulkay, *Science Observed: Perspectives on the Social Study of Science* (Beverly Hills: Sage Publications, 1983); and Karen D. Knorr-Cetina, *The Manufacture of Knowledge: An Essay on the Constructivist and Contextual Nature of Science* (New York: Pergamon Press, 1981).

4. Ilya Prigogine, *From Being to Becoming: Time and Complexity in the Physical Sciences* (San Francisco: W. H. Freeman, 1980); Ilya Prigogine and Isabelle Stengers, *Order Out of Chaos* (Toronto: Bantam Books, 1984); Erich Jantsch, *Self-Organizing Universe* (New York: Pergamon, 1980). On the implications of Prigogine's approach for the study of history see Toffler's forward to Prigogine and Stengers, *Order Out of Chaos*, pp. xi–xxvi, especially pp. xv–xvi.

5. On "generation," see *Compact Edition of the Oxford English Dictionary*, 2 vols. (Oxford: Oxford University Press, 1971), vol. 1, p. 1128; on "reproduction," see ibid., vol. 2, p. 2501.) Until the eighteenth century, biological reproduction, following Aristotle, was called generation, or the production of plants, animals, and other substances by natural means. The process of generation was contrary to that of corruption and the two processes together described all changes in the cosmos. Buffon, *Histoire Naturelle* (Paris: Imprimerie nationale, 1749) vol. 2, p. 16 used the term reproduction to mean the general phenomenon of generation in all species. In 1776, Adam Smith (*An Inquiry into the Nature and Causes of the Wealth of Nations* [London: Strahan and Cadell, 1776]), Bk. I, Ch. 8, sec. 40, p. 98 wrote that "the demand for men regulates the production of men," thus tying production to reproduction. Friedrich Engels in his *The Origin of Family, Private Property, and the*

State linked the production and reproduction of immediate life with the production of food, clothing, and shelter, on the one hand, and the production of the human species, on the other. (See Karl Marx and Friedrich Engels, *Selected Works* (New York: International Publishers, 1968), p. 455). I am grateful to Barbara Dudden for pointing out these changes in the use of the term generation and reproduction. On reproduction as an organizing category see Abby Peterson, "Gender-Sex Dimension in Swedish Politics," *Acta Sociologica* 27, no. 1 (1984): 3–17. On the application of the concept of reproduction to capitalist cultures see Women's Work Study Group, "Loom, Broom, and Womb: Producers, Maintainers, and Reproducers," *Radical America* 10 (March–April 1976): 29–45; Veronica Beechey, "On Patriarchy," *Feminist Review* 10 (March–June 1980): 66–82; Iris Young, "Socialist Feminism and the Limits of Dual Systems Theory," *Socialist Review* 10, nos. 2-3 (March-June 1980): 169–88. For an argument that reproduction should be reduced to production, see Alison Jaggar and William McBride, "'Reproduction' as Male Ideology," *Women's Studies International Forum* 8, no. 4 (1985): 185–96.

6. Claude Meillassoux, *Maidens, Meal, and Money: Capitalism and the Domestic Community* (Cambridge, England: Cambridge University Press, 1981; originally published, 1975). Critiques of Meillassoux include Bridget O'Laughlin, "Production and Reproduction: Meillassoux's *Femmes, Greniers et Capitaux*," *Critique of Anthropology* 2 (Spring 1977): 3–33; and Maureen Mackintosh, "Reproduction and Patriarchy: A Critique of Claude Meillassoux, *Femmes, Greniers et Capitaux*," *Capital and Class* 2 (Summer 1977): 114–27.

7. Meillassoux, *Maidens, Meal, and Money*, pp. 36, 39.

8. Abby Peterson, "Gender-Sex Dimension in Swedish Politics," *Acta Sociologica* 27, no. 1 (1984): 6, 3–17. Quotation on p. 6. Peterson's fourfold taxonomy of political interests included (1) Issues related to the interests of intergenerational reproduction; (2) Issues related to the interests of intragenerational reproduction in the family; (3) Issues related to the interests of intragenerational reproduction in the public sector; (4) Issues related to the interests of reproduction workers (women), i.e., so-called women's liberation issues. Peterson also applied her taxonomy to the politics of reproduction in the Swedish environmental movement. See Abby Peterson and Carolyn Merchant, "'Peace with the Earth': Women and the Environmental Movement in Sweden," *Women's Studies International Forum* 9, no. 5–6 (1986): 465–79, esp. 472–4.

9. Renate Bridenthal, "The Dialectics of Production and Reproduction in History," *Radical America* 10 (March–April 1976): 3–11. For a feminist analysis of reproduction in American culture see Women's Work Study Group, "Loom, Broom, and Womb: Producers, Maintainers, and Reproducers," pp. 29–45; Veronica Beechley, "On Patriarchy," *Feminist Review* 10 (March–June 1980): 66–82.

10. Charles Taylor, "Neutrality in Political Science," in Alan Ryan, ed., *The Philosophy of Social Explanation* (London: Oxford University Press, 1973), pp. 139–70, see pp. 144–6, 154–5.

11. On mimetic, participatory consciousness see Morris Berman, *The Reenchantment of the World* (Ithaca: Cornell University Press, 1981); Eric Havelock, *Preface to Plato* (Cambridge, MA: Harvard University Press, 1963); and Max Horkheimer, *The Eclipse of Reason* (New York: Oxford University Press, 1947), pp. 92–127. On the disenchantment of the world and religion, see Marcel Gauchet, *The Disenchantment of the World: A Political History of Religion*, trans. Oscar Burge, foreword by Charles Taylor (Princeton, NJ: Princeton University Press, 1997). On the gaze, see *Compact Oxford English Dictionary*, s.v. gaze, p. 1123: "said of a deer, also of persons, especially in wonder, expectancy, bewilderment." "The hart, stag, buck, or hind when borne in coat-armour, looking affrontée or full faced is said to be at gaze. . . but all other beasts in this attitude are called guardant." William Berry, *Encyclopedia Heraldica* (London: Sherwood, Gilbert, and Piper, 1828–40), s.v. "gaze." On the Koyukon Indian versus white methods of hunting deer see Richard K. Nelson, "The Gifts," in Daniel Halpern, ed., *Antaeus*, no. 57 (Autumn 1986), pp. 117–31, esp. 122. On imitation of animals by

humans in hunting, see Randall L. Eaton, "Hunting and the Great Mystery of Nature," *Utne Reader* 19 (January–February 1987): 42–49.

12. On the dominance of vision in Western consciousness see Hans Jonas, "The Nobility of Sight," *Philosophy and Phenomenological Research* 14 (1954): 507–19; Evelyn Fox Keller and Christine Grontkowski, "The Mind's Eye," in Sandra Harding and Merrill B. Hintikka, eds., *Discovering Reality* (Dordrecht, Holland: D. Reidel, 1983), pp. 207–24; James Axtell, "The Power of Print in the Eastern Woodlands," *William and Mary Quarterly* 44 (2) 3rd ser. (April 1987): 300–309.

FIGURE 11.1 American Progress (1872). By John Gast. The advance of civilization is represented by a female figure floating westward bearing the gifts of light, knowledge, and communication while pushing native peoples and buffalo into darkness.

Source: Courtesy of the Autry Museum of the American West, Los Angeles; 92.126.1.

11

SHADES OF DARKNESS*

Race and Environmental History

In *The Hidden Wound*, published in 1989, environmentalist Wendell Barry writes that "the psychic wound of racism has resulted inevitably in wounds in the land, the country itself." When he began writing the book in 1968 during the Civil Rights movement, he tells us, "I was trying to establish the outlines of an understanding of myself, in regard to what was fated to be the continuing crisis of my life, the crisis of racial awareness." Berry's book is an effort to come to terms with the environmental history of race as reflected in his family's history as slaveholders, in his own childhood on a Kentucky farm in the segregated South, and in his adult life as a conservationist and environmentalist.[1]

In recent years, environmental historians too have reflected on the crisis of racial awareness for the field and have collectively begun the process of writing an environmental history of race. The negative connections between wilderness and race, cities and race, toxics and race, and their reversal in environmental justice have been explored by numerous scholars who have analyzed the ideology and practice of environmental racism. Throughout the country many courses are now including multicultural perspectives on the environment.[2] We have learned important new ways to think about the relationship between race and environmental history. These include the following perspectives:

- Slavery and soil degradation are interlinked systems of exploitation and deep seated connections exist between the enslavement of human bodies and the enslavement of the land. Blacks resisted that enslavement in complex ways that maintained African culture and created unique African American ways of living on the land.[3]

- Native Americans were removed from the lands they had managed for centuries, not only during settlement as is well known, but during the creation of the national parks and national forests. Indians resisted these moves in an effort to maintain autonomy and access to resources.[4]

- American Indians and African Americans perceived wilderness in ways that differed markedly from those of white Americans.[5]

- A "coincidental order of injustice" reigned in post-Civil War America as emancipated Blacks in the South were expected to pay for land with wages at the same time that free lands taken from Indians were being promoted to whites via the Homestead Act and other land acts.[6]

- African Americans bore the brunt of early forms of environmental pollution and disease as whites fled urban areas to the new streetcar suburbs. Black neighborhoods became toxic dumps and black bodies became toxic sites. Out of such experiences arose African American environmental activism in the Progressive Era and the environmental justice movement of the late twentieth century.[7]

All of this work is an auspicious beginning to compiling an environmental history of race. But we need to do much more in integrating multicultural history and environmental justice into our courses and frameworks. We especially need more research on the roles of African Americans in the southern and western U.S. environment and early urbanization and on Asian and Hispanic practices and perceptions of nature.[8]

I hope to contribute to this growing body of literature by looking at views held about American Indians and African Americans in environmental history. If an environmental justice perspective is to permeate the field of environmental history, we need to be aware of the ideas of the contributions of the founders of the conservation and environmental movements. I will argue that whiteness and blackness were redefined environmentally in ways that reinforced institutional racism.

INDIANS AND WILDERNESS

The 1964 Wilderness Act defined wilderness as areas where "man is a visitor who does not remain." As environmental historians have pointed out, this characterization reads Native Americans out of the wilderness and out of the homelands they had managed with fire, hunting, and gathering for centuries. By the late nineteenth century, following the move to eliminate Native Americans and their food supplies, Indians were moved to reservations. National Parks and wilderness areas were set aside for the benefit of white

American tourists. By redefining wilderness as the polar opposite of civilization, wilderness in its ideal form could be viewed as free of people, while
civilization by contrast was filled with people. Yet this was a far different
view of Indians than had been the case for most of American history, where
Indian presence in the landscape was very prominent. For William Bradford
the New England forests had been filled with "wild beasts and wild men." For
Henry David Thoreau, forests and parks were areas where native vegetation
would be restored and where even the "red man" might walk again. National
parks had initially been conceived by George Catlin as places where Indians
would be free to roam and carry on their way of life. In the mid-nineteenth
century, travelers going west expected to see Indians as part of the untamed
wilderness.[9]

By the end of the century, Indian removal had become part of a program to
provide tourists with access to wild animals and scenery, but without danger-
ous and negative encounters with Indians. The national parks were config-
ured as living Edens containing beautiful scenery, rivers, animals, flowering
trees, and carpets of wildflowers. They were "virgin" places of rebirth in
which people could be spiritually renewed. The new wilderness areas were
managed places in which the wilderness encounter was predictable within
given parameters. There were "wild beasts," but no "wild men." Unpredictable elements such as Indians were removed or carefully managed for tourists
so that they became part of the total "wilderness experience." The parks were
vast managed gardens in which the wild was contained for viewing. People
could have a wilderness experience in a protected environment.

But at the same time that parks and wilderness were being reconstructed
as white and pure for the benefit of white tourists, Indians were being characterized as dark and dirty. John Muir envisioned national parks as pristine
wilderness, without containing domesticated animals or Indians. In *My First
Summer in the Sierra* (1911), a saga of his Sierra Nevada travels in 1868, he
wrote disparagingly of the Indians he encountered there, equating Indians
with unclean animals which did not belong in the wilderness. In 1868, he
visited Brown's Flat near Yosemite's Merced River where he encountered
a group of Indians denigrated as Diggers whom he found dirty and unclean.
On another occasion, he was visited by Indians from Mono and commented
that the clean air and water of the mountains "cover and cure the grossness
of their lives." He wrote: "A strangely dirty and irregular life these dark-eyed
dark-haired, half-happy savages lead in this clean wilderness." He described
a band of Indians from Mono collecting acorns on their way to Yosemite:
"They were wrapped in blankets made of the skins of sage-rabbits. The dirt
on some of the faces seemed almost old enough and thick enough to have
a geological significance. . . . How glad I was to get away from the gray,
grim crowd and see them vanish down the trail! Yet it seems sad to feel such

desperate repulsion from one's fellow beings, however degraded. To prefer the society of squirrels and woodchucks to that of our own species must surely be unnatural."[10]

Muir continually contrasted Indians with wilderness, writing of them as polar opposites of the pristine lands in which he found them. He was particularly appalled by Indian women, writing of one: "Her dress was calico rags, far from clean. In every way she seemed sadly unlike Nature's neat well-dressed animals, though living like them on the bounty of the wilderness. Strange that mankind alone is dirty. Had she been clad in fur or cloth woven of grass or shreddy bark, she might then have seemed a rightful part of the wilderness; like a good wolf at least, or bear." On another occasion, he happened upon some Indian women collecting wild grain and beating the out the seed, commenting, "the women were evidently enjoying it, laughing and chattering and looking almost natural. . . . Perhaps if I knew them better I should like them better. The worst thing about them is their uncleanliness. Nothing truly wild is unclean. Down on the shore of Mono Lake I saw a number of their flimsy huts on the banks of streams that dash swiftly into that dead sea,—mere brush tents where they lie and eat at their ease."[11]

In his excursions into southeastern Alaska in 1879 and 1880, in the company of Indian guides and a missionary, S. Hall Young, Muir moderated his view of the Indians he encountered there. He expressed admiration for their totem poles, ideas of the world, and dignity, while nevertheless preferring the "clean wilderness," to Indian encampments and the depravity of Indian fighting and addiction to alcohol. He was especially moved by the oratorical ability of his guide Toyatte and deplored the latter's subsequent sacrifice of his own life to save his people. When questioned by Indians as to his purpose there, Muir insisted that he had only come to see their glaciers, forests, and mountains, but assured them of God's love of all of them and of "the brotherhood of all races of people." While Muir did not become an advocate for Indians, he came to appreciate those whom he considered as living closer to a state of wildness than those degraded by their encounters with "over-civilized" whites. In preparing his Sierra journals for subsequent publication in 1911 and his Alaska journals for publication (posthumously) in 1915, he did not modify his earlier impressions of either Indian group.[12]

Muir's responses to the Indians he found during his first summer in the Sierras, contrasted sharply with those of another writer of the same period and place, Helen Hunt Jackson. Jackson wrote about her experiences in Yosemite National Park and the California "wilderness," where her initial negative reactions to the Indians, as Rebecca Solnit points out, were soon altered, and she became an activist on their behalf. On her visit to Yosemite Valley in 1872, Jackson had characterized the Digger Indians as "loathsome," "half-naked," and "dirty," while admiring their legends, poetry, and language.

But in 1881, she completed *A Century of Dishonor: A Sketch of the United States Government's Dealings with Some of the Indian Tribes*, a volume so critical of broken treaties and inhumane treatment of Indians that it shocked the nation. *Ramona*, her novel of the southern California mission Indians, was written in 1883 and serialized in the *Christian Union* in May 1884. Its elegant literary style and ethical message of Indian mistreatment surpassed her earlier work in arousing the public to the cause of Indians.[13]

Another environmental writer of the same period who championed the cause of American Indians was Mary Austin. In 1903, Austin published *The Land of Little Rain*. Like a number of other environmental advocates around the turn of the nineteenth century, Austin was also an advocate for Indians. She began her book with an appreciation for the Indians of the western deserts whose lives blended with the limits of the West's arid lands in the Country of Lost Borders. "Ute, Paiute, Mojave, and Shoshone inhabit its frontiers, and as far into the heart of it as man dare go," she wrote. "Not the law, but the land sets the limit." It was a land that "will not be lived in except in its own fashion," a land which the Shoshone Indians called their home, a place of awesome beauty, with sculpted vermillion hills and radiant flowers that bloomed in the rare rains. In contrast to Muir, Austin wrote, "Not the weathered hut is his home, but the land, the winds, the hill front, the stream." Here the Indians were not removed from the land or written out of the narrative as "visitors who did not remain," but were integral to a sense of the land as home.[14]

BLACKS, BLACKNESS, AND THE ENVIRONMENT

African Americans presented more difficult problems for European colonizers than did Indians. Although both Indians and Blacks were regarded as savage, Africans and Indians were constructed differently and treated differently. Although Indians were of a different color than whites, white–black differences seemed more pronounced than those between Indians and whites. Whereas the English colonizers' "errand into the wilderness" of America was to live there, civilize the land, and Christianize the Indian, their business in Africa was to trade and enslave. Europeans associated blackness with witchcraft, Satan, beasts, and putrid, decaying matter. The concept of whiteness itself emerged as a contrast and "other" to blackness.[15]

The slave system caused both the destruction of black bodies and the rapid degradation of southern soils, as tobacco, rice, sugar, and cotton became cash crops in an expanding world market. Environmental justice advocate Robert Bullard put it bluntly: "The nation was founded on the principles of "free land" (stolen from Native Americans and Mexicans), "free labor" (cruelly extracted from African slaves), and "free men" (white men with property)."[16]

Like Indians, Blacks resisted their enslavement and degradation. Slave rebellions such as those of Denmark Vesey in 1822 and Nat Turner in 1831 were overt demonstrations against repression. But slaves also covertly appropriated food from their masters' gardens and kitchens, slacked off or ran away from field work, and even retaliated against their owners when the latter became too old or sick to enforce their superiority. In addition, blacks, like Indians, retained many of their own cultural traditions, foods, stories, religious practices, songs, clothing, and dance. Many believed that their owners would receive due punishment after death, while they themselves would end up in paradise.

But one environmentalist protested slavery. Henry David Thoreau refused to pay poll taxes that supported the Mexican War and a government "which buys and sells men, women, and children like cattle at the door of its senate-house." As Patricia Nelson Limerick argues, "Nature-loving and slavery-hating were compatible and matched projects in Thoreau's mind." While living at Walden Pond in July 1846, Thoreau was arrested and spent a night in jail as a consequence. He wrote "Civil Disobedience" (1849), "Slavery in Massachusetts" (1854) and "A Plea for Captain John Brown" (1859) in defiance of slavery. "I cannot for an instant recognize that political organization as my government which is the slave's government also," he wrote. More reprehensible even than southerners, Thoreau asserted, were Massachusetts farmers and merchants, who were far more interested in making money than they were "in humanity, and are not prepared to do justice to the slave and to Mexico, *cost what it may*." Thoreau argued vehemently against a citizen's utilitarian duty to submit to civil government and insisted instead that "this people must cease to hold slaves, and to make war on Mexico, though it cost them their existence as a people." Thoreau's concept of community not only included minorities, it encompassed both humanity and nature; he "regarded sunfish, plants, skunks, and even stars as fellows and neighbors—members, in other words, of his community." His ethic was one of the individual self in partnership with the entire human community and the natural world.[17]

During the 1850s, northern and southern abolitionists joined in the moral condemnation of slavery. Abraham Lincoln's Emancipation Proclamation of 1863 freed the slaves and the American Civil War (fought between 1861 and 1865) released slaves from bodily bondage and reconstituted the nation. But a new system of oppressive sharecropping and segregation of free blacks ensued.

With increasing urbanization after the Civil War, many African Americans found themselves living in segregated areas in America's cities. While the intermingling of races existed in the three decades following the war, by the 1890s, neighborhoods began to organize themselves along color lines. Black mainstreets co-existed with white downtowns and racial zoning arose as Jim

Crow laws were enacted in southern cities. By the turn of the century, rigid separations occurred with segregated black and white parks, schools, train stations, and streetcars. In the minds of many Americans, the valence of wilderness had been reversed. The city had become a dark, negatively charged wilderness filled with Blacks and southern European immigrants, while mountains, forests, waterfalls, and canyons were viewed as sublime places of white light. Robert Woods wrote *The City Wilderness* in 1898 to describe deteriorating urban neighborhoods that were morally and socially depraved, while Booth Tarkington in *The Turmoil* (1914) portrayed them as sooty, polluted, and diseased.

During the same period that John Muir was describing Indians as dirty and unclean, cities were perceived as dirty and polluted. Dark, smoke-filled cities contrasted with the purity of mountain air and the clarity of whitewater rivers, waterfalls, and lakes. Sublime nature was white and benign, available to white tourists; cities were portrayed as black and malign, the home of the unclean and the undesirable.[18]

ENVIRONMENTALISM AND AFRICAN AMERICANS

The conservation movement at the turn of the nineteenth century emerged during the same period in which cities became negatively signed black areas and as Blacks struggled for advancement in post-Civil War America. As environmental policy advocate Jeffrey Romm argues, the two movements existed in separate spheres, but were tightly bound together in ways that produced negative consequences for African Americans. The creation of the Forest Reserves (1891), the founding of the Sierra Club (1892) with John Muir as its first president, the progressive conservation movement (1900–1913), and passage of the Antiquities Act (1906) that preserved Mesa Verde by removing the Ute from their homelands occurred during the same period as Booker T. Washington, Louis Hughes, George Washington Carver, and W.E. B. DuBois were engaged in struggles to liberate Blacks from the oppressions of post-Civil War sharecropping, soil degradation, and racial prejudice.

Romm maintains that a "coincidental order of environmental injustice," evident in the late nineteenth century, hardened existing forms of institutional racism. "The Supreme Court's 'separate but equal' doctrine of its *Plessy v. Ferguson* decision [1896] legitimized racial segregation in the United States for the next seventy years. . . . While the forest reservations reduced people's access to land, racial segregation reserved ownership of the remaining private land for whites." In the South, freed slaves were expected to purchase land with wages at a time when lands in the West were promoted to whites as free lands. Boundaries created by natural resource regulations restrained opportunities for people of color, while protecting white power and privilege.[19]

African American environmentalist Carl Anthony points out that John Muir's encounters in the pristine wilderness of Canada and the Cotton South were actually made possible by the "occupied wilderness" of the Civil War and Native American battles. Muir, Anthony states, had been a Civil War draft-dodger who went to the Canadian wilds rather than fight. Environmental historian Roderick Nash concurs: "Muir's first encounter with the idea that nature had rights came as a consequence of draft-dodging. . . . Muir who was twenty-six and single, felt certain he would be called, and he apparently had no interest in the fight to save the Union or free the slaves." Biographer Stephen Fox portrays him instead as a pacifist who "was paralyzed by the threat of conscription" and who "had no strong feelings about the moral aspects of war." As a consequence, Muir fled to Canada after Lincoln signed an order to draft 500,000 men and spent the war years as a fugitive, seeking peace in the "wilderness" north of Lake Huron, failing to communicate with family and friends for fear of being discovered. While whites and blacks alike lost their lives fighting for freedom, Muir worried about maintaining his solitude: "Only once in my long Canada wanderings," Muir wrote, "was the deep peace of the wilderness savagely broken. . . . I was awakened by the awfully dismal howling of the wolves."[20]

After the war, in 1867, Muir made his "Thousand Mile Walk to the Gulf" to study natural history through war-torn lands protected by soldiers of the U.S. Government, but whose wilderness delights seemed to him Edenic. Here he encountered mountainous streams lined with "forest walls vine-draped and flowery as Eden," in the very place where "General Scott had his headquarters when he removed the Cherokee Indians to a new home in the West."[21]

Muir was unsympathetic toward the "savages" he encountered on his thousand-mile walk. Of his visit to Murphy, North Carolina, he wrote: "For the first time since leaving home I found a house decked with flowers and vines, clean within and without and stamped with the comforts of culture and refinement in all its arrangements. Striking contrast to the uncouth transitionist establishments from the wigwams of savages to the clumsy but clean log castle of the thrifty pioneer."[22]

Muir's account of his walk likewise reflected cultural prejudices against Blacks. Although he described some as "well trained," extremely polite," and very "civil," he viewed most as lazy and noisy. He wrote that "the Negroes are easy-going and merry, making a great deal of noise and doing little work. One energetic white man, working with a will, would easily pick as much cotton as half a dozen Sambos and Sallies." He described an evening campfire he attended as akin to deviltry: "In the center of this globe of light sat two Negroes. I could see their ivory gleaming from the great lips, and their smooth cheeks flashing off light as if made of glass. Seen anywhere but in the South, the glossy pair would have been taken for twin devils, but here it was only a Negro and his wife at their supper." Muir's environmental ethic included wilderness, but, unlike Thoreau, he was insensitive to much of humanity. He embraced non-human nature from bears to orchids to rattlesnakes as "fellow mortals," but his theocentric ethic, which was grounded in a God manifested within nature, did not explicitly include the entire human community.[23]

In contrast to John Muir's descriptions of Blacks and nature in the South as disconnected opposites, African American writer Zora Neale Hurston wrote of Blacks as part of Florida's environment. In *Their Eyes Were Watching God* (1937), Hurston portrayed Blacks who were planting and harvesting beans in the Florida Everglades as engaging with a wild, animate, spiritualized nature that produced "big beans, big cane, big weeds, big everything." The dirt was "so rich and black that a half mile of it would have fertilized a Kansas Wheat Field. Wild cane on either side of the road. . . . People wild too." While waiting for the beans to grow, Blacks fished and hunted alligators as did the local Indians, who were "calmly winning their living in the trackless ways of the 'Glades." But Indians left the Everglades in an impending hurricane, while Blacks stayed to combat and succumb to the fury of its winds.[24]

Hurston's unpredictable chaotic forces were male not female. "The two hundred miles an hour wind had loosed his chains. He seized hold of his dikes and ran forward until he met the quarters; uprooted them like grass and rushed on after his supposed to be conquerors, rolling the dikes, rolling the houses, rolling the people in the houses along with other timbers. The sea was walking the earth with a heavy heel." Here nature and the human community are at odds, life hanging by a thread, a time of dying for all that lived. A time to face the desolation, a time to bury the dead and go on. "The time of dying was over." Here too was an ethic at odds with Muir's ecstatic experience of a lightning storm in a sublime Sierra wilderness apart from civilization. Hurston's ethic was one of living on the land and of acceptance of nature as active and alive—"a bloom time, and a green time and an orange time."[25]

Patricia Limerick argues that Aldo Leopold's 1949 "Land Ethic," which advocated enlarging the bounds of the community to include "soils, waters, plants, and animals," ignored communities of people of color. Leopold, Limerick asserts, began his essay with the sentence, "When god-like Odysseus returned from the wars in Troy, he hanged all on one rope a dozen slave-girls of his household whom he suspected of misbehavior during his absence. This hanging involved no question of propriety. The girls were property." To Leopold, both slavery (and gender violence) seemed to exist only in the deep past, rather than in twentieth-century America in which segregation and patriarchy were both alive and well. "Not a word of the essay," Limerick writes, "suggested that the end of slavery left any unfinished business in the United States." Leopold's obliviousness to the legacy of slavery in Jim Crow America, she argues, echoed the conservation movement's own obliviousness to a legacy that excluded people of color from equal access to natural and recreational resources.[26]

Yet in Leopold's writings, there is neither evidence of the exclusion of minorities from his ethic, as in the case of Muir, nor of inclusion, as in the case of Thoreau. Leopold's early skepticism toward Indian uses of fire and game predation evolved to one of admiration for Indian insights into ecological management. Moreover, he seems to have implicitly assumed the equality of all persons and biota in an era when slavery had officially been abolished. Although Leopold was not an advocate for the rights of minorities, he was neither insensitive to minorities nor a racist by the sin of omission as Limerick implies. His wife and her family were of Hispanic and Jewish descent. He was appalled by the "near pogram in Germany," that exterminated Jews during World War II. And his ethical sequence decried the slavery of both humanity and the earth.[27]

In his elaboration of the ethical sequence proposed by Leopold, environmental historian Roderick Nash argues that Leopold's ethic does in fact extend to African American emancipation and American Indian citizenship. Nash explicates an environmental ethic that expanded rights to oppressed minorities first in Great Britain and then in the United States. The Magna Carta of 1215 and the Declaration of Independence in 1776 were followed by Abraham Lincoln's Emancipation Proclamation of 1863, the nineteenth amendment giving women the right to vote in 1920, the Indian Citizenship Act of 1924, the Fair Labor Standards Act of 1938, the Civil Rights Act of 1957, and the Endangered Species Act of 1973.

Nash made explicit the connections between the rights of minorities and the rights of nature implicit in Leopold's ethical sequence. "Assuming one regarded slaves as people," Nash wrote, "the new natural-rights philosophy made a strong case for including them in the ethical community. The abolitionists quickly seized on this idea as a powerful argument for terminating an institution that denied slaves something all people possessed by birth and which could never be alienated—namely their right to life and liberty." Those who extended the natural rights principles across the boundaries of species, he noted, "employed the same liberal faith that had served the antislavery partisans." My own view is that Leopold's "Land Ethic" which is based on "the tendency of interdependent individuals or groups to evolve modes of cooperation" might be viewed, not as an extension of a Eurocentric rights-based ethic, but as one foundation for an ethic of partnership among humans and between human and non-human communities, an ethic that explicitly includes minorities.[28]

Limerick points to two positive junctions between environmentalism and civil rights. In 1964, two acts were passed by the exact same Congress: The Wilderness Act and the Civil Rights Act. And thirty years later, in 1994, President William Jefferson Clinton created a federal mandate for environmental justice with the issuance of Executive Order 12898. He directed all federal agencies to "make achieving environmental justice part of its mission by identifying and addressing as appropriate, disproportionately high and adverse human health or environmental effects of its programs, policies, and activities on minority populations and low-income populations."[29]

COLONIZED "OTHERS"

Legislative and legal victories that linked human rights and nature's rights, however, are belied by the realities of life in twenty-first century America. Segregation and poverty still militate against equal access to resources and encourage toxic waste "Dumping in Dixie." Wilderness has been redefined in ways that exclude Native Americans and discourage access by minorities and disadvantaged peoples.[30]

With the taming of wilderness, the removal of Indians, and the repression of Blacks, the American Eden became a colonized Eden that could be extended to other countries. The control of the wild represented the kind of state that Western societies could export throughout the world to colonized "Other" lands. That state was the "Self" of Western European countries, in particular, those that exported their science, technologies, and methods of controlling resources to the "Others." The "Others" were the colonized indigenous people, immigrants, and people of color who were outside the controlled, managed garden. Throughout the world, as land was transformed into irrigated gardens filled with monocultures controlled by agribusiness, what lay beyond the periphery were wastelands and deserts, the place of outcasts, of waste, of people of color, and of immigrants—in short, those colonized "Others" not admitted into the enclosed space of the reinvented garden.[31]

From the perspective of the Western European "Subject," such wastelands are the locales of the "Others." The sequence—first the forest, then the city, then the desert—intimates an impending decline if cities and civilizations are not managed properly. The idea of the desert encroaching on the city—of wastelands arriving at the city borders—is symptomatic of the global ecological crisis, exemplified by desertification, the failure of irrigation systems, and the salinization of soils.

The crisis of racial awareness continues in the current reaction against multiculturalism and affirmative action. Other symptoms of crisis are policies directed against the environment—the property rights movement, erosion of the Endangered Species Act, efforts by ranchers to preserve "free" grazing on the Western range, and the persistence of lumber companies in cutting old-growth forests.

Waste, pollution, landfills, and incinerators have been located in deserts, in inner cities, in ghettos, and on American Indian reservations and are often targeted for the neighborhoods of people of color. This became particularly apparent in 1987 when the United Church of Christ released its report on "Toxic Waste and Race in the United States." The struggles have taken place in various geographical and bodily locations. The bodies of women and men are sites of local contestation. When bodies are sick, polluted, or cancerous, people fight against the illness. The home, where many women and children spend much of their time, is polluted. Many communities, especially those of poor people, such as rural communities in Appalachia and Hispanic communities in California, Indian reservations, and urban inner cities are toxic. They have become sites of local contestation and local movements for environmental justice. On a more hopeful level, many grassroots organizations that arose in opposition to toxic dumping have become multiethnic and multiracial. Many local movements are woman based and many are led by minority women. The mainstream environmental movement, however, remains largely white and environmental organizations, with some exceptions, still work on issues most relevant to white communities.[32]

CONCLUSION

In conclusion, many people of color found themselves colonized or enslaved as European civilization spread throughout the globe over the past several centuries. As the Western narrative of progress has taken shape, they have been left out or victimized. Indians who lost their lands and blacks whose forced labor helped to create degraded soils find themselves again threatened by wastes dumped on their homelands and in their neighborhoods. For them the progressive story is a decline. They envision, instead, a new story—the possibility of a post-colonial world that could be a better place for indigenous peoples and people of color.[33]

The environmental justice movement includes justice for people of color, justice for women, and justice for nature. It reverses past environmental injustices disproportionately experienced by minorities. Environmental justice is the righting of the inequities of the past through laws, regulations, compensation, and removal of the causes of eco-injustice. Ecojustice entails the redistribution of wealth through the redistribution of environmental goods and services. With hard work and awareness, the crisis of environmental injustice, noted by Wendell Barry and a host of environmental historians, could result instead in justice restored.

NOTES

* From Carolyn Merchant, "Shades of Darkness: Race and Environmental History," *Environmental History* 8, no. 3 (July 2003): 380–94. Reprinted by permission of Oxford University Press.

1. Wendell Berry, *The Hidden Wound* (Berkeley, CA: Northpoint Press, 1989), quotations on pp. 112, 48.

2. For example, the University of California, Berkeley, has an American Cultures requirement that can be fulfilled by "American Environmental and Cultural History," see www.ecohistory.org. The requirement states: "The courses focus on themes or issues in United States history, society or culture; address theoretical or analytical issues relevant to understanding race, culture, and ethnicity in our society; take substantial account of groups drawn from at least three of the following: African-Americans, indigenous peoples of the United States, Asian Americans, Chicano/Latino Americans, and European Americans; and are integrative and comparative in that students study each group in the larger context of American society, history, or culture. The courses also provide students with the intellectual tools to understand better their own identity and the cultural identity of others in their own terms." "Berkeley Campus American Cultures Breadth Requirement," *General Catalog*, University of California, Berkeley.

3. Mart A. Stewart, *What Nature Suffers to Groe: Life, Labor, and Landscape on the Georgia Coast, 1680–1920* (Athens: University of Georgia Press, 1996); Mart A. Stewart, "Rice, Water, and Power: Landscapes of Domination and Resistance in the Lowcountry, 1790–1880," *Environmental History Review* 15, no. 3 (1991): 47–64; Timothy Silver, *A New Face on the Countryside: Indians, Colonists, and Slaves in South Atlantic Forests, 1500–1800* (New York: Cambridge University Press, 1990); Judith A. Carney, *Black Rice: The African Origins of Rice Cultivation in the Americas* (Cambridge, MA: Harvard University Press, 2001); Carl Anthony, "The Big House and the Slave Quarters: Part II, African Contributions to the New World," *Landscape* 21, no. 1 (Autumn 1976): 9–15; Dianne D. Glave, "Fields and Gardens: An Environmental History of African American Farmers in the Progressive South," Doctoral Dissertation, State University of New York at Stony Brook, 1998; Dianne D. Glave, "The African American Cooperative Service: A Folk Tradition in Conservation and Preservation in the Early Twentieth Century," *International Journal of Africana Studies* 6, no.1 (November–December 2000): 85–100; Carolyn Merchant, "The Tobacco and Cotton South, 1600–1900," in Carolyn Merchant, ed., *The Columbia Guide to American Environmental History* (New York: Columbia University Press, 2002), pp. 39–58.

4. Mark David Spence, *Dispossessing the Wilderness: Indian Removal and the Making of the National Parks* (New York: Oxford University Press, 1999); J. Baird Callicott, "The Wilderness Idea Revisited: The Sustainable Development Alternative," *The Environmental Professional* 13 (1991): 235–47; William Cronon, "The Trouble with Wilderness: Or Getting Back to the Wrong Nature," in William Cronon, ed., *Uncommon Ground: Rethinking the Human Place in Nature* (New York: W. W. Norton, 1996; originally published, 1995), pp. 69–90; Philip Burnham, *Indian Country, God's Country: Native Americans and the National Parks* (Washington, DC: Island Press, 2000); Robert H. Keller and Michael F. Turek, *American Indians and National Parks* (Tucson, AZ: University of Arizona Press, 1998); Rebecca Solnit, "Up the River of Mercy," *Sierra* 77 (November–December 1992): 50–84; Rebecca Solnit, *Savage Dreams: A Journey into the Hidden Wars of the American West* (San Francisco: Sierra Club Books, 1994); Carolyn Merchant, "Indian Land Policy, 1800–1900," in Merchant, *Columbia Guide to American Environmental History*, pp. 140–58.

5. Elizabeth D. Blum, "Power, Danger, and Control: Slave Women's Perceptions of Wilderness in the Nineteenth Century," *Women's Studies* 31 (2002): 247–65; Callicott, "The Wilderness Idea Revisited."
6. Jeffrey Romm, "The Coincidental Order of Environmental Injustice," in Kathryn M. Mutz, Gary C. Bryner, and Douglas S. Kenny, eds., *Justice and Natural Resources: Concepts, Strategies, and Applications* (Washington, DC: Island Press, 2002), pp. 117–38; Patricia Nelson Limerick, "Hoping against History," in Kathryn M. Mutz, Gary C. Bryner, and Douglas S. Kenny, eds., *Justice and Natural Resources: Concepts, Strategies, and Applications* (Washington, DC: Island Press, 2002), pp. 337–54; Roderick Nash, *The Rights of Nature: A History of Environmental Ethics* (Madison, WI: University of Wisconsin Press, 1989).
7. Eileen McGurty, "From NIMBY to Civil Rights: The Origins of the Environmental Justice Movement," *Environmental History* 2, no. 3 (July 1997): 301–23; Edie Yuen, Lisa J. Bunin, and Tim Stroshane, "Multicultural Ecology: An Interview with Carl Anthony," *Capitalism, Nature, Socialism* 8, no 3 (September 1997): 41–62; Robert Gottlieb, "Reconstructing Environmentalism: Complex Movements, Diverse Roots," *Environmental History Review* 17, no. 4 (Winter 1993): 1–19; Robert Bullard, ed., *Confronting Environmental Racism: Voices from the Grassroots* (Boston: South End Press, 1993); Andrew Hurley, *Environmental Inequalities: Class, Race, and Industrial Pollution in Gary, Indiana, 1945–1980* (Chapel Hill: University of North Carolina Press, 1995); Martin Melosi, "Equity, Eco-Racism, and Environmental History," *Environmental History Review* 19 (1995): 1–16; Dorceta Taylor, "American Environmentalism: The Role of Race, Class, and Gender in Shaping Activism 1820–1995," *Race, Gender and Class* 5, no. 1 (1997): 16–62; Elizabeth D. Blum, "Pink and Green: A Comparative Study of Black and White Women's Environmental Activism in the Twentieth Century," Doctoral Dissertation, University of Houston, 2000; Elizabeth D. Blum, "Protecting Home and Race: Black Women's Environmental Activism During the Progressive Era," Paper presented to the annual meeting of the American Historical Association, San Francisco, CA, January 3–6, 2002; Colin Fisher, "African Americans and the Frontier of Leisure: The 1919 Chicago Race Riot and Access to Nature," Paper presented to the annual meeting of the American Historical Association, San Francisco, CA, January 3–6, 2002.
8. On African and Asian Americans in the American West, see William Loren Katz, *The Black West: A Documentary and Pictorial History of the African American Role in the Westward Expansion of the United States* (New York: Simon and Schuster, 1996; originally published, 1971); Sucheng Chan, *This Bittersweet Soil: The Chinese in California Agriculture, 1860–1910* (Berkeley, CA: University of California Press, 1986); Sylvia Sun Minnick, *Samfow: The San Joaquin Chinese Legacy* (Fresno, CA: Panorama West, 1988); Silvia Anne Sheafer, *Chinese and the Gold Rush* (Whittier, CA: Journal Publications, 1979); Devra Weber, *Dark Sweat, White Gold: California Farm Workers, Cotton, and the New Deal* (Berkeley, CA: University of California Press, 1994).
9. William Bradford, *Of Plimoth Plantation* (Boston: Wright and Potter, 1901), pp. 94–5; George Catlin, *North American Indians* (Philadelphia: Leary, Stuart, 1913; originally published, 1844), vol. 1, pp. 294–5.
10. John Muir, *My First Summer in the Sierra* (New York: Penguin Books, 1987; originally published, 1911), pp. 205, 218.
11. Ibid., pp. 58–9, 226.
12. John Muir, *Travels in Alaska* (New York: AMS Press, 1978; originally published, 1915), pp. 31, 71–2, 77, 123, 131, 133–8, 163, 171, 197–204, quotations on pp. 239, 136. On Muir's "sermons," see pp. 135–6, 171–3. On Muir's attitudes toward Indians, see Richard F. Fleck, *Henry Thoreau and John Muir among the Indians* (Hamden, CT: Archon Books, 1985). Fleck reprints Muir's unpublished typescript from about 1908 containing one of his "sermons" in Alaska (referred to, but not included by Muir in his *Travels in Alaska*, pp. 135–6, 171–2), with words in brackets either added ([ ]) or crossed out (< >) by Muir: "Then I spoke of the brotherhood of man—how we were all children of one father; sketched

the characteristics of the different races of mankind, showing that no matter [how far apart their countries were], how they differed in color, [size, language] etc and no matter how <different and how> various the ways in which they got a living, that the white man [& all the people of the world] were essentially alike, <and that all the races of the world were alike; that> we all had ten fingers and ten toes, and in general [our bodies were the same whether] <whether our limbs were the same, although we might have] [white or brown or black different color and speak different languages,> just as though one family of [Thlinkit] boys and girls [has been scattered far abroad, formed] <should be sent abroad to different places and> [different tribes] forget their own language, and were so changed in <each form a habit of talking of their own after be> [color by the winds & sunshine of different climates that when after a long] <ing separated so long. . . ." (Fleck, *Henry Thoreau and John Muir*, pp. 89–90). For more on Muir's view of Indians in Alaska, see Linnie Marsh Wolfe, ed., *John of the Mountains: The Unpublished Journals of John Muir* (Boston: Houghton Mifflin, 1938), pp. 270–5.

13. Rebecca Solnit, personal communication. Helen Hunt Jackson, *Ah-Wah-Ne Days: A Visit to the Yosemite Valley in 1872* (San Francisco, CA: Book Club of California, 1971), pp. 39, 46, 47, 70, quotations on pp. 20, 38–9; Helen Hunt Jackson, *My Day in the Wilderness: Six California Tales* (San Francisco, CA: Book Club of California, 1939), no. 6; Helen Hunt Jackson, *A Century of Dishonor: A Sketch of the United States Government's Dealings with Some of the Indian Tribes* (Boston: Roberts Brothers, 1888; originally published, 1881); Helen Hunt Jackson, *Ramona: A Story* (Boston, MA: Little Brown and Co., 1899; originally published, 1884); Ruth Odell, *Helen Hunt Jackson (H.H.)* (New York: D. Appleton-Century Co., 1939), pp. 155–70; Carlyle Channing Davis and William A. Alderson, *The True Story of "Ramona"* (New York: Dodge Publishing Co., 1914); Valerie Sherer Mathes, *Helen Hunt Jackson and Her Indian Reform Legacy* (Austin: University of Texas Press, 1990), pp. 21–54.

14. Mary Austin, *The Land of Little Rain* (Boston: Houghton Mifflin, 1950; originally published, 1903), quotations on pp. 1, 33, 63. On Austin's view of Indians and the desert see Vera Norwood, "Heroines of Nature: Four Women Respond to the American Landscape," *Environmental Review* 8, no. 1 (Spring 1984): 34–56, see pp. 41–4. In 1873, Joaquin Miller who had lived with the Modoc Indians wrote *Life Amongst the Modoc*, about the simultaneous defeat of the Indians during the 1873 Modoc War and the destruction of the California environment from gold mining. See Joaquin Miller, *Life Amongst the Indians* (Chicago: Moril, Higgins & Co., 1892; originally published, 1873), pp. 18–22, 54–5. Another environmentalist sympathetic to Indians was John Wesley Powell, author of the *Report on the Lands of the Arid Region of the United States* (Washington, DC, 1878) and director of the Bureau of Ethnology (1879–1902). Powell's attitudes, however, were complex. On the one hand, he agonized over Indian poverty and hunger and desired to help Indians adapt to what he considered inevitable change, and, on the other hand, he believed that civilization meant the displacement of a nomadic, hunting lifestyle and the dispelling of Indian animism and myths. He was fascinated by Indian languages and lifestyles, but believed that their way of life was doomed and that Indians must adapt to white ways in order to survive. See Donald Worster, *A River Running West: The Life of John Wesley Powell* (New York: Oxford University Press, 2001), pp. 261–96.

15. Winthrop Jordan III, *White over Black: American Attitudes Toward the Negro, 1550–1812* (New York: W. W. Norton, 1977; originally published, 1968), pp. 23–8; Carl Anthony, personal communication.

16. Robert Bullard, "Environmental Racism and the Environmental Justice Movement," in Robert Bullard, ed., *Confronting Environmental Racism: Voices from the Grassroots* (Boston: South End Press, 1993), pp. 15–16.

17. Henry David Thoreau, *Walden and Civil Disobedience* (New York: Penguin, 1983), introduction, pp. 29–36, quotation from "Walden" on p. 216, from "Civil Disobedience," on pp. 389, 390, 391. On Thoreau's concept of community see Nash, *The Rights of Nature*, quotation on p. 37. On Thoreau as an opponent of slavery, see Limerick, "Hoping against

History," quotation on p. 343. The English actress Frances Anne Kemble (wife of Phila-delphian Pierce Butler, who owned a Sea Island Cotton plantation off the coast of Georgia) was likewise an opponent of slavery and an advocate for nature. See Frances Anne Kemble, *Journal of a Residence on a Georgian Plantation in 1838–1839* (New York: Alfred A. Knopf, 1961; originally published, 1863), pp. 3–4, 10–11, 202–3, 215–16. Frederick Law Olmsted traveled through the South in 1853 and in 1856 published *A Journey in the Sea-board Slave States*, noting both the brutal treatment of slaves and the exhaustion of soils. See Frederick Law Olmsted, *The Slave States* (New York: G.P. Putnam's Sons, 1959; origi-nally published, 1856).

18. Thomas W. Hanchett, *Sorting Out the New South City: Race, Class, and Urban Develop-ment in Charlotte, 1875–1975* (Chapel Hill, NC: University of North Carolina Press, 1998), pp. 116–44; Robert Woods, ed., *The City Wilderness: A Settlement Study* (Boston: Hough-ton Mifflin, 1898), pp. 1–2; Booth Tarkington, *The Turmoil, a Novel* (New York: Harper & Brothers, 1915; originally published, 1914), pp. 1–5.

19. Jeffrey Romm, "The Coincidental Order of Environmental Injustice," in Kathryn M. Mutz, ed., *Justice and Natural Resources* (Washington, DC: Island Press, 2002), pp. 117–38, quotations on pp. 122–3.

20. Yuen, Bunin, and Stroshane, "Interview with Carl Anthony," p. 50; Nash, *The Rights of Nature*, quotation on pp. 38–9; Stephen Fox, *John Muir and His Legacy: The American Conservation Movement* (Boston: Little, Brown and Co., 1981), pp. 41–3, quotations on p. 42; John Muir, *A Thousand-Mile Walk to the Gulf* (San Francisco: Sierra Club Books, 1991), quotation on p. xvi.

21. Muir, *A Thousand-Mile Walk to the Gulf*, quotations on p. 25.

22. Ibid.

23. Ibid., quotations on pp. 30, 31, 60.

24. Zora Neale Hurston, *Their Eyes Were Watching God* (New York: HarperCollins, 1990, originally published 1937), quotations on pp. 129, 130.

25. Ibid., quotations on pp. 161–2, 169, 25.

26. Limerick, "Hoping against History," pp. 340–2; Aldo Leopold, "The Land Ethic," in Aldo Leopold, ed., *A Sand County Almanac* (New York: Oxford University Press, 1949), pp. 201-226, quotation on p. 204.

27. On Leopold's changing attitudes toward Indians, see his 1937 essay, "Conservationist in Mexico," in Susan L. Flader and J. Baird Callicott, eds., *The River of the Mother of God and Other Essays by Aldo Leopold* (Madison, WI: University of Wisconsin Press, 1991), pp. 239–44. In the "Conservation Ethic" an early draft of the "Land Ethic" written in 1933, Leopold wrote: The "sense of right and wrong may be aroused quite as strongly by the desecration of a nearby woodlot as by a famine in China, a near pogrom in Germany, or the murder of the slave-girls in ancient Greece." Aldo Leopold, "The Conservation Ethic," in Flader and Callicott, eds., *The River of the Mother of God*, quotation on p. 182. The legacy of slavery as extended to the earth led Leopold to an ethic of cooperation among people and between people and nature. He wrote: "Civilization is not . . . the enslavement of a stable and constant earth. It is a state of mutual and interdependent cooperation between human animals, other animals, plants, and soil, which may be disrupted at any moment by the failure of any of them." ("The Conservation Ethic," ibid., p. 183)

28. Nash, *The Rights of Nature*, pp. 6–7, 200–13, quotations on pp. 202, 203; Leopold, "The Land Ethic," in *A Sand County Almanac*, p. 202. Nash points out that: "slavery in the United States was not negotiated away. For similar reasons it might be unreasonable to expect that what Aldo Leopold was the first to call 'the enslavement of . . . earth' could be abolished without profound social disruption." (Nash, *The Rights of Nature*, p. 8.) Arthur L. Herman, *Community, Violence, and Peace* (Albany: State University of New York Press, 1999) argues that Aldo Leopold, like Martin Luther King Jr., Mohandas Gandhi, and Gautama the Buddha each developed an ethic rooted in a concept of community that arose from a transformative experience within the individual.

29. Limerick, "Hoping against History," in Mutz, ed., *Justice and Natural Resources*, pp. 344–5.

30. Robert Bullard, *Dumping in Dixie: Race, Class, and Environmental Quality* (Boulder, CO: Westview Press, 1990).
31. Gayatri Chakravorty Spivak, "Can the Subaltern Speak?," in Carly Nelson and Lawrence Grossberg, eds., *Marxism and the Interpretation of Culture* (London, England: Macmillan, 1988), pp. 271-318, reprinted in Bill Ashcroft, Gareth Griffiths, and Helen Tiffin, eds., *The Post-Colonial Studies Reader* (New York: Routledge, 1995), pp. 24–8.
32. Hawley Truax, "Minorities at Risk," *Environmental Action* 21 (January–February 1990): 20–1; Charles Lee, *Toxic Wastes and Race in the United States: A National Report on the Racial and Socio-Economic Characteristics of Communities with Hazardous Waste Sites* (New York: United Church of Christ Commission for Racial Justice, 1987); Jesus Sanchez, "The Environment: Whose Movement?" *Green Letter* 5, no. 1 (Spring 1989): 3–4, 14–16; Philip Shabecoff, "Environmental Groups Faulted for Racism," *San Francisco Chronicle*, February 1, 1990, A2; Robbin Lee Zeff, Marsha Love, and Karen Stults, *Empowering Ourselves: Women and Toxics Organizing* (Arlington, VA: Citizen's Clearing House for Hazardous Wastes, 1989); Andrew Szasz, *Ecopopulism: Toxic Waste and the Movement for Environmental Justice* (Minneapolis, MN: University of Minnesota Press, 1994).
33. James M. Blaut, *The Colonizer's Model of the World: Geographical Diffusionism and Eurocentric History* (New York: Guilford Press, 1993); Ashcroft, et al., *The Post-Colonial Studies Reader*.

FIGURE 12.1 Aldo Leopold (1887–1948). Proponent of the science of restoration ecology and author of "The Land Ethic," in *A Sand County Almanac* (1949). Leopold and his family began replanting pines and restoring the prairies around their "shack" in Baraboo, Wisconsin in 1935.

Source: Courtesy of the Aldo Leopold Foundation, www.aldoleopold.org.

FIGURE 12.2 Curtis Prairie. University of Wisconsin, Madison, Arboretum. Aldo Leopold's vision of restoration led botanist John Curtis (1913–1961) and others in the 1930s to restore a native prairie from abandoned farmland.

Source: Paul Jenkins, Wildflower Farm, Coldwater, Ontario, Canada, used by permission.

12

RESTORING NATURE*

Restoration is a backward-looking philosophy. But unlike romanticism, which is a longing for the past, or preservation, which seeks to save what already exists, restoration implies an active participation in bringing the past back to life. It recognizes that, while humans may be part of nature, they also have more power to alter it than do other species. Admitting this, it goes on to provide ways to use that power responsibly and ethically by going back in time to heal what has been changed or damaged. But this very act, even as in some ways it reaches into the past, also creates a new future.[1]

In reconstructing natural ecosystems such as prairies, forests, rivers, and lakes, humans are imitators of nature. By studying and mimicking natural patterns they can recover not only the communities themselves but some of the wisdom inherent in both cultural and biological evolution. Rather than taking nature apart and simplifying ecosystems, as the past three centuries of mechanistic science have taught us to do supremely well, restorationists are actively putting them back together. Rather than analyzing nature for the sake of dominating and controlling it, restorationists are synthesizing it for the sake of living symbiotically within the whole.[2]

A major pioneer of restoration ecology was Aldo Leopold (1887–1948) who used his family's land in Baraboo, Wisconsin as a demonstration area for replanting the surrounding prairies and woodlands with native species. Leopold's vision and that of other University of Wisconsin botanists also led to the creation during the 1930s of the university's 1200-acre Arboretum containing restored woods, prairies, and wetlands out of abandoned farmlands. In his now classic book, *A Sand County Almanac* (1949) published the year after his death in 1948 fighting a forest fire in Baraboo, he set forth his chapter on "The Land Ethic." He wrote: "The land ethic simply enlarges the boundaries of the community to include soils, waters, plants, and animals or simply the land." And "a land ethic changes the role of *homo sapiens* from conquer of the land-community to plain citizen of it." "A thing is right," Leopold said, "when it tends to preserve the integrity, beauty, and stability of the biotic community. It is wrong when it tends otherwise."[3]

Restoration ecology draws on Leopold's land ethic in the process of renewing degraded ecosystems by human intervention. Scientists study the history of a piece of land and the plants, animals, fungi, and bacteria that used to populate it. They then reintroduce, replant, and regroup the plant and animal communities that existed at a chosen point in time. Ecological processes and relationships take over and the community is eventually restored. In the practice of restoration, they are imitating what existed in a prior time at a particular place.

Mimesis, the process of imitation through which restoration takes place, has had an important history. Indian hunters mimicked the sounds, smells, and behavior of the animals they captured for food. Forest clearings planted with corn, beans, and squash by Indian women mimicked nature's polycultural patterns. The Indian's oral-aural culture of myths, songs, and poems by which tribal values were preserved were grounded in the mimetic, oral mode of knowing. In peasant agriculture, peasants danced in the fields to awaken the generative powers of nature and spread cider, cake, or corn on the ground to influence the seasonal cycles. The alchemist who followed in nature's footsteps to imitate her ways was participating in the natural cycles in order to hasten them. The miner who cajoled nature through prayer before following a vein of ore, and the smith who abstained from drinking and eating before shaping a metal on the anvil, were artists uncovering nature's own hidden patterns.[4]

Platonism in ancient Greece and mechanistic science in early modern Europe both undermined the mimetic tradition by elevating analysis to a position of reverence. To Plato, mimesis was simply a catalogue of responses learned by rote. The knower should be separated from the known; the subject from the object. Not recollection and participation, but problem-solving and analysis were what mattered most. The song and narrative were replaced by logic, arithmetic, and science. Two millennia later, Newtonian scientists undertook to understand nature by dividing it into atomic parts and changing it through external forces. To Francis Bacon, imitation meant obeying nature in order to command her. Nature was to be dominated, not by following but by prodding and ferreting out her secrets. The organic cosmos of Aristotle, in which nature acted and developed from within, gave way to a worldview that sanctioned external manipulation and control. The model of the technician repairing the clock from the outside superseded that of the artist who revealed the form inherent in the matter, or the doctor, whose herbs healed the body because their inner knowledge (*scientia*) became one with the body's own knowledge.[5]

Drawing on the mechanistic model, modern agriculture has increasingly moved in the direction of artificial ecosystems occupied by monocultures that are vulnerable to pest outbreaks and catastrophic collapse. Identical fields, outlined in precise geometric patterns for efficient cultivation and harvesting, replicate lattice-like atomic patterns, replacing the diversity of small, haphazard patchworks of fields created in forest clearings. Further stimulated by urbanization and industrialization, traditional agriculture was profoundly altered during the agricultural improvement movements of the eighteenth and nineteenth centuries by the introduction of more efficient machinery and irrigation technology and by improvements in crop and animal breeding, artificial fertilizers, and chemical pesticides. As a result, the external energy needed to produce the chemicals; operate the farm machinery; and process, store, and transport the products often surpasses the calories the foods themselves supply.

Today, restoration is part of a spectrum of emerging disciplines based on imitation, synthesis, and a creative reciprocity between humans and non-human nature. Both restoration and agroecology look back to traditional agriculture, combining it with ecology in order to design sustainable systems by mimicking nature. Together, these disciplines represent a spectrum of practices based on reestablishing contact with nature through imitation. Thus much is being learned by studying the polycultural methods of traditional farmers, combining the wisdom of traditional agriculture developed over generations of trial and error with an understanding of local ecology. In the resulting agroecosystems, the spatial arrangements and seasonal development of wild plant species are used as models; the farmer imitates the arrangement of local species of grass, vine, shrub and tree to design integrated cereal, vegetable, fruit, and tree crop systems.[6]

Similarly, agroforestry restores complementary arrangements of trees, crops, and animals in accord with ecological principles in order to maintain productivity without environmental degradation. Orchards are planted with a ground cover of legumes or berries and foraged by poultry, pigs, and bees to keep down pests and produce well-mulched and manured soil.[7]

Permaculture carries the process of imitation a step further. As an agriculture for the future, it imitates ecosystem evolution toward climax states by designing perennial plant and animal crop interactions. In contrast to monocultural agriculture, permaculture uses several stories of trees, shrubs, vines, and perennial ground crops to absorb more light and nutrients, increasing the total yield. Plants and animals coexist in separate niches that reduce competition and promote symbiosis among species. Complexity not only helps to ward off catastrophes but increases the variety of foods produced. External energy and physical labor decrease as perennials mature, so that energy needs are provided from within.[8]

As a form of agriculture, restoration, too, is based on the capacity of both humans and nature for action. While restoration is oriented toward the reconstruction of authentic replicas of natural habitats, agriculture traditionally aims at the production of food, clothing, and shelter. In either ease, however, the principle of mimesis is important: people can use the environment to fulfill real needs, while non-human nature acts reciprocally as a partner. In this way nature is used with respect, not as something passive and manipulable as in the mechanistic model but as a partner that is active and alive.

At a deeper level, a number of scientists in the past few years have proposed alternatives to the mechanistic framework based on nature's inherent activity, self-organization, permeable boundaries, and resilience. These deep structural changes in science itself may be indicative of the emergence of a new paradigm compatible with the recognition that a global crisis exists in current patterns of resource use.[9]

The Gaia hypothesis of British chemist James Lovelock proposes that the earth's biota as a whole maintain an optimal, life-supporting chemical composition within the atmosphere and oceans. Gaia, the name of the Greek earth goddess, is a metaphor for a self-regulating system that controls the functioning of the earth's chemical cycles.[10]

The thermodynamics of Ilya Prigogine contrasts the equilibrium and near-equilibrium dynamics of the closed, isolated physical systems described by the mechanistic model with open, biological and social systems in which matter and energy are constantly being exchanged with their surroundings. In a similar spirit, the new physics of David Bohm contrasts the older world picture of atomic fragmentation with a new philosophy of wholeness expressed in the unfolding and enfolding of moments within a "holomovement." Bohm's cosmology emphasizes the primacy of process rather than the domination of parts.[11]

These new theoretical frameworks share with action-oriented disciplines, such as restoration and permaculture, a participatory form of consciousness rooted in ecology. In opposition to the subject/object, mind/body, and nature/culture dichotomies basic to mechanistic science, ecological consciousness recognizes mind and skin as permeable boundaries that integrate organism with environment, tacit knowing and learning through visceral imitation, and complexity and process as a merging of nature with culture. Opposed to the abstract concepts of a disembodied intellect imposed on agriculture is the embeddedness of design in gardens that mimic natural patterns. Humans are neither helpless victims nor arrogant dominators of nature but active participants in the destiny of the systems of which they are a part.

The biological control of insects also uses natural ecosystems as models. Uncultivated land surrounding fields harbors birds and insect enemies as well as pests. Hedges and flowers along roadsides are attractive to beneficial insects. Diversity in crops and surroundings and arrangements of beneficial plants mimic natural conditions making crops less visible to insect enemies and acting as barriers to pest dispersal. Thus by imitating nature, agricultural systems can be designed both to suppress pests and maximize total yield. By integrating these methods with new theoretical frameworks, ecosystems can be restored and agriculture can be made sustainable.[12]

NOTES

*   From Carolyn Merchant, "Perspective: Restoration and Reunion with Nature," *Restoration and Management Notes* 4 (Winter 1986): 68–70. Copyright 1986 by the Board of Regents of the University of Wisconsin System. Reproduced courtesy of the University of Wisconsin Press; edited with additions for this volume.
1. William R. Jordan III, "Thoughts on Looking Back," *Restoration & Management Notes* 1, no. 3 (Winter 1983): 2.
2. Carolyn Merchant, *The Death of Nature: Women, Ecology, and the Scientific Revolution* (San Francisco: Harper & Row, 1980), Ch. 1.
3. Aldo Leopold, "The Land Ethic" in Aldo Leopold, ed., *A Sand County Almanac* (New York: Oxford University Press, 1949), pp. 201-226, quotations on pp. 224–5. On Aldo Leopold's family shack in Baraboo Wisconsin see www.aldoleopold.org/visit/the-shack/. On Leopold's role in creating the Curtis Prairie, see www.wildflowerfarm.com/blog/?p=2768 and http://news.wisc.edu/birthplace-of-ecological-restoration-celebrates-75-years/
4. Morris Berman, *The Reenchantment of the World* (Ithaca: Cornell University Press, 1981); Merchant, *The Death of Nature*, Ch. 4.
5. Merchant, *The Death of Nature*, Ch. 7, 9.
6. William R. Jordan III, "On Ecosystem Doctoring," *Restoration & Management Notes* 1, no. 4 (Fall 1983): 2; Miguel Altieri, *Agroecology: The Scientific Basis of Alternative Agriculture* (Berkeley, CA: University of California, Berkeley, Division of Biological Control, 1983).
7. John Farrell, "Agroforestry Systems," in Miguel Altieri, *Agroecology: The Scientific Basis of Alternative Agriculture*. Berkeley, CA: University of California, Division of Biological Control, 1983), pp. 77–83.
8. Bill Mollison and David Holmgren, *Permaculture One: A Perennial Agriculture for Human Settlements* (Maryborough, Australia: Dominion Press-Hedges & Bell, 1984); Bill Mollison, *Permaculture Two: Practical Design for Town and Country in Permanent Agriculture* (Maryborough, Australia: Dominion Press-Hedges & Bell, 1984).
9. Erich Jantsch, *The Self-Organizing Universe* (New York: Pergamon, 1980); Bill Devall and George Sessions, *Deep Ecology: Living as if Nature Mattered* (Salt Lake City: Peregrine Smith Books, 1985); Murray Bookchin, *The Ecology of Freedom: The Emergence and Dissolution of Hierarchy* (Palo Alto: Cheshire Books, 1982).

10. James Lovelock, *Gaia: A New Look at Life on Earth* (Oxford: Oxford University Press, 1979).

11. Ilya Prigogine and Isabelle Stengers, *Order Out of Chaos: Man's New Dialogue with Nature* (Toronto: Bantam Books, 1984); David Bohm, *Wholeness and the Implicate Order* (Boston: Routledge & Kegan Paul, 1980).

12. Altieri, *Agroecology*.

Part V

ENVIRONMENTAL ETHICS

I began thinking and writing about environmental history and ethics as the environmental movement gained momentum following the Earth Day demonstrations of 1970. During the succeeding two decades as I wrote my first books on environmental history—*The Death of Nature* (1980) and *Ecological Revolutions* (1989)—I also began developing a framework for environmental ethics. In Chapter 13, in a keynote address to the entering freshman class at Vassar College (my *alma mater*) in 1989, I ask "Is it Time for an Earth Ethic?" Here I address the global ecological crisis facing humanity through disasters ranging from the 1989 Alaska Oil Spill to Antarctic ozone depletion and from atmospheric pollution to the loss of tropical rainforests. I argue that we not only need a new ethic but a new metaphysics that contrasts with that inherited from the Scientific Revolution.

Integral to environmental ethics are feminist theories and feminist ethics. In Chapter 14, "Ecofeminism and Feminist Theory," I present a framework for understanding approaches to ecofeminism arising from liberal, radical, social, and socialist politics. I examine underlying assumptions about nature and human nature, as well as critiques feminists have made of environmentalism and their images of a feminist environmentalism. Since the 1970s, ecofeminism has thrived in many new and different forms with numerous articles and books appearing that illustrate its use over many areas of the globe including Europe, Australia, India, and Latin America. Other topics include ecofeminism and other animals; ecofeminism and systems thinking; ecofeminism and literary criticism, and ecofeminist theologies. Recent dimensions embrace ecofeminism and environmental justice as manifested in Lesbian, Gay, Bisexual, Transgender, and Queer (LGBTQ) identities.

At the Earth Summit in Rio de Janeiro in 1992, after teaching and thinking about environmental ethics for over a decade, I formulated a new ethic of human partnership with nature. My partnership ethic states that "the greatest good for the human and the non-human communities is to be found in their mutual, living interdependence." As elaborated in Chapter 15, treating nature as a partner with humanity means that we take from nature what we need for life (food, clothing, shelter, and energy), but we also give back to nature what it needs in order to survive. We restrict and reduce our use of non-renewable resources, we recycle renewable resources, and we reuse without waste everything we take from nature. In this chapter, I illustrate the three main forms of environmental ethics—egocentric, homocentric, and ecocentric— and show how partnership ethics both derives from and supersedes these three earlier forms. I also give examples of how partnership ethics can be applied to real world situations and how it can help us make decisions about living with the earth.

As a whole, the three chapters of Part V present a vision of how humans and nature can overcome the problems of degradation and exploitation and how both can survive and thrive on the earth in the twenty-first century and beyond.

FIGURE 13.1 Earth Image. The beauty and tranquility of the Earth as viewed from outer space suggests that it is indeed time for an Earth Ethic to save the planet.

Source: Public domain.

13

IS IT TIME FOR
AN EARTH ETHIC?*

In 1958 a group of senior science majors was preparing to leave Vassar College to enter life beyond the stone walls adjoining Taylor Gate. One was heading for a year of study at Wood's Hole Oceanographic Institute. Another was off to Harvard University's Medical School. A third was set to enroll in the graduate program in Biological Chemistry at the University of Michigan. A fourth decided on advanced work in mathematics and another was set to enroll in graduate work in Physics at the University of Pennsylvania. Two others decided to forsake Chemistry for careers in graduate work in Philosophy at Columbia University. These seniors were all moving out into a world of expanding scientific opportunities propelled by the successful launch of the Russian satellite *Sputnik*—a world in which science seemed to hold the key to human progress on earth and hope of success for American democracy in the Cold War over nuclear energy.

As I sat in Professor Vernon Venable's philosophy class in 1957, the year the Russians launched Sputnik, I learned from him that Galileo and Newton in the seventeenth century had discovered all the fundamental principles necessary for a successful satellite program. Only the technology remained to be developed. Back then, life seemed simpler and solutions possible, although philosophy of course was neither. Science seemed to provide a cohesive social, almost religious, force. An expansive sense of optimism prevailed that science and technology could solve most of the world's pressing social problems, even as it was also creating the most devastating one of all—the possibility of nuclear holocaust.

Within thirty years, however, a global environmental crisis—only dimly apparent in 1958—had become painfully visible. In January 1989, *Time* magazine's person of the year award went to "The Endangered Earth," graphically illustrated by sculptor Christo as a suffocating globe wrapped in plastic and bound with twine. With increasing public awareness of global problems, public concern mounted. The 1989 Alaskan Oil Spill alerted millions of Americans to the tragic transformation of a pristine Alaskan shoreline surrounded by lush rainforest into black, motionless, silent beaches of dead birds, seals, sea otters, and contaminated waters devoid of the life that sustained local fishers and their families. A *New York Times*/CBS poll found that an astonishing 80% of all those questioned overwhelmingly agreed with the statement: "Protecting the environment is so important that requirements and standards cannot be too high, and continuing environmental improvements must be made regardless of cost."[1]

Examples of those environmental concerns included:

CLIMATE CHANGE

Perhaps the most widely felt evidence of the global crisis was the intense hot weather experienced by Americans during the summer of 1988. "The Greenhouse Effect is already here and it will worsen," warned scientists and policy analysts at Congressional hearings held that summer. According to then Colorado Senator Timothy Wirth, "The greenhouse effect is the most significant economic, political, environmental, and human problem facing the twenty-first century."[2] As the amount of carbon dioxide and other gases in the atmosphere increased from the burning of fossil fuels and other industrial processes, global temperatures were predicted to rise 3 to 10 degrees Fahrenheit. By 2016, four countries, China (29%), the United States (15%), the European Union (10%), and India (6%) together produced 60% of all carbon dioxide emissions, but worldwide growth was beginning to slow.[3] With climate change, winters are becoming stormier and summers hotter and drier. Seas are predicted to rise one to three feet over the next half century and hurricanes will become more powerful as the oceans warm. Waterfront homes will be flooded, mid-western droughts will increase in severity, grain growing regions will move north, and whole forests and wild species will be lost.[4] Although there has been much debate over the timing of the effect, a series of measures to slow it have been recommended, such as stopping global deforestation, planting trees, conserving heating fuel, and shifting to alternative energy sources.[5]

OZONE DEPLETION

In 1985 scientists reported a hole in the ozone layer over the Antarctic. As a result of worldwide concern 24 countries met at Montreal in 1987 and agreed to reduce production of the prime culprit, chlorofluorocarbons (CFC's), by 35% by 1999. CFC's used as refrigerator and air conditioner coolants, as primary components of styrofoam, and as propellant gases in spray cans were banned in the U.S. in the 1970s, but were still used in other countries. Alternatives to CFCs in disposable cups, fast food containers, and packing were researched and introduced, but much work still needs to be done by science, by Congress in regulating CFCs, and by all of us in changing the habits of our everyday lives. By 2016, through worldwide efforts at control of chlorofluorocarbons, the ozone hole was beginning to heal.[6]

TROPICAL FORESTS / AMERICAN REDWOODS

Tropical forests, which cover 2.3 million square miles of the earth's surface are disappearing at a rapid rate. If the destruction continued, it was predicted that little would be left by the year 2040. Rainforests, which once covered fourteen percent of the earth's surface now cover only six percent.[7] In Indonesia 500,000 acres of tropical rainforest were converted to Eucalyptus plantations to produce toilet paper for North America. Much of the rainforest is being used to construct throw-away construction forms, boxes for shipping, and disposable chopsticks. At the June 1989 "The Fate and Hope of the Earth" conference held in Managua, Nicaragua, Martin Khor of Indonesyia admonished, "There are enough world resources for everyone's need, but not for everyone's greed." In the United States, Pacific old-growth redwood and Douglas Fir forests were threatened by logging for export to the Far East. While much has been done to save the remaining stands of old growth trees and alternatives to redwood are now being used, illegal poaching continues.[8]

SPECIES EXTINCTIONS

In the words of *Time* magazine, "the death of birth" poses another immense global threat to all non-human species. A National Science Foundation study predicted that a quarter of the earth's species of plants, animals, microbes, and fungi would become extinct over the next several years unless extraordinary measures are taken to protect the ecosystems in which they live. Only

1.4 of the 5 to 10 million species of life in the world had even been named. Increased efforts must be taken to identify them, understand their ecology, and to educate the public.[9] International agreements were reached on halting some of the most visible threats. The United States and Europe banned imports of ivory from the African elephant. Japan followed suit and reduced its imports of endangered species such as the Hawksbill Turtle used for exotic ornaments and wedding gifts. China pledged to ban its imports of ivory by 2017. Policies and practices are changing, but they may not be in time to preserve the lives of known endangered species, much less those not even identified.[10]

OCEANS

Eight million tons of plastic wastes end up in oceans each year and gather into giant gyres such as the Great Pacific Garbage Patch. Together, they cause the deaths of tens of thousands of birds and marine mammals a year. Dead and dying birds entangled in plastic six-pack rings wash up on beaches every day. The plastic rings will go on for another 450 years, outliving the generations they are extinguishing. Seabirds, fish, turtles, and whales lunch on small plastic pellets produced as wastes in the plastics industries. Diving birds and mammals are entrapped in plastic drift nets 6 to 30 miles in length used primarily by Japanese and other East Asian fishermen. Seven hundred miles of nets are lost each season in the Pacific ocean. When these nets escape they go on trapping marine life until they sink under their own weight.[11]

EROSION

Soil erosion in the United States is threatening one-third of all croplands. If allowed to continue over the next 50 years, U.S. grain production will sink to about half of what the U.S. exported in 1980, affecting millions of people around the world.[12] In India, land has been used to feed people for over forty centuries, with only 5–10% of the surpluses leaving the local villages. According to conservationist Vandana Shiva, Green Revolution farming techniques replaced traditional methods, teaching Indian farmers "to forget about the hunger of the soil and the stomach and to go after their own hunger for profits."[13]

TOXICS

Humans and other living things were being invaded by an immense number of toxic chemicals unknown to biological evolution. According to environmentalist Barry Commoner, "an organic compound that does not occur in nature [is] one that has been rejected in the course of evolution as incompatible with living systems." Because of their toxicity, "they have a very high probability of interfering with living processes." Toxic chemicals range from factory emissions, smog, and radon in the air, to pesticides in the soil, to trichloroethylene in drinking water. Some scientists believe that even if we do not destroy ourselves with a nuclear bang, we will poison ourselves in a toxic whimper. Concerns such as these led California citizens to pass Proposition 65, an anti-toxics initiative, in 1986 with a 63% vote. The state's list of chemicals linked to cancer or birth defects is updated every year.[14]

The words of seventeenth century poet John Donne that I first read in my English Literature class at Vassar pertain just as well to our world today as to his own in the seventeenth. Donne compared the death of the Renaissance living earth and organic cosmos, enlivened by the world soul and spirit, to the death of a young woman Elizabeth Drury.

Sicke World, yea, dead, yea putrified, since shee
Thy intrinsique balme, and thy preservative,
Can never be renewed, thou never live.[15]

Every section of Donne's poem, describing the dying world as a cripple, an ugly monster, a wan ghost, and a dry cinder, was followed by the dirge-like refrain, "Shee, Shee is dead; shee's dead." Is this refrain also appropriate to a small dying blue planet in the twenty-first century?

Since the time of my graduation from Vassar in 1958, skepticism about the ability of science to solve the world's problems has increased. Classical science as we learned it in the 1950s came to be viewed not only as part of the problem, but also as essential to the solution. What happened to erode the optimism over science that prevailed during the age of Sputnik?

In the 1960s, the country underwent a revolutionary challenge to the values of the post-World War II era. The Civil Rights movement erupted in the South and spread across the country sparking sit-ins, demonstrations, and a wave of legislation aimed at providing equal opportunities for minorities. The Vietnam War protests called into question the principle of a just war, sacred to the World War II mobilization against fascism, anti-Semitism, and the holocaust. The women's movement emerged in part from women's efforts to play leadership roles in the new social movements and in part from their need to get out of the home and to engage in meaningful creative work. Many lives were changed irrevocably, either in sympathy with these social movements or in opposition to them.

In 1970, the first Earth Day galvanized an incipient environmental movement into national action. An outpouring of citizen concern resulted in the passage of environmental laws and tighter regulations. The National Environmental Policy Act (NEPA) was passed in 1970 and with it the President's Council on Environmental Quality was created. The Clean Air Amendments of 1970 strengthened the Clean Air Act first passed in 1955.[16] In 1972 water regulation was also brought under stricter federal control. Then in 1973 long thirty-minute lines at the corner gas station curtailed people's weekend and vacation excursions. A national energy crisis brought forth an array of alternative energy proposals from solar heating sources and wind energy supplements, to shale oil extraction, and home energy conservation.

During the 1970s, I was teaching History of Science at the University of San Francisco. My students were aroused by the issues of science and society raised by the environmental and energy crises. They wanted to know how we got into these problems historically and what science had to do with them. Excited by the questions they were asking, I began to rethink the history of science as I had learned it in graduate school in the sixties. What were the historical roots of the environmental crisis? What did the Scientific Revolution on which I had done my doctoral dissertation contribute to the worldview of the twentieth century? What was the role of women in science and how were society's concepts of women reflected in it? Rethinking the roots of modern science and its role in today's world resulted in my book, *The Death of Nature* (1980).

NATURE DOMINATES HUMANS

Through my teaching, I came to understand that when nature ceased to be viewed as alive and the earth to be perceived as a nurturing mother, a profound transformation took place in human ways of relating to the earth. For millennia, most premodern peoples experienced the world as alive, filled with spirits, and responsive to human action. If a deer was to be shot for food, a tree cut for fuel, a brook dammed for water, seed sown on a freshly plowed field, or even a mine shaft dug for ore, a ritual of propitiation was made to the living spirit of the animal, plant, or earth mother. If the deer escaped, if plants died, or wells ran dry, humans and their rituals were at fault. In European culture, too, the world was treated as a living organism down through the Renaissance of the sixteenth century. It had a body, soul, and spirit, and the earth had respiratory, circulatory, and reproductive systems just as humans did. If a harvest failed or disease struck a village, people had not behaved properly toward nature or toward God. They accepted their fate and tried to live better lives.

SCIENCE DOMINATES NATURE

With the rise of a capitalist market economy and of modern science in the seventeenth century, human attitudes toward the earth changed. Francis Bacon and the experimental scientists of the seventeenth century taught that the earth should be examined to reveal her secrets for the sake of humankind. Rather than following nature in her footsteps and learning from her as had farmers, alchemists, and miners, Bacon argued that nature should be "forced out of her natural state and squeezed and molded." Miners and smiths should "search into the bowels of nature" and "shape her on the anvil." Technology should not just "exert a gentle guidance over nature's course," but should "conquer and subdue her," and "shake her to her foundations."[17]

Other philosophers and scientists such as René Descartes and Isaac Newton conceptualized nature as dead, inert corpuscles moved by external forces. They removed the soul from the world and the *spiritus mundi* from the heavens. They left the earth as dead matter, devoid of any resemblance to the human being. Nature was described by mathematical laws, God was a mathematician and engineer, human bodies and animals were miniature machines, and the mind resembled a calculating machine that added up perceptions of the outside world in a logical sequence. The "death of nature" metaphorically gave humans the power to control and manipulate it for their own benefit. They could intervene in the earth and repair it from outside, just as God repaired the world machine from on high. Newton believed that God periodically had to set the planets back on their elliptical courses when their orbits were disturbed by a passing comet entering from outside the solar system.

The Enlightenment of the eighteenth century accepted this philosophy of domination and turned it into tremendous optimism over the capacity of the human beings to control their own destinies. This faith in science and its power over nature has continued into the twenty-first century with the discovery and harnessing of nuclear energy, the space program, large scale hydropower projects, and medical advances. Today it is reflected most strongly in the new field of biotechnology, as scientists search for ways to combat cancer and AIDS and to engineer more resilient crops and livestock.[18]

NATURE AND SCIENCE AS PARTNERS

Yet offsetting these hopes for new medicines and technologies is a profound skepticism about the style of classical science as it was done in the Sputnik era. Optimism about the progressive implications of the mechanistic worldview of the Scientific Revolution is being questioned. Many people believe that we are witnessing a major shift in values and assumptions about science and its role in the world.

Today, the world is searching for a new relationship between humans and nature. Today we may be experiencing a scientific revolution as profound as that of the seventeenth century that casts Nature and Science as partners on the stage of history. The machine image and its control of nature seem to be giving way to something new. Some call the transformation a "new paradigm;" others call it "deep ecology;" still others call it a postmodern ecological worldview. I suggest that a partnership ethic in which "the greatest good for the human and non-human communities is to be found in their mutual, living, interdependence." (see Ch 15, this book).[19]

How can we meet the environmental challenges of the 1990s using a partnership ethic? In addition to chemistry and physics, a number of new scientific fields have emerged in recent years that are based on an ecological philosophy that everything is related to everything else and that there are no free lunches whenever nature is invited as a guest. All of these fields will require the kinds of skills and commitments that young people with understanding and fresh ideas can bring to them.

1. **Sustainable Development.** In developing countries there is a great need for agricultural science and environmental analysis. Working with local peoples, science and policies must be formulated that provide for basic human needs and food security, while preserving ecosystemic diversity.[20]

2. **Restoration Ecology** is the human act of reconstructing original ecosystems that have been polluted or destroyed by human activities. Scientists physically replant and rebuild prairies, forests, rivers, and lakes, not as dominators of nature, but as imitators of ecological patterns. Restorationists are dedicated, not to taking nature apart by analysis, but to recreating ecosystems by synthesis (see Ch 12, this book).[21]

3. **Conservation Biology** is the effort to preserve biological diversity through saving ecosystems all over the world. This includes saving human communities that have used and preserved plant and animal species for hundreds of years through successful subsistence ways of life. These *in situ* conservation activities preserve whole ecosystems for future generations. Such efforts require talented scientists, anthropologists, and policy analysts willing to work sensitively with indigenous peoples and local governments.[22]

4. **Agroecology and agroforestry** both attempt to combine the wisdom of traditional peoples and the principles of ecological science to create

sustainable methods of producing crops, animals, and trees. They imitate natural patterns by using wild plant systems as models.[23]

5. **Feminist science and ecofeminism** attempt to apply women's perspectives to ecological problems. During the past decade, women over the entire globe have emerged as ecological activists. In Sweden, they used their traditional talents in gathering and preserving berries to protest the use of herbicides on forests by offering jam made from tainted berries to members of Parliament. In India, they joined the Chipko, or "tree hugging" movement, to preserve fuelwood for cooking in protest over market lumbering. In Kenya's Greenbelt movement, they planted millions of trees in an effort to reverse desertification. Native American women protested uranium mining linked with an increased number of cancer cases on their reservations. At Love Canal near Niagara Falls, housewives demanded action from New York State officials over an outbreak of birth defects and miscarriages in a neighborhood built on the site of a former hazardous chemical dump.[24]

6. **New scientific theories.** But Sputnik era science has also been challenged at the level of theory. Emerging over the past decade are a number of scientific proposals that question the Scientific Revolution's mechanistic view of nature.

THE GAIA HYPOTHESIS

In 1980 atmospheric scientist James Lovelock revived the Greek goddess Gaia as a metaphor for a living earth. He proposed that the earth's biota as a whole maintain an optimal, life-supporting chemical composition within the atmosphere and oceans. Since then a number of conferences have been called to scrutinize his theory and further develop its implications.[25]

PROCESS PHYSICS

Theoretical physicist David Bohm likewise draws on some older ideas about nature held by ancient Indian and Chinese philosophers in challenging the assumptions of mechanistic science. He argues that instead of starting with atomic parts as primary and building up wholes from them, a physics is needed that starts with a flow of energy called the holomovement. The Newtonian world described by classical physics in which we live and work actually unfolds from a higher "implicate" order contained in the underlying flow of energy.[26]

ORDER OUT OF CHAOS

Another challenge to mechanism comes from the new thermodynamics of Ilya Prigogine. Nineteenth-century thermodynamics had beautifully described closed, isolated systems such as steam engines and refrigerators. Prigogine's far-from-equilibrium thermodynamics suggests that higher levels of organization can spontaneously emerge when a system breaks down. His approach applies to social and ecological systems, which are open rather than closed, and helps to account for biological and social evolution.[27]

CHAOS THEORY

Chaos theory in mathematics proposes that a cause as small as a butterfly flapping its wings in Brazil can result in an effect as large as a hurricane in Texas. Chaos, in which a small effect may lead to a large effect, may be the usual, while the equations we learn in freshman calculus may apply only to the unusual. Most environmental and biological systems, such as changing weather, population, noise, aperiodic heart fibrillations, and ecological patterns, may in fact be governed by non-linear chaotic relationships (on these ideas, see Conclusion to this book).[28]

What all these developments suggest is the possibility that a new science and a new worldview could guide us in finding an ecologically sustainable way of life. A new approach to science and a new ecological ethic, however, must be accompanied by a commitment to the recycling of renewable resources, the conservation of non-renewable resources, and the restoration of sustainable ecosystems that fulfill basic human physical and spiritual needs.

Every year, on April 22, communities and colleges across the country celebrate the anniversary of the first Earth Day in 1970. Local, national, and global environmental issues focus the celebrations. Among the activities to be considered should be a nationwide signature campaign endorsing an environmental amendment to the Constitution of the United States. It would read, "Every person has a right to a clean, healthful environment. The Congress and the individual states shall have the power to enforce this article by appropriate legislation." With enough citizen backing it could be introduced in Congress and passed by a two-thirds majority. State after state would ratify the amendment and people could live in the twenty-first century with constitutionally protected environmental rights. In this way, we could bequeath to our children and to our grandchildren in the twenty-first century and beyond the possibility of a clean, healthful, beautiful earth on which to live.

Biologist Lewis Thomas listening late one night to Gustav Mahler's Ninth Symphony speculated on what it would be like to be seventeen going into the world that our generation will leave to our children. "The life of the earth," he said, "is like the life of an organism: the great round being possesses a mind: the mind contains an infinite number of thoughts and memories: when I reach my time I may find myself still hanging around in some sort of midair, one of those small thoughts, drawn back to the memory of the earth: in that peculiar sense I will be alive." But, "if I were sixteen or seventeen," he concluded, "I would want to give up listening and reading. I would begin thinking up new kinds of sounds, different from any music heard before, and I would be twisting and turning to rid myself of human language."[29]

NOTES

* Revised from Carolyn Merchant, "Is It Time for an Earth Ethic?" *Vassar Quarterly* 86, no. 2 (Spring 1990): 10–14," by permission of *Vassar Quarterly* and from Carolyn Merchant, "Fish First!: The Changing Ethics of Ecosystem Management," *Human Ecology Review*, special issue on "Emerging Ecological Policy: Winners and Losers," 4, no. 1 (Spring/Summer, 1990): 25–30. Reproduced with permission.

1. Anonymous, "Planet of the Year: Endangered Earth," *Time*, January 2, 1989; Anonymous, "The Environment: A Higher Priority," *The New York Times*, July 2, 1989.

2. Associated Press, "Senators Unveil Legislative Plan to Combat Greenhouse Effect," *San Francisco Chronicle*, July 29, 1988.

3. CDIAC (Carbon Dioxide Information Analysis Center) Communications, "Fossil Fuels CO_2 Emissions: Three Countries Account for 50% in 1986," Oak Ridge National Laboratory, TN, Winter 1989: Global Carbon Budget, www.globalcarbonproject.org/carbonbudget/16/files/GCP_CarbonBudget_2016.pdf

4. Charles Petit, "Why the Earth's Climate Is Changing Drastically," *San Francisco Chronicle*, August 8, 1988.

5. "EPA Urges Drastic Action to Slow Greenhouse Effect," *San Francisco Chronicle*, March 14, 1989.

6. Michael D. Lemonick, "Deadly Danger in a Spray Can," *Time*, January 2, 1989, p. 42; Kara Swisher, "Refrigerators New CFC Issue," *Star Bulletin and Advertiser*, Honolulu, July 16, 1989, p. D-3.

7. Peter Raven, "The Global Ecosystem in Crisis," *A MacArthur Foundation Occasional Paper* (1987): 7; Rainforest Action Network, "An Emergency Call to Action for the Forests and Their Peoples," http://rain-tree.com/facts.htm#.WIy_tJJCCQo

8. Frederic P. Sutherland, Executive Director of the Sierra Club Legal Fund, *San Francisco Chronicle*, August 21, 1989, www.huffingtonpost.com/2013/03/11/chopstick-china-forests_n_2853033.html.

9. Anonymous, *San Francisco Chronicle*, August 20, 1989.

10. Eugene Linden, "Putting the Heat on Japan," *Time* (July 10, 1989): 50–2.

11. Daniel Keith Conner and Robert O'Dell, "The Tightening Net of Marine Plastics Pollution," *Environment* 30, no. 1 (January–February 1988): 17–20, 33–6; Anastasia Toufexis, "The Dirty Seas," *Time*, 132 (August 1, 1988): 44.

12. Norman Myers, ed., *Gaia: An Atlas of Planet Management* (Garden City, NY: Anchor, 1984), p. 40.

13. Vandana Shiva, "Address," Fate and Hope of the Earth Conference, Managua, Nicaragua, June 1989.

14. Elliot Diringer, "U.S. Awash in Toxic Chemicals: And Fear of Them," *San Francisco Chronicle*, October 17, 1988; Elliot Diringer, "Science Is Anything But Exact on Toxic Risks," *San Francisco Chronicle*, October 18, 1988; Elliot Diringer, "Prop 65 Begins to Affect Products, Buying Habits," *San Francisco Chronicle*, October 20, 1988 (Proposition 65 is the Safe Drinking Water and Toxic Enforcement Act of 1986, http://oehha.ca.gov/media/downloads/proposition-65//p65single01272017.pdf).

15. John Donne, "An Anatomie of the World: The First Anniversary," in Herbert Grierson, ed., *The Poems of John Donne* (London: Oxford University Press, 1933), pp. 206–26, quotation on p. 209.

16. Roger W. Findley and Daniel A. Farber, *Environmental Law in a Nutshell*, 2nd ed. (St. Paul, MN: West Publishing Co., 1988).

17. Carolyn Merchant, *The Death of Nature: Women, Ecology, and the Scientific Revolution* (San Francisco: Harper & Row, 1980; 2nd ed. 1990), pp. 168–90.

18. Ibid., pp. 216–35, 275–81.

19. Bill Devall and George Sessions, *Deep Ecology: Living as if Nature Mattered* (Salt Lake City: Peregrine Smith Books, 1985); David Ray Griffin, ed., *The Reenchantment of Science: Postmodern Proposals* (Albany: State University of New York Press, 1988); Marcus Raskin and Herbert J. Bernstein, *New Ways of Knowing: The Sciences, Society, and Reconstructive Knowledge* (Totowa, NJ: Roman & Littlefield, 1987). See this book, Ch 15.

20. John Mellor, "Sustainable Agriculture in Developing Countries," *Environment* 30, no. 9 (November 1988): 7. See also entire issue. John Ross, Coordinator, "Environment and Development: Building Sustainable Societies: Lectures from the 1987 Summer Forum at the University of Wisconsin-Madison," Institute for Environmental Studies Report 135, November 1988.

21. Carolyn Merchant, "Perspective: Restoration and Reunion with Nature," *Restoration and Management Notes* 4, no. 2 (Winter 1986): 68–70. See Ch 12, this book. See also other issues of the journal and John Berger, *Restoring the Earth* (New York: Knopf, 1985).

22. Michael Soulé, ed., *Conservation Biology: The Science of Scarcity and Diversity* (Sunderland, MA: Sinauer, 1986).

23. Miguel Altieri, *Agroecology: The Scientific Basis of Alternative Agriculture* (Berkeley, CA: University of California, Division of Biological Control, 1983).

24. Sandra Harding, *The Science Question in Feminism* (Ithaca: Cornell University Press, 1986); Carolyn Merchant, "Earthcare: Women and the Environmental Movement," *Environment* 23, no. 5 (June 1981): 6–13, 38–40; Vandana Shiva, *Staying Alive: Women, Ecology, and Development* (London: Zed Books, 1988).

25. James Lovelock, *Gaia: A New Look at Life on Earth* (Oxford, England: Oxford University Press, 1979).

26. David Bohm, *Wholeness and the Implicate Order* (Boston: Routledge & Kegan Paul, 1980); John Briggs and F. David Peat, *Looking Glass Universe: The Emerging Science of Wholeness* (New York: Simon and Schuster, 1984).

27. Ilya Prigogine and Isabelle Stengers, *Order Out of Chaos: Man's New Dialogue with Nature* (Toronto: Bantam Books, 1984).

28. James Gleick, *Chaos: Making a New Science* (New York: Viking, 1987).

29. Lewis Thomas, *Late Night Thoughts on Listening to Mahler's Ninth Symphony* (New York: Viking Press, 1980), pp. 165, 168.

FIGURE 14.1 Ellen Swallow Richards (1842–1911). Introduced the term "ecology" to the United States in 1892.

Source: Photograph from Caroline L. Hunt. *The Life of Ellen H. Richards*. Boston: 1912, frontispiece. Public domain.

FIGURE 14.2 Françoise d'Eaubonne (1920–2005). Founded the Ecology-Feminism Center in Paris in 1972 and introduced the term "ecofeminism" in 1974 in her book *Feminism or Death*.

Source: Photograph by Ruth Hottell, 1995, used by permission.

14

ECOFEMINISM AND
FEMINIST THEORY*

Ecofeminism emerged in the 1970s with an increasing consciousness of the connections between women and nature. French writer Françoise d'Eaubonne (1920–2005) founded the Ecology-Feminism (*Ecologie-Féminisme*) Center in Paris in 1972 and in 1974 used the term, "*ecofeminisme*," in her book, *Feminism or Death*, in which she called upon women to lead an ecological revolution to save the planet. (Fig. 14.2) Such an ecological revolution would entail new gender relations between women and men and between humans and nature. D'Eaubonne saw pollution, destruction of the environment, and run-away population growth as problems created by a male culture. The planet itself was in danger of dying, taking humanity along with it. A society recast in the "feminine," however, would not mean power in the hands of women, but no power at all.[1] Threats to planetary life were also the grounds for a 1974 conference in Berkeley, California, organized by geographers Sandra Marburg and Lisa Watkins, entitled "Women and Environment" (a gathering of interested persons meeting and discussing solutions to the most urgent threats to life). Connections between women and nature and women and ecology were made in works by Sherry Ortner (1974), Rosemary Radford Ruether (1974), Susan Griffin (1978), and Carolyn Merchant (1980).[2]

In the United States, "eco-feminism" was developed in courses by Ynestra King at the Institute for Social Ecology in Vermont around 1976, and it became a movement in 1980 as a result of a major conference that King and others organized on "Women and Life on Earth: Ecofeminism in the '80s" and the ensuing 1980 Women's Pentagon Action in which 2,000 women encircled the Pentagon to protest anti-life nuclear war and weapons development. A West Coast ecofeminist conference was held at Sonoma State University in 1981 and a WomanEarth Feminist Peace Institute took place in 1986. In 1987, in celebration of the twenty-fifth anniversary of Rachel Carson's *Silent Spring*, Irene Diamond and Gloria Orenstein organized the "Ecofeminist Perspectives: Culture, Nature, Theory" conference at the University of Southern California and published a book of articles from the conference entitled, *Reweaving the World: The Emergence of Ecofeminism*. Women in the United States and other countries (such as England, Australia, Sweden, Germany, India, Africa, and Brazil) continued to inject new life into ecofeminism through anthologies, conferences, and political actions that further developed the connections between women, nature, ecology, development, and threats to life on earth.[3]

In the 1990s, the organization WEDO (Women, Environment, and Development Organization) held the 1991 World Women's Congress for a Healthy Planet in Miami in preparation for the 1992 Rio de Janeiro Earth Summit and since then has continued to engage women internationally for other United Nations conferences. In 1995, the "Ecofeminist Perspectives" conference was held at Ohio State University and later that year, Irene Diamond and Carolyn Merchant organized an "Ecofeminist Encampment" at Mountain Grove, Oregon. Numerous books and newsletters continue to appear and conferences and environmental actions have taken place around the world as women embrace ecofeminism or engage in actions dealing directly with women's connections to nature and the environment.[4]

In what follows, I show how women have made connections to nature, how they have used those connections as motivations to justify their actions, and how their actions, often in coalitions and partnerships, have helped to identify and create pathways toward resolving environmental problems. I use the categories of liberal, radical, social, and socialist feminism to illustrate different approaches to the ways women have been concerned with improving the human/nature relationship and to show how each approach has contributed to an ecofeminist perspective.[5] Liberal feminism is consistent with the objectives of reform environmentalism to alter human relations with nature through the passage of new laws and regulations. Radical (later called cultural) ecofeminism analyzes environmental problems from within its critique of patriarchy and offers alternatives that could liberate both women and nature. The social and socialist forms of ecofeminism are based on a critique of capitalist patriarchy as underlying economic and political structures that need to be transformed, the first as a form of anarchist social ecology, the second as an ecological socialist society. (Table 14.1)

TABLE 14.1 Feminism and the Environment

	Nature	Human Nature	Feminist Critique of Environmentalism	Image of a Feminist Environmentalism
Liberal Feminism	Atoms Mind/Body dualism Domination of nature	Rational agents Individualism Maximization of self-interest	"Man and his environment" leaves out women	Women in natural resources and environmental sciences
Marxist Feminism	Transformation of nature by science and technology for human use	Creation of human nature through mode of production, praxis Historically specific, not fixed Species nature of humans	Critique of capitalist control of resources and accumulation of goods and profits	Socialist society will use resources for good of all men and women Resources will be controlled by workers Environmental pollution could be minimal since no surpluses would be produced Environmental research by men and women
Radical (Cultural) Feminism	Nature is spiritual and personal Conventional science and technology problematic because of their emphasis on domination	Biology is basic Humans are sexual reproducing bodies Sexed by biology/ gendered by society	Unaware of interconnectedness of male domination of nature and women Male environmentalism retains hierarchy Insufficient attention to environmental threats to women's reproduction (chemicals, nuclear war, radiation)	Woman/Nature both valorized and celebrated Reproductive freedom Against pornographic depictions of both women and nature
Social Feminism	Nature is material basis of life: food, clothing, shelter, energy should be derived from local renewable sources Domination of nature stems from domination of human by human	Humans are sexed by biology/all genders are equal Women are oppressed by public/private dichotomies in society No gender hierarchies should exist in society	Human hierarchies are cause of domination of nature Irrationality of goddess worship Men and women are both equally capable of caring for nature	All systems of oppression must be ended All hierarchies must be overturned Decentralized accountable face-to-face societies Women's intellectual, sexual, economic, and moral freedoms

(Continued)

TABLE 14.1 (Continued)

	Nature	Human Nature	Feminist Critique of Environmentalism	Image of a Feminist Environmentalism
Socialist Feminism	Nature is material basis of life: food, clothing, shelter, energy Nature is socially constructed Transformation of nature by production and reproduction	Human nature created through biology and praxis (sex, race, class, age) Historically specific and socially constructed	Leaves out nature as active and responsive Leaves out women's role in reproduction and reproduction as a category Systems approach is mechanistic not dialectical	Both nature and human production are active Centrality of biological and social reproduction Dialectic between production and reproduction Multileveled structural analysis Dialectical (not mechanical) systems

Liberal feminism characterized the history of feminism from its beginnings in the seventeenth century until the 1960s. Its roots are liberalism, the political theory that incorporates the scientific analysis that nature is composed of atoms moved by external forces with a theory of human nature that views humans as individual rational agents who maximize their own self-interest and capitalism as the optimal economic structure for human progress. Historically, liberal feminists have argued that women do not differ from men as rational agents and that exclusion from educational and economic opportunities have prevented them from realizing their own potential for creativity in all spheres of human life.[6]

In the United States, chemist Ellen Swallow Richards (1842–1911, Fig. 14.1) introduced to the term ecology in 1892 to a meeting of the Boston Boot and Shoe Club. Headlines in the Boston Globe read: "New Science: Mrs. Richards Names It Ecology." Seventy years later, in 1962 biologist Rachel Carson (1907–1964) made the care of the environment a public issue. Her book *Silent Spring* focused attention on the death-producing effects of DDT, chlorinated hydrocarbons, and organophosphates.[7]

For liberal ecofeminists (as for liberalism generally), environmental problems result from the overly rapid development of natural resources and the failure to regulate environmental pollutants. Better science, conservation, and laws are the proper approaches to resolving resource problems. Given equal educational opportunities to become scientists, natural resource managers, regulators, lawyers, and legislators, women like men can contribute to the improvement of the environment, the conservation of natural resources, and the higher quality of human life. Women, therefore, can transcend the social stigma of their biology and join men in the cultural project of environmental conservation.

Radical feminism developed in the late 1960s and 1970s with the second wave of feminism. The radical (cultural) form of ecofeminism is a response to the perception that women and nature have been mutually associated and devalued in Western culture and that both can be elevated and liberated through direct political action. In prehistory an emerging patriarchal culture dethroned the mother Goddesses and replaced them with male gods to whom the female deities became subservient.[8] The Scientific Revolution of the seventeenth century further degraded nature by replacing Renaissance organicism and a nurturing earth with the metaphor of a machine to be controlled and repaired from the outside. The Earth was to be dominated by male-developed and male-controlled technology, science, and industry.

Radical feminism instead celebrates the relationship between women and nature through the revival of ancient rituals centered on Goddess worship, the moon, animals, and the female reproductive system. A vision in which nature is held in esteem as mother and Goddess is a source of inspiration and empowerment for many ecofeminists. Spirituality is seen as a source of both personal and social change. Goddess worship and rituals centered around the lunar and female menstrual cycles, lectures, concerts, art exhibitions, street and theater productions, and direct political action (web weaving in anti-nuclear protests) are all examples of the re-visioning of nature and women as powerful forces. Radical ecofeminist philosophy embraces intuition, an ethic of caring, and weblike human/nature relationships.

For radical feminists, human nature is grounded in human biology. Humans are biologically sexed and socially gendered. Sex/gender relations give men and women different power bases. Hence the personal is political. Radical feminists object to the dominant society's perception that women are limited by being closer to nature because of their ability to bear children. The dominant view is that menstruation, pregnancy, nursing, and nurturing of infants and young children should tie women to the home, decreasing their mobility and inhibiting their ability to remain in the work force. Radical feminists argue that the perception that women are totally oriented toward biological reproduction degrades them by association with a nature that is itself devalued in Western culture. Women's biology and nature should instead be celebrated as sources of female power.

Turning the perceived connection between women and biological reproduction upside down becomes the source of women's empowerment and ecological activism. Women argue that male-designed and -produced technologies neglect the effects of nuclear radiation, pesticides, hazardous wastes, and household chemicals on women's reproductive organs and on the ecosystem. They argue that radioactivity from nuclear wastes, power plants, and bombs is a potential cause of birth defects, cancers, and the elimination of life on Earth.[9] They expose hazardous waste sites near schools and homes as permeating soil and drinking water and contributing to miscarriage, birth defects, and leukemia. They object to pesticides and herbicides being sprayed on crops and forests as potentially affecting children and the child-bearing women living near them. Women frequently spearhead local actions against spraying and power plant siting and organize others to demand toxic cleanups. When coupled with an environmental ethic that values rather than degrades nature, such actions have the potential both for raising women's consciousness of their own oppression and for the liberation of nature from the polluting effects of industrialization. For example, many lower-middle-class women who became politicized through protests over toxic chemical wastes at Love Canal in New York simultaneously became feminists when their activism spilled over into their home lives.[10]

Yet in emphasizing the female, body, and nature components of the dualities male/female, mind/body, and culture/nature, radical ecofeminism runs the risk of perpetuating the very hierarchies it seeks to overthrow. Critics point to the problem of women's own reinforcement of their identification with a nature that Western culture degrades.[11] If "female is to male as nature is to culture," as anthropologist Sherry Ortner argues,[12] then women's hopes for liberation are set back by association with nature. Any analysis that makes women's essence and qualities special ties them to a biological destiny that thwarts the possibility of liberation. A politics grounded in women's culture, experience, and values can be seen as reactionary.

In contrast to liberal and radical (or cultural) ecofeminism, the social and socialist strands of ecofeminism are based on a critique of capitalism and patriarchy as underlying economic and political structures that need to be transformed in order to liberate women and nature.

Building on the social ecology of Murray Bookchin, social ecofeminism envisions the restructuring of society as humane decentralized communities. "Social ecofeminism," stated Janet Biehl in 1988, "accepts the basic tenet of social ecology, that the idea of dominating nature stems from the domination of human by human. Only ending all systems of domination makes possible an ecological society, in which no states or capitalist economies attempt to subjugate nature, in which all aspects of human nature—including sexuality and the passions as well as rationality—are freed."[13]

Social ecofeminism advocates the liberation of women through overturning economic and social hierarchies that turn all aspects of life into a market society that today even invades the womb. It envisioned a society of decentralized communities that would transcend the public-private dichotomy necessary to capitalist production and the bureaucratic state. In them women would emerge as free participants in public life and local municipal workplaces. Rejecting all forms of determinism, it advocated women's reproductive, intellectual, sensual, and moral freedom. Biology, society, and the individual interact in all human beings giving them the capacity to choose and construct the kinds of societies in which they wish to live.

But in her 1991 book, *Rethinking Ecofeminist Politics*, Janet Biehl withdrew her support from ecofeminism, and likewise abandoned social ecofeminism, on the grounds that the concept had become so fraught with irrational, mythical, and self-contradictory meanings that it undercut women's hopes for a liberatory, ecologically sane society. While early radical feminism had sought equality in all aspects of public and private life, based on a total restructuring of society, the cultural feminism that lies at the root of much of ecofeminism seemed to her to reject rationality by embracing goddess worship, to biologize and essentialize the caretaking and nurturing traits assigned by patriarchy to women, and to reject scientific and cultural advances just because they were advocated by men. While Biehl's approach is a much-needed critique of the inconsistencies within ecofeminism, it fails to recognize the historicity and different political bases of the various strands within ecofeminism, feminism, green politics, and social ecology and to allow for a political and self-critical development of the ecofeminist movement.[14]

Nevertheless, social ecofeminism continued to be taught at Murray Bookchin's Institute for Social Ecology by Ynestra King and Chaia Heller. In "Feminism and the Revolt of Nature" (1981), King argued that ecofeminism unites the repressed and bridges the theoretical gap by addressing all forms of oppression, including male and female, human and non-human nature. King distinguished between radical-cultural feminism and rational-materialist feminism and called for a transformative feminism that moves beyond the culture-nature debate, is neither fully natural or fully cultural, and that is non-hierarchical.[15]

For socialist feminists, the source of male domination of women is the complex of social patterns called capitalist patriarchy, in which men bear the responsibility for labor in the marketplace and women for labor in the home. Yet the potential exists for a socialist ecofeminism that would push for an ecological, economic, and social revolution that would simultaneously liberate women, working-class people, and nature.

For socialist ecofeminism, environmental problems are rooted in the rise of capitalist patriarchy and the ideology that the Earth and nature can be exploited for human progress through technology. Historically, the rise of capitalism eroded the subsistence-based farm and city workshop in which production was oriented toward use values and men and women were economic partners. The result was a capitalist economy dominated by men and a domestic sphere in which women's labor in the home was unpaid and subordinate to men's labor in the marketplace. Both women and nature are exploited by men as part of the progressive liberation of humans from the constraints imposed by nature. The consequence is the alienation of women and men from each other and both from nature.

Socialist feminism incorporates many of the insights of radical feminism, but views both nature and human nature as historically and socially constructed. Human nature is seen as the product of historically changing interactions between humans and nature, men and women, classes, and races. Any meaningful analysis must be grounded in an understanding of power not only in the personal but also in the political sphere. Like radical feminism, socialist feminism is critical of mechanistic science's treatment of nature as passive and of its male-dominated power structures. Similarly, it deplores the lack of a gender analysis in history and the omission of any treatment of women's reproductive and nurturing roles. But rather than grounding its analysis in biological reproduction alone, it also incorporates social reproduction. Biological reproduction includes the reproduction of the species and the reproduction of daily life through food, clothing, and shelter; social reproduction includes socialization and the legal/political reproduction of the social order.[16]

Like Marxist feminists, socialist feminists see non-human nature as the material basis of human life, supplying the necessities of food, clothing, shelter, and energy. Materialism, not spiritualism, is the driving force of social change. Nature is transformed by human science and technology for use by all humans for survival. Socialist feminism views change as dynamic, interactive, and dialectical, rather than as mechanistic, linear, and incremental. Non-human nature is dynamic and alive. As a historical actor, nature interacts with human beings through mutual ecological relations. Socialist feminist environmental theory gives both reproduction and production central places. A socialist feminist environmental ethic involves developing sustainable, non-dominating relations with nature and supplying all peoples with a high quality of life.

In politics, socialist feminists participate in many of the same environmental actions as radical feminists. The goals, however, are to direct change toward some form of an egalitarian socialist state, in addition to resocializing men and women into non-sexist, non-racist, non-violent, anti-imperialist forms of life. Socialist ecofeminism deals explicitly with environmental issues that affect working-class women, Third World women, and women of color. Examples include support for the women's *Chipko* (tree-hugging) movement in India that protects fuel resources from lumber interests, for the women's Green Belt movement in Kenya that has planted more than 2 million trees into years, and for Native-American women and children exposed to radioactivity from uranium mining.[17]

Although the ultimate goals of liberal, radical, social, and socialist feminists may differ as to whether capitalism, women's culture, or socialism should be the ultimate objective of political action, shorter-term objectives overlap. In this sense there is perhaps more unity than diversity in women's common goal of restoring the natural environment and quality of life for people and other living and non-living inhabitants of the planet.

NOTES

* From Carolyn Merchant, "Ecofeminism and Feminist Theory," in Irene Diamond and Gloria Orenstein eds., *Reweaving the World: The Emergence of Ecofeminism* (San Francisco: Sierra Club Books, 1990), pp. 100–5. Copyright 1990 by Irene Diamond and Gloria Feman Orenstein. Reprinted by permission of the publisher. Revised with excerpts from Carolyn Merchant, *Radical Ecology: The Search for a Livable World*, 2nd ed. (New York: Routledge, 2005), pp. 194–5, 205–12, and Carolyn Merchant, *Earthcare: Women and the Environment* (New York: Routledge, 1996), pp. 139–40, used by permission of Routledge.

1. Françoise D'Eaubonne, "Feminism or Death," in Elaine Marks and Isabelle de Courtivron, eds., *New French Feminisms: An Anthology* (Amherst: University of Massachusetts Press, 1980), pp. 64–7, but see especially p. 25; Françoise D'Eaubonne, *Le Féminisme ou la Mort* (Paris: Pierre Horay, 1974), pp. 213–52; Françoise D'Eaubonne, "The Time for Ecofeminism," trans. Ruth Hottell, in Carolyn Merchant, ed., *Key Concepts in Critical Theory: Ecology* (Atlantic Highlands, NJ: Humanities Press, 1994), pp. 174–97.

2. Sherry Ortner, "Is Female to Male as Nature Is to Culture?" in Michelle Rosaldo and Louise Lamphere, eds., *Women, Culture, and Society* (Stanford, CA: Stanford University Press, 1974), pp. 67–87; Rosemary Radford Ruether, *New Woman/New Earth: Sexist Ideologies and Human Liberation* (New York: Seabury Press, 1975); Susan Griffin, *Woman and Nature: The Roaring Inside Her* (New York: HarperCollins, 1978); Carolyn Merchant, *The Death of Nature: Women, Ecology, and the Scientific Revolution* (San Francisco: Harper & Row, 1980).

3. Ynestra King, "Toward an Ecological Feminism and a Feminist Ecology," in Joan Rothschild, ed., *Machina Ex Dea* (New York: Pergamon Press, 1983), pp. 118–29; Leonie Caldecott and Stephanie Leland, eds., *Reclaim the Earth: Women Speak Out for Life on Earth* (London: The Women's Press, 1983); Irene Dankelman and Joan Davidson, *Women and Environment in the Third World* (London: Earthscan Publications, 1988); Vandana Shiva, *Staying Alive: Women, Ecology and Development* (London: Zed Books, 1988); Judith Plant, *Healing the Wounds: The Promise of Ecofeminism* (Philadelphia, PA: New Society Publishers, 1989); Irene Diamond and Gloria Orenstein, eds., *Reweaving the World: The Emergence of Ecofeminism* (San Francisco: Sierra Club Books, 1990).

4. Maria Mies and Vandana Shiva, *Ecofeminism* (London: Zed Books, 1993); Greta Gaard, ed., *Ecofeminism: Women, Animals, Nature* (Philadelphia, PA: Temple University Press, 1993); Val Plumwood, *Feminism and the Mastery of Nature* (New York: Routledge, 1993); Rosi Braidotti, Ewa Charkiewics, Sabine Häusler, and Saskia Wieringa, *Women, the Environment, and Sustainable Development* (London: Zed Books, 1994); Karen Warren, ed., *Ecological Feminism* (New York: Routledge, 1994); Karen Warren, ed., *Ecological Feminist Philosophies* (Indianapolis: Indiana University Press/Hypatia, 1996); Merchant, *Earthcare*; Karen Warren, ed., *Ecofeminism: Women, Nature, Culture* (Bloomington, IN: Indiana University Press, 1997); Ariel Salleh, *Ecofeminism as Politics: Nature, Marx, and the Postmodern* (London: Zed Books, 1997); Noel Sturgeon, *Ecofeminist Natures: Race, Gender, Feminist Theory and Political Action* (New York: Routledge, 1997); Karen Warren, *Ecofeminist Philosophy* (Lanham, MD: Roman and Littlefield, 2000); Val Plumwood, *Environmental Culture: The Ecological Crisis of Reason* (New York: Routledge, 2002).

5. Alison Jaggar, *Feminist Politics and Human Nature* (Totawa, NJ: Roman & Allanheld, 1983); Karen Warren, "Feminism and Ecology: Making Connections," *Environmental Ethics* 9, no. 1 (1987): 3–10.

6. Jaggar, *Feminist Politics and Human Nature*, pp. 27–47.

7. Merchant, *Earthcare*, pp. 139–40.
8. Ortner, "Is Female to Male as Nature Is to Culture?" pp. 67–87.
9. Dorothy Nelkin, "Nuclear Power as a Feminist Issue," *Environment* 23, no. 1 (1981): 14–20, 38–9.
10. Merchant, *Earthcare*.
11. Susan Prentice, "Taking Sides: What's Wrong with Eco-Feminism?" *Women and Environments* 10 (Spring 1988): 9–10.
12. Ortner, "Is Female to Male as Nature Is to Culture?" pp. 67–87.
13. Janet Biehl, "What is Social Ecofeminism?" *Green Perspectives*, issue no. 11 (October 1988): 1–8, quotation on p. 7.
14. Janet Biehl, *Rethinking Ecofeminist Politics* (Boston: South End Press, 1991), pp. 1–7, 9–19.
15. Ynestra King, "Feminism and the Revolt of Nature," *Heresies* 13 (1981): 12–15; Chaia Heller, *Ecology of Everyday Life* (Montreal: Black Rose Books, 1999).
16. Carolyn Merchant, *Ecological Revolutions: Nature, Gender, and Science in New England* (Chapel Hill: University of North Carolina Press, 1989), see Figure I.1.
17. Shiva, *Staying Alive*, p. 76; Wangari Maathai, *The Green Belt Movement: Sharing the Approach and the Experience* (Nairobi, Kenya: Environment Liaison Centre International, 1988), pp. 5–24, quotation on p. 5. On socialist ecofeminism see, Vandana Shiva and Maria Mies, *Ecofeminism* (1993; Mary Mellor, *Feminism and Ecology* (1997); Ariel K. Salleh, *Ecofeminism as Politics: Nature, Marx, and the Postmodern* (1997). On ecofeminism in the developing world, see Jytte Nhanenge, Ecofeminism: Towards Integrating the Concerns of Women, Poor People, and Nature into Development (Lanham, MD: University Press of America, 2011); Mary Judith Ress, Ecofeminism from Latin America (Women from the Margins) (Maryknoll, NY: Orbis Books, 2006); Heather Eaton and Lois Ann Lorentzen, Ecofeminism and Globalization: Exploring Culture, Context, and Religion (Lanham, MD: Roman and Littlefield, 2003). Numerous works and websites on aspects of ecofeminism have appeared in recent years. See especially those on queer and LGBTQ ecofeminism.

FIGURE 15.1 Partnership with the Earth. Partnership with each other.

Source: Public domain.

15

PARTNERSHIP ETHICS*

Partnership is a word that is experiencing a renaissance in the discourse of the business and environmental communities. Successful environmental partnerships, focused on resolving policy conflicts surrounding local issues, are forming among corporations, local communities, government agencies, and environmental organizations. Trees, rivers, endangered species, tribal groups, minority coalitions, and citizen activists all find representation along with business at the negotiating table. The partnership process offers a new approach to collaboration.[1]

Equally innovative is the idea that partners refer not only to societal entities and institutions, but to individuals and even natural entities. Domestic partners with legal status may include not only married couples but stable relationships between men and women, women and women, and men and men. A partnership ethic may offer guidelines for moving beyond the rhetoric of environmental conflict and toward a discourse of cooperation. And as I will argue here, the term partner can also be used to represent gnatcatchers, coho salmon, grizzly bears, and checkerspot butterflies. Indeed non-human nature itself can be our partner.

Partnership ethics differs from the three major forms of environmental ethics that currently dominate human-environment relations—egocentric, homocentric, and ecocentric. Each ethic reflects a different discourse stemming from conflicts among underlying modernist institutions. The 1992 Earth Summit in Rio de Janeiro illustrates the underlying assumptions of the three ethical frameworks and their associated discourses. The egocentric ethic is exemplified by GATT—the General Agreement on Tariffs and Trade; the homocentric by UNCED—the United Nations Commission on Environment and Development and its *Agenda 21* program; and the ecocentric by many environmental organizations involved in sustainable development. While conflicts arise from the different discourses associated with the institutional arrangements of capitalism, the state, and environmentalism, a new transcendent ethic of partnership may help to resolve them. Partnership should include not only human-human relationships, but human-nature interactions as well.[2]

Egocentric ethics: The Uruguay round of GATT, which began in 1986 and by 1994 was concluded and undergoing ratification, assumes a free market model of world trade and an egocentric ethic. Based on the idea of trickle-down economic benefits, an egocentric ethic is the idea that what is good for the individual, or the corporation acting as an individual, is good for society as a whole. Here a discourse of individual freedom to act in one's own self-interest, rhetoric that lies at the very heart of modernism, promotes human actions in which nature is represented as mere "raw material." Nature comprises resources that can be turned into commodities for trade. It consists of free goods from an inexhaustible tap whose wastes go into an inexhaustible sink. Based on the model of a factory, nature is conceptualized as a dead machine, isolated from its environment, whose parts are manipulated for assembly-line production. Resource depletion (the tap) and environmental pollution (the sink) are not part of the profit-loss accounts, hence there is no accountability to or for nature. Because the individual, or individual corporation, is free to profit, there are no ethical restraints on nature's "free" goods or on free trade. The result is the Hobbesian Good Society, an egocentric ethic, and a discourse rooted in individual gain.[3]

Homocentric ethics: In contrast to GATT's egocentric ethic, the ethic of UNCED's sustainable development program is a homocentric ethic. Here new terms of discourse enter the vocabulary of national representatives. A utilitarian ethic based on the precept of the greatest good for the greatest number promotes a discourse whose terms of debate are in potential conflict with those of individualism. Developed by Jeremy Bentham and John Stuart Mill in the nineteenth century, utilitarian ethics became the conservation ethic of Theodore Roosevelt and Gifford Pinchot during the Progressive Era in the early twentieth century with the addition of the phrase "for the longest time." The idea of "the greatest good of the greatest number for the longest time," is a public-interest, social-interest ethic that considers conservation of natural resources to be consistent with the needs and interests of the majority over those of the individual. In Bentham and Mill's formulations it promotes the general good, the greatest happiness for the greatest number, and freedom from pain and suffering. In its purest form, it is the ethic of federal and state agencies, acting free of political forces and private lobbyists, on behalf of the people for the common good. The utilitarian calculus of benefits and costs, rather than the bottom line of profits, guides the ethical choices made. In reality, however, the discourse of homocentric ethics is always in conflict with the egocentric discourse of private individuals and lobbyists who promote monopoly-capitalist interests. Conflicts of interest stem from underlying institutions and are expressed in the rhetoric of GATT versus the rhetoric of UNCED.

For the homocentric ethic of UNCED, as for the egocentric ethic of GATT, nature is viewed primarily as a resource for humans and as a source of commodities. But in contrast to GATT, the United Nations is dedicated to promoting the general good of all nations and all peoples in the world community. Its policies reflect the principle of the greatest good for the greatest number. Like the Progressive Era's conservation ethic, UNCED's sustainable development ethic adds the principle of the longest time. Sustainable development is development that fulfills the needs of the present generation without compromising the needs of future generations. This principle brings future generations into the accountability calculus. The Earth Summit's goal is to promote greater democracy for more people for a longer time by developing and conserving resources sustainably. Yet a cultural politics of social good conflicts with a cultural politics of individual good as expressed through egocentric and homocentric discourse and ethics.[4]

Ecocentric ethics: Many (but not all) environmentalists attending the Earth Summit, subscribed to the assumptions of a third ethic—ecocentrism. Here a new discourse of what is good for non-human entities enters the conversation. Developed by ecologist Aldo Leopold, who formulated the land ethic in the 1940s, and elaborated as ecocentric (and biocentric) ethics by environmental philosophers over the past three decades, ecocentrism includes the entire biotic and abiotic world. Leopold's land ethic had expanded the human community to include "soils, waters, plants, animals, or collectively the land." "A thing is right," Leopold said, "when it tends to preserve the integrity, beauty, and stability of the biotic community. It is wrong when it tends otherwise." Ecocentrism, as elaborated in the 1970s and 1980s, went a step further to assert that all things have intrinsic worth—value in and of themselves—not just instrumental or utilitarian value. Because biota have evolved over millennia, all organisms have a right to exist and should be preserved for future generations. Biodiversity is necessary not only for utilitarian and humanitarian reasons (for maintaining the present and future health of the entire biosphere, for enhancing the quality of life, and for aesthetic enjoyment), but for its own sake. Ecocentrism expands the good of the human community to embrace and include within it the good of the biotic community. From an ecocentric point of view, accountability must include the rights of all other organisms, as well as humans, to continue to exist.[5]

Ethical dilemmas occur when real world situations produce conflicts among the three forms of ethics. Acting on the basis of GATT's egocentric ethic, with the goal of maximizing profits through free trade in natural resources, transnational corporations harvest rainforests for timbers and turn cutover areas into range lands for grazing cattle. Acting on the basis of ecocentric ethics, with the goal of saving rainforests and endangered species, environmentalists engineer debt-for-nature swaps that preserve and value whole ecosystems. Both ethics, however, can negatively affect communities of indigenous peoples by forcing them out of long-inhabited areas onto marginal lands, where they increase their populations to obtain the labor to survive, or migrate to cities where they end up jobless and homeless. In this example, the social-interest ethic of these communities to fulfill their basic needs conflicts with the egocentric ethic of transnational corporations and the ecocentric ethic of nature preservationists. From one point of view nature is victimized at the expense of people, from another people are victimized at the expense of nature.[6]

The three dominant forms of environmental ethics all have conceptual and practical shortcomings. Egocentric ethics are criticized for privileging the few at the expense of the many (narcissistic, cut-throat individualism), homocentric ethics for privileging majorities at the expense of minorities (tyranny of the majority, environmental racism), and ecocentric ethics for privileging the whole at the expense of the individual (holistic fascism). Egocentric and homocentric ethics are often lumped together as anthropocentrism (by deep ecologists, for example). But this approach masks the role of economics and particularly of capitalism, placing the onus on human hubris and domination rather than the capitalist appropriation of both nature and labor. Moreover, it fails to recognize the positive aspects of the social-justice approach of homocentric ethics. On the other hand, the ecocentric approach of many environmentalists suggests the possibility of incorporating the intrinsic value of nature into an emancipatory green politics.[7]

Partnership ethics: An alternative that transcends many of these problems is a partnership ethic. A partnership ethic sees the human community *and* the biotic community in a mutual relationship with each other. It states that "the greatest good for the human and the non-human community is to be found in their mutual, living interdependence."

A partnership ethic draws on the principles and advantages of both the homocentric social-interest ethic and the ecocentric environmental ethic, while rejecting the egocentric ethic associated with capitalist exploitation of people and nature. The term partnership avoids gendering nature as a mother or a goddess (sex-typing the planet), avoids endowing either males or females with a special relationship to nature or to each other (essentialism), and admits the anthropogenic, or human-generated (but not anthropocentric, or human-centered) nature of environmental ethics and metaphor. A partnership ethic of earthcare means that both women and men can enter into mutual relationships with each other and the planet independently of gender and does not hold women alone responsible for "cleaning up the mess" or individual men of creating male-dominated science, technology and capitalism.

Just as egocentric ethics is grounded in the principle of self-interest, homocentric ethics in the concept of utility, and ecocentric ethics in intrinsic value, so partnership ethics is grounded in the concept of relation. A relation is a mode of connection. This connection can be between people or kin in the same family or community, between men and women, between people, other organisms, and inorganic entities, or between specific places and the rest of the earth. A relation is also a narrative; to relate is to narrate. A narrative connects people to a place, to its history, and to its multileveled meanings. It is a story that is recounted and told, in which connections are made, alliances and associations established. A partnership ethic of earthcare is an ethic of the connections between a human and a non-human community. The relationship is situational and contextual within the local community, but each community is also embedded in and connected to the wider earth, especially the national and global economies.[8]

A partnership ethic has the following precepts:

1. Equity between the human and non-human communities.
2. Moral consideration for humans and non-human nature.
3. Respect for cultural diversity and biodiversity.
4. Inclusion of women, minorities, and non-human nature in the code of ethical accountability.
5. An ecologically sound management that is consistent with the continued health of both the human and non-human communities.

A partnership ethic goes beyond egocentric and homocentric ethics in which the good of the human community wins out over the good of the biotic community (as in egocentric and homocentric ethics). It likewise transcends ecocentric ethics in which the good of the biotic community may take precedence over the good of the human community. In contrast to Leopold's extensionist ethic, in which the community is extended to encompass non-human nature, partnership ethics recognizes both continuities and differences between humans and non-human nature. It admits that humans are dependent on non-human nature and that non-human nature has preceded and will postdate human nature. But also it recognizes that humans now have the power, knowledge, and technology to destroy *life as we know it* today.

For millennia, Nature held the upper hand over humans. People were subordinate to nature and fatalistically accepted the hand that nature dealt. Since the seventeenth century, the balance of power has shifted and humans have gained the upper hand over Nature. We have an increasing ability to destroy nature as we know it through mechanistic science, technology, capitalism, and the Baconian hubris that the human race should have dominion over the entire universe. In the late twentieth century, however, the environmental crisis and developments in postmodern science and philosophy have called into the question the efficacy of the mechanistic worldview, the idea of Enlightenment progress, and the ethics of unrestrained development as a means of dominating nature.

A partnership ethic calls for a new balance in which both humans and non-human nature are equal partners, neither having the upper hand, yet cooperating with each other. Both humans and nature are active agents. Both the needs of nature to continue to exist and the basic needs of human beings must be considered. As George Perkins Marsh put it in 1864, humanity should "become a co-worker with nature in the reconstruction of the damaged fabric," by restoring the waters, forests, and bogs "laid waste by human improvidence or malice." While thunderstorms, tornados, volcanos, and earthquakes represented nature's power over humanity to rearrange elementary matter, humans equally had the power "irreparably to derange the combinations of inorganic matter and of organic life, which through the night of aeons she had been proportioning and balancing."[9] In the 1970s, Herbert Marcuse conceptualized nature an opposing partner, emphasizing the differences, as well as the continuities that people share with nature. Nature is an ally, not mere organic and inorganic matter—a "life force in its own right," appearing as "subject-object." Nature as subject "may well be hostile to man, in which case the relation would be one of struggle; but the struggle may also subside and make room for peace, tranquility, fulfillment." A non-exploitative relation would be a "surrender, 'letting-be,' acceptance."[10]

A partnership ethic therefore has two components—a homocentric social-interest ethic of partnership among human groups and an ecocentric ethic of partnership with non-human nature. The first component, the idea of a partnership among human groups, is reflected in both the preamble to UNCED's *Agenda 21* of "a global partnership for sustainable development" and in the opening paragraph of the "Rio Declaration on Environment and Development" proclaiming that the conference met "with the goal of establishing a new and equitable global partnership through the creation of new levels of cooperation among states, key sectors of societies, and people." Article 7 of the Rio Declaration asserts that "States shall cooperate in a spirit of global partnership to conserve, protect, and restore the health of the Earth's Ecosystem." The concept of partnership is also called forth in the title of the Miami

"Global Assembly of Women and the Environment–Partners in Life."[11] The document from the second Miami conference, the World Women's Congress for a Healthy Planet, exemplifies ways of actually putting the human side of the partnership into practice.

But a partnership ethic also entails a new consciousness and a new discourse about nature. Living with and communicating with nature as a partner, rather than as a passive resource, opens the possibility of a non-dominating, non-hierarchical mode of interaction between humanity and nature. Rather than speaking about nature as a machine to be manipulated, a resource to be exploited, or an object to be studied and transformed, nature becomes a subject. As in any partnership, nature will sometimes win out; in other cases, humanity's needs will receive greater consideration. But both will have equal voice and both voices will be heard. The new postmodern sciences of ecology, chaos, and complexity theory help to make this partnership possible.

Postmodern science reconstructs the relationship between humans and nature. While mechanistic science assumes that nature is divided into parts and that change comes from external forces (a billiard-ball model), ecology emphasizes nature as continuous change and process. Chaos theory goes a step further, suggesting that the human ability to predict the outcome of those processes is limited. Disorderly order, the world represented by chaos theory, becomes a component of the partnership ethic.[12]

While many aspects of nature can indeed be represented by linear, deterministic equations, and are therefore predictable (or can be subjected to probabilities, stochastic approximations, and complex systems analysis), a very large domain can be represented only through non-linear equations that do not admit of solutions. The closed systems and determinism of classical physics described by mechanistic science and probabilities give way to a postclassical physics of open complex systems and chaos theory. These theories suggest that there are limits to the knowable world. This is not the same as saying there is a Kantian noumenal world behind the phenomena. It says there is a real, material, physical world, but a world that can never be totally known by means of mathematics. It is a world that is primarily chaotic and unpredictable and therefore cannot be totally controlled by science and technology. Science can no longer impose a view of everything from nowhere. It cannot offer the totalizing viewpoint associated with modernism, the Enlightenment, and mechanistic science. The real world is both orderly and disorderly, predictable and unpredictable, controllable and uncontrollable (see "Conclusion" to this book).[13]

This disorderly, ordered world of non-human nature must be acknowledged as a free autonomous actor, just as humans are free autonomous agents. But Nature limits human freedom to totally dominate and control it, just as human power limits Nature's and other humans' freedom. Science and technology can tell us that an event such as a hurricane, earthquake, flood, or fire is likely to happen in a certain locale, but not when it will happen. Because nature is fundamentally chaotic, it must be respected and related to as an active partner through a partnership ethic.

If we know that an earthquake in Los Angeles is likely in the next 75 years, a utilitarian, homocentric ethic would state that the government ought not to license the construction of a nuclear reactor on the faultline. But a partnership ethic would say that, we, the human community, ought to respect nature's autonomy as an actor by limiting building and leaving open space. If we know there is a possibility of a one-hundred-year flood on the Mississippi River, we respect human needs for navigation and power, but we also respect nature's autonomy by limiting our capacity to dam every tributary that feeds the river and build homes on every flood plain. We leave some rivers wild and free and leave some flood plains as wetlands, while using others to fulfill human needs. If we know that forest fires are likely in the Rockies, we do not build cities along forest edges. We limit the extent of development, leave open spaces, plant fire resistant vegetation, and use tile rather than shake roofs. If cutting tropical and temperate old-growth forests creates problems for both the global environment and local communities, but we cannot adequately predict the outcome or effects of those changes, we need to conduct partnership negotiations in which non-human nature and the people involved are equally represented.

Each of these difficult, time-consuming ethical and policy decisions will be negotiated by a human community in a particular place, but the outcome will depend on the history of people and nature in the area, the narratives they tell themselves about the land, vital human needs, past and present land-use patterns, the larger global context, and the ability or lack of it to predict nature's events. Each human community is in a changing, evolving relationship with a non-human community that is local, but also connected to global environmental and human patterns. Each ethical instance is historical, contextual, and situational, but located within a larger environmental and economic system.

Consensus and negotiation should be attempted as partners speak together about the short and long-term interests of the interlinked human and non-human communities. The meetings will be lengthy and may continue over many weeks or months. As in any partnership relationship, there will be give and take as the needs of each party, including those representing non-human nature, are expressed, heard, and acknowledged. If the partners identify their own egocentric, homocentric, and ecocentric ethical assumptions and agree to start anew from a partnership ethic of mutual obligation and respect for each other and for non-human nature, there is hope for consensus. A partnership ethic does not mean that all dams must be blasted down, electrical production forfeited, and irrigation curtailed for the sake of salmon. It means that the vital needs of humans and the vital needs of fish and their mutually linked aqueous and terrestrial habitats must both be given equal consideration. Indeed there is no other choice, for failure means a regression from consensus, into contention, and thence into litigation.

A partnership ethic offers a new approach to relationships between the business community and the environment that can transcend the egocentric ethic's emphasis on the domination of nature and the get-ahead, individualistic mentality. Environmental partnerships are "voluntary collaborations among organizations working toward a common objective." Partnerships are formed, often among formerly contesting parties, to solve a specific problem and to avoid the acrimony and costs of litigation. Furthermore, the cooperative agreement that emerges from the process is one to which all parties have agreed and in which all have a stake. Hence the outcome may have the prospect of lasting longer than one settled through a series of courtroom battles.[14]

For example, a manufacturing company in the mid-western United States is approached by a wildlife conservation organization about creating a wildlife reserve on 3200 acres of company owned grounds. The company has recently decided not to use the area for a formerly planned expansion. Employees are enthusiastic about developing the land for jogging, wildlife-viewing, photography, and perhaps limited seasonal fishing and hunting. Schools and local Audubon societies are eager to have an educational wildlife area. The company and the conservation organization agree to form a voluntary partnership and begin to hold regular meetings with the specific goal of "protecting, restoring, and enhancing the 3200 acres as a wildlife conservation area with recreational facilities." Seated at the table (situated off of each of the partners' home grounds) are not only company representatives, wildlife biologists, planners, and employees who wish to hunt and fish, but also people who speak on behalf of deer and trout.[15] The discourse begins by asking questions:

1. Will the partnership project solve or significantly impact a problem?
2. Are the goals consistent with the company's mission and objectives?
3. Are cooperation and collaboration needed to do the project?
4. Do the partners all have a reason to participate in the partnership?
5. Has the partnership identified all groups needed for the project to succeed?
6. Will the partnership be voluntary and equitable?[16]

After much discussion, the partners decide that a wildlife area will be established on the 3200 acre plot for a minimum of twenty years. The company's image will be enhanced within the community; employees will have an area for jogging and hiking; wildlife viewing areas will be set aside. The interests of deer and fish have been heard and, after an intensely passionate discussion, their needs for survival are made compatible with limited hunting and fishing through a well-defined management plan. The conservation group has acquired an addition to a migratory bird flyway, an educational site for school children, a refuge for birdwatchers, and a recreational area for the surrounding community. While it has not set aside the area in perpetuity, it has achieved a green zone in place of potential concrete and pollution and time to become involved in and respond to a longer-term company and community planning-process.[17]

What are some examples of actual, successful environmental partnerships and how has business participated in them?

- On the Cooper River, near Charleston, S.C. the Wildlife Habitat Enhancement Council (WHEC) worked with the Amoco and DuPont Chemical companies to develop wildlife management programs on company lands. Landholders in the vicinity then developed a "wildlife corridor" running 10 miles between the two companies.[18]
- In 1989, a group of leading corporations that use CFCs as solvents collaborated with each other and the U.S. Environmental Protection Agency in order to become CFC-free in advance of the time-lines established by regulaton. Several companies have used the new technologies to replace CFC use in plants in developing countries.[19]
- In the Columbia River Basin, where salmon runs have declined from 16 million per year in the 1800s to less than two million in the early 1990s, the Northwest Power Planning Council (NPPC) initiated a partnership negotiating group comprising American Indian tribes, environmental groups, corporations, and agencies to plan and implement harvesting reductions, habitat restoration, hatchery projects, water flow changes, and other means of enhancing the salmon's survival.[20]
- The East Bay Conservation Corps of the San Francisco Bay Area formed a partnership with public agencies that resulted in funds for developing an environmental ethic in minority and lower income youth through a summer program employing young people to assist with public land maintenance work.[21]

In these examples, the partnership process focuses mainly on human-human interactions, but it opens the way for the inclusion of persons representing non-human entities and the chaotic patterns of nature. Partnerships are a new form of cooperative discourse aimed at reaching consensus rather than creating winners and losers. Partnerships can be formed between women and women, men and men, women and men, people and nature, and north and south to solve specific problems and to work toward a socially just, environmentally sustainable world.

The partnership process draws on many of the skills and goals long advocated and practiced by women's groups. While not essentialist (i.e., the position that cooperation is an essential trait of being female), partnership discourse is nevertheless rooted in many women's social experiences and attitudes toward problem-solving. But this cooperative discourse does not claim that women have a special knowledge of nature or a special ability to care for nature. Nor is it a case where "some" women are speaking for "all" women or for "other" women who are capable of speaking for themselves. Here women and minorities participate in the process. But "nature," which often speaks in a different voice, is also heard at the table.

In addition to feminist discourse, partnership ethics draw on social and socialist ecology in making visible the connections between economic systems, people, and the environment in an effort to find new economic forms that fulfill basic needs, provide security, and enhance the quality of life without degrading the local or global environment. Finally, a partnership ethic relates work in the sciences of chaos and complexity to possibilities for nondominating relationships between humans and non-human nature.

Many difficulties exist in implementing a partnership ethic. The free market economy's growth-oriented ethic that uses both natural and human resources inequitably to create profits presents the greatest challenge. The power of the global capitalist-system to remove resources, especially those in Third World countries, without regard to restoration, reuse, or recycling is a major roadblock to reorganizing relations between production and ecology. Even as capitalism continues to undercut the grounds of its own perpetuation by using renewable resources, such as redwoods and fish, faster than the species or stock's own recruitment, so green capitalism attempts to bandaid the decline by submitting to some types of regulation and recycling. Ultimately new economic forms will need to found that are compatible with sustainability, intergenerational equity, and a partnership ethic.

Another source of resistance to a partnership ethic is the property rights movement, which in many ways is a backlash against both environmentalism and ecocentrism. The protection of private property is integral to the growth and profit-maximization approaches of capitalism and egocentrism and to their preservation by government institutions and laws. While individual, community, or common ownership of "appropriate" amounts of property is not inconsistent with a partnership ethic, determining what is sustainable and hence appropriate to the continuation of human and non-human nature is both challenging and important.

So, as we move forward in the twenty-first century, the idea of a partnership between human beings and the non-human community in which both are equal and share in mutual relationships is the ethic that I would propose. A partnership ethic will not always work, but it is a beginning, and with it there is hope.

NOTES

* From Carolyn Merchant, "Partnership Ethics: Business and the Environment," in Joel Reichart and Patricia Werhane, eds., *Environmental Challenges to Business*, 1997 Ruffin Lectures, University of Virginia Darden School of Business (Bowling Green, OH: Society for Business Ethics, Ruffin Series No. 2, 2000), pp. 7–18. Reprinted by permission of the Ruffin Series of the Society for Business Ethics. Portions appeared previously in Carolyn Merchant, *Reinventing Eden: The Fate of Nature in Western Culture* (New York: Routledge, 1996), Ch. 11, used by permission.

1. This article draws on the following five books on environmental partnerships and stakeholder negotiations: Frederick J. Long and Matthew Arnold, *The Power of Environmental Partnerships* (Fort Worth, TX: Dryden Press, 1994); Management Institute for Environment and Business, *Environmental Partnerships: A Business Handbook* (Fort Worth, TX: Dryden Press, 1994); Management Institute for Environment and Business, *Environmental Partnerships: A Field Guide for Governmental Agencies* (Fort Worth, TX: Dryden Press, 1994); Management Institute for Environment and Business, *Environmental Partnerships: A Field Guide for Nonprofit Organizations and Community Interests* (Fort Worth, TX: Dryden Press, 1994); Alan R. Beckenstein, Frederick J. Long, Matthew B. Arnold, and Thomas N. Gladwin, *Stakeholder Negotiations: Exercises in Sustainable Development* (Chicago, IL: Richard D. Irwin, 1995).

2. On egocentric, homocentric, and ecocentric ethics see Carolyn Merchant, "Environmental Ethics and Political Conflict," in Carolyn Merchant, *Radical Ecology* (New York: Routledge, 1992), pp. 63–82.

3. Environmental News Network, *GATT, the Environment, and the Third World: An Overview* (Berkeley, CA: The Tides Foundation, 1992); Anonymous, *GATT vs. UNCED: Can Free Trade and Sustainable Development Coexist?* (San Francisco, CA: Rainforest Action Network, 1992); World Wide Fund for Nature, *The GATT Report on Trade and Environment: A Critique* (Gland, Switzerland: WWF International, 1992); Third World Network, *Earth Summit Briefings* (Penong, Malaysia: Third World Network, 1992); Marcia Stepanek, "GATT Group Turns Up the Heat," *San Francisco Examiner*, August 7, 1994, B-1, 9; Kristin Dawkins, *NAFTA, GATT and the World Trade Organization: The Emerging World Order* (Westfield, NJ: Open Pamphlet Series, 1994).

4. The Preamble to UNCED's *Agenda 21* states: "[the] integration of environment and development concerns and greater attention to them will lead to the fulfillment of basic needs, improved living standards for all, better protected and managed ecosystems and a safer, more prosperous future. No nation can achieve this on its own; but together we can—in a global partnership for sustainable development." Quoted in Michael Grubb, et al., *The Earth Summit Agreements: A Guide and Assessment* (London: Earthscan, 1993), p. 101.

5. On Aldo Leopold's land ethic and ecocentric ethics more generally see Aldo Leopold, *A Sand County Almanac* (New York: Oxford University Press, 1949); J. Baird Callicott, *In Defense of the Land Ethic: Essays in Environmental Philosophy* (Albany: State University of New York Press, 1989); Holmes Rolston III, *Philosophy Gone Wild: Essays in Environmental Ethics* (Buffalo, NY: Prometheus Books, 1986).

6. Harold Gilliam, "The Real Price of Free Trade," and "The Bottom Line for Indigenous Cultures," *This World, San Francisco Examiner*, January 2, 1994, pp. 13–14.

7. On the land ethic as a case of "environmental fascism," see Tom Regan, *The Case for Animal Rights* (Berkeley, CA: University of California Press, 1983), p. 262. For a response see

Callicott, *In Defense of the Land Ethic*, pp. 92–4 and J. Baird Callicott, "Moral Monism in Environmental Ethics Defended," *Journal of Philosophical Research* 19 (1994): 51–60, see p. 53. On ecocentrism as the ground for an emancipatory green politics, see Robyn Eckersley, *Environmentalism and Political Theory: Toward an Ecocentric Approach* (Albany: State University of New York Press, 1992).

8. The idea of a partnership between women and men as the basis for a new society, but without explicit attention to environmental ethics, has been developed by Riane Eisler, *The Chalice and the Blade* (San Francisco: Harper & Row, 1988). The concept of relation as a foundation for ecofeminism and the relational self has been developed by Val Plumwood, *Feminism and the Mastery of Nature* (London: Routledge, 1993). On the connections between ethics and narrative, see Jim Cheney, "Postmodern Environmental Ethics: Ethics as Bioregional Narrative," *Environmental Ethics* 11 (1989): 117–34. On the importance of seeing the local community as connected to a global capitalist system see, James O'Connor, "Socialism and Ecology," *Capitalism, Nature, Socialism* 2, no. 3 (1991): 1–12.

9. George Perkins Marsh, *Man and Nature* (New York: Charles Scribner's, 1864), pp. 35–36.

10. Herbert Marcuse, "Nature and Revolution," in Herbert Marcuse, *Counterrevolution and Revolt* (Boston: Beacon Press, 1972), pp. 59-78, see pp. 65, 69.

11. "Preamble to *Agenda 21*" and "The Rio Declaration on Environment and Development," in Grubb, et al., *The Earth Summit Agreements*, pp. 101, 87.

12. On chaos theory see, James Gleick, *Chaos: The Making of a New Science* (New York: Viking, 1987); Edward Lorenz, *The Essence of Chaos* (Seattle, WA: University of Washington Press, 1993); Lorenz, "Irregularity: A Fundamental Property of the Atmosphere." *Crafoord Prize Lecture, Tellus* 36A (1984): 98-110; N. Katherine Hayles, *Chaos Bound: Orderly Disorder in Contemporary Literature and Science* (Ithaca, NY: Cornell University Press, 1990); N. Katherine Hayles, ed., *Chaos and Order: Complex Dynamics in Literature and Science* (Chicago: University of Chicago Press, 1991); Ralph Abraham, *Chaos, Eros, and Gaia* (San Francisco: Harper & Row, 1994). On the difference between chaos theory and complexity theory, see Mitchell Waldrop, *Complexity: The Emerging Science at the Edge of Order and Chaos* (New York: Simon and Schuster, 1992).

13. On the god-trick of seeing everything from nowhere, see Donna Haraway, "Situated Knowledges," in Donna Haraway, *Simians, Cyborgs, and Women: The Reinvention of Nature* (New York: Routledge, 1991), pp. 183–201, esp. pp. 189, 191, 193, 195.

14. Management Institute for Environment and Business, *Environmental Partnerships: A Business Handbook*, quotation on p. 3.

15. In constructing this example I have drawn on a hypothetical case presented in Management Institute for Environment and Business, *Environmental Partnerships: A Business Handbook*, pp. 11–12, but I have added representatives of affected natural entities.

16. Ibid.

17. Ibid., p. 12.

18. Management Institute for Environment and Business, *Environmental Partnerships: A Field Guide for Nonprofit Organizations and Community Interests*, p. 11.

19. Long and Arnold, *The Power of Environmental Partnerships*, p. 5.

20. Ibid.

21. Management Institute for Environment and Business, *Environmental Partnerships: A Field Guide for Government Agencies*, p. 32.

Part VI

CONCLUSION

In the Conclusion to *Science and Nature*, I explore twentieth-century theoretical frameworks, such as chaos and complexity theories, that supersede the mechanistic philosophy of the Scientific Revolution—and suggest that we are living in a far less predictable world than that bequeathed to us by classical physics. These new theories challenge the mainstream narrative of the Scientific Revolution that although humans fell from a biblical Garden of Eden, they can dominate and control the earth through mechanistic science. As Francis Bacon put it (see Chapter 2): "Man by the Fall, fell at the same time from his state of innocency and from his dominion over creation. Both of these losses can in this life be in some part repaired; the former by religion and faith, the latter by arts and science." Humans, he asserted, could "recover that right over nature which belongs to it by divine bequest." The most noble of human ambitions was "to endeavor to establish and extend the power and dominion of the human race itself over the universe."[1]

But Bacon's narrative plot which gives hope to human progress via the domination of nature through science and technology depends on the predictability, control, and determinism of mechanistic science. Today Bacon's narrative of the recovery of Eden is challenged by the new sciences of chaos and complexity theory that argue that in open systems (such as ecological and social systems) outcomes are far less predictable than those described by the classical sciences of the nineteenth century.

The Earth of the twenty-first century is a world in which nature is far more autonomous and uncontrollable than that described by classical science and one in which ecological transformations, weather patterns, and climate change make it far more difficult to predict and hence to control. Working with nature through sciences such as sustainable agriculture, restoration ecology, and the use of renewable energy sources gives hope for a livable world. That new world is one of human partnership with nature.

NOTE

1. Francis Bacon, "Novum Organum," in James Spedding, Robert Leslie Ellis, and Douglas Devon Heath, eds., *Works*, 14 vols. (London: Longmans Green, 1870), vol. 4, Bk. II, aphorism 52, pp. 247–8; Bk. I, aphorism 129, pp. 114–15.

FIGURES 16.1 AND 16.2 Biologist Stuart Kauffman (b. 1939) (left) and Physicist Günter Mahler (1945–2016), colleagues who investigated complex adaptive systems while working together at the Santa Fe Institute in New Mexico.

Source: Public domain.

CONCLUSION*

Science for the Twenty-First Century

Biologist Stuart Kauffman (b. 1939) and physicist Günter Mahler (1945–2016) are sitting on a sunny terrace outside the Santa Fe Institute overlooking northern New Mexico's Rio Grande Valley and its juniper-piñon pine mesas. They are discussing new views of cosmic chaos and complex adaptive systems which are challenging the narratives by which people have immemorially defined their role in the natural order. Here in the shadow of the *Sangre de Christo* mountains, Native American origin stories have contended for nearly four centuries with the Biblical story of the creation and loss of Eden. And here, as elsewhere, narratives of modern science have contested those of earlier traditions. Now, at the Santa Fe Institute where the two scientists sit, the stories wrought by classical science are again being challenged by new views of chaos and complexity.

Suddenly Mahler, gazing out over the rolling hills asks Kauffman what his image of paradise is. Without waiting for an answer, he suggests that the surrounding landscape, similar in form to that of East Africa, may carry for us some genetic imprint of our species' African origins, its first home—the original "Eden." Recent genetic analysis even traces the anthropological "Adam" and "Eve" to that same East African landscape. What new narrative(s) about human origins and humanity's "home in the universe" are implied by the new scientific focus on chaos and complexity? Can they also foster a new ethic of human interaction with non-human nature—an ethic of partnership?[1]

Kauffman argues that complex systems theory can in fact turn around the fall from Eden initiated not by Eve's sin, but by science itself.

"Somewhere along our path, paradise has been lost, lost to the Western mind, and in the spreading world civilization, lost to our collective mind. John Milton must have been the last superb poet of Western civilization who could have sought to justify the ways of God to man in those early years foreshadowing the modern era. Paradise has been lost, not to sin, but to science."[2]

It was Copernican, Newtonian, and Darwinian science, Kauffman asserts, that removed humanity as God's chosen people from its Edenic home. Copernicus's sun-centered universe displaced our terrestrial home from the center of the cosmos. Moreover, Leibniz's universe removed the need for God's continuous action and presence. He merely created the universe, wound up the clock, and left it to tick away into eternity. Seventeenth-century mechanics assumed that nature is divided into parts and that change comes from external forces (a billiard ball model). Classical physics, as consolidated in the nineteenth century with the development of thermodynamics, electricity and magnetism, and astrophysics, accurately predicts events in the three-dimensional world. But equilibrium thermodynamics (the basis for the steam engine and refrigerator) implies a continual running down of that world into a terminal heat death as entropy (or the energy unavailable to do work) increases. Moreover, Darwinian evolution, operating by natural selection on chance mutations, makes human life an accidental outcome of the emergence of life. If the drama were replayed, humans might not be around at all. Such science makes for a depressing human story of decline from an original Eden.[3]

"How far we have come," Kauffman laments, "from the blessed children of God, at the center of the universe, walking among creatures created for our benefit, in a garden called Eden. Science, not sin, has indeed lost us our paradise." The science of complex systems, however, offers hope for a new story. By seeing the emergence of life as a complex adaptive system that reflects an underlying cosmic order, we could once again be "at home in the universe." A new science could counter some of the problems of modernity.[4]

The classical sciences of the modern era, while displacing humanity as God's chosen children, at the same time empowered humans with a God-like hubris capable of recreating Eden on earth. Mechanistic, deterministic science gave people the ability to predict the outcome of mathematically described events through algebra, calculus, and linear differential equations. It is prediction that leads to the possibility of control and hence to the domination of nature. The eighteenth-century Enlightenment brought hope of progress through rational thought, science, and capitalist economic development. Mechanistic science became a powerful tool in the technological reclamation of the earth, turning forests into farms and deserts into irrigated gardens, reversing the fall from Eden by reinventing the earth in the image of the original garden. Yet that very success has led to the widespread destruction of ancient forests, other species, entire ecosystems, and vital products of biological evolution.[5]

Like Kauffman, environmentalists want a new recovery. As environmental historian Steven Pyne sees it: "The real future of environmentalism is in rehabilitation and restoration. Environmentalists have told the story of the Garden of Eden and the fall from grace over and over again. But we haven't yet told the story of redemption. Now we need to tell that story." Having seen the plot as declensionist rather than progressive, environmentalists nevertheless opt for a recovery that must be put in place by the mid-twenty-first century.[6]

"Sustainability" is a new vision of the recovered garden, one in which humanity will live in a dynamically balanced relationship with the natural world. Environmentalists who press for sustainable development see the recovery as achievable through the spread of non-degrading forms of agriculture and industry. Preservationists and deep ecologists strive to save pristine nature as wilderness before it can be destroyed by development. Restoration ecologists wish to marshal human labor to restore an already degraded nature to an earlier pristine state. Social ecologists and green parties devise new economic and political structures that overcome the domination of human beings and non-human nature. The regeneration of nature and people will be achieved through social and environmental justice. The End Drama envisions a sustainable, socially just ecotopia for the post-millennial world of the twenty-first century.

Seeing Western history as a recovery narrative, with environmentalism as a reversal of the plot, brings up the question of the character of the plot itself. The progressive and declensionist plots that underlie the meta-narrative of recovery both gain power from their linearity. Linearity is not only conceptually easy to grasp, but it is also a property of modernity itself. Mechanistic science, progress, and capitalism all draw power from the linear functions of mathematical equations—the upward and downward slopes of straight lines and curves. To the extent that these linear slopes intersect with a real material world, they refer to a limited domain only. But chaos theory suggests that only the unusual domain of mechanistic science can be described by linear differential equations. The usual—the domain of everyday occurrences— such as the weather, turbulence, the shapes of coastlines, the arrhythmic fibrillations of the human heart cannot be so easily described. The world is more complex than we know or indeed can ever know. The comfortable predictability of the linear slips away into the uncertainty of the indeterminate, into discordant harmonies and disorderly order.

POSTMODERN NARRATIVES

The sciences of chaos and complexity suggest new narratives that are influenced at least in part by skepticism about determinism, prediction, and control. While chaos theory disrupts hopes for complete prediction in certain domains of the everyday world, complexity theory operates in the realm between order and chaos to bring chance and necessity into new relationships. The Enlightenment hope of an orderly, upward trajectory is punctured by a recognition of the roles of unforeseen events, chance encounters, and branching histories to which communities and societies respond by adaptation, struggle, or disintegration. How did these changes come about and how do the sciences of chaos and complexity suggest new stories about the universe, humanity, and the individual's place in the world?

Emerging over the past decade are a number of scientific proposals that challenge the Scientific Revolution's mechanistic view of nature. According to physicist David Bohm, a mechanistic science based on the assumption that matter is divisible into parts (such as atoms, electrons, or quarks) moved by external forces may be giving way to a new science based on the primacy of process. In the early twentieth century, he argues, relativity and quantum theory began to challenge mechanism. Relativity theory postulated that fields with varying strengths spread out in space. Strong, stable areas, much like whirlpools in a flowing stream, represented particles. They interacted with and modified each other, but were still considered external to and separate from each other. Quantum mechanics mounted a greater challenge. Motion was not continuous, as in mechanistic science, but occurred in leaps. Particles, such as electrons, behaved like waves, while waves, such as light waves, behaved like particles, depending on the experimental context. Context dependence, which was antithetical to mechanism and part of the organic worldview, was a fundamental characteristic of matter.

Bohm's process physics challenges mechanism still further. He argues that instead of starting with parts as primary and building up wholes as secondary phenomena, a physics is needed that starts with undivided, multidimensional wholeness (a flow of energy called the holomovement) and derives the three-dimensional world of classical mechanics as a secondary phenomenon. The explicate order of the Newtonian world in which we live unfolds from the implicate order contained in the underlying flow of energy.

Another challenge to mechanism comes from the new thermodynamics of Ilya Prigogine. The clock-like machine model of nature and society that dominated the past three centuries of western thought may be winding down. While Newtonian classical physics is still valid, it is nonetheless limited to a clearly defined domain of the total world. It was extended in the nineteenth century to include theories of thermodynamics that developed out of the needs of a steam-engine society, electricity and magnetism that supplied the light and electricity that powered that society, and hydrodynamics or the science associated with the dams and water power that generated its electricity. The equilibrium and near-equilibrium thermodynamics of nineteenth-century classical physics had beautifully described closed, isolated systems such as steam engines and refrigerators.

In dealing with the emergence of order out of chaos, Prigogine's theory helped to clarify an apparent contradiction between two nineteenth-century scientific developments. Classical thermodynamics, which says that the universe is moving toward a greater state of chaos, is based on two laws. The first law states that the total energy of the universe is constant and only changes its form as it is transferred from mechanical, to chemical, to hydrodynamic, to metabolic, and so on. But the second law states that the energy available for work—the useful energy—is decreasing. The universe is running down, just as a clock unwinds over time when no one is there to rewind it. The second law implies that the world proceeds from order to disorder, that people grow older, and that in billions of years the whole universe will reach a uniform temperature. The classical model of reality deals very adequately with closed systems that are isolated from their environments—situations in which small inputs result in small outputs that can be described by linear mathematical relationships.

Yet the very concept of an unwinding clocklike universe is apparently contradicted by another startling nineteenth-century theory—evolution, or the motion toward greater order. Darwinian evolution says that biological systems are evolving, not running down. They are moving from disorder to order; they are becoming more organized rather than disorganized. The direction of change over time is from simple to more complex life forms. The apparent contradiction lies in the domain in which the laws applied. Mechanical systems are closed systems isolated from the natural environment. In contrast, most biological and social systems are open, not closed. They exchange matter and energy with the environment.

Prigogine argued that classical thermodynamics holds in systems that are in equilibrium or near-equilibrium, such as pendulum clocks, steam engines, and solar systems. These are stable systems in which small changes within the system lead to adjustments and adaptations. They are described mathematically by the great seventeenth- and eighteenth-century mathematical advances in calculus and linear differential equations. But what happens when the input is so large that a system cannot adjust? In these far-from-equilibrium systems, non-linear relationships take over. In such cases small inputs can produce new and unexpected effects.

Prigogine's far-from-equilibrium thermodynamics allows for the possibility that higher levels of organization can spontaneously emerge out of disorder when a system breaks down. His approach applies to social and ecological systems, which are open rather than closed, and helps to account for biological and social evolution. In the biological realm, when old structures break down, small inputs can (but do not necessarily) lead to positive feedbacks that may produce new enzymes or new cellular structures. In social terms, revolutionary changes can take place. On a large scale, a social or economic revolution can occur in which a society regroups around a different social or economic form, such as the change from gathering-hunting to horticulture, or from a feudal society to a pre-industrial capitalist society. In the field of science, a revolutionary change could entail a paradigm shift toward new explanatory theories, such as the change from a geocentric Ptolemaic cosmos to a heliocentric Copernican universe.[7]

The recent emergence of chaos theory in mathematics suggests that deterministic, linear, predictive equations which form the basis of mechanism, may apply to unusual rather than usual situations. Instead, chaos, in which a small effect may lead to a large effect, may be the norm. Chaos theory reveals patterns of complexity that lead to a greater understanding of global behaviors, but militate against over-reliance on the simple predictions of linear differential equations.

Edward Lorenz, Professor of Meteorology at the Massachusetts Institute of Technology, described chaos theory as a phenomenon of sensitive dependence on initial conditions. In a talk entitled, "Predictability: Does the Flap of a Butterfly's Wings in Brazil Set Off a Tornado in Texas?" he wrote: "The question which really interests us is whether . . . for example, two particular weather situations differing by as little as the immediate influence of a single butterfly will generally after sufficient time evolve into two situations differing by as much as the presence of a tornado. In more technical language, is the behavior of the atmosphere unstable with respect to perturbations of small amplitude?"

Lorenz's work, for which he won the 1983 Crafoord Prize of the Royal Swedish Academy of Sciences, led him to question the possibility of finding suitable linear prediction formulas for weather forecasting and instead to develop models based on non-linear equations. He argued that irregularity is a fundamental property of the atmosphere and that the rapid doubling of errors from the effects of physical features precludes great accuracy in real-world forecasting. Most environmental and biological systems, such as changing weather, population, noise, aperiodic heart fibrillations, and ecological patterns, may in fact be governed by non-linear chaotic relationships.[8]

CHAOS AND COMPLEXITY

Quantum mechanics and relativity theory challenged the determinism of classical mechanics at the atomic and nuclear levels. Heisenberg's uncertainty principle emphasized the impossibility of simultaneously predicting both the momentum and position of a subatomic particle. But chaos theory then went a step further, questioning the determinism of processes in the everyday world and suggesting that the human ability to predict the outcome of those processes, even when lawlike regularities are well described, is limited. It presented, instead, a world of disorderly order and uncertain outcomes. What does chaos theory mean for the environment?

The appearance of chaos as an actor in science and history in the late twentieth century fundamentally destabilizes the very concept of nature as a standard or referent. It disrupts the idea of nature as resilient actor or mother who will repair the errors of human actors and continue as fecund garden (Eve as mother). It questions the possibility that humans as agents can control and master nature through science and technology, undermining the myth of nature as virgin female to be developed (Eve as virgin). Chaos is the reemergence of nature as power over humans, nature as active, dark, wild, turbulent, and uncontrollable (fallen Eve). Ecologists characterize "Mother Nature" as a "strange attractor" while turbulence is seen to be encoded with gendered images of masculine channels and feminine flows. In the chaotic narrative, humans lose the hubris of fallen Adam that the garden can be recreated on earth. The world is not created by a patriarchal God *ex nihilo*, but emerges out of chaos. Thus the very possibility of the recovery of a stable original garden—the plot of the recovery meta-narrative—is itself challenged.[9]

While a certain domain of nature can be represented by linear, deterministic equations, and is therefore predictable (or can be subjected to probabilities, stochastic approximations, and systems analysis), a very large domain can be represented only through non-linear equations that do not admit of solutions. The closed systems and determinism of classical physics described by Isaac Newton and Pierre Simon Laplace give way to a postclassical physics of open complex systems and chaos theory. These theories suggest that there are limits to the knowable world. This is not the same as saying there is a non-knowable noumenal world behind the phenomena. Rather there is a real, material, physical world, but a world that can never be fully known by means of mathematics. It is a world that is chaotic and unpredictable and therefore cannot be totally controlled by science and technology. Science can no longer perform the God-trick—imposing the view of everything from nowhere. It cannot offer the totalizing viewpoint associated with modernism, the Enlightenment, and mechanistic science. The real world is both orderly and disorderly, predictable and unpredictable, controllable and uncontrollable, depending on context and situation.[10]

Complexity theory not only reconstructs the relationship between humans and nature, but also suggests the possibility of a non-linear narrative that is more complicated than that of the Enlightenment recovery story. The emerging science of complex systems bridges the gap between order and chaos and suggests a narrative of lawlike regularities, branching histories, "frozen accidents," and adaptive reorganizations—or failures to adapt. A range of entities and possibilities exists that moves from simplicity, to complexity, to complex adaptive systems. The quark, according to Nobel physicist Murray Gell-Mann who invented it, exemplifies a simple entity, the jaguar a complex organism, humanity itself a complex adaptive system. "A complex adaptive system is a system that learns or evolves by utilizing acquired information. . . . It compresses regularities into concise packages that are often called schemata. . . . In biological evolution, the genome of an organism is a schema. In the scientific enterprise, a theory is a schema. In the evolution of a society, such things as laws, traditions, kinship rules, and myths constitute schemata." The environment, societies, and the economy are all complex adaptive systems. The emergence of life, biological and cultural evolution, and computers are examples of the ways in which one complex system gives rise to another.[11]

According to Gell-Mann, we live in a quasiclassical world governed by quantum mechanical laws that because of the limitations of our senses and instruments can only be experienced as coarse-grained—like the graininess of a blown-up photograph. Deviations from classically determined events can nevertheless be described by probabilities. But just as Heisenberg's uncertainty principle injects indeterminacy at the micro (or atomic level), so chaotic processes, or sensitive dependence on initial conditions (as in weather phenomena—Edward Lorenz's "butterfly effect") inject indeterminacy at the macro (or everyday world) level. Alternative, often unpredictable pathways of development result. These branching histories, or "gardens of forking paths" (a metaphor created by Jorge Luis Borges) are mutually exclusive alternatives that result in the evolution of complex adaptive systems. From the beginning of the universe, through all of time, the initial expansion branches into alternatives for which there are well-defined probabilities. But these alternative branches are mutually exclusive. In one branch a planet may ultimately result from a quantum accident billions of years ago, but in another no planet can occur.[12]

Chance operates in the realm between order and chaos to create complexity. Fundamental laws combine with chance to generate "frozen accidents"—events that could have been different, but because of the way they turn out produce a multitude of specific results, as when a vice-president becomes president after an assassination. "Complex adaptive systems," says Gell-Mann, "function best in a regime intermediate between order and disorder. They exploit the regularities provided by the approximate determinism of the quasiclassical domain, and at the same time they profit from . . . indeterminacies (describable as noise, fluctuations, heat, uncertainty, and so on)."[13]

Complex biological and social systems are not controlled by central mechanisms and do not change in a linear manner. Their internal dynamics, operating in response to external conditions, can result in rapid change from a small input (the introduction of a disease or a natural disaster, for example). In biology, a genome responding favorably to selection pressure will survive and reproduce. In science, a theory or schema that explains empirical data and predicts verifiable results will be selected over those that fail in some major respect. In cultural development, societies that respond creatively to changing environmental and social conditions by successfully applying existing rules (moving to a new location when drought occurs) or developing new schemata (religious rituals or new agricultural techniques) will survive; those that fail will die out.[14]

Throughout the history of the earth, complex adaptive biological and social systems have developed which exhibit regularities in efficient organization and distribution of resources that allow them to persist over time, accumulate and exchange information, and continue to evolve. They interact with each other and with other parts of non-human nature, persisting in transition zones between order and disorder. Today many of these diverse biological systems and human cultures are threatened with decline or extinction. We need to try to imagine what an ecologically sustainable planet, in which both biological and cultural diversity are preserved, would look like. Gell-Mann urges: "It is worthwhile to try to construct models of the future—not as blueprints but as aids to the imagination—and see if paths can be sketched out that may lead to such a sustainable and desirable world late in the next century, a world in which humanity as a whole and the rest of nature operate as a complex adaptive system to a much greater degree than they do now."[15]

ECOLOGY

Ecology is based on open, rather than closed, systems and emphasizes nature as continuous change and process. But chaos and complexity theories challenge two basic assumptions of ecology as it developed in the 1950s and 1960s that formed the basis of environmental management—the ideas of the balance of nature and the diversity-stability hypothesis. These theories question the idea of the constancy and stability of nature, the idea that every organism has a place in the harmonious workings of nature, and that nature itself is fixed in time and space—like the environment in a petri dish in a modern scientific laboratory. Many ecologists also argue that diversity does not necessarily lead to stability, as seems to be the case in tropical rainforests which, while extremely diverse, can easily be destroyed by natural and human interventions.

The idea of a balance of nature that humans could disrupt implied that people could repair damaged ecosystems with better practices. The idea that biodiversity led to ecosystem stability meant that species conservation and ecological restoration could improve ecosystem health. But chaos theory suggests that natural disturbances and mosaic patches that do not exhibit regular or predictable patterns are the norm rather than the aberration. Moreover, the seemingly stable world that is the object of socially-constructed representations can be destabilized by human social practices (as when pesticides produce mutant insects or antibiotics produce resistant bacteria). Such theories undercut assumptions of a stable, harmonious nature and question holism as a foundation for ecology. They reinforce the idea that predictability, while still useful, is more limited than previously assumed and that nature, while in part a human construct and a representation, is also a real, material, autonomous agent. A postclassical, postmodern science is a science of limited knowledge, of the primacy of process over parts, and of imbedded contexts within complex, open, ecological systems.[16]

Ecologist Daniel Botkin proposes the idea of discordant harmonies as an alternative to the concept of the balance of nature. Botkin argues that we must move to a deeper level of thought and "confront the very assumptions that have dominated perceptions of nature for a very long time. This will allow us to find the true idea of a harmony of nature, which as Plotinus wrote so long ago, is by its very essence discordant, created from the simultaneous movements of many tones, the combination of many processes flowing at the same time along various scales, leading not to a simple melody, but to a symphony sometimes harsh and sometimes pleasing."[17]

The idea of discordant harmonies, theories of the chaotic and complex behavior of nature, and the consideration that natural disturbances are perhaps equally important to and, in some cases, more rapid and drastic (as in fires, tornadoes, and hurricanes) than disturbances by human beings (forest harvesting, real estate development, and dam construction, for example), have led to a questioning of earlier ethical approaches to environmental management. Self-interested, or egocentric ethics (what is good for the individual is good for society); social-interest, or homocentric ethics (the greatest good for the greatest number); and even earth-centered, or ecocentric ethics (all living and non-living things are morally considerable and have rights) all have problematical implications for a sustainable world. The growth-oriented capitalistic economy from which the egocentric ethic arises and the anthropocentric focus of the utilitarian cost-benefit approach from which the homocentric ethic arises both have negative implications for the environment. On the other hand, the idea that all non-human organisms have moral consideration equal to human beings—the ecocentric approach—undercuts the real struggles of the poor and of disadvantaged minorities for a better life. What is called for is a new ethic of partnership that arises out of both the needs of nature and the needs of humanity (see Ch 15 of this book).

The disorderly, ordered world of non-human nature must be acknowledged as a free autonomous actor, just as humans are free autonomous agents. Nature limits human freedom to totally dominate and control it, just as human power limits Nature's and other humans' freedom. Science and technology can tell us that an event such as a hurricane, earthquake, flood, or fire is likely to happen in a certain locale, but not when it will happen. Because nature is fundamentally chaotic, it must be respected and related to as an active partner.

These new approaches to science are consistent with a new narrative about the natural world and humanity's place within it. They are based on a different set of assumptions about the nature of reality than mechanism: wholeness rather than atomistic units, process rather than the rearrangement of parts, internal rather than external relations, the non-linearity and unpredictability of fundamental change, and pluralism rather than reductionism. But could a postclassical science embodying such a vision be socially created and accepted? If so, it might be consistent with new ethical guidelines for humanity's relationship with the environment—an ethic of partnership among humans and between humanity and nature.

NOTES

* Revised from Carolyn Merchant, *Reinventing Eden: The Fate of Nature in Western Culture* (New York: Routledge, 2013; originally published 2003), pp. 175–187. Used by permission of Routledge.

1. The narrative laid out above is drawn from Stuart Kauffman, *At Home in the Universe: The Search for the Laws of Self-Organization and Complexity* (New York: Oxford University Press, 1995), see p. 1. Günter Mahler (d. Oct. 12, 2016) was a professor at the Institute for Theoretical Physics, University of Stuttgart, Germany and author of *Quantum Thermodynamic Processes: Energy and Information Flow at the Nanoscale* (Boca Raton, FL: CRC Press, 2015).

2. Kauffman, *At Home in the Universe*, quotation on p. 4.

3. Ibid., pp. 9–16.

4. Ibid., quotation on p. 10; M. Mitchell Waldrop, *Complexity: The Emerging Science at the Edge of Order and Chaos* (New York: Simon and Schuster, 1992).

5. Carolyn Merchant, *The Death of Nature: Women, Ecology, and the Scientific Revolution* (San Francisco: Harper & Row, 1980).

6. Ed Marston, "Experts Line Up on All Sides of the Tree-Grass Debate," *High Country News* 28, no. 7 (1996): 12–13, quotation on p. 13.

7. Ilya Prigogine and Isabelle Stengers, *Order Out of Chaos: Man's New Dialogue with Nature* (New York: Bantam, 1984).

8. James Gleick, *Chaos: The Making of a New Science* (New York: Viking, 1987), pp. 9–32. Edward Lorenz, "Predictability: Does the Flap of a Butterfly's Wings in Brazil Set Off a Tornado in Texas?" Paper presented to the annual meeting of the American Association for the Advancement of Science, Washington, DC, December 29, 1972. Edward Lorenz, "Irregularity: A Fundamental Property of the Atmosphere." Crafoord Prize Lecture, *Tellus* 36A (1984): 98–110; Edward Lorenz, *The Essence of Chaos* (Seattle: University of Washington Press, 1993), pp. 181–4.

9. Prigogine and Stengers, *Order Out of Chaos*; Gleick, *Chaos*; Lorenz, *The Essence of Chaos*, op. cit. note 8; N. Katherine Hayles, *Chaos Bound: Orderly Disorder in Contemporary Literature and Science* (Ithaca, NY: Cornell University Press, 1990); N. Katherine Hayles, ed., *Chaos and Order: Complex Dynamics in Literature and Science* (Chicago, IL: University of Chicago Press, 1991); N. Katherine Hayles, "Gender Encoding in Fluid Mechanics: Masculine Channels and Feminine Flows," *Differences* 4, no. 2 (1992): 16–44.

10. On the God-trick of seeing everything from nowhere, see Donna Haraway, "Situated Knowledges," in Haraway, *Simians, Cyborgs, and Women: The Reinvention of Nature* (New York: Routledge, 1991), pp. 183–201, esp. pp. 189, 191, 193, 195.

11. Murray Gell-Mann, *The Quark and the Jaguar* (New York: W. H. Freeman, 1994), pp. 367–71; George J. Gumerman and Murray Gell-Mann, eds., *Understanding Complexity in the Prehistoric Southwest*, Santa Fe Institute Studies in the Sciences of Complexity, vol. 16 (Reading, MA: Addison-Wesley, 1994), quotation on p. 3.

12. Gell-Mann, *The Quark and the Jaguar*, pp. 149–50, 369.

13. Ibid., pp. 367–9, 371, quotation on p. 369.

14. Gumerman and Gell-Mann, eds., *Understanding Complexity*, pp. 345, 344.

15. Gell-Mann, *The Quark and the Jaguar*, pp. 374–5, quotation on p. 375.

16. For the diversity-stability hypothesis, see Eugene P. Odum, *Fundamentals of Ecology* (Philadelphia: W.B. Saunders, 1953); Eugene P. Odum, "The Strategy of Ecosystem Development," *Science* 164 (1969): 262–70. On shortcomings of equilibrium theories in ecology, see Seth R. Reice, "Nonequilibrium Determinants of Biological Community Structure," *American Scientist* 82 (September–October 1994): 424–35. On the history and disruption of the balance of nature theory, see Daniel Botkin, *Discordant Harmonies: A New Ecology for the Twenty-First Century* (New York: Oxford University Press, 1990); Stuart T. A. Pickett and Peter S. White, eds., *The Ecology of Natural Disturbance and Patch Dynamics* (Orlando, FL: Academic Press, 1985). On the problem of a stable world behind socially constructed representations, see Elizabeth Ann R. Bird, "The Social Construction of Nature: Theoretical Approaches to the History of Environmental Problems," *Environmental Review* 11, no. 4 (1987): 255–64. On the history of chaos theory in ecology, see Donald Worster, "Ecology of Order and Chaos," *Environmental History Review* 14, no. 1–2 (1990): 4–16.

17. Botkin, *Discordant Harmonies*, quotation on p. 25.

Nobel Prize Medal. Shows Swedish chemist Alfred Nobel (1833–1896), inventor of dynamite, on the facing side and *Scientia* (Science) and *Natura* (Nature) on the reverse.

Source: Designed by Eric Lindberg, 1902, for the Royal Swedish Academy of Sciences, used by permission © ® The Nobel Foundation

EPILOGUE

Can Science Know Nature?

Like all medals, the Nobel Prize for physics and chemistry has two sides. On the front is the image of Swedish chemist Alfred Nobel (1833–1896), inventor of dynamite, whose will endowed the Nobel prizes for peace, literature, medicine, chemistry, and physics. Turn it over and a very different image prevails. On the left side is *Natura*, symbol of nature, holding a cornucopia of fruit. On the right side is *Scientia*, symbol of science, removing the veil from the head of a bare-breasted *Natura*. At the feet of the two women is inscribed the name of the laureate and year of the prize. Together, the two goddesses imply that Science can indeed know Nature.[1]

In the foregoing chapters of *Science and Nature*, I have examined these two topics as they have emerged over the course of my academic career. But the relationships between the two ideas are becoming increasingly complex. The assumption that Science can know Nature has been made in Western culture over many years. But recent work suggests that humanity has entered a new era called the "Anthropocene" in which human impacts on nature from the burning of fossil fuels mean that the planet has been significantly changed by humanity. This raises the question, has nature in the Anthropocene been so altered by human science that it can no longer be thought to exist separately from humanity? Are science and nature now so completely intertwined and merged that we can no longer even use the two words separately? What is the future of the relationship between science and nature?[2]

In 1830, August Comte outlined *A Course of Positive Philosophy* based on experimentation and mathematics, stemming from the advances of the seventeenth century. The goal of positive philosophy was to understand all phenomena in terms of the smallest number of natural laws based on observed facts as manifested by experiments. Observation and experimentation combined with mathematics were the keys to positive knowledge of nature. "Since Bacon's time," Comte wrote, "there can be no real knowledge but that which is based on observed facts," while Descartes' discovery of analytical geometry "changed the whole aspect of mathematical science and yielded the germ of all future progress."[3]

The logical positivism (or logical empiricism) of the Vienna Circle, during the first-half of the twentieth century, held that the only ways in which science could know nature were through two kinds of statements. Logical, including mathematical, statements were true by virtue of being tautologies, but needed empirical content to be scientific truths. Empirical statements were true be virtue of being testable through experimentation and observation. Together, the two types constituted scientific knowledge of the natural world.[4]

But the positivist response to the question, "Can Science Know Nature?" came under intense scrutiny in the last quarter of the twentieth century. In the 1960s, the internalist-externalist debates within the history of science questioned the idea of the growth of science as an outcome of efforts to solve theoretical problems. The externalists argued that social and economic changes in society, such as the rise of pre-industrial capitalism in the late sixteenth century, influenced the types of problems that scientists chose to investigate.[5]

In addition, Thomas Kuhn's *Structure of Scientific Revolutions* (1962) questioned the idea of the progress of science as an accumulation of knowledge about nature. Kuhn set out the concept of a scientific paradigm as a set of ideas, theories, and practices that were accepted by a scientific community until anomalies within the paradigm forced the development of a new theory. Scientific knowledge about nature developed not as an accumulation of truths, but as revolutions in what scientific communities accepted as knowledge. The transition from a Ptolemaic earth-centered cosmos to a Copernican sun-centered universe in early modern Europe or from the wave theory of light to the photon theory in the early twentieth century were cases in point.[6]

During the 1980s, the problem of "knowing nature" moved to encompass the social construction of both science and nature—in particular, knowledge of the environment. In her 1987 article on "The Social Construction of Nature," Elizabeth Ann R. Bird argued that "scientific knowledge should not be regarded as a representation of nature, but rather as a socially constructed interpretation [of] an already socially constructed natural-technical object." The practices of scientists, she noted, have altered the very "nature" that they study, as in the role of DDT in creating chemically induced mutations and the introduction of genetically-engineered life forms into the environment.[7]

Within the history of science, feminist historians and philosophers of science, such as Evelyn Fox Keller, Sandra Harding, Londa Schiebinger,

Ruth Bleier, and Margaret Rossiter questioned the possibility of a scientific knowledge system independent of the culture-bound influences of gender and wrote on the contributions of women to the various branches of science.[8] Ellen Swallow Richards (1892) and Rachel Carson (1962) were two women scientists who, as founders and contributors to the science of human ecology, shaped our understanding of the ways in which humans can both benefit from and disrupt nature itself.[9] The rise of ecofeminism in the 1970s and 1980s examined the linkages between women and nature and the impacts of a biologically and chemically-altered nature on women's bodies.[10]

Similarly, claims about the theory and practice of science in white Western ways of knowing has been challenged by an examination of ways in which race and racism privilege concepts associated with Western and First World societies over and above those of non-Western cultures.[11] In the ancient Near East and in other Eastern and indigenous cultures, the concepts of "science and nature" as we know them today did not even exist.[12]

As social constructs, race and racism have shaped the ways in which science and nature have omitted the scientific influences and responses of people of color to nature.[13] Thus African Americans made unique contributions to agricultural development (e.g., tobacco, rice, turpentine, sugar, and cotton), to exploration and resource use in ranching and mining, and to industrial production (e.g., mining, textiles, and manufacturing). Moreover, Blacks have related to nature, wilderness, and national parks in historically specific ways, such as using forests for subsistence, as places of escape from the oppressions of slavery, as opportunities for worship, or as places to be avoided for fear of capture and lynching. Opportunities exist for further research and collaboration at the intersection of the fields of science and nature.[14]

Chaos and complexity theories in science reveal new and complicated aspects of nature's responses to science and new ways in which science can know nature. These new sciences question the human ability to control nature through science and technology and hence challenge the mechanistic ideal of the domination of nature.[15] Likewise, current issues, such as the history of climate change, biotechnology, and toxic environments, especially in racially segregated neighborhoods and Third World environments, suggest a convergence of interests in which the social construction of gender, race, and nature all play critical roles.

Examining the interactions between science and nature in the question "Can Science know Nature?" is a way to engage in a productive conversation. An emphasis on the dialectical interaction between science and nature brings out ways in which *Natura* as an actress resists and reacts to *Scientia's* scientific and technological innovations. The inclusion of gender in investigations of science and nature, the fight against racism, and a renewed emphasis on economic equalities can move us all toward a more democratic future.

These dialectical, gendered, socially, and racially-conscious approaches to the Age of the Anthropocene can help to shed new light on the relationships between *Scientia* and *Natura* and to the complex question, "Can Science know Nature?" and, if so, with what consequences.[16]

NOTES

1. I am grateful to Elizabeth Ann R. Bird, Montana State University, Bozeman, for conversations in which she posed the question, "Can Science know Nature?" and for her article, "The Social Construction of Nature: Theoretical Approaches to the History of Environmental Problems," *Environmental Review* 11, no. 4 (Winter 1987): 255–264. On the Nobel prize medal, see Londa Schiebinger, *The Mind Has No Sex? Women in the Origins of Modern Science* (Cambridge, MA: Harvard University Press, 1989), pp. 149–150: "On the Nobel prize medals for chemistry and physics designed in 1902 we encounter familiar symbols and messages. On the front of the medal is a profile of the inventor and patron, Alfred Nobel. On the back we find a scene in which a female *Natura* holds a horn of plenty as *Scientia* (also female) lifts away the veil from her face." For numerous images of Science unveiling Nature, see Pierre Hadot, *The Veil of Isis: An Essay on the History of the Idea of Nature*, trans. Michael Chase (Cambridge, MA: Harvard University Press, 2006; originally published 2004). See illustrations to Epilogue and Figure 2.1, this book.
2. Paul J. Crutzen, and Eugene F. Stoermer, "The Anthropocene," *IGPB (International Geosphere-Biosphere Programme) Newsletter*, 41 (2000): 17.
3. Gertrud Lenzer, ed., *Auguste Comte and Positivism: The Essential Writings* (New York: HarperCollins, 1975), pp. 71–86.
4. Victor Kraft, *The Vienna Circle: The Origins of Neo-Positivism*, trans. Arthur Pap (New York: Philosophical Library, 2015; originally published 1953); Friedrich Stadler, ed., *The Vienna Circle and Logical Positivism: Reevaluation and Future Perspectives* (Boston: Dordrecht, 2003).
5. George Basalla, ed., *The Rise of Modern Science: External or Internal Factors?* (Lexington, MA: D.C. Heath, 1968); Boris Hessen, *The Social and Economic Roots of Newton's "Principia,"* with an introduction by Robert S. Cohen (New York: Howard Fertig, 1971 [1931]); Steven Shapin, "Discipline and Bounding: The History and Sociology of Science as Seen through the Externalism-Internalism Debate," *History of Science* 30 (1992): 333–69.
6. Thomas Kuhn, *The Structure of Scientific Revolutions* (Chicago: University of Chicago Press, 1962 [1970, 1996]).
7. Bird, "The Social Construction of Nature," op. cit., note 1, quotation on p. 255. "Since the publication of Thomas Kuhn's work, *The Structure of Scientific Revolutions*, it has become philosophically unacceptable for scientists to claim to know the *Truth* about nature. The most that they can claim to know is a *relative* truth about nature, one whose meaning and articulation are governed by a particular scientific paradigm" (Bird, p. 255).
8. Evelyn Fox Keller, *A Feeling for the Organism: The Life and Work of Barbara McClintock* (New York: W. H. Freeman, 1983); Keller, *Reflections on Gender and Science* (New Haven, CT: Yale University Press, 1985); Ruth Bleier, *Science and Gender: A Critique of Biology and Its Theories on Women* (New York: Pergamon, 1984); Schiebinger, *The Mind has No Sex?*; Sandra Harding, *The Science Question in Feminism* (Ithaca: Cornell University, 1986); Nancy Tuana, ed., *Feminism and Science* (Bloomington: Indiana University Press, 1989); Margaret W. Rossiter, *Women Scientists in America: Struggles and Strategies to 1940* (Baltimore: John Hopkins University Press, 1982); idem, *Women Scientists in America: Before Affirmative Action, 1940–1972* (Baltimore: John Hopkins University Press, 1995); Helen Longino, *Science as Social Knowledge* (Princeton: Princeton University Press, 1990).

9. Robert Clarke, *Ellen Swallow: The Woman Who Founded Ecology* (New York: Follett, 1973); Linda Lear, "Rachel Carson's *Silent Spring*," *Environmental History Review* 17, no. 4 (Summer 1993): 23–42; Linda Lear, *Rachel Carson: Witness for Nature* (New York: Henry Holt, 1997); Linda Lear, ed., *Lost Woods: The Discovered Writings of Rachel Carson* (Boston: Beacon, 1998); Kathleen Kudlinski, *Rachel Carson: Pioneer of Ecology* (New York: Viking, 1988); Patricia Hynes, "Ellen Swallow, Lois Gibbs, and Rachel Carson: Catalysts of the American Environmental Movement," *Women's Studies International Environmental Forum* 8, no. 4 (1985): 291–298; Michael B. Smith, "Silence Miss Carson!: Science, Gender, and the Reception of Silent Spring," *Feminist Studies* 27, no. 3 (Fall 2001): 733–752; Jean Langenheim, "The Path and Progress of American Women Ecologists," *Journal of the Ecological Society of America* 69 (1988): 184–197; Vera Norwood, *Made from This Earth* (Chapel Hill: University of North Carolina Press, 1993).

10. On "Ecofeminism," see Merchant, Ch. 14 of this book.

11. Londa Schiebinger, *Nature's Body: Gender in the Making of Modern Science* (Boston: Beacon Press, 1993); Sandra Harding, ed., *The Racial Economy of Science: Toward a Democratic Future* (Bloomington: Indiana University Press, 1993); Donna Haraway, *Primate Visions: Gender, Race, and Nature in the World of Modern Science* (New York: Routledge, 1993). On African American scientists and mathematicians, see Kenneth Manning, *Black Apollo of Science: The Life of Ernest Everett Just* (New York: Oxford University Press, 1983). On African Americans and nature, see Merchant, "Shades of Darkness: Race and Environmental History," Ch. 11, this book.

12. Francesca Rochberg, *Before Nature: Cuneiform Knowledge and the History of Science* (Chicago: University of Chicago Press, 2016), esp. Ch. 1, "Science and Nature." Laura Nader, ed., *What the Rest Think of the West: Since 600 A.D.* (Berkeley, CA: University of California Press, 2015); J. Baird Callicott and James McRae, eds., *Environmental Philosophy in Asian Traditions of Thought* (Albany: SUNY Press, 2014).

13. On blacks and the environment see Dianne Glave and Mark Stoll, eds., *To Love the Wind and the Rain: African Americans and Environmental History* (Pittsburgh: University of Pittsburgh Press, 2005); Sylvia Hood Washington, *Packing Them In: An Archeology of Environmental Racism, 1865–1954* (Lanham, MD: Lexington Books, 2005); idem, ed., *Echoes from the Poisoned Well: Global Memories of Environmental Injustice* (Lanham, MD: Lexington Books, 2006); Dorceta Taylor, "American Environmentalism: The Role of Race, Class and Gender. 1820–1995," *Race, Gender and Class*, 5, no. 1 (1997): 16-62; idem, *The Environment and the People in American Cities, 1600–1900s: Disorder, Inequality, and Social Change* (Durham: Duke University Press, 2009); Mart Stewart, *What Nature Suffers to Groe: Life, Labor, and Landscape on the Georgia Coast, 1680–1920* (Athens: University of Georgia Press, 1996); Elizabeth Blum, "Power, Danger, and Control: Slave Women's Perceptions of Wilderness in the Nineteenth Century," *Women's Studies* 31 (2002): 247–265; Earl Leatherberry, "An Overview of African Americans' Historical, Religious, and Spiritual Ties to Forests," Proceedings of the Society of American Foresters 1999 National Convention, 2000; Cassandra Y. Johnson, "A Consideration of Collective Memory in African American Attachment to Wildland Recreation Places," *Human Ecology Review* 5, no. 1, 1998: 5-15; Kimberly K. Smith, *African American Environmental Thought: Foundations* (Lawrence: University Press of Kansas, 2007); Carolyn Finney, *Black Faces, White Spaces: Reimagining the Relationship of African Americans to the Great Outdoors* (Chapel Hill: University of North Carolina Press, 2014); Michael Omi and Howard Winant, *Racial Formation in the United States: From the 1960s to the 1990s*, 2nd ed. (New York: Routledge, 1994); William J. Wilson, *The Declining Significance of Race: Blacks and Changing American Institutions* (Chicago: University of Chicago Press, 1978); Evelynn Hammonds and Rebecca Herzig, eds., *The Nature of Difference: Sciences of Race in the United States from Jefferson to Genomics* (Cambridge, MA: MIT Press, 2008); Helen Longino and Evelynn Hammonds, "Conflicts and Tensions in the Feminist Study of Gender and Science," in Marianne Hirsch and Evelyn Fox Keller, eds., *Conflicts in Feminism* (New York: Routledge, 1990), pp. 164-183.

14. See note 8.
15. James Gleick, *Chaos: The Making of a New Science* (New York: Viking, 1987); M. Mitchell Waldrop, *Complexity: The Emerging Science at the Edge of Order and Chaos* (New York: Simon and Schuster, 1992); Jennifer Wells, *Complexity and Sustainability* (New York: Routledge, 2014). See also "Conclusion" to this volume.
16. Omi and Winant, *Racial Formation in the United States*; Donald Moore, Jake Kosek, and Anand Pandian, eds., *Race, Nature, and the Politics of Difference* (Durham, NC: Duke University Press, 2003); Haraway, *Primate Visions*.

BIBLIOGRAPHY

Abraham, Ralph. *Chaos, Eros, and Gaia*. San Francisco: Harper & Row, 1994.

Adorno, Theodor, et al. *The Positivist Dispute in German Sociology*. Trans. Glyn Adey and David Frisby. New York: Harper & Row, 1976.

Agrippa, Henry Cornelius. *De Nobilitate et Praecellentia foeminei sexus*. 1529.

Agrippa, Henry Cornelius. *Female Pre-Eminence; or the Dignity and Excellency of That Sex, Above the Male*. London, 1670.

Agrippa, Henry Cornelius. *The Glory of Women: Or a Looking-Glasse for Ladies*. London, 1652.

Agrippa, Henry Cornelius. *The Vanity of Arts and Sciences*. London, 1694; first published 1530.

AHR Forum. "The Old History and the New." *The American Historical Review* 94, no. 3 (June 1989): 581–698.

Aiton, Eric J. *The Vortex Theory of Planetary Motions*. New York: Elsevier, 1972.

Alain de Lille. *The Complaint of Nature*. Trans. Douglas Moffat. New York: Henry Holt, 1908.

Alanus de Insulis. "De Planctu Naturae." In Thomas Wright, ed. *The Anglo-Latin Satirical Poets and Epigrammatists of the Twelfth Century*. Vol. 2. London: Longman & Trubner, 1892.

Algarotti, Francesco. *Il Newtonianismo per le Dame*. Naples, 1737.

Algarotti, Francesco. *Sir, Isaac Newton's Philosophy Explain'd for the Use of the Ladies: In Six Dialogues on Light and Colours: From the Italian of Sig: Algarotti*. London, 1739.

Allemand, Jean. "Histoire de la vie et des ouvrages de M 's Gravesande." In William 's Gravesande, ed. *Oeuvres philosophiques et mathématiques*. Vol. 1. Amsterdam, 1774.

Altieri, Miguel. *Agroecology: The Scientific Basis of Alternative Agriculture*. Berkeley, CA: University of California, Division of Biological Control, 1983.

Altieri, Miguel. *Agroecology: The Scientific Basis of Alternative Agriculture*. Berkeley, CA, 1983, 2nd ed. London: Westview Press, 1987.

Anonymous. "John Eames." In Leslie Stephan and Sidney Lee, eds. *Dictionary of National Biography*. Vol. 6, 63 vols. London: Oxford University Press, 1917, 313.

Anonymous. "The Environment: A Higher Priority." *The New York Times*, July 2, 1989.

Anonymous. "EPA Urges Drastic Action to Slow Greenhouse Effect." *San Francisco Chronicle*, March 14, 1989.

Anonymous. "Freemasonry." In *Encyclopedia Britannica*. Chicago, 1954.

Anonymous. *La Physique Experimentale et Raisonnée*. Paris, 1756.

Anonymous. "Planet of the Year: Endangered Earth." *Time*, January 2, 1989, cover.

Anthony, Carl. "The Big House and the Slave Quarters: Part II, African Contributions to the New World." *Landscape* 21, no. 1 (Autumn 1976): 9–15.

Applebaum, Wilbur. *The Scientific Revolution and the Foundations of Modern Science*. Westport, CT: Greenwood Press, 2005.

Aristotle. *De Generatione Animalium*. Trans. Arthur Platt. Oxford, England: Clarendon Press, 1910.

Ashcroft, Bill, Gareth Griffiths, and Helen Tiffin, eds. *The Post-Colonial Studies Reader*. New York: Routledge, 1995.

Associated Press. "Senators Unveil Legislative Plan to Combat Greenhouse Effect." *San Francisco Chronicle*, July 29, 1988.

Astell, Mary. *A Serious Proposal to the Ladies for the Advancement of Their True and Greatest Interest*. London, 1694.

Austin, Mary. *The Land of Little Rain*. Boston: Houghton Mifflin, 1950; originally published, 1903.

Bacon, Francis. *Le Progrez et avancement aux sciences diuines & humaines*. Paris: Pierre Billaine, 1624.

Bacon, Francis. *The New Organon and Related Writings*. Ed. Fulton Anderson. New York: Liberal Arts Press, 1960.

Bacon, Francis. *The New Organon*. Ed. Lisa Jardine and Michael Silverthorne. Cambridge, England: Cambridge University Press, 2000.

Bacon, Francis. *Works*. Ed. James Spedding, Robert Leslie Ellis, and Douglas Devon Heath. 14 vols. London: Longmans Green, 1875.

Balz, Albert G.A. "Cartesian Doctrine and the Animal Soul: An Incident in the Formation of the Modern Philosophical Tradition." In Columbia Department of Philosophy, ed. *Studies in the History of Ideas*. New York: Columbia University Press, 1935, vol. 3, pp. 117–180.

Barber, William H. *Leibniz in France: From Arnauld to Voltaire: A Study in French Reactions to Leibnizianism, 1670–1760*. Oxford: Clarendon Press, 1955.

Barber, William H. "Mme. du Châtelet and Leibnizianism: The Genesis of the *Institutions de Physique*." In William H. Barber, et al., eds. *The Age of the Enlightenment: Studies Presented to Theodore Besterman*. Edinburgh and London: Oliver & Boyd, 1967, 200–222.

Basalla, George, ed. *The Rise of Modern Science: External or Internal Factors?* Lexington, MA: D.C. Heath, 1968.

Battigelli, Anna. *Margaret Cavendish and the Exiles of the Mind*. Lexington, KY: University Press of Kentucky, 1998.

Beckenstein, Alan R., Frederick J. Long, Matthew B. Arnold, and Thomas N. Gladwin. *Stakeholder Negotiations: Exercises in Sustainable Development*. Chicago, IL: Richard D. Irwin, 1995.

Beechley, Veronica. "On Patriarchy." *Feminist Review* 10 (March–June 1980): 66–82.

Berger, John. *Restoring the Earth*. New York: Knopf, 1985.

Berkhofer, Robert F., Jr. "A New Context for a New American Studies?" *American Quarterly* 41, no. 4 (December 1989): 588–613.

Berman, Morris. *The Reenchantment of the World*. Ithaca: Cornell University Press, 1981.

Bernal, Martin. *Black Athena*. New Brunswick, NJ: Rutgers University Press, 1987, 1991.

Bernoulli, Jean. "Discours sur les loix de la communication du movement." *Recueil des pieces qui a remporté les prix de l'Académie royale des sciences* 2 (1727): 1–108.

Berry, Wendell. *The Hidden Wound*. Berkeley, CA: Northpoint Press, 1989.

Berry, William. *Encyclopedia Heraldica*. London: Sherwood, Gilbert, and Piper, 1828–1840.

Besterman, Theodore, ed. *Les Lettres de la Marquise du Châtelet*. Geneva: Institut et Musée Voltaire, Las Delices, 1958.

Biagioli, Mario. *Galileo, Courtier: The Practice of Science in the Culture of Absolutism*. Chicago: University of Chicago Press, 1993.

Biehl, Janet. *Rethinking Ecofeminist Politics*. Boston: South End Press, 1991.

Biehl, Janet. "What Is Social Ecofeminism?" *Green Perspectives*, no. 11 (October 1988): 1–8.

Bird, Elizabeth Ann R. "Social Construction of Nature: Theoretical Approaches to the History of Environmental Problems." *Environmental Review* 11 (Winter 1987): 255–264.

Bitter, Heinrich. *Geschichte der Philosophie*. Hamburg, 1853.

Blaut, James M. *The Colonizer's Model of the World: Geographical Diffusionism and Eurocentric History*. New York: Guilford Press, 1993.

Bleier, Ruth. *Science and Gender: A Critique of Biology and Its Theories on Women*. New York: Pergamon, 1984.

Blum, Elizabeth D. "Pink and Green: A Comparative Study of Black and White Women's Environmental Activism in the Twentieth Century." Doctoral Dissertation, University of Houston, 2000.

Blum, Elizabeth D. "Power, Danger, and Control: Slave Women's Perceptions of Wilderness in the Nineteenth Century." *Women's Studies* 31 (2002): 247–265.

Blum, Elizabeth D. "Protecting Home and Race: Black Women's Environmental Activism During the Progressive Era." Paper presented to the annual meeting of the American Historical Association, San Francisco, CA, January 3–6, 2002.

Bohm, David. *Wholeness and the Implicate Order*. Boston: Routledge & Kegan Paul, 1980.

Bookchin, Murray. *The Ecology of Freedom: The Emergence and Dissolution of Hierarchy*. Palo Alto: Cheshire Books, 1982.

Borgmann, Albert. *Crossing the Postmodern Divide*. Chicago: University of Chicago Press, 1992.

Boscovich, Roger. *A Theory of Natural Philosophy*. Trans. James M. Child, from the second edition of 1763. London: Open Court, 1922.

Boscovich, Roger. *De Viribus Vivis*. Rome: Komarek, 1745.

Bradford, William. *Of Plimoth Plantation*. Boston: Wright and Potter, 1901.

Bridenthal, Renate. "The Dialectics of Production and Reproduction in History." *Radical America* 10 (March–April 1976): 3–11.

Briggs, John C. *Francis Bacon and the Rhetoric of Nature*. Cambridge, MA: Harvard University Press, 1989.

Briggs, John C. and F. David Peat. *Looking Glass Universe: The Emerging Science of Wholeness*. New York: Simon and Schuster, 1984.

Bronfenbrenner, Martha [Ornstein]. *The Role of Scientific Societies in the Seventeenth Century*. New York: Arno Press, 1975.

Brown, Harcourt. *Science and the Human Comedy: Natural Philosophy in French Literature from Rabelais to Maupertuis*. Toronto: University of Toronto Press, 1979.

Buchdahl, Gerd. *Metaphysics and the Philosophy of Science*. Oxford: Blackwell, 1969.

Bullard, Robert, ed. *Confronting Environmental Racism: Voices from the Grassroots*. Boston: South End Press, 1993.

Bullard, Robert. *Dumping in Dixie: Race, Class, and Environmental Quality*. Boulder, CO: Westview Press, 1990.

Burnham, Philip. *Indian Country, God's Country: Native Americans and the National Parks*. Washington, DC: Island Press, 2000.

Cajori, Florian. "Madame du Châtelet on Fluxions." *Mathematical Gazette* 13 (1926): 252.

Callicott, J. Baird. *In Defense of the Land Ethic: Essays in Environmental Philosophy*. Albany: State University of New York Press, 1989.

Callicott, J. Baird. "Moral Monism in Environmental Ethics Defended." *Journal of Philosophical Research* 19 (1994): 51–60.

Callicott, J. Baird. "The Wilderness Idea Revisited: The Sustainable Development Alternative." *The Environmental Professional* 13 (1991): 235–247.

Callicott, J. Baird and James McRae, eds. *Environmental Philosophy in Asian Traditions of Thought*. Albany: SUNY Press, 2014.

Capefigue, Jean-Baptiste. *La Marquise du Châtelet et les amies: des philosophes du XVIIIᵉ Siecle*. Paris: Amyot, 1868.

Carney, Judith A. *Black Rice: The African Origins of Rice Cultivation in the Americas*. Cambridge, MA: Harvard University Press, 2001.

Carson, Rachel. *Silent Spring*. Boston: Houghton Mifflin, 1962.

Cassirer, Ernst. *The Platonic Renaissance in England*. Trans. James P. Pettegrove. Austin: University of Texas Press, 1953.

Catalan, Abbé. "Courte Remarque de M. l'Abbé D. C. où l'on montre à M. G. G. Leibnits le paralogisme contenu dans l'objection précédente." *Nouvelles de la republique des lettres* 8 (September 1686): 1000–1005.

Catalan, Abbé. "Remarque sur la réplique de M. L. touchant le principe mechanique de M. Descartes, contenue dans l'article VII de ces nouvelles, mois de Février, 1687." *Nouvelles de la republique des lettres* 10 (June 1687): 577–590.

Catlin, George. *North American Indians*. Philadelphia: Leary, Stuart, 1913; originally published, 1844.

Cavendish, Margaret. *The Description of a New World Called the Blazing-World*. London, 1666; reprinted 1668.

Cavendish, Margaret. *Grounds of Natural Philosophy*. London, 1668.

Cavendish, Margaret. *Observations Upon Experimental Philosophy*. Ed. Eileen O'Neill. New York: Cambridge University Press, 2001; originally published, London, 1666.

Cavendish, Margaret. *The Philosophical and Physical Opinions*. London: Martin and Allestrye, 1655.

Cavendish, Margaret. *Philosophical Letters, or, Modest Reflections Upon Some Opinions in Natural Philosophy Maintained by Several Famous and Learned Authors of This Age, Expressed by Way of Letters/by the Thrice Noble, Illustrious, and Excellent Princess the Lady Marchioness of Newcastle*. London, 1664.

Cavendish, Margaret. *Poems and Fancies*. London: Martin and Allestrye, 1653.

CDIAC (Carbon Dioxide Information Analysis Center) Communications. *Oak Ridge National Laboratory*, Oak Ridge, TN. "Fossil Fuels CO_2 Emissions: Three Countries Account for 50% in 1986." Winter 1989.

Chan, Sucheng. *This Bittersweet Soil: The Chinese in California Agriculture, 1860–1910*. Berkeley, CA: University of California Press, 1986.

Châtelet, Gabrielle Emilie Marquise du. *Dissertation sur la nature et propagation du feu*. Paris, 1744.

Châtelet, Gabrielle Emilie Marquise du. *Institutions de Physique*. Paris, 1740.

Châtelet, Gabrielle Emilie Marquise du. "Réponse de Madame la Marquise du Châtelet à la lettre que M. de Mairan, secretaire perpetuel de l'académie royale des sciences, lui à écrite le 18. Février, 1741, sur la question des forces vives." Brussels, 1741.

Chaucer, Geoffrey. "The Merchant's Tale." In Fred N. Robinson, ed. *The Complete Works of Geoffrey Chaucer*. Boston, MA: Houghton Mifflin, 1933, pp. 612-627.

Cheney, Jim. "Postmodern Environmental Ethics: Ethics as Bioregional Narrative." *Environmental Ethics* 11 (1989): 117–134.

Chui, Glennda. "The Mother Earth Theory." *San Jose Mercury News*, March 8, 1988, pp. 1C, 2C.

Clarke, Robert. *Ellen Swallow: The Woman Who Founded Ecology*. New York: Follett, 1973.

Clarke, Samuel. *A Collection of Papers Which Passed between the Late Learned Mr. Leibniz and Dr. Clarke*. London, 1717.

Clarke, Samuel. "A Letter from the Rev. Dr. Samuel Clarke to Mr. Benjamin Hoadly, F.S.R. Occasion'd by the Present Controversy among Mathematicians, Concerning the Proportion of Velocity and Force in Bodies in Motion." *Philosophical Transactions* 35 (1728): 381–389.

Cohen, I. Bernard. "The French Translation of Isaac Newton's *Philosophiae naturalis principia mathematica* (1756, 1759, 1966)." *Archives Internationales d'Histoire Des Sciences* 21 (1968): 261–290.

Cohen, J. Bernard. "Newton's Second Law and the Concept of Force in the *Principia*." *Texas Quarterly* 10 (1967): 127–157.

Cohen, Leonora D. "Descartes and Henry More on the Beast-Machine: A Translation of their Correspondence Pertaining to Animal Automatism." *Annals of Science* 1 (1936): 48–61.

Conner, Daniel Keith and Robert O'Dell. "The Tightening Net of Marine Plastics Pollution." *Environment* 30, no. 1 (January–February 1988): 17–20, 33–36.

Conway, Anne. *The Principles of the Most Ancient and Modern Philosophy*. Ed. with an Introduction by Peter Loptson. The Hague: Martinus Nijhoff, 1982.

Coolidge, Julian L. "Six Female Mathematicians." *Scripta Mathematica* 17 (1951): 20–31.
Costabel, Pierre. "Le De Viribus Vives de R. Boscovich ou de la Vertu des Querrelles de Mot." *Archives Internationales d'Histoire des Sciences* 14 (1961): 54–57.
Costabel. Pierre. *Leibniz et la dynamique: Les textes de 1692.* Paris: Hermann, 1960.
Cottegnies, Line and Nancy Weitz, eds. *Authorial Conquests: Essays on Genre in the Writings of Margaret Cavendish.* Madison, NJ: Fairleigh Dickinson University Press, 2003.
Coudert, Alison. "A Cambridge Platonist's Kabbalist Nightmare." *Journal of the History of Ideas* 36 (1975): 633–652.
Coudert, Alison. "A Quaker-Kabbalist Controversy." *Journal of the Warburg and Courtauld Institutes* 39 (1976): 171–189.
Cronon, William. "The Trouble with Wilderness: Or Getting Back to the Wrong Nature." In William Cronon, ed. *Uncommon Ground: Rethinking the Human Place in Nature.* New York: W. W. Norton, 1996; originally published, 1995, 69–90.
Crookes, Sir William. "Modern Views on Matter." *Scientific American Supplement* 56 (July 1903): 23014.
Crutzen, Paul J. and Eugene F. Stoermer. "The Anthropocene." *IGPB (International Geosphere-Biosphere Programme) Newsletter* 41 (2000): 17.
D'Alembert, Jean. *Traité de Dynamique.* 1st ed. Paris: David l'Ainé, 1743.
D'Alembert, Jean. *Traité de Dynamique.* 2nd ed. 1758. Paris: Gauthier-Villars, 1921.
Daniels, Stephen. *Joseph Wright.* Princeton, NJ: Princeton University Press, 1999.
Daston, Lorraine and Katharine Park. *Wonders and the Order of Nature, 1150–1750.* New York: Zone Books, 1998.
Davies, Nina de Garis. *Ancient Egyptian Paintings, Selected, Copied, and Described.* 3 vols. Chicago, IL: University of Chicago Press, 1936.
Dawkins, Kristin. *NAFTA, GATT and the World Trade Organization: The Emerging World Order.* Westfield, NJ: Open Pamphlet Series, 1994.
d'Eaubonne, Françoise. "Feminism or Death." In Elaine Marks and Isabelle de Courtivron, eds. *New French Feminisms: An Anthology.* Amherst: University of Massachusetts Press, 1980, pp. 64–67.
d'Eaubonne, Françoise. *Le Féminisme ou la Mort.* Paris: Pierre Horay, 1974.
d'Eaubonne, Françoise. "The Time for Ecofeminism." Trans. Ruth Hottel. In Carolyn Merchant, ed. *Key Concepts in Critical Theory: Ecology.* Atlantic Highlands, NJ: Humanities Press, 1994, 174–197.
Debus, Allen G. *The English Paracelsians.* London: Oldbourne, 1965.
Deidier, Abbé. *Nouvelle refutation de l'hypotheses des force vives.* Paris, 1741.
Della Porta, Giambattista. *Natural Magic.* Facsimile of 1658 edition. Ed. D. J. Price. New York: Basic Books, 1957; first published 1558.
Desaguliers, John Theophilus. *A Course of Experimental Philosophy.* 2 vols. London, 1734.
Desaguliers, John Theophilus. "An Account of Some Experiments Made to Prove That the Force of Moving Bodies Is Proportionable to Their Velocities." *Philosophical Transactions* 32 (1723): 269–279.
Desaguliers, John Theophilus. "Animadversions Upon Some Experiments Relating to the Force of Moving Bodies; with Two New Experiments on the Same Subject." *Philosophical Transactions* 32 (1723): 285–290.
Descartes, René. *Meditations and Selections from the Principles of Philosophy.* La Salle, IL: Open Court, 1952.
Descartes, René. "Principia philosophiae." In Charles Adam and Paul Tannery, eds. *Oeuvres de Descartes.* 13 vols. Paris: Cerf, 1897–1913.
Devall, Bill and George Sessions. *Deep Ecology: Living as if Nature Mattered.* Salt Lake City: Peregrine Smith Books, 1985.
Diamond, Irene and Gloria Feman Orenstein. *Reweaving the World: The Emergence of Ecofeminism.* San Francisco, CA: Sierra Club Books, 1990.
Dijksterhuis, Eduard J. *The Mechanization of the World Picture.* Trans. C. Dikshoorn. Oxford: Clarendon Press, 1964; originally published, 1950.

Diop, Cheikh Anta. *The Cultural Unity of Black Africa*. Chicago, IL: World Press, 1990; originally published, 1959.

Diringer, Elliot. "Prop 65 Begins to Affect Products, Buying Habits." *San Francisco Chronicle*, October 20, 1988.

Diringer, Elliot. "Science Is Anything but Exact on Toxic Risks." *San Francisco Chronicle*, October 18, 1988.

Diringer, Elliot. "U.S. Awash in Toxic Chemicals—and Fear of Them." *San Francisco Chronicle*, October 17, 1988.

Donne, John. *The Poems of John Donne*. Ed. Herbert Grierson. London: Oxford University Press, 1933.

Dorothy Smith, "Women's Perspective as a Radical Critique of Sociology." *Sociological Inquiry* 44 (1974): 7–13.

Dreyfus, Hubert. *What Computers Can't Do*. New York: Harper & Row, 1972.

Eames, John. "A Remark upon the New Opinion Relating to the Forces of Moving Bodies, in the Case of the Collision of Non-Elastic Bodies." *Philosophical Transactions* 34 (1726): 183–187.

Eames, John. "Remarks upon a Supposed Demonstration, That the Moving Forces of the Same Body Are Not as the Velocities, but as the Squares of the Velocities." *Philosophical Transactions* 34 (1726): 188–191.

Eamon, William. *Science and the Secrets of Nature: Books of Secrets in Medieval and Early Modern Culture*. Princeton: Princeton University Press, 1994.

Easlea, Brian. *Science and Sexual Oppression: Patriarchy's Confrontation with Woman and Nature*. London: Weidenfeld and Nicholson, 1981.

Easlea, Brian. *Witch-Hunting, Magic, and the New Philosophy*. Sussex: Harvester, 1980.

Eaton, Randall L. "Hunting and the Great Mystery of Nature." *Utne Reader* 19 (January/February 1987): 42–49.

Eckersley, Robyn. *Environmentalism and Political Theory: Toward an Ecocentric Approach*. Albany: State University of New York Press, 1992.

Ecole, Jean. "Cosmologie wolffienne et dynamique leibnizienne." *Les Etudes philosophiques* 19 (1964): 3–10.

Economou, George. *The Goddess Natura in Medieval Literature*. Cambridge, MA: Harvard University Press, 1972.

Edwards, Samuel [pseud. Noel Bertram Gerson]. *The Divine Mistress*. New York: David McKay, 1970.

Ehrard, Jean. *L'Idée de nature en France dans la première moitieé du XVIIIe siècle*. Paris: S.E.V.P.E.N. 1964.

Ehrenreich, Barbara and Deirdre English. *Witches, Midwives, and Nurses*. Old Westbury, NY: Feminist Press, 1973.

Eisler, Riane. *The Chalice and the Blade*. San Francisco: Harper & Row, 1988.

Elkana, Yehuda. "Helmholtz's Kraft: An Illustration of Concepts in Flux." *Historical Studies in the Physical Sciences* 2 (1970): 263–298.

Environmental News Network. *GATT, the Environment, and the Third World: An Overview*. Berkeley, CA: The Tides Foundation, 1992.

Estienne, Charles. *De dissectione partium corporis humani*. Paris, 1545.

Farrington, Benjamin. *The Philosophy of Francis Bacon*. Liverpool, England: Liverpool University Press, 1964.

Fausto-Sterling, Anne. "The Dissection of Race and Gender in the Nineteenth Century." Paper presented to the annual meeting of the History of Science Society, Seattle, October 26, 1990.

Ferguson, James. *Lectures on Select Subjects*. London: W. Strahan, 1776; originally published, 1761.

Fieser, James and Bradley Dowden. "Internet Encyclopedia of Philosophy." URL: www.iep.utm. edu.

Findley, Roger W. and Daniel A. Farber. *Environmental Law in a Nutshell*. 2nd ed. St. Paul, MN: West Publishing Co., 1988.

Finney, Carolyn. *Black Faces, White Spaces: Reimagining the Relationship of African Americans to the Great Outdoors*. Chapel Hill: University of North Carolina Press, 2014.

Fisher, Colin. "African Americans and the Frontier of Leisure: The 1919 Chicago Race Riot and Access to Nature." Paper presented to the annual meeting of the American Historical Association, San Francisco, CA, January 3–6, 2002.

Flader, Susan L. and J. Baird Callicott, eds. *The River of the Mother of God and Other Essays by Aldo Leopold*. Madison, WI: University of Wisconsin Press, 1991.

Fleck, Richard F. *Henry Thoreau and John Muir among the Indians*. Hamden, CT: Archon Books, 1985.

Fludd, Robert. *Utriusque Cosmi Maioris Scilicet et Minoris Metaphysica.* Oppenheim, 1617.

Fontenelle, Bernard de. *A Discovery of New Worlds, from the French, Made English by Mrs. Aphra Behn . . . Wholly New*. London, 1688.

Fontenelle, Bernard de. *Entretiens sur la Pluralité des Mondes*. Paris, 1686.

Fontenelle, Bernard de. *Week's Conversation on the Plurality of Worlds*. Trans. William Gardiner. London, 1737.

Foucault, Michel. *Discipline and Punish: The Birth of the Prison*. Trans. Alan Sheridan. New York: Pantheon, 1977.

Foucault, Michel. *Power/Knowledge*. New York: Pantheon, 1980.

Fowler, Thomas, ed. *Bacon's Novum Organum*. With introduction and notes. 2nd ed. Oxford: Clarendon Press, 1889; originally published, 1878.

Fox, Stephen. *John Muir and His Legacy: The American Conservation Movement*. Boston: Little, Brown and Co., 1981.

Frängsmyr, Tore. "Science or History: George Sarton and the Positivist Tradition in the History of Science." *Lychnos* 37 (1973–4): 104–144.

Friedan, Betty. *The Feminine Mystique*. New York: Dell, 1963.

Gabbey, Alan. "Anne Conway et Henri More, *Lettres sur Descartes*." *Archives de Philosophie* 40 (1977): 379–404.

Garb, Yaakov. "The Use and Misuse of the Whole Earth Image." *Whole Earth Review* no. 45 (March 1985): 18–25.

GATT vs. UNCED: Can Free Trade and Sustainable Development Coexist? San Francisco, CA: Rainforest Action Network, 1992.

Gauchet, Marcel. *The Disenchantment of the World: A Political History of Religion*. Trans. Oscar Burge. Foreword by Charles Taylor. Princeton, NJ: Princeton University Press, 1997.

Gilliam, Harold. "The Real Price of Free Trade, and The Bottom Line for Indigenous Cultures." *This World, San Francisco Examiner*, January 2, 1994, pp. 13–14.

Gillispie, Charles Coulston. *The Edge of Objectivity*. Princeton: Princeton University Press, 1960.

Glanvill, Joseph. *Plus Ultra*. Gainesville, FL: Scholar's Facsimile Reprints, 1958; originally published, 1668.

Glanvill, Joseph. *The Vanity of Dogmatizing*. New York: Columbia University Press, 1931; originally published, 1661.

Glave, Dianne D. "The African American Cooperative Service: A Folk Tradition in Conservation and Preservation in the Early Twentieth Century." *International Journal of Africana Studies* 6, no.1 (November/December 2000): 85–100.

Glave, Dianne D. "Fields and Gardens: An Environmental History of African American Farmers in the Progressive South." Doctoral Dissertation, State University of New York at Stony Brook, 1998.

Glave, Dianne and Mark Stoll, eds. *To Love the Wind and the Rain: African Americans and Environmental History*. Pittsburgh: University of Pittsburgh Press, 2005.

Gleick, James. *Chaos: The Making of a New Science*. New York: Viking, 1987.

Goethe, Johann Wolfgang von. *Maximen und Reflexionen. Nach den Handschriften des Goethe-und Schiller-Archivs herausgegeben von Max Hecker*. Weimar: Goethe-Gesellschaft, 1907.

Goethe, Johann Wolfgang von. *Maxims and Reflections*. Trans. Elisabeth Stopp. Ed. Peter Hutchinson. London: Penguin, 1998.

Golinski, Jan. "The Theory of Practice and the Practice of Theory: Sociological Approaches in the History of Science." *Isis* 81, no. 3 (September 1990): 492–505.

Gottesman (Coudert), Alison. "Francis Mercurius Van Helmont: His Life and Thought." Doctoral Dissertation, University of London, 1972.

Gottlieb, Robert. "Reconstructing Environmentalism: Complex Movements, Diverse Roots." *Environmental History Review* 17, no. 4 (Winter 1993): 1–19.

Graffigny, Mme de. *La vie privée de Voltaire et de Mme du Châtelet.* Paris: Treuttel and Wurtz 1820.

Grant, Douglass. *Margaret the First: A Biography of Margaret Cavendish, Duchess of Newcastle, 1623–1673.* London: Hart-Davis, 1957.

Green, Monica H. "Bodies, Gender, Health, Disease: Recent Work on Medieval Women's Medicine." *Studies in Medieval and Renaissance History,* 3rd ser, 2 (2005): 1–46.

Griffin, David Ray, ed. *The Reenchantment of Science: Postmodern Proposals.* Albany: State University of New York Press, 1988.

Griffin, Susan. *Woman and Nature: The Roaring Inside Her.* New York: Harper Collins, 1978.

Grubb, Michael, et al. *The Earth Summit Agreements: A Guide and Assessment.* London: Earthscan, 1993.

Gumerman, George J. and Murray Gell-Mann, eds. *Understanding Complexity in the Prehistoric Southwest.* Santa Fe Institute Studies in the Sciences of Complexity. Vol. 16. Reading, MA: Addison-Wesley, 1994.

Habermas, Jürgen. *The Philosophical Discourse of Modernity.* Cambridge, MA: MIT Press, 1990.

Habermas, Jürgen. *Toward a Rational Society.* London: Heineman, 1971.

Hadot, Pierre. *Le Voile d'Isis: Essai sur l'histoire de l'idée de Nature.* Paris: Éditions Gallimard, 2004.

Hadot, Pierre. *The Veil of Isis: An Essay on the History of the Idea of Nature.* Trans. Michael Chase. Cambridge, MA: Harvard University Press, 2006.

Hall, A. Rupert. "Desaguliers." In *Dictionary of Scientific Biography.* Ed. Charles Coulston Gillespie. Vol. 4, 8 vols. New York: Scribner, 1971, 43.

Hamel, Frank. *An Eighteenth Century Marquise: A Study of Emile du Châtelet and Her Time.* London: Stanley Paul and Company, 1910.

Hamel, Jean Baptiste du. *Regiae Scientiarum Academiae Historia.* 2nd ed. Paris: J. B. Delespine, 1701.

Hammonds, Evelynn and Rebecca Herzig, eds. *The Nature of Difference: Sciences of Race in the United States from Jefferson to Genomics.* Cambridge, MA: MIT Press, 2008.

Hanchett, Thomas W. *Sorting out the New South City: Race, Class, and Urban Development in Charlotte, 1875–1975.* Chapel Hill, NC: University of North Carolina Press, 1998.

Hankins, Thomas L. "Eighteenth Century Attempts to Resolve the *Vis Viva* Controversy." *Isis* 56, no. 3 (Fall 1965): 281–297.

Hankins, Thomas L. "The Influence of Malebranche on the Science of Mechanics during the Eighteenth Century." *Journal of the History of Ideas* 28 (1967): 193–210.

Hankins, Thomas L. *Jean d'Alembert: Science and the Enlightenment.* Oxford: Clarendon Press, 1970.

Haraway, Donna. *Primate Visions: Gender, Race, and Nature in the History of Modern Science.* New York: Routledge, 1989.

Haraway, Donna. "Situated Knowledges: The Science Question in Feminism and the Privilege of Partial Perspective." *Feminist Studies* 14, no. 3 (Fall 1988): 575–599.

Haraway, Donna. *Simians, Cyborgs, and Women: The Reinvention of Nature.* New York: Routledge, 1991, pp. 183–201.

Harding, Sandra, ed. *The "Racial" Economy of Science: Toward a Democratic Future.* Bloomington, IN: University of Indiana Press, 1993.

Harding, Sandra. *The Science Question in Feminism.* Ithaca: Cornell University Press, 1986.

Harvey, William. *Works.* London: Sydenham Society, 1847.

Hatch, Robert. "The Scientific Revolution." URL: www.clas.ufl.edu/users/rhatch/pages/03-Sci-Rev/SCI-REV-Home/.

Havelock, Eric. *Preface to Plato.* Cambridge, MA: Harvard University Press, 1963.

Hayles, N. Katherine, ed. *Chaos and Order: Complex Dynamics in Literature and Science*. Chicago, IL: University of Chicago Press, 1991.

Hayles, N. Katherine. *Chaos Bound: Orderly Disorder in Contemporary Literature and Science*. Ithaca, NY: Cornell University Press, 1990.

Hayles, N. Katherine. "Gender Encoding in Fluid Mechanics: Masculine Channels and Feminine Flows." *Differences* 4, no. 2 (1992): 16–44.

Heidegger, Martin. "The Age of the World Picture." In Heidegger, *The Question Concerning Technology*. Trans. William Lovitt. New York: Harper & Row, 1977, pp. 115–154.

Heimann, Peter M. "Helmholz and Kant: The Metaphysical Foundations of *Uber die Erhaltung der Kraft*." *Studies in the History and Philosophy of Science* 5 (1974): 205–238.

Heimann, Peter M. "Nature Is a Perpetual Worker." *Ambix* 20 (1973): 1–25.

Heimann, Peter M. and James E. McGuire. "Newtonian Forces and Lockean Powers: Concepts of Matter in Eighteenth-Century Thought." In Russell McCormmach, ed. *Historical Studies in the Physical Sciences*. Philadelphia: University of Pennsylvania Press, 1971. Vol. 3, pp. 233–306.

Hein, Hilda. "The Endurance of the Mechanism–Vitalism Controversy." *Journal of the History of Biology* 5, no. 1 (Spring 1972): 159–188.

Hein, Hilda. "Mechanism and Vitalism as Theoretical Commitments." *The Philosophical Forum*, n.s., 1, no. 1 (Fall 1968): 185–205.

Heller, Chaia. *Ecology of Everyday Life*. Montreal: Black Rose Books, 1999.

Heller, Erich. *The Disinherited Mind: Essays in Modern German Literature and Thought*. Cambridge: Bowes & Bowes, 1952.

Helsham, Richard. *A Course of Lectures in Natural Philosophy*. London, 1743.

Herodotus. *The History of Herodotus*. New York: Tudor, 1928.

Hessen, Boris. *The Social and Economic Roots of Newton's "Principia"*. With a new Introduction by Robert S. Cohen. New York: Howard Fertig, 1971; originally published, 1931.

Hiebert, Erwin. *Historical Roots of the Conservation of Energy*. Madison, WI: State Historical Society of Wisconsin, 1962.

Hirsch, Marianne and Evelyn Fox Keller, eds. *Conflicts in Feminism*. New York: Routledge, 1990.

Hiscock, Walter George. *David Gregory, Isaac Newton, and Their Circle*. Oxford, UK: Oxford University, Press, 1937.

Hobbes, Thomas. *Leviathan*. Intro. by A.D. Lindsay. New York: Dutton, 1950.

Hodges, Devon L. *Renaissance Fictions of Anatomy*. Amherst: The University of Massachusetts Press, 1985.

Hogarth, William. "Four Stages of Cruelty 1751." URL: www.haleysteele.com/hogarth/plates/four_stages.html.

Horkheimer, Max. *The Eclipse of Reason*. New York: Oxford University Press, 1947.

Horkheimer, Max and Theodor Adorno. *Dialectic of Enlightenment*. Trans. John Cumming. New York: Herder & Herder, 1972.

Horney, Karen. "The Flight from Womanhood." In Jean Strouse, ed. *Women and Analysis*. New York: Grossman, 1974. URL: www.mezzo-mondo.com/arts/mm/wright/wright.html.

Hunter, William H., Jr. "The Seventeenth Century Doctrine of Plastic Natures." *Harvard Theological Review* 43 (1950): 212.

Hurley, Andrew. *Environmental Inequalities: Class, Race, and Industrial Pollution in Gary, Indiana, 1945–1980*. Chapel Hill: University of North Carolina Press, 1995.

Hurst, Wilfred Reginald. *An Outline of the Career of John Theophilus Desaguliers*. London: Edson, 1928.

Hurston, Zora Neale. *Their Eyes Were Watching God*. New York: HarperCollins, 1990, originally published 1937.

Huygens, Christiaan. "A Summary Account of the Laws of Motion." *Philosophical Transactions of the Royal Society* 4 (1669): 925–928.

Huygens, Christiaan. "Extract d'une Lettre de M. Huygens." *Journal de sçavans* (March 18, 1669): 22–24.

Huygens, Christiaan. *Horologium oscillatorium sive de motu pendulorum ad horologia aptato dem-onstrationes geometricae*. Paris: F. Muguet, 1673.

Huygens, Christiaan. *Oeuvres complètes de Christiaan Huygens*. 22 vols. La Haye: Martinus Nijhoff, 1888–1950.

Huygens, Christiaan. "Regles du mouvement dans la rencontre des corps." *Journal de sçavans* (March 18, 1669): 22–24.

Hynes, Patricia. "Ellen Swallow, Lois Gibbs, and Rachel Carson: Catalysts of the American Envi-ronmental Movement." *Women's Studies International Environmental Forum* 8, no. 4 (1985): 291–298.

Iltis, Carolyn [Merchant]. "The Controversy Over Living Force: Leibniz to D'Alembert." Doctoral Dissertation, University of Wisconsin, 1967. URL: https://nature.berkeley.edu/departments/espm/env-hist/dissertation.html.

Iltis, Carolyn [Merchant]. "D'Alembert and the *Vis Viva* Controversy." *Studies in History and Phi-losophy of Science* 1, no. 2 (August 1970): 135–144.

Iltis, Carolyn [Merchant]. "The Decline of Cartesianism in Mechanics: The Leibnizian-Cartesian Debates." *Isis* 64, no. 3 (Fall 1973): 356–373.

Iltis, Carolyn [Merchant]. "Leibniz and the *Vis Viva* Controversy." *Isis* 62, no. 1 (Spring 1971): 25–35.

Iltis, Carolyn [Merchant]. "The Leibnizian-Newtonian Debates: Natural Philosophy and Social Psychology." *British Journal for the History of Science* 6, no. 4 (December 1973): 343–377.

Iltis, Carolyn [Merchant]. "Madame du Châtelet's Metaphysics and Mechanics." *Studies in History and Philosophy of Science* 8 (1977): 29–48.

Jackson, Helen Hunt. *A Century of Dishonor: A Sketch of the United States Government's Dealings with Some of the Indian Tribes*. Boston, MA: Roberts Brothers, 1888; originally published, 1881.

Jackson, Helen Hunt. *Ah-Wah-Ne Days: A Visit to the Yosemite Valley in 1872*. San Francisco, CA: Book Club of California, 1971.

Jackson, Helen Hunt. *My Day in the Wilderness: Six California Tales*. San Francisco, CA: Book Club of California, 1939.

Jackson, Helen Hunt. *Ramona: A Story*. Boston, MA: Little Brown and Co., 1899; originally pub-lished, 1884.

Jaggar, Alison. *Feminist Politics and Human Nature*. Totawa, NJ: Roman & Allanheld, 1983.

Jaggar, Alison and William McBride. "'Reproduction' as Male Ideology." *Women's Studies Interna-tional Forum* 8, no. 4 (1985): 185–96.

Jammer, Max. *Concepts of Force*. Cambridge, MA: Harvard University Press, 1957.

Jantsch, Erich. *The Self-Organizing Universe*. New York: Pergamon, 1980.

Jay, Martin. *Downcast Eyes: The Denigration of Vision in Twentieth Century French Thought*. Berkeley, CA: University of California Press, 1993.

Johnson, Cassandra Y. "A Consideration of Collective Memory in African American Attachment to Wildland Recreation Places." *Human Ecology Review* 5, no. 1, 1998: 5–15.

Jonas, Hans. "The Nobility of Sight." *Philosophy and Phenomenological Research* 14 (1954): 507–519.

Jordan, William R., III. "On Ecosystem Doctoring." *Restoration & Management Notes* 1, no. 4 (Fall 1983): 2.

Jordan, William R., III. "Thoughts on Looking Back." *Restoration & Management Notes* 1, no. 3 (Winter 1983): 2.

Jordan, Winthrop. *White over Black: American Attitudes toward the Negro, 1550–1812*. New York: W. W. Norton, 1977; originally published, 1968.

Kant, Immanuel. "Gedanken von der wahren Schätzung der lebendigen Kräfte." In *Immanuel Kant's Werke*. Berlin: Bruno Cassirer Verlag, 1922, vol. 1, pp. 1–187.

Kant, Immanuel. *The Philosophy of Law*. Trans. William Hastie. Edinburgh: T. & T. Clark, 1887.

Kargon, R[obert] H. *Atomism in England from Hariot to Newton*. Oxford, England: Clarendon Press, 1966.

Katz, Daniel and Robert L. Kahn. *The Social Psychology of Organizations*. New York: Wiley, 1966.

Katz, William Loren. *The Black West: A Documentary and Pictorial History of the African American Role in the Westward Expansion of the United States*. New York: Simon and Schuster, 1996; originally published, 1971.

Kauffman, Stuart. *At Home in the Universe: The Search for the Laws of Self-Organization and Complexity*. New York: Oxford University Press, 1995.

Keill, John. *An Introduction to Natural Philosophy*. 4th ed. Trans. from 3rd Latin ed. London: Henry Woodfall, 1745.

Keller, Evelyn Fox. "Gender and Science." *Psychoanalysis and Contemporary Thought* 1 (1978): 409–433.

Keller, Evelyn Fox. *Reflections on Gender and Science*. New Haven, CT: Yale University Press, 1985.

Keller, Evelyn Fox and Christine Grontkowski. "The Mind's Eye." In Sandra Harding and Merrill B. Hintikka, eds. *Discovering Reality*. Dordrecht, Holland: D. Reidel, 1983, pp. 207–224.

Keller, Robert H. and Michael F. Turek. *American Indians and National Parks*. Tucson, AZ: University of Arizona Press, 1998.

Kemble, Frances Anne. *Journal of a Residence on a Georgian Plantation in 1838–1839*. New York: Alfred A. Knopf, 1961; originally published, 1863.

Kevles, Daniel. *The Physicists*. New York: Knopf, 1978.

King, Ynestra. "Feminism and the Revolt of Nature." *Heresies* 13 (1981): 12–15.

Kirchner, James. "The Gaia Hypothesis: Can It be Tested?" *Reviews of Geophysics* 27, no. 2 (May 1989): 223–235.

Knorr-Cetina, Karen D. *The Manufacture of Knowledge: An Essay on the Constructivist and Contextual Nature of Science*. New York: Pergamon Press, 1981.

Koertge, Noretta, ed. *A House Built on Sand: Exposing Postmodernist Myths about Science*. New York: Oxford University Press, 1998.

Koyré, Alexandre. *From the Closed World to the Infinite Universe*. New York: HarperCollins, 1958.

Koyré, Alexandre and I. Bernard Cohen. "Newton and the Leibniz-Clarke Correspondence." *Archives Internationales d'Histoire des Sciences* 15 (1962): 63–126.

Kraft, Victor. *The Vienna Circle: The Origins of Neo-Positivism*. Trans. Arthur Pap. New York: Philosophical Library, 2015; originally published 1953.

Kubrin, David. "How Sir Isaac Newton Helped Restore Law 'n' Order to the West." *Liberation* 16, no. 10 (March 1972): 32–41.

Kubrin, David. "Newton and the Cyclical Cosmos: Providence and the Mechanical Philosophy." *Journal of the History of Ideas* 28 (July–September, 1967): 325–346.

Kubrin, David. "Newton's Inside Out! Magic, Class Struggle, and the Rise of Mechanisms in the West." In Harry Woolf, ed. *The Analytic Spirit: Essays on the History of Science in Honor of Henry Guerlac*. Ithaca, NY: Cornell University Press, 1981.

Kudlinski, Kathleen. *Rachel Carson: Pioneer of Ecology*. New York: Viking, 1988.

Kuhn, Thomas S. "Mathematical vs. Experimental Traditions in the Development of Physical Science." *Journal of Interdisciplinary History* 7, no. 1 (Summer 1976): 1–3.

Kuhn, Thomas S. "Energy Conservation as an Example of Simultaneous Discovery." In Marshall Clagett, ed. *Critical Problems in the History of Science*. Madison: University of Wisconsin Press, 1959, 321–356.

Kuhn, Thomas S. *The Structure of Scientific Revolutions*. Chicago: University of Chicago Press, 1970; originally published, 1962.

Lakoff, George and Mark Johnson. *Metaphors We Live by*. Chicago: University of Chicago Press, 1980.

Lakoff, Robin. *Language and Woman's Place*. New York: Harper & Row, 1975.

Landau, Iddo. "Feminist Criticisms of Metaphors in Bacon's Philosophy of Science." *Philosophy* 73 (1998): 47–61.

Langenheim, Jean. "The Path and Progress of American Women Ecologists." *Journal of the Ecological Society of America* 69 (1988): 184–197.

LaPorte, Dierdre. "Theories of Fire and Heat in the First Half of the Eighteenth Century." Doctoral Dissertation, Cambridge, MA: Harvard University, 1970.

Latour, Bruno. "Visualization and Cognition." In Henrika Kuklick and Elizabeth Long, eds. *Knowledge and Society: Studies in the Sociology of Culture Past and Present*. Vol. 6. Greenwich, CT: JAI Press, 1986.

Laudan, L[arry] L. "The *Vis Viva* Controversy, a Post-Mortem." *Isis* 59, no. 2 (Summer 1968): 131–143.

Lear, Linda. "Rachel Carson's *Silent Spring*." *Environmental History Review* 17, no. 4 (Summer 1993): 23–42.

Lear, Linda. *Rachel Carson: Witness for Nature*. New York: Henry Holt, 1997.

Lear, Linda, ed. *Lost Woods: The Discovered Writings of Rachel Carson*. Boston: Beacon, 1998.

Leatherberry, Earl. "An Overview of African Americans' Historical, Religious, and Spiritual Ties to Forests." *Proceedings of the Society of American Foresters 1999 National Convention*, Portland, OR, 2000.

Lee, Charles. *Toxic Wastes and Race in the United States: A National Report on the Racial and Socio-Economic Characteristics of Communities with Hazardous Waste Sites*. New York: United Church of Christ Commission for Racial Justice, 1987.

Leibniz, Gottfried Wilhelm. "Brevis demonstratio erroris memorabilis Cartesii et aliorum circa legem naturalem, secundum quam volunt a Deo eandem semper quantitatem motus conservari; qua et in re mechanica abutuntur." *Acta Eruditorum* (1686): 161–163.

Leibniz, Gottfried Wilhelm. *Correspondance de Leibniz avec l'Electrice Sophie de Brunswick-Lunebourg*. Ed. Onno Klopp. Hanover: Klindworth, 1874.

Leibniz, Gottfried Wilhelm. "De Causa gravitatis et defensio sententiae sua veris naturae legibus contra Cartesianos." *Acta Eruditorum* (May 1690): 228–239.

Leibniz, Gottfried Wilhelm. "De Legibus naturae et vera aestimatione virium motricium contra Cartesianos. Responsio ad rationes a Dn. Papino mense Januarii proxima in *Actis* hisce p. 6. Propositas." *Acta Eruditorum* (September 1691): 439–447.

Leibniz, Gottfried Wilhelm. *Discourse on Metaphysics and Correspondence with Arnauld*. La Salle: Open Court, 1957.

Leibniz, Gottfried Wilhelm. *Mathematische Schriften*. Ed. C. I. Gerhardt. 9 vols. in 5. Halle: H. W. Schmidt, 1860.

Leibniz, Gottfried Wilhelm. *New Essays Concerning Human Understanding*. Ed. and Trans. Alfred G. Langley. La Salle: Open Court, 1949.

Leibniz, Gottfried Wilhelm. *Opera Omnia*. Ed. Ludovici Datens. Geneva, 1768.

Leibniz, Gottfried Wilhelm. *Philosophical Papers and Letters*. Ed. Leroy E. Loemker. 2 vols. Chicago: University of Chicago Press, 1956.

Leibniz, Gottfried Wilhelm. *Philosophische Schriften*. Ed. C. I. Gerhardt. 7 vols. Berlin: Akademie-Verlag, 1875–1890.

Leibniz, Gottfried Wilhelm. "Réplique à M. l'Abbé D. C. contenue dans une lettre écrite a l'auteur de ces nouvelles le 9. de Janr. 1687, touchant ce qu'a dit M. Descartes que Dieu conserve toujours dans la nature la même quantité de mouvement." *Nouvelles de la République des Lettres* 9 (February 1687): 131–144.

Leiss, William. *The Domination of Nature*. New York: George Braziller, 1972.

Lemonick, Michael D. "Deadly Danger in a Spray Can." *Time*, January 2, 1989, p. 42.

Lenzer, Gertrud, ed. *Auguste Comte and Positivism: The Essential Writings*. New York: HarperCollins, 1975.

Leopold, Aldo. "The Land Ethic." In Aldo Leopold, ed. *A Sand County Almanac*. New York: Oxford University Press, 1949, pp. 201–226.

Limerick, Patricia Nelson. "Hoping Against History." In Kathryn M. Mutz, Gary C. Bryner, and Douglas S. Kenny, eds. *Justice and Natural Resources: Concepts, Strategies, and Applications*. Washington, DC: Island Press, 2002, pp. 337–354.

Linden, Eugene. "Putting the Heat on Japan." *Time* (July 10, 1989): 50–2.

Long, Frederick J. and Matthew Arnold. *The Power of Environmental Partnerships*. Fort Worth, TX: Dryden Press, 1994.

Longino, Helen. *Science as Social Knowledge*. Princeton: Princeton University Press, 1990.

Lorenz, Edward. "Irregularity: A Fundamental Property of the Atmosphere." *Crafoord Prize Lecture, Tellus* 36A (1984): 98-110.

Lorenz, Edward. *The Essence of Chaos*. Seattle, WA: University of Washington Press, 1993.

Lorenz, Edward. "Predictability: Does the Flap of a Butterfly's Wings in Brazil Set Off a Tornado in Texas?" Paper presented to the annual meeting of the American Association for the Advancement of Science in Washington, DC, December 29, 1972.

Louville, Jacque Eugène de. "Sur la théorie des Mouvements varies." *Histoire de l'Académie Royale des Sciences* (1729): 154.

Lovelock, James. *The Ages of Gaia: A Biography of Our Living Earth*. New York: W. W. Norton, 1988.

Lovelock, James. *Gaia: A New Look at Life on Earth*. Oxford, England: Oxford University Press, 1979.

Lower, Richard. "Extrait du Journal d'Angleterre, contenant la manière de faire passer le sang d'un animal dans un autre." *Journal des sçavans* (January 31, 1667).

Lower, Richard. *Tractatus de corde (1665): Philosophical Transactions of the Royal Society of London*. December, 1666.

Maathai, Wangari. *The Green Belt Movement: Sharing the Approach and the Experience*. Nairobi, Kenya: Environment Liaison Centre International, 1988.

Mach, Ernst. *Science of Mechanics*. 6th ed. La Salle, IL: Open Court, 1960.

Mackintosh, Maureen. "Reproduction and Patriarchy: A Critique of Claude Meillassoux, *Femmes, Greniers et Capitaux*." *Capital and Class* 2 (Summer 1977): 114–127.

Maclaurin, Colin. "Démonstration des loix du choc des corps." *Recueil des pièces qui a remporté les prix de l'academie royale des sciences* 1 (1724): 1–24.

Magie, W[illiam] F[rancis]. *A Source Book in Physics*. New York: McGraw Hill, 1935.

Mairan, Jean Jacques de. "Dissertation sur l'estimation et la mesure des forces motrices des corps." In *Mémoires de l'Académie des Sciences de Paris*. Paris, 1728, pp. 1–49.

Mairan, Jean Jacques de. *Lettre à Madame [du Chastelet] sur la question des forces vives en réponse aux objections*. Paris: Jombart, 1741.

Makin, Bathsua. *An Essay to Revive the Antient Education of Gentle-Women, in Religion, Manners, Arts, and Tongues*. London, 1673.

Management Institute for Environment and Business. *Environmental Partnerships: A Business Handbook*. Fort Worth, TX: Dryden Press, 1994.

Management Institute for Environment and Business. *Environmental Partnerships: A Field Guide for Governmental Agencies*. Fort Worth, TX: Dryden Press, 1994.

Management Institute for Environment and Business. *Environmental Partnerships: A Field Guide for Nonprofit Organizations and Community Interests*. Fort Worth, TX: Dryden Press, 1994.

Manning, Kenneth. *Black Apollo of Science: The Life of Ernest Everett Just*. New York: Oxford University Press, 1983.

Manuel, Frank. *A Portrait of Sir Isaac Newton*. Cambridge, MA: Harvard University Press, 1968.

Marcuse, Herbert. "Nature and Revolution." In Herbert Marcuse. *Counterrevolution and Revolt*. Boston: Beacon Press, 1972, pp. 59–78.

Marsh, George Perkins. *Man and Nature*. New York: Charles Scribner's, 1864.

Marshall, Eugene. "Margaret Cavendish (1623–1673)." *Internet Encyclopedia of Philosophy*. URL: www.iep.utm.edu/cavend-m/.

Marston, Ed. "Experts Line Up on All Sides of the Tree-Grass Debate." *High Country News* 28, no. 7 (1996): 12–13.

Marx, Karl. "Preface to *A Contribution to the Critique of Political Economy* (1859)." In Karl Marx and Friedrich Engels, eds. *Selected Works*. New York: International Publishers, 1968, pp. 182–183.

Marx, Karl and Friedrich Engels. *Selected Works*. New York: International Publishers, 1968.

Mathes, Valerie Sherer. *Helen Hunt Jackson and Her Indian Reform Legacy*. Austin: University of Texas Press, 1990.

Mathews, Nieves. "Francis Bacon, Slave-Driver or Servant of Nature? Is Bacon to Blame for the Evils of Our Polluted Age?" URL: http://itis.volta.alessandria.it/episteme/madar1.html.

Mauner, George. *Manet: Peintre-philosophe*. University Park, PA: Pennsylvania State University Press, 1975.

Maurel, André. *La Marquise du Châtelet, Amie de Voltaire*. Paris: Librairie Hachette, 1930.

Mayer, J. Robert. "Bemerkungen über die Kräfte der unbelebten Natur." *Annalen der Chemie und Pharmacie* 41–42 (Winter 1842).

McGuire, J. E. "Atoms and the 'Analogy of Nature'." *Studies in History and Philosophy of Science* 1 (1970): 4–6.

McGuire, J. E. "Boyle's Conception of Nature." *Journal of the History of Ideas* 33 (1972): 523–542.

McGuire, J. E. "Force, Active Principles, and Newton's Invisible Realm." *Ambix* 15 (1968): 154–208.

McGuire, J. E. "*Labyrinthus continui*: Leibniz on Substance, Activity and Matter." In P. K. Machamer and R. G. Turnbull, eds. *Matter, Motion and Time, Space and Matter*. Columbus: Ohio State University Press, 1976, pp. 290–326.

McGuire, J. E. and P. M. Rattansi. "Newton and the 'Pipes of Pan'." *Notes and Records of the Royal Society of London* 21 (1966): 108–143.

McGurty, Eileen. "From NIMBY to Civil Rights: The Origins of the Environmental Justice Movement." *Environmental History* 2, no. 3 (July 1997): 301–323.

McLaughlin, J. and Ebenezer Clifton. *A New Dictionary of the French and English Languages*. New Rev. ed. New York: David McKay, 1904.

Meillassoux, Claude. *Maidens, Meal, and Money: Capitalism and the Domestic Community*. Cambridge, England: Cambridge University Press, 1981; originally published, 1975.

Mellor, John. "Sustainable Agriculture in Developing Countries." *Environment* 30, no. 9 (November 1988): 6–30.

Mellor, Mary. *Feminism and Ecology*. New York: NYU Press, 1997.

Melosi, Martin. "Equity, Eco-Racism, and Environmental History." *Environmental History Review* 19 (1995): 1–16.

Merchant, Carolyn. *Autonomous Nature: Problems of Prediction and Control from Ancient Times to the Scientific Revolution*. New York: Routledge, 2016.

Merchant, Carolyn. *The Columbia Guide to American Environmental History*. New York: Columbia University Press, 2002.

Merchant, Carolyn. *The Death of Nature: Women, Ecology, and the Scientific Revolution*. London: Wildwood House, 1983.

Merchant, Carolyn. *The Death of Nature: Women, Ecology, and the Scientific Revolution*. 2nd ed. 1990. San Francisco, CA: HarperCollins, 1980.

Merchant, Carolyn. *The Death of Nature: Women, Ecology, and the Scientific Revolution*. Japanese translation. Tokyo: Kousakusha, 1985.

Merchant, Carolyn. *The Death of Nature: Women, Ecology, and the Scientific Revolution*. Chinese translation. Beijing: Jilin Peoples' Publishing House, 1999.

Merchant, Carolyn. *Der Tod der Natur: Ökologie, Frauen und neuzeitliche Naturwissenschaft*. Munich: C.H. Beck, 1987; mass market paperback, 1994.

Merchant, Carolyn. *Earthcare: Women and the Environment*. New York: Routledge, 1996.

Merchant, Carolyn. "Earthcare: Women and the Environmental Movement." *Environment* 23, no. 5 (June 1981): 6–13, 38–40.

Merchant, Carolyn. "Ecofeminism and Feminist Theory." In Irene Diamond and Gloria Orenstein, eds. *Reweaving the World: The Emergence of Ecofeminism*. San Francisco: Sierra Club Books, 1990, 100–105.

Merchant, Carolyn. *Ecological Revolutions: Nature, Gender, and Science in New England*. Chapel Hill: University of North Carolina Press, 1989.

Merchant, Carolyn. "Environmental Ethics and Political Conflict: A View from California." *Environmental Ethics* 12, no. 1 (Spring 1990): 45–68.

Merchant, Carolyn. "Indian Land Policy, 1800–1900." In Carolyn Merchant, ed. *Columbia Guide to American Environmental History*. New York: Columbia University Press, 2002, 140–158.

Merchant, Carolyn. *La Morte Della Natura: Donne, Ecologia e Rivoluzione Scientifica*. Milan: Garzanti Editorial, 1988.

Merchant, Carolyn. *Naturens Död: Kvinnan, Ekologin och den Vetenskapliga Revolutionen*. Stockholm (Stegag): Symposion, 1994.

Merchant, Carolyn. "Perspective: Restoration and Reunion with Nature." *Restoration and Management Notes* 4, no. 2 (Winter 1986): 68–70.

Merchant, Carolyn. *Radical Ecology: The Search for a Livable World*. New York: Routledge, 1992.

Merchant, Carolyn. *Reinventing Eden: The Fate of Nature in Western Culture*. 2nd ed. 2013. New York: Routledge, 2003.

Merchant, Carolyn. "The Scientific Revolution and the Death of Nature: Special Focus section on Carolyn Merchant's *the Death of Nature*." *Isis* 97 (September 2006): 513–533.

Merchant, Carolyn. "The Theoretical Structure of Ecological Revolutions." *Environmental Review* 11, no. 4 (Winter 1987): 265–274.

Merriam, Thomas. "The Disenchantment of Science." *The Ecologist* 7, no. 1 (1977): 23–28.

Meyer, Gerald Dennis. *The Scientific Lady in England*. Berkeley and Los Angeles: University of California Press, 1955.

Meyerson, Emil. *Identity and Reality*. New York: Dover, 1962.

Michell, John. *The Earth Spirit*. New York: Avon, 1975.

Miller, Joaquin. *Life Amongst the Indians*. Chicago: Moril, Higgins & Co., 1892; originally published, 1873.

Minnick, Sylvia Sun. *Samfow: The San Joaquin Chinese Legacy*. Fresno, CA: Panorama West, 1988.

Mitford, Nancy. *Voltaire in Love*. London: Hamilton, 1957.

Mollison, Bill. *Permaculture Two: Practical Design for Town and Country in Permanent Agriculture*. Maryborough, Australia: Dominion Press-Hedges & Bell, 1984.

Mollison, Bill and David Holmgren. *Permaculture One: A Perennial Agriculture for Human Settlements*. Maryborough, Australia: Dominion Press-Hedges & Bell, 1984.

Montucla, Jean-Etienne. *Histoire des Mathématiques*. 3 vols. Paris, 1799–1802.

Moore, Donald, Jake Kosek, and Anand Pandian, eds. *Race, Nature, and the Politics of Difference*. Durham, NC: Duke University Press, 2003.

More, Henry. "Conjectura Cabbalistica: Or a Conjectural Essay of Interpreting the Mind of Moses in the Three First Chapters of Genesis According to a Threefold Cabbala: viz. Literal Philosophical, Mystical, or, Divinely Moral (first published 1653)." In *A Collection of Several Philosophical Writings of Dr. Henry More*. London, 1712.

Mornet, Daniel. *Les sciences de la nature en France XVIIIe siècle*. Paris: Armand Cohn, 1911.

Mouy, Paul. *Le developpement de la physique cartesienne, 1646–1712*. Paris: Vrin, 1934.

Muir, John. *A Thousand-Mile Walk to the Gulf*. San Francisco: Sierra Club Books, 1991.

Muir, John. *My First Summer in the Sierra*. New York: Penguin Books, 1987; originally published, 1911.

Muir, John. *Travels in Alaska*. New York: AMS Press, 1978; originally published, 1915.

Myers, Norman, ed. *Gaia: An Atlas of Planet Management*. Garden City, NY: Anchor, 1984.

Nader, Laura, ed. *What the Rest Think of the West: Since 600 A.D.* Berkeley, CA: University of California Press, 2015.

Nash, Roderick. *The Rights of Nature: A History of Environmental Ethics*. Madison, WI: University of Wisconsin Press, 1989.

Needham, Joseph. *Science and Civilization in China*. 7 vols. Cambridge, England: Cambridge University Press, 1956.

Nelkin, Dorothy. "Nuclear Power a Feminist Issue." *Environment* 23, no. 1 (1981): 14–20, 38–39.

Nelson, Richard K. "The Gifts." In Daniel Halpern, ed. *Antaeus*. no. 57, Autumn 1986), 117–131.

Newton, Isaac. *Chronology of Ancient Kingdoms*. London, 1727.

Newton, Isaac. *Mathematical Principles of Natural Philosophy*. Trans. Andrew Motte and Florian Cajori. Berkeley, CA: University of California Press, 1960.

Newton, Isaac. *Opticks*. Based on 4th ed. London, 1730. New York: Dover, 1952.

Nicholson, Linda, ed. *Feminism/Postmodernism*. New York: Routledge, 1990.

Nicolson, Marjorie. *Conway Letters: The Correspondence of Anne, Viscountess Conway, Henry More, and Their Friends, 1642–1684*. New Haven, CT: Yale University Press, 1930.

Nicolson, Marjorie. "Milton and the *Conjectura Cabbalistica*." *Philological Quarterly* 6 (1927): 1–18.

Nicholson, Marjorie. "The Real Scholar Gipsy." *Yale Review* 18 (January 1929): 347–363.

Norcia, Vincent di. "From Critical Theory to Critical Ecology." *Telos*, no. 22 (1974/75): 85–95.

Norwood, Vera. "Heroines of Nature: Four Women Respond to the American Landscape." *Environmental Review* 8, no. 1 (Spring 1984): 34–56.

Norwood, Vera. *Made from This Earth*. Chapel Hill: University of North Carolina Press, 1993.

Nunn, Hillary. *Staging Anatomies: Dissection and Spectacle in Early Stuart Tragedy*. Burlington, VT: Ashgate, 2005.

O'Connor, James. "Socialism and Ecology." *Capitalism, Nature, Socialism* 2, no. 3 (1991): 1–12.

Odell, Ruth. *Helen Hunt Jackson (H.H.)*. New York: D. Appleton-Century Co., 1939.

Odum, Eugene P. *Fundamentals of Ecology*. Philadelphia: W. B. Saunders, 1953.

Odum, Eugene P. "The Strategy of Ecosystem Development." *Science* 164 (1969): 262–270.

Oelschlager, Max. *The Idea of Wilderness: From Prehistory to the Age of Ecology*. New Haven: Yale University Press, 1991.

O'Faolain, Julia and Lauro Martines, eds. *Not in God's Image*. New York: Harper & Row, 1973.

O'Laughlin, Bridget. "Production and Reproduction: Meillassoux's *Femmes, Greniers et Capitaux*." *Critique of Anthropology* 2 (Spring 1977): 3–33.

Olmsted, Denison. *A Compendium of Natural Philosophy*. New Haven, CT, 1833.

Olmsted, Frederick Law. *The Slave States*. New York: G. P. Putnam's Sons, 1959; originally published, 1856.

Omi, Michael and Howard Winant. *Racial Formation in the United States: From the 1960s to the 1990s*. 2nd ed. New York: Routledge, 1994.

Ortner, Sherry. "Is Female to Male as Nature Is to Culture?" In Michelle Rosaldo and Louise Lamphere, eds. *Woman, Culture, and Society*. Stanford, CA: Stanford University Press, 1974, 67–87.

Owen, Gilbert Roy. "The Famous Case of Lady Anne Conway." *Annals of Medical History* 9 (1937): 567–571.

Oxford English Dictionary. Compact Edition. 2 vols. Oxford, UK: Oxford, 1971.

Pagel, Walter. *Paracelsus: An Introduction to Philosophical Medicine in the Era of the Renaissance*. New York: Karger, 1958.

Pagel, Walter. "The Religious and Philosophical Aspects of van Helmont's Science and Medicine." *Bulletin of the History of Medicine*, Supp. no. 2 (1944): 1–43.

Papin, Denis. "De Gravitatis causa et proprietatibus observations." *Acta Eruditorum* (April 1689): 183–188.

Papin, Denis. "Mechanicorum de viribus motricibus sententia, asserta adversus cl. GGL. Objections." *Acta Eruditorum* (January 1691): 6–13.

Paracelsus. *Hermetic and Alchemical Writings*. Ed. A. E. Waite. 2 vols. London, 1894.

Park, Katharine. "Nature in Person: Medieval and Renaissance Allegories and Emblems." In Lorraine Daston and Fernando Vidal, eds. *The Moral Authority of Nature*. Chicago: University of Chicago Press, 1994, pp. 50–73.

Park, Katharine. *Secrets of Women: Gender, Generation, and the Origins of Human Dissection*. New York: Zone Books, 2006.

Parry, Leonard A. *The History of Torture in England*. Montclair, NJ: Patterson Smith, 1975; originally published, 1934.

Pemberton, Henry. "A letter to Dr. Mead ... Concerning an Experiment, Whereby It Has Been Attempted to Shew the Falsity of the Common Opinion in Relation to the Force of Bodies in Motion." *Philosophical Transactions* 32 (1722): 57–66.

Pemberton, Henry. *A View of Sir Isaac Newton's Philosophy*. London, 1728.

Penrose, S. Beasley Linnard, Jr. *The Reputation and Influence of Francis Bacon*. Doctoral Dissertation, New York: Columbia University, 1934.

Pesic, Peter. "Nature on the Rack, Leibniz's Attitude towards Judicial Torture and the 'Torture' of Nature." *Studia Leibnitiana* 39, no. 2 (1997): 189–197.

Peterson, Abby. "Gender-Sex Dimension in Swedish Politics." *Acta Sociologica* 27, no. 1 (1984): 6, 3–17.

Peterson, Abby and Carolyn Merchant. "'Peace with the Earth': Women and the Environmental Movement in Sweden." *Women's Studies International Forum* 9, no. 5–6 (1986): 465–479.

Petit, Charles. "Why the Earth's Climate is Changing Drastically." *San Francisco Chronicle*, August 8, 1988.

Phanjas, Abbé Para du. *Théorie des Etres sensibles ou Cours complet de Physique*. Paris: C.A. Jombert, père, 1772.

Pickett, Stuart T. A. and Peter S. White, eds. *The Ecology of Natural Disturbance and Patch Dynamics*. Orlando, FL: Academic Press, 1985.

Plumwood, Val. *Feminism and the Mastery of Nature*. London: Routledge, 1993.

Plutarch. "Isis and Osiris (1–2)." In Jeffrey Henderson, ed. *Moralia*. 15 vols. Loeb Classical Library. Vol. 5. Cambridge, MA: Harvard University Press, 1935.

Poleni, Giovanni. *Epistolarum mathematicarum fasciculus*. Padua, 1729.

Poleni, Giovanni. "Recueil de Lettres sur divers Sujets de mathématique, second Extrait." *Journal Historique de la République des Lettres* (March–April, 1733): 220–229.

Poleni, Johannis Marchionis. *De Castellis per quae derivantur fluviorum latera convergentia*. Padua, 1718.

Politella, Joseph. *Platonism, Aristotelianism, and Cabalism in the Philosophy of Leibniz*. Philadelphia: Politella, 1938.

Poster, Mark. *Critical Theory and Poststructuralism: In Search of a Context*. Ithaca, NY: Cornell University Press, 1989.

Poulain de la Barre, François. *The Woman as Good as the Man; or the Equality of Both Sexes*. Trans. A. L. London: N. Brooks, 1677; first published, 1673.

Powell, John Wesley. *Report on the Lands of the Arid Region of the United States*. Washington, DC, 1878.

Prentice, Susan, "Taking Sides: What's Wrong with Eco-Feminism?" *Women and Environments* 10 (Spring 1988): 9–10.

Prigogine, Ilya and Isabelle Stengers. *Order Out of Chaos: Man's New Dialogue with Nature*. Toronto: Bantam Books, 1984.

Rainforest Action Network. "An Emergency Call to Action for the Forests and Their Peoples." URL: http://rain-tree.com/facts.htm#.WIy_tJJCCQo.

Raskin, Marcus and Herbert J. Bernstein. *New Ways of Knowing: The Sciences, Society, and Reconstructive Knowledge*. Totowa, NJ: Roman & Littlefield, 1987.

Rattansi, Piyo M. "Newton's Alchemical Studies." In Allen G. Debus, ed. *Science, Medicine and Society: Essays to Honor Walter Pagel*. New York: Science History Publications, 1972, pp. 167–182.

Raven, Peter. "The Global Ecosystem in Crisis." *A MacArthur Foundation Occasional Paper* Chicaco, IL: The John D. and Catherine T. MacArthur Foundation, December 1987: 7.

Redd, Danita. "Black Madonnas of Europe: Diffusion of the African Isis." In Ivan Van Sertima, ed. *African Presence in Early Europe, 1985*. New Brunswick, NJ: Transaction Publishers, Rutgers—The State University, 1993, pp. 106–133.

Rees, Emma L. E. *Margaret Cavendish: Gender, Genre, Exile*. Manchester, UK: Manchester University Press, 2003.

Regan, Tom. *The Case for Animal Rights*. Berkeley, CA: University of California Press, 1983.

Reice, Seth R. "Nonequilibrium Determinants of Biological Community Structure." *American Scientist* 82 (September–October 1994): 424–435.

Reichenbach, Hans. *Atom and Cosmos: The World of Modern Physics*. Trans. and Rev. Edward S. Allen. New York: MacMillan, 1933.

Reid, Thomas. "An Essay on Quantity." *Philosophical Transactions of the Royal Society of London* 45 (1748): 505–520.

Renwick, James. *First Principles of Natural Philosophy*. New York, 1842.

Reuther, Rosemary Radford. *New Woman/New Earth: Sexist Ideologies and Human Liberation*. New York: Seabury Press, 1975.

Reuther, Rosemary Radford. "Women's Liberation, Ecology & Social Revolution." *WIN* 9 (October 4, 1973): 4–7.

Reynolds, Myra. *The Learned Lady in England, 1650–1760*. Boston: Houghton Mifflin, 1920.

Rochberg, Francesca. *Before Nature: Cuneiform Knowledge and the History of Science*. Chicago: University of Chicago Press, 2016.

Rohault, Jacques. *System of Natural Philosophy, Illustrated with Dr. Samuel Clarke's Notes Taken Mostly out of Sir Isaac Newton's Philosophy*. London, 1733.

Rolston, Holmes, III. *Philosophy Gone Wild: Essays in Environmental Ethics*. Buffalo, NY: Prometheus Books, 1986.

Romm, Jeffrey. "The Coincidental Order of Environmental Injustice." In Kathryn M. Mutz, Gary C. Bryner, and Douglas S. Kenny, eds. *Justice and Natural Resources Concepts, Strategies, and Applications*. Washington, DC: Island Press, 2002, pp. 117–138.

Ross, John. "Environment and Development: Building Sustainable Societies: Lectures from the 1987 Summer Forum at the University of Wisconsin-Madison." Institute for Environmental Studies Report 135. Madison, WI: University of Wisconsin Institute for Environmental Studies Office of Publications, November 1988.

Rossi, Paolo. *Francis Bacon: From Magic to Science*. Chicago: University of Chicago Press, 1968.

Rossiter, Margaret W. *Women Scientists in America: Before Affirmative Action, 1940–1972*. Baltimore: John Hopkins University Press, 1995.

Rossiter, Margaret W. *Women Scientists in America: Struggles and Strategies to 1940*. Baltimore: John Hopkins University Press, 1982.

Roszak, Theodore. *Where the Wasteland Ends: Politics and Transcendence in Post-Industrial Society*. Garden City, NY: Doubleday, 1972.

Salleh, Ariel K. *Ecofeminism as Politics*. London: Zed Books, 1997.

Sanchez, Jesus. "The Environment: Whose Movement?" *Green Letter* 5, no. 1 (Spring 1989): 3–4, 14–16.

Sarasohn, Lisa. *The Scientific Revolution*. Boston: Houghton Mifflin, 2006.

Sarton, George. *A History of Science*. 2 vols. Cambridge, MA: Harvard University Press, 1959.

Sarton, George. *The Study of the History of Mathematics*. New York: Dover, 1936.

Sarton, George. *The Study of the History of Science*. New York: Dover, 1936.

Sawday, Jonathan. *The Body Emblazoned: Dissection and the Human Body in Renaissance Culture*. London: Routledge, 1995.

Sawday, Jonathan. "The Fate of Marsyas: Dissecting the Renaissance Body." In Lucy Grant and Nigel Llewellyn, eds. *Renaissance Bodies: The Human Figure in English Culture, c. 1540–1660*. London: Reaktion, 1990, pp. 112–135.

Schiebinger, Londa. "The Anatomy of Difference: Race and Sex in Eighteenth Century Science." *Eighteenth Century Studies* 23 (1990): 387–406.

Schiebinger, Londa. "Feminine Icons: The Face of Early Modern Science." *Critical Inquiry* 14, no. 4 (Summer 1988): 661–691.

Schiebinger, Londa. *The Mind Has No Sex? Women in the Origins of Modern Science*. Cambridge, MA: Harvard University Press, 1989.

Schiebinger, Londa. *Nature's Body: Gender in the Making of Modern Science*. Boston: Beacon Press, 1993.

Schuster, John A. "(New) Master Narratives, Yes: 'Scientific Revolution', No Thanks." Paper presented at the annual meeting of the History of Science Society, Seattle, October 26, 1990.

Scott, George Ryley. *The History of Torture throughout the Ages*. 2nd ed. London: Kegan Paul, 2003.

Scott, Wilson L. *The Conflict between Atomism and Conservation Theory, 1644 to 1860*. London: MacDonald; New York: Elsevier, 1970.

The Second Citizen's Report. 1985. *The State of India's Environment, 1984–85*. New Delhi: Centre for Science and Environment, 370.

Seidel, Michael A. "The Woman as Good as the Man." *Journal of the History of Ideas* 35 (July–September 1974): 499–508.

's Gravesande, William. "Essai d'une nouvelle théorie sur le choc des corps." *Journal Litteraire, de La Haye* 12 (1722): 1–54.

's Gravesande, William. *Mathematical Elements of Natural Philosophy*. Trans. J. T. Desaguliers. 5th ed. London, 1737.

's Gravesande, William. *Oeuvres philosophiques et mathématiques*. Amsterdam: M. M. Rey, 1774.

's Gravesande, William. "Remarques sur la Force des Corps en Mouvement et sur Choc; précédées de quelques Réflexions sur la Maniere d'Ecrire, de Monsieur le Docteur Samuel Clarke." *Journal Litteraire, de La Haye* 13 (1729): Pt. 1, 189–197 and Pt. 2, 407–432.

Shabecoff, Philip. "Environmental Groups Faulted for Racism." *San Francisco Chronicle*, February 1, 1990, A2.

Shapin, Steven. "Discipline and Bounding: The History and Sociology of Science as Seen through the Externalism-Internalism Debate." *History of Science* 30 (1992): 333–69.

Shapin, Steven and Simon Schaffer. *Leviathan and the Air-Pump: Hobbes, Boyle, and the Experimental Life*. Princeton, NJ: Princeton University Press, 1985.

Sheafer, Silvia Anne. *Chinese and the Gold Rush*. Whittier, CA: Journal Publications, 1979.

Shiva, Vandana. "Address." Fate and Hope of the Earth Conference, Managua, Nicaragua, June 1989.

Shiva, Vandana. *Staying Alive: Women, Ecology, and Development*. London: Zed Books, 1988.

Siegfried, Brandie R. and Lisa T. Sarasohn, eds. *God and Nature in the Thought of Margaret Cavendish*. Burlington, VT: Ashgate, 2014.

Silver, Timothy. *A New Face on the Countryside: Indians, Colonists, and Slaves in South Atlantic Forests, 1500–1800*. New York: Cambridge University Press, 1990.

Sjöö, Monica and Barbara Mor. "The Original Black Mother." In Monica Sjöö and Barbara Mor, eds. *The Great Cosmic Mother: Rediscovering the Religion of the Earth*. San Francisco: Harper & Row, 1987, pp. 21–32.

Smith, Adam. *An Inquiry into the Nature and Causes of the Wealth of Nations*. London: Strahan and Cadell, 1776.

Smith, Hilda. *Reason's Disciples: Seventeenth Century Feminists*. Urbana: University of Illinois Press, 1982.

Smith, Kimberly K. *African American Environmental Thought: Foundations*. Lawrence: University Press of Kansas, 2007.

Smith, Michael B. "Silence Miss Carson! Science, Gender, and the Reception of Silent Spring." *Feminist Studies* 27, no. 3 (Fall 2001): 733–752.

Smith, Sir William. *A Smaller Latin-English Dictionary*. Rev. Ed. John F. Lockwood. New York: Barnes & Noble, 1960.

Soble, Alan. "In Defense of Bacon." *Philosophy of the Social Sciences* 25 (1995): 192–215.

Solnit, Rebecca. *Savage Dreams: A Journey into the Hidden Wars of the American West*. San Francisco: Sierra Club Books, 1994.

Solnit, Rebecca. "Up the River of Mercy." *Sierra* 77 (November/December 1992): 50–84.

Soulé, Michael, ed. *Conservation Biology: The Science of Scarcity and Diversity*. Sunderland, MA: Sinauer, 1986.

Spence, Mark David. *Dispossessing the Wilderness: Indian Removal and the Making of the National Parks*. New York: Oxford University Press, 1999.

Spivak, Gayatri Chakravorty. "Can the Subaltern Speak?" In Carly Nelson and Lawrence Grossberg, eds. *Marxism and the Interpretation of Culture*. London, England: Macmillan, 1988, pp. 271–318.

Sprat, Thomas. *History of the Royal Society* [1667]. Ed. Jackson I. Cope and Harold Whitmore Jones. St. Louis: Washington University Press, 1958.

Stadler, Friedrich, ed. *The Vienna Circle and Logical Positivism: Reevaluation and Future Perspectives*. Boston: Dordrecht, 2003.

Stallo, J. Bernard. *The Concepts and Theories of Modern Physics*. New York: Appleton, 1884.

Stein, Ludwig. *Leibniz and Spinoza*. Berlin: Reimer, 1890.

Stepan, Nancy Leys. *The Idea of Race in Science: Great Britain, 1800–1960*. Hamden, CT: Archon Books, 1982.

Stepanek, Marcia. "GATT Group Turns up the Heat." *San Francisco Examiner*, August 7, 1994, pp. B-1, 9.

Stewart, Mart A. "Rice, Water, and Power: Landscapes of Domination and Resistance in the Low-country, 1790–1880." *Environmental History Review* 15, no. 3 (1991): 47–64.

Stewart, Mart A. *What Nature Suffers to Groe: Life, Labor, and Landscape on the Georgia Coast, 1680–1920*. Athens: University of Georgia Press, 1996.

Stewart, Stanley. *The Enclosed Garden: The Tradition and Image in Seventeenth Century Poetry*. Madison, WI: University of Wisconsin Press, 1966.

Stimson, Dorothy. *Scientists and Amateurs: A History of the Royal Society*. New York: Greenwood Press, 1968.

Sutherland, Frederic P. "Executive Director of the Sierra Club Legal Fund." *S. F. Chronicle* (August 21, 1989). Available online at: www.huffingtonpost.com/2013/03/11/chopstick-china-forests_n_2853033.html.

Swisher, Kara. "Refrigerators New CFC Issue." *Star Bulletin and Advertiser*. Honolulu, July 16, 1989, D-3.

Szasz, Andrew. *Ecopopulism: Toxic Waste and the Movement for Environmental Justice*. Minneapolis, MN: University of Minnesota Press, 1994.

Takaki, Ronald. *Iron Cages*. New York: Alfred Knopf, 1979.

Talvacchia, Bette. *Taking Positions: On the Erotic in Renaissance Culture*. Princeton: Princeton University Press, 1999.

Tarkington, Booth. *The Turmoil, a Novel*. New York: Harper & Brothers, 1915; originally published, 1914.

Taton, René. "Gabrielle Emilie du Châtelet." In Charles Coulston Gillispie, ed. *Dictionary of Scientific Biography*. Vol. 3. New York: Charles Scribner's Sons, 1970, pp. 215–217.

Taylor, Charles. "Neutrality in Political Science." In Alan Ryan, ed. *The Philosophy of Social Explanation*. London: Oxford University Press, 1973, pp. 139–170.

Taylor, Dorceta. "American Environmentalism: The Role of Race, Class, and Gender in Shaping Activism 1820–1995." *Race, Gender and Class* 5, no. 1 (1997): 16–62.

Taylor, Dorceta. *The Environment and the People in American Cities, 1600-1900s: Disorder, Inequality, and Social Change*. Durham: Duke University Press, 2009.

Third World Network. *Earth Summit Briefings*. Penong, Malaysia: Third World Network, 1992.

Thomas, Lewis. *Late Night Thoughts on Listening to Mahler's Ninth Symphony*. New York: Viking Press, 1980.

Thoreau, Henry David. *Walden and Civil Disobedience*. New York: Penguin, 1983.

Toufexis, Anastasia. "The Dirty Seas." *Time* 132, (August 1, 1988): 44.

Truax, Hawley. "Minorities at Risk." *Environmental Action* 21 (January–February 1990): 20–21.

Tuana, Nancy, ed. *Feminism & Science*. Bloomington, IN: Indiana University Press, 1989.

Vann, Richard T. *The Social Development of English Quakerism 1655–1755*. Cambridge, MA: Harvard University Press, 1969.

Vann, Richard T. "Toward a New Lifestyle: Women in Preindustrial Capitalism." In Renate Bridenthal and Claudia Koonz, eds. *Becoming Visible*. Boston: Houghton Mifflin, 1977, pp. 192–216.

Varignon, Pierre. *Nouvelle mécanique ou statique*. Paris, 1725.

Vickers, Brian. "Francis Bacon, Feminist Historiography, and the Dominion of Nature." *Journal of the History of Ideas* 69, no. 1 (January 2008): 117–141.

Volney, Constantin-François. *Voyage en Syrie et Egypte*. Paris: Mouton & Co., 1959; originally published, 1787.

Voltaire, François. "Doutes sur la mesure des force motrices et sur leur nature, presentés à l'academie des sciences de Paris, en 1741." In *Oeuvres completes*. Paris, 1819–1825.

Wade, Ira O. *Studies on Voltaire*. Princeton: Princeton University Press, 1947.

Wade, Ira O. *Voltaire and Madame du Châtelet: An Essay on the Intellectual Activity at Cirey*. Princeton: Princeton University Press, 1941.

Waldrop, Mitchell. *Complexity: The Emerging Science at the Edge of Order and Chaos*. New York: Simon and Schuster, 1992.

Wallis, John. "A Summary Account of the General Laws of Motion." *Philosophical Transactions of the Royal Society* 3 (1669): 864–866.

Wallis, John. *Mechanica sive de Motu*. 2 vols. London, 1669–1671.

Walters, Lisa. *Margaret Cavendish: Gender, Science, and Politics*. Cambridge, UK: Cambridge University Press, 2014.

Walters, Robert L. "Chemistry at Cirey." *Studies on Voltaire and the 18th Century* 58 (1967): 1807–1827.

Warren, Karen. "Feminism and Ecology: Making Connections." *Environmental Ethics* 9, no. 1 (1987): 3–10.

Washington, Sylvia Hood. *Packing Them In: An Archeology of Environmental Racism, 1865–1954*. Lanham, MD: Lexington Books, 2005.

Washington, Sylvia Hood, ed. *Echoes from the Poisoned Well: Global Memories of Environmental Injustice*. Lanham, MD: Lexington Books, 2006.

Watson, Richard A. *The Downfall of Cartesianism, 1673–1712: A Study of Epistemological Issues in Late 17th Century Cartesianism*. The Hague: Martinus Nijhoff, 1966.

Weber, Devra. *Dark Sweat, White Gold: California Farm Workers, Cotton, and the New Deal*. Berkeley, CA: University of California Press, 1994.

Webster, Charles. *The Great Instauration: Science, Medicine, and Reform, 1626–1660*. London: Duckworth, 1975.

Wells, Jennifer. *Complexity and Sustainability*. New York: Routledge, 2014.

Westfall, Richard S. *Force in Newton's Physics*. London: MacDonald, 1971.

Westfall, Richard S. "Newton and the Hermetic Tradition." In Allen G. Debus, ed. *Science, Medicine and Society: Essays to Honor Walter Pagel*. New York: Science History Publications, 1972, pp. 183–198.

Westkott, Marcia. "Feminist Criticism of the Social Sciences." *Harvard Educational Review* 49 (November 1979): 422–430.

Wheeler, Leonard R. *Vitalism: Its History and Validity*. London: Witherby, 1939.

Whewell, William. *A History of the Inductive Sciences*. 3rd ed., 2 vols. New York: D. Appleton, 1872.

Whewell, William. *Elementary Treatise on Mechanics*. Cambridge, 1824.

Whiston, William. *Historical Memoirs of the Life of Dr. Samuel Clarke*. London, 1730.

Wilkins, Emma. "Margaret Cavendish and the Royal Society." *Notes and Records, The Royal Society Journal of the History of Science* (2014). URL: http://rsnr.royalsocietypublishing.org.

Wilson, James. *A Course of Chemistry, Formerly Given by the Late and Learned Dr. Henry Pemberton*. London: J. Nourse, 1771.

Wilson, Margaret D. "Leibniz and Locke on First Truths." *Journal of the History of Ideas* 28 (1967): 847–866.

Wilson, William J. *The Declining Significance of Race: Blacks and Changing American Institutions*. Chicago: University of Chicago Press, 1978.

Wolfe, Linnie Marsh, ed. *John of the Mountains: The Unpublished Journals of John Muir*. Boston: Houghton Mifflin, 1938.

Wolff, Christian. *Cosmologia generalis*. Francofurti et Lipsiae, 1737.

Wolff, Christian. *Philosophia Prima Sive Ontologia*. 1st ed. Frankfurt, 1729. Critical ed. In Jean Ecole, ed. *Gesammelte Werke, Abt. II, Bd. 3*. Hidesheim: Georg Olms, 1962.

Women's Work Study Group. "Loom, Broom, and Womb: Producers, Maintainers, and Reproducers." *Radical America* 10 (March–April 1976): 29–45.

Woods, Robert, ed. *The City Wilderness: A Settlement Study*. Boston: Houghton Mifflin, 1898.

Wooley, Hannah. *The Gentlewomen's Companion*. London, 1673; first published, 1655.

World Wide Fund for Nature. "The GATT Report on Trade and Environment: A Critique." Gland, Switzerland: WWF International, 1992.

Worster, Donald. *A Passion for Nature: The Life of John Muir*. New York: Oxford University Press, 2008.

Worster, Donald. *A River Running West: The Life of John Wesley Powell.* New York: Oxford University Press, 2001.

Worster, Donald. "Ecology of Order and Chaos." *Environmental History Review* 14, no. 1–2 (1990): 4–16.

Worster, Donald. *Nature's Economy: A History of Ecological Ideas.* New York: Cambridge University Press, 1994; originally published, 1977.

Worster, Donald. *Rivers of Empire: Water, Aridity, and the Growth of the American West.* New York: Oxford University Press, 1992; originally published, 1985.

Wren, Christopher. "Lex Naturae de Collisione Corporum." *Philosophical Transactions of the Royal Society* 3 (1669): 867–868.

Wright, Joseph. "An Experiment on a Bird in the Airpump." 1768. URL: www.nationalgallery.org. uk/cgi-bin/WebObjects.dll/CollectionPublisher.woa/wa/largeImage?workNumber=NG725.

Wylde, James. *The Circle of the Sciences.* 4 vols. London, 1862–1869.

Yates, Frances A. *Giordano Bruno and the Hermetic Tradition.* Chicago: University of Chicago Press, 1964.

Yates, Frances A. "The Hermetic Tradition in Renaissance Science." In Charles S. Singleton, ed. *Art, Science, and History in the Renaissance.* Baltimore: Johns Hopkins Press, 1968.

Young, Iris. "Socialist Feminism and the Limits of Dual Systems Theory." *Socialist Review* 10, nos. 2–3 (March-June 1980): 169–88.

Young, Robert, ed. *Untying the Text: A Post-Structuralist Reader.* Boston: Routledge & Kegan Paul, 1981.

Young, Thomas. *A Course of Lectures on Natural Philosophy and the Mechanical Arts.* 2 vols. London: J. Johnson, 1807.

Yuen, Edie, Lisa J. Bunin, and Tim Stroshane. "Multicultural Ecology: An Interview with Carl Anthony." *Capitalism, Nature, Socialism* 8, no. 3 (September 1997): 41–62.

Zagorin, Perez. *Francis Bacon.* Princeton, NJ: Princeton University Press, 1998.

Zalta, Edward N., ed. *Stanford Encyclopedia of Philosophy.* URL: plato.stanford.edu.

Zeff, Robbin Lee, Marsha Love, and Karen Stults. *Empowering Ourselves: Women and Toxics Organizing.* Arlington, VA: Citizen's Clearing House for Hazardous Wastes, 1989.

Zilsel, Edgar. "The Genesis of the Concept of Scientific Progress." In Philip P. Wiener and Aaron Noland, eds. *Roots of Scientific Thought.* New York: Basic Books, 1953.

INDEX

Page numbers in italics indicate figures